HISTORY OF
GERMAN LITERATURE

ABOUT THE AUTHORS

Werner Paul Friederich is Professor of German and Compara-tive Literature at the University of North Carolina, where he has taught since 1935. Dr. Friederich obtained both his Master's and his Doctor's degree at Harvard University, and has studied and lectured in Switzerland, France, Italy, and Spain. He has taught at MIT, Yale, and Middlesex school, and in 1955 was a Fulbright lecturer to Australia.

Dr. Friederich is the Editor of the University of North Caro-lina *Studies in Comparative Literature*, and of the *Yearbook of Comparative Literature*. He is also Associate Editor of *Compara-tive Literature*, and a member of the executive committee of the International Comparative Literature Association. He is the author of nine books and more than thirty articles on the subject of literature.

Professor Philip Shelley is Chairman of the German Depart-ment at Pennsylvania State College. He has taught Comparative and German Literature there since 1939.

Oskar Seidlin is Professor of German, at Ohio State University, whose staff he joined in 1946.

COLLEGE OUTLINE SERIES

HISTORY OF GERMAN LITERATURE

BY

WERNER P. FRIEDERICH

with the collaboration of

PHILIP A. SHELLEY

OSKAR SEIDLIN

New York

BARNES & NOBLE, INC.

PREFACE

This book is meant to serve both as an introduction to German literature for beginners and as a quick reference manual for more advanced students. This twofold purpose has often led to conflicts of presentation, because for the former I should have preferred to give as few names and titles as possible, whereas the needs of the latter seemed to call for a short enumeration even of minor authors. I trust that the compromise achieved between these two aims will prove satisfactory.

A book of this size and character cannot, of course, claim any originality of interpretation; its sole merits—if any—lie in its arrangement, in a logical and clear build-up, of the absolute necessity for which years of experience in the teaching of literature have convinced me.

The chapter on Contemporary German Literature has grown beyond the scope first envisaged by me; yet in view of the multitude and the popularity of English translations of modern German authors it seemed advisable to classify and describe as many as possible and to leave the task of unavoidable eliminations to later generations.

Various discussions and many bibliographical data have branched out into the field of Comparative Literature. This corresponded not only to my own personal predilection, but also to the wish of the publishers, who hope that this Outline may thus be of help also to students in allied literatures. For the latter's convenience short lists of English translations have been added at the end of each chapter. Both these lists and the bibliographical data are meant to serve as guides only; they do not in any way aim at completeness.

Besides being indebted to my two friends and collaborators, Professors Seidlin and Shelley, I owe many thanks also to the kindly and untiring help of my friend and colleague, Professor William Wells, and of Messrs. David H. Malone and William R. Barrett, two graduate students in our university.

PREFACE

In dedicating this book to my native Switzerland, I am mindful not only of the values she has contributed to German and French literature—the emphasis on nature and simplicity in Haller and Rousseau, the truly cosmopolitan and tolerant attitude of Bodmer and Mme. de Staël, the kindly didacticism and homespun humor in Gotthelf, the scholarly understanding of the past in Sismondi and Burckhardt, the immortal faith in democracy and human decency in Keller, the striving for high individual standards by Meyer and Spitteler; I am thinking even more of the great moral strength of Switzerland during the past decades: her unyielding integrity in the face of immense external dangers, and her endeavors, ever since the days of Henri Dunant, to alleviate her neighbors' sufferings and, in the midst of chaos, never to lose sight of human values and of the dignity of man. Her intrepidity and her loyalty to her tolerant and liberal political ideas will last on in the hard postwar years that will finally settle over strife-torn Europe; and thereby this land of two races, of three religious faiths, and of four languages may yet prove the truth of Victor Hugo's hopeful and prophetic assertion that "La Suisse, dans l'histoire, aura le dernier mot."

W. P. F.

Chapel Hill, N. C.

CONTENTS

CONTENTS

CHAPTER I

INTRODUCTION

THE GERMAN LANGUAGE

Like most European tongues the several Germanic languages, of which German is one, belong to the great Indo-European family of languages. They can be subdivided into three groups:

a. The east Germanic languages: Burgundian, Vandalian, and (especially) Gothic, in the last of which has been preserved the earliest extant text in any Germanic language. This is a portion of the translation of the Bible made about 360 A.D. by Bishop ULFILAS or Wulfila (311–381) and preserved in the so-called *Codex Argenteus*. All of these languages are extinct today.

b. The north Germanic or Scandinavian languages: Swedish, Danish, Norwegian, and Icelandic. In the twelfth and thirteenth centuries Old Norse literature reached its highest peak, particularly in Iceland, e.g. in the *Eddas*.

c. The west Germanic languages: High German, Low German, Dutch, and English, the last of which affords in its oldest form, Anglo-Saxon, the second oldest literary monument in a Germanic language, viz., the *Beowulf* (eighth century).

Beginning about 500 A.D. a special sound-shift served to separate the Old High German speech in southern and central Germany from the other west Germanic languages in north Germany, Holland, and England. However, this linguistic division of the German language into High German and Low German is today of relatively little importance because, through Luther's translation of the Bible into the former and through its consequent use in the great works of the German writers, especially from the eighteenth century onward, High German has become the standard literary language even in northern Germany.

1

PERIODS OF GERMAN LITERATURE

Largely determined by continuing linguistic change in
High German, three periods of literary production are
commonly distinguished:

a Old High German literature (OHG), 800–1050.
b. Middle High German literature (MHG), 1050–1500.
c. New High German literature (NHG), 1500 to the present.

More or less Christianized monks and their mentality con-
ditioned the bulk of OHG literature. Knights and their ideals
and adventures constituted the subject matter of MHG literature. From the thirteenth century on, German literature
ceased to be the exclusive privilege of a religious or a social
group. In the course of the centuries, burghers, aristocrats,
intellectuals, and proletarians came to the fore and gave
expression to their thoughts and ideals, successively or
simultaneously.

THE MIGRATIONS (c. 375–500)

The east Germanic peoples early moved their domain from
the Baltic to the Black Sea; but with the invasion of Europe
by the Asiatic Huns under King Attila in the last quarter of
the fourth century, they were compelled to resume their
wanderings and were soon sweeping over the entire continent. A great number of the Burgundians were annihilated
by the Huns in the vicinity of the Rhine in 437 and the rem-
nants driven on to the French-Swiss border regions. The
East Goths under the powerful King Theodoric the Great
(c. 454–526) established a kingdom in Italy with capitals ∂
Ravenna and Verona, and the Vandals, after having crossed
Spain and North Africa, founded a kingdom in what was
formerly Carthage; yet both these realms, around the middle
of the sixth century, were conquered by the East Roman
Emperor from Byzantium. The West Goths, finally, having
established a kingdom in Spain, were overwhelmed by the
Arabic invasion of Spain in 711 A.D.

After the defeat of the Roman legions by several united
west Germanic tribes under Hermann or Arminius, the chief
of the Cherusci, in the Teutoburg Forest in 9 A.D., the Rhine

remained for centuries the boundary between Germany and the Roman Empire; yet with the collapse of the latter in 476, the west Germanic tribes also began to sweep into Gaul and Italy. In contrast with the east Germanic tribes who moved swiftly and were quickly exterminated, the west Germanic peoples moved slowly and settled permanently: the Anglo-Saxons landed in Britain (449), the Lombards moved into northern Italy, the Alemanni into Switzerland. Most important were the Franks who, under Clovis around 490, established a kingdom on both banks of the lower Rhine, and then spread southward and eastward.

EARLIEST REPORTS ABOUT THE GERMANIC PEOPLES

Julius Caesar in his *Bellum Gallicum* (*c.* 50 B.C.) included accounts of the sturdy Germanic tribes which even then were beginning to press against the Rhine.

Tacitus in his *Germania* (*c.* 98 A.D.) added interesting details about the primitive manners and religious customs of these tribesmen, implying that the Romans should fear and emulate their austere strength and valor.

The East Roman historian Procopius described in *The Vandalic War* and *The Gothic War* the bloody battles of annihilation which the Byzantine generals, Belisar and Narses, waged in the sixth century against the exposed east Germanic tribes in North Africa and in Italy.

TRANSLATIONS

CAESAR: *The Gallic War.* London (Loeb Classical Library), 1939.
PROCOPIUS: *History of the Wars.* London (Loeb Classical Library), 1914–1940.
TACITUS: *Dialogues, Agricola, Germania.* London (Loeb Classical Library), 1932.

CHAPTER II

OLD HIGH GERMAN LITERATURE,
800–1050

THE HISTORICAL BACKGROUND

In the chaos that prevailed in western Europe following the collapse of the Roman Empire and during the migrations and the accompanying internecine strife and feuds of the Germanic tribes, the kingdom of the Franks under the Merovingian dynasty (486–751) became an increasingly important force for unification, consolidation, and stabilization. In 496 the Franks were converted to Christianity under Clovis; later, Winfrid of Wessex or Bonifacius (d. 755) and other Anglo-Saxon and Irish missionaries contributed much to the conversion of other Germanic tribes beyond the Rhine.

The Carolingian dynasty (751–911) produced two worthy representatives in Charles Martel, who in 732 beat back the Arabs at Tours, and in his son Pepin the Short, who defeated the Lombards and helped the Pope to establish what later became the Church State; but the greatest of all Carolingians was Charlemagne (*Karl der Grosse*), who ruled from 768 to 814 and who by his wars with the Saxons in the north, the Lombards in Italy, and the Arabs in Spain extended his realm over most of western Europe. Therewith a new and firm European unity was finally established, and on Christmas morning in the year 800 Charlemagne was crowned Emperor of the German-French-Italian empire of the Franks, which later came to be called the Holy Roman Empire of the German Nation. Charlemagne worked in close collaboration with the Pope, as was clearly demonstrated in the case of Widukind, chief of the Saxons, who at his defeat in 785 was the last pagan and free leader of a west Germanic tribe to submit to the new imperialism and the new religious creed of the Franks.

This new European unity began to totter under Charle-

4

magne's son, Louis the Pious (814–840), and upon his death his three sons by the significant Treaty of Verdun (843) split the Empire into Germany, France, and a so-called Middle Realm which extended from Holland through Switzerland into Italy. In 870 most of this *Mittelreich,* with the exception of Italy, was absorbed by Germany. Thus it is proper only from 843 on to speak of German, rather than Germanic, history.

Internal weaknesses arising from the rebellions of local feudal lords and external dangers threatening through the attacks of Viking pirates from the north, Arabian or Saracen pirates from the south, and Hungarian invaders from the east were finally removed by a new dynasty: the Saxon Emperors (919–1024). Their greatest representative was Otto I, or the Great (936–973), who defeated the Hungarians, reconquered north and central Italy, and firmly established his imperial power over the rebellious barons and an increasingly restless Church.

OLD HIGH GERMAN LITERATURE

Only with the establishment of stability by about 800, socially through the conclusion of the Migrations, politically through the unification of the Germanic domains, and linguistically through the completion of the (second) sound-shift which separated OHG from the other west Germanic languages, did a recorded literature become possible. Previously, as early as the beginning of the Christian era, the Germanic tribes are known to have produced heroic and historic ballads as well as other types of poetic composition. These, however, consigned to oral transmission, have not survived. The earliest recorded compositions, which, to be sure, often reveal evidence of survival through oral tradition from origins in the Germanic period, date from the ninth century.

The literary problem of the OHG period was to reconcile the warlike, primitive, and valiant spirit of the old heroic songs with the heretofore not clearly understood teachings and the alien tenets of the Christian Church. In making these necessary adjustments OHG literature often became guilty of strange inconsistencies and queer mixtures.

Heroic Literature

Heroic Sagas. Among the warriors and minstrels, scores of old ballads about Germanic and Hunnish heroes, such as Dietrich von Bern (Theodoric of Verona), Gunther, Hagen, Gudrun, Kriemhilde, Siegfried, and Attila (Etzel), lived on from generation to generation, until after many centuries they found perfect expression in the *Nibelungen* and the *Gudrun* epics. The influence of these Germanic heroic sagas produced such early masterpieces as *Beowulf* in eighth century England and *La Chanson de Roland* (The Song of Roland) in tenth century France.

Hildebrandslied. Outstanding is the *Hildebrandslied* (Lay of Hildebrand), a fragment dating back to about 800, a splendid illustration of Germanic valor, honor, and fatalism. It tells of Hildebrand, arms bearer of Dietrich, who, with his master, has spent so many years in the land of the Huns that upon his return to Italy even his son Hadubrand does not recognize him and challenges him to combat. With a heavy heart the old man agrees to this fight in which, after so many years of separation, he is bound to kill his own son. A later, more modern version of this theme, which is of frequent occurrence in world literature, leads to a reconciliation: it is the so-called *Younger Lay of Hildebrand*.

Merseburger Zaubersprüche. As an example of the pagan rites and superstitions of the early tribes can be mentioned the so-called *Merseburger Zaubersprüche* (Merseburg Charms), two magic formulas telling of the power of the gods in warfare and in the healing of wounds.

Religious Literature

Monasteries constituted the centers of learning and of literature; monks tried to impart their knowledge and their religion to the masses. The monasteries of St. Gall in Switzerland, Weissenburg in Alsace, and Fulda in central Germany were particularly important.

Early religious documents include such works as *Das Wessobrunner Gebet,* a prayer from the Bavarian monastery of Wessobrunn; the *Evangelienharmonie,* a translation, made at Fulda, of the Gospel Harmony of Tatian, a Syrian of the second century; and the *Muspilli* (World Destruction), a hundred-odd alliterative lines in which pagan and Christian conceptions of the end of the world are intermixed.

OTFRIED VON WEISSENBURG'S *Evangelienbuch* (Book of Gospels, *c.* 870) is a good example of a didactic paraphrase of the Gospels with which the author tried to impress his readers. Otfried's work is neither great nor beautiful; yet he is important, first because his is the first known name in the history of German literature, and second because, instead of the customary alliteration, his Gospel-Harmony for the first time uses end-rime.

Of a distinctly religious tenor is also the *Ludwigslied* (Song of Ludwig), a glorification of Louis III's victory over the Normans at Saucourt in 881.

Around the year 1000, the monk NOTKER in St. Gall was an outstanding scholar and translator who, through his essays on music and his interpretations and translations of works by Aristotle and Boethius, contributed greatly towards making the as yet unwieldy German language pliable enough to be a suitable medium for abstract thought.

LITERATURE IN OTHER LANGUAGES

Low German

Heliand. Compared with Otfried's work, the *Heliand* (i.e. *Heiland* or Savior), likewise a Messiad, is a much finer composition and a more interesting example of a priest's effort to recount the Christian story to a Germanic people, in this case to the recently converted Saxons, who were now presented with a description of Christ as a Germanic chieftain and of his disciples as doughty thanes. Unlike the *Evangelienbuch,* but like the *Hildebrandslied,* the *Heliand* (*c.* 830) is anonymous and also alliterative.

Latin

The so-called Carolingian Renaissance centering at the court of Charlemagne in Aachen (Aix-la-Chapelle) at the end of the eighth and the beginning of the ninth century represents a first effort to revive classical learning and to cultivate a purer form of Latin. Associated in this effort, which involved the establishment of better schools and the encouragement of literature, were also English and Italian scholars, such as Alcuin of York and Peter of Pisa. A noteworthy product of this activity is Charlemagne's biography, the *Vita Karoli Magni* by EINHART or Eginhart. Although the Emperor likewise liked the old Germanic sagas and caused them to be collected, most of these collections of pagan literature were destroyed under his bigoted son and successor, Louis the Pious.

Of comparable importance is the so-called Ottonian Renaissance of the tenth century, so named after the leading rulers of the Saxon dynasty. During this century of scholarly endeavor the beginnings of OHG literature were almost completely replaced by works written in Latin.

Ekkehard. The *Waltharius Manufortis* (Walter of the Strong Hand) was written in Latin hexameters under the influence of Virgil's *Aeneid* about 930 by the monk Ekkehard at the monastery of St. Gall. It relates how the hero, Walter of Aquitania, and his bride, Hildegund of Burgundy, who have been held as hostages at the court of Attila, escape from the Huns, are waylaid by Gunther, the greedy king of the Franks, but finally reach home and happiness after a mighty and unequal struggle between Walter and Gunther with twelve vassals. Chief among these was Hagen, who had earlier been a comrade in exile with Walter and Hildegund, and whose subsequent internal conflict between fealty to his liege lord and affection for his former friend constitutes for modern readers the most impressive aspect of the epic.

Ecbasis Captivi. The *Ecbasis Captivi* (Flight of the Captive) is a Latin poem written by a German monk in Lorraine around 940, which represents the first example of the beast epic in German literature. Under the guise of a calf which has escaped from its stall and falls into the power of a wolf, the author presumably relates his own adventures and temptations in running away from his monastery.

Roswitha. In the dramas of Roswitha or Hrosvitha of Gandersheim in the second half of the tenth century, the good nun endeavored to imitate and improve upon the Roman playwright Terence, whose works, read as texts in rhetoric during the Middle Ages, seemed too immoral for the purposes

8

of devout nuns. Roswitha's six little dramas, including in
Paphnutius the earliest treatment of the story of Thais, since
they dealt with the perennial struggle between the spirit and
the flesh as well as with the early conflict between Christianity and paganism, were meant to be very moral and edifying. Although these glorifications of Christian virtues were
probably never produced on the stage, their author is remembered as the first dramatist and also as the first poetess
in the history of German literature. In addition to the dramas
she wrote eight religious legends and two historical epics, all
of them like the dramas in the Latin language.

Ruodlieb. The story of *Ruodlieb* was written down in
Bavaria towards the middle of the eleventh century. It is an
anonymous and fragmentary novel in Latin, the first freely
invented tale of adventures in European literature, dealing
with the foreign travels of a young German hero and his
experiences at home after his return from abroad.

TRANSLATIONS

GENERAL COLLECTIONS

Grant, A. J. *Early Lives of Charlemagne by Eginhard and the Monk
of St. Gall.* London, 1926.
Hawthorne, Julian. *The Masterpieces and the History of Literature.*
New York, 1906. (Vol. I: *Song of Hildebrand, Muspilli, Wessobrunner Prayer,* etc.)

INDIVIDUAL AUTHORS

EKKEHARD: Scheffel, J. V. von. *Ekkehard, A Tale of the Tenth
Century* (containing a translation of the *Waltharius Manufortis*).
New York (Everyman's Library), 1940.

ROSWITHA: St. John, Christopher, tr. *The Plays of Roswitha.*
London, 1923.
Wiegand, Sister M. G., O. S. F. *The Non-dramatic Works of Hros-
vitha: Text, Translation, and Commentary.* Saint Louis, Mo., 1936.

CHAPTER III

MIDDLE HIGH GERMAN LITERATURE, 1050–1300 (–1500)

GENERAL OBSERVATIONS

The old German heroic sagas, as well as the earliest Christian writings of fervent monks, had been equally devoid of great artistic accomplishment. The former displayed a somber beauty that does not fail to impress us, even in the Latinized form of the *Waltharilied;* but they dwelt too much on martial virtues, manly loyalty, and untarnished honor, and paid little or no heed to love or other tender emotions. Nor did the religious texts distinguish themselves through beauty or elegance; heavy didacticism and ardent sincerity are their chief characteristics.

French Influence

However, this was all changed in the MHG period. The cultural influence of France now became very important. The innate French genius for ease and elegance of form could not but accelerate the German attempts, noticeable already in Notker, to make the German language richer, more flexible, and more expressive. More than that: French aristocracy had gradually abandoned the martial spirit of the originally Germanic *chansons de geste* of the type of the *Song of Roland* for the gentler, more civilized atmosphere of court life. Woman and love, which had been so completely neglected by the oldest German bards, now became the center of life and literature, thus reflecting a truly revolutionary change in man's way of thinking. Not battles, but love affairs and tournaments were now the main themes of literature; not bold external activity, but delicate analysis of hearts and souls was now important. The knight was no longer primarily a battling warrior, but a tender lover. The Christian spirit of mercy and humility at last fully possessed him, so that he was no longer a pagan in disguise, but a dauntless hero striving for a perfect synthesis of worldly activity and religious sincerity, of chivalric adventure and Christian virtue.

Anglo-Celtic Influence

Through France a second influence began to make itself felt: the Anglo-Celtic stories centering around King Arthur and the Knights of the Round Table. Having been brilliantly treated by such French authors as Chrétien de Troyes and Marie de France, these colorful tales of love and chivalry now were introduced into German literature. In the hands of German poets they underwent a valuable improvement through the introduction of a moral earnestness and a religious fervor which were not found in the often rather shallow and glittering French models.

Provençal Influence

Further French transmission of foreign influence occurred in connection with the lyric poetry and courtly manners which, partly under Arabic influence exerted through Spain, flourished especially in the Provence, at the time one of the leading cultural centers of Europe. The troubadours of southern France, with their almost abject adoration of ladies, usually married, who were their benefactresses, were also imitated in Germany, although here, too, the German poets usually enriched the often empty formalism of the French with a more sincere personal ardor of their own.

Oriental Influence

Still another source of foreign influence upon German life, literature, and culture was opened with the beginning of the Crusades (1096 ff.). Though these Crusades tended to increase Christian zeal, they also served to make European knighthood truly international and tolerant, because not only did the knights of western Europe come into close contact with one another on such expeditions, but they also learned to know and to respect foreign races and religions—Mohammedan culture, for example. Commercially the Crusades opened up new and valuable trade routes to the Orient;

11

culturally they were of utmost importance in opening up new intellectual horizons and in kindling man's fancy and imagination. Exotic tales about wondrous adventures, strange peoples, and fantastic occurrences now became quite frequent in German literature. The new "historical sense" as promoted by the Crusades manifested itself in the so-called *Weltchroniken* (World Chronicles) by RUDOLF VON EMS and by JANSEN ENIKEL, although their almost exclusive "historical" source was still the Bible.

Transitional Works

Among the transitional works which indicate the growing French and Oriental influences and the increasing emphasis on amatory adventure and psychological analysis, these may be mentioned:

a. *Das Alexanderlied* (The Song of Alexander), a secular epic treating the miraculous expedition of Alexander the Great into the Oriental wonderlands of Persia and India, is the first example of a German translation of a French epic. It was made by a priest, LAMPRECHT, between 1120 and 1130.

b. *Das Rolandslied* (The Song of Roland), also a secular epic likewise translated from a French original by a priest, KONRAD, around 1130, made known to the descendants of the East Franks one of the great heroes of the West Franks, Roland, paladin of Charlemagne, who died at Roncevaux (778) in battling an overwhelming force of Basques.

c. *König Rother* (King Rother), an epic written by a wandering minstrel between 1150 and 1160, presents a favorite medieval motif, a bridal abduction, and other adventures and Odyssean journeys in the Near East of the hero, king of the Lombards and supposedly grandfather of Charlemagne.

d. *Herzog Ernst* (Duke Ernest), written between 1170 and 1180, also shows the influence of the Crusades upon German literature. This amalgam of historical and legendary lore tells the story of a Swabian Robin Hood who was finally captured by the Emperor; in trying to explain his sudden disappearance, the epic insists that the valiant duke was never really imprisoned in Germany but that, instead, he had undertaken a great and adventurous journey into the Orient.

e. *Eneit,* commenced by HEINRICH VON VELDEKE before 1174 and completed after 1184, endeavors to give a courtly analysis of the unhappy passion between Aeneas and Dido, Queen of Carthage, such as was told in Virgil's great epic.

These five works helped to prepare the Golden Age of MHG literature. Heinrich von Veldeke's *Eneit* is the most important work among these forerunners.

THE HISTORICAL BACKGROUND

Under the Franconian dynasty (1024–1125) and the Hohenstaufen dynasty (1138–1254) the compact and unchallenged unity of the Empire as it had existed under Otto the Great was exposed to many stresses. Because the Catholic Church, inspired by the ascetic and ambitious order of Cluny, became increasingly unwilling to accept second place, there now began a titanic struggle between Emperor and Pope, between the secular ruler and the spiritual ruler of Christendom, between the conception of a universal monarchy and the conception of a universal theocracy. This struggle for supremacy in Europe reached a climax in 1077 at the monastery of Canossa in northern Italy where the Emperor Henry IV had to humble himself before Pope Gregory VII.

Yet the struggle with the Popes continued even among the Hohenstaufen Emperors (Frederick I, called Barbarossa, Henry VI, and Frederick II), and numerous times German armies were led into Italy in order to chastise refractory Popes and subdue restless Italian cities. In addition, rebellious German princes, under the leadership of the family of the Guelfs (Henry the Proud, Henry the Lion, and Otto IV), joined the insurrection against the Hohenstaufen or Ghibelline Emperors; yet even though Barbarossa and Henry VI were successful in defeating their enemies and establishing a period of peace, which witnessed the culmination of MHG culture, the brilliant dynasty of the Hohenstaufens, unrelentingly pursued by the hatred of the Popes, was finally doomed.

After Frederick II's death in 1250, the Empire was for

twenty-three years without an Emperor; civil wars were raging, club law and robber barons terrorized the country, and arrogant princes, who had become very powerful during the Emperor's altogether too frequent absences in Italy, destroyed the precarious unity of the Empire. The dire consequences of the dream of a German-Italian Empire now became clear: the Emperors had failed to consolidate their power at home, local princes had become too autonomous within the Empire, and the pressing problem of a real political unification of Germany was delayed till the nineteenth and twentieth centuries. The two succeeding new dynasties of Hapsburg and Luxemburg Emperors, who ruled intermittently from 1273 on, no longer possessed a fraction of the power that had once belonged to Otto the Great.

THE POPULAR EPIC

The Golden Age of MHG literature lasted from about 1180 to 1220 and found expression especially in three types of poetic works:

a. The Popular Epic: *Nibelungenlied, Gudrun.*
b. The Court Epic: Hartmann von Aue, Wolfram von Eschenbach, Gottfried von Strassburg.
c. The Lyric Poetry: Walther von der Vogelweide.

Das Nibelungenlied. Now at last the century-old heroic tales about the Migrations were collected and the many ballads were fitted together by some great but anonymous author into what was to become the great German national epic, *The Song of the Nibelungs.* The poem is the residue of old and originally unrelated sagas and cycles (the Brunhilde story, the Siegfried story, the story of the downfall of the Burgundians, the stories centering around the heroic deeds of Dietrich von Bern, a poetic transfiguration of the East Gothic king Theodoric the Great) which, in the course of centuries, had grown together and, by so doing, had developed new motivations and modifications. The basis of these tales, Siegfried's adventures and the deadly struggle of the Burgundians against the Huns, was still essentially pagan and Germanic; but under the more recent influences of French chivalry the author (or possibly some of his forerunners) felt obliged to superimpose some very slight and not wholly

14

convincing Christian and courtly elements upon this powerful old tale of loyalty and revenge.

The adventures of Siegfried with Brunhilde, Gunther's marriage to Brunhilde and Siegfried's marriage to Gunther's sister, Kriemhilde, and the growing rivalry between the two queens constitute the first part of the epic. It ends with the murder of Siegfried, who is killed at the request of Brunhilde and of Gunther by the latter's fiercely loyal vassal, Hagen. The second part tells of Kriemhilde's slow but determined and cruel revenge; how she marries Etzel (Attila), the king of the Huns, and then invites her kinsfolk to Etzel's court; and how all these Burgundians are finally slaughtered in a grandiose and gruesome finale of the epic, in which at last even Kriemhilde herself is slain.

The central figure of Kriemhilde alone holds together the Siegfried and Etzel parts of the epic. The study of her character is masterful: it shows the development of a tender maiden into a loving wife, in turn into a grief-stricken widow, and, finally, into a merciless fury. Siegfried departs too soon from her life; Brunhilde is soon forgotten; Gunther is a weakling; Etzel, a mere tool; and the only character besides Kriemhilde who is either grandiose or cruel enough to be worthy of any special emphasis is Hagen, the grimmest and yet most impressive representative of old Germanic warriordom.

The main theme of this epic, as of the *Waltharilied,* is the cruel conflict between two opposing loyalties: the conflict in Kriemhilde as to whether to avenge her dead husband or to forgive her treacherous brother; or, to mention another example, the conflict in Rüdiger as to whether to support his lord Etzel or his newly-won Burgundian relatives. Only in Hagen's breast is there no conflict, no moment of hesitation: in unswerving obedience he murders Siegfried, whose indiscretion has offended his queen, Brunhilde; with a grim joy he accompanies the Burgundian host to Etzel's court, though he knows that Kriemhilde has neither forgotten nor forgiven and that not one of them will ever return alive to the Rhine. Neither blood nor carnage is the main theme in this great epic; it is loyalty alone—a supreme loyalty that is above former friendships, above fear and death. No cheap compromises here; inexorably these giant characters act as act they must.

Gudrun. Second only to the *Nibelungenlied* is *Gudrun,* again a great glorification of woman's loyalty. The unity of action is less well preserved here, because the agglomeration of ballads really embraces the tale of three generations, in which Gudrun's story is only a part and not the absolute center, as Kriemhilde's love and hatred had been. The tale of Gudrun is incomparably more modern, more Christian, more courtly than the tale of Kriemhilde had been; and a woman's undying loyalty is represented here not in hating and killing but in loving, hoping, and enduring. Kidnapped by Hartmut, an unsuccessful suitor, Gudrun is kept a captive for over thirteen years before her former fiancé, Herwig, finds and saves her. Not active battling but faith and steadfastness are the chief traits which give force to Gudrun's character.

On account of its sea background, its many ships and ocean battles, *Gudrun* has often been called the German *Odyssey,* and the *Nibelungenlied,* the tale of the extermination of an entire people because of a woman, can be likened to the *Iliad.*

THE COURT EPIC

Of the three great poets of the court epic, we can say that Wolfram von Eschenbach was unexcelled in the whole realm of medieval European literature (with the exception of Dante and his *Divina Commedia*) in depth of thought and earnestness of ethical striving; that Gottfried von Strassburg was the great master of fluent versification and elegant, colorful style; and that Hartmann von Aue happily combined the talents of these two men by blending religious earnestness with picturesque and fashionable chivalry. Real classical perfection seems to be possible in German literature only when irregular and ardent German thought is tempered by French or Graeco-Latin influences of stylistic restraint and smoothness.

Hartmann von Aue. He was the first major German poet to deal with Arthurian romances and was chronologically the first great representative of those upper German districts around the Rhine and the Danube (including Alsace, Swabia,

16

Bavaria, Austria, and Switzerland) where MHG literature was to develop its finest blossoms.

His two Arthurian epics, *Erec* and *Iwein,* illustrate best the knightly maxim that, besides valor and piety, every true knight should also especially practice *mâze,* i.e., restraint and moderation—a virtue which keeps him from excesses and preserves in him a harmonious balance between the spirit and the flesh, between his worldly duties and his domestic affairs. Erec has sinned against this principle because he loves his wife so much that he stays with her all the time and forgets his knightly duties; Iwein, on the other hand, sins by being such an enthusiastic and untiring knight-errant that he completely neglects his wife and fails to return to her. Both knights are punished for their excesses, for their lack of *mâze;* and they have to suffer much before they strike the ideal and happy balance. *Iwein* especially is a masterpiece of an Arthurian tale in German literature.

In addition to wordly subjects Hartmann also presented religious problems. *Gregorius* is a religious legend of a great though unwitting sinner, a Christian Oedipus, who is involved in double incest through being the son of a brother and sister and becoming the husband of his mother and who, by his fervent penance for his sins, moves God to forgive him and, moreover, make him Pope.

Most famous, however, of Hartmann's works is *Der arme Heinrich* (Poor Henry), another religious tale of sin and forgiveness. It may be considered an early short story, and it is also one of the finest idyls in medieval literature. Heinrich von Aue, model of knighthood and a medieval Job, is for the fault of pride suddenly stricken with leprosy. Told by physicians at Salerno in Italy that he can be cured only if a pure and innocent maiden voluntarily sacrifices her heart's blood for him, the desperate man is inclined to accept such an offer which is actually made by the daughter of one of his tenants. When preparations are made to kill the child, however, Heinrich repents his egotism and rejects the sacrifice. Having learned the lesson of humility which God had sought to teach him, Heinrich returns to his native Swabia, is forgiven by God and cured by him, and thus enabled to marry the unselfish girl who had been willing to die for him.

17

Wolfram von Eschenbach. He is undoubtedly the greatest literary figure in that Golden Age of MHG culture. His masterpiece, *Parzival,* a long epic of almost 25,000 lines completed about 1210, is a superlative example of the way in which the worldly Anglo-French romances about King Arthur and the Knights of the Round Table were rendered more deeply earnest and religious by German poets and adaptors. In this epic, brilliant knighthood and colorful pageantry are reproduced in the adventures of Gawain, while a spiritual counterpoise is provided in the symbolic and significant career of Parzival, the primary hero of the work.

Parzival presents the story of the development of a naive youth (*ein tumber knappe*) into a mature man and perfect knight; it depicts the ups and downs, the successes and discouragements, and the men and women he meets on his wanderings. Furthermore, with marvelous symbolism and deep significance, it relates in all its changing fortunes the hero's quest for the Holy Grail, the miraculous source of spiritual powers, which is guarded by the noblest of knights. In the guise of this quest, which is symbolic of man's everlasting quest for God, is related how the hero at first fails, how he becomes embittered, how he still errs and yet perseveres, how he is eventually encouraged and gradually cleansed of his shortcomings and sins, and how finally he achieves his high purpose and becomes King of the Grail.

In Parzival, the perfect knight, are happily blended the spiritual and the worldly elements of chivalry, and nowhere has the deep mystical yearning of medieval religion found a more intense and sincere expression. Wolfram's broad canvas of Arthurian knighthood is beautiful and fascinating to behold; the women especially, such as Herzeloyde, Parzival's mother, and Kondwiramurs, his wife, are masterfully drawn; yet its ethical significance and religious implication, which are much deeper and more valuable than the meanings to be derived from the ordinary romances and tales of chivalry, are its supreme attraction. Thus *Parzival,* as the story of a God-seeker, a Christian whom no obstacle can divert or deter on his Pilgrim's Progress, may be considered the earliest example of a *Bildungsroman* or apprenticeship novel in German literature. Wolfram's language may at times be too heavy with thought and some of his verses may tend to become obscure; but the aesthetic and, above all, the ethical greatness of his epic is undisputed.

In a second work of his, *Willehalm,* in which he reproduced an old French *chanson de geste* about the bitter battles between Christians and Mohammedans during the reign of Charlemagne, Wolfram again displayed his ennobling genius: instead of blood-thirsty hatred, which permeates his source, he shows gentleness and restraint; and instead of fanatical bigotry he imparts a spirit of religious and racial tolerance which clearly reveals the cosmopolitan and more enlightened influence of the age of the Crusades.

Gottfried von Strassburg. Stylistically Gottfried is the most skillful and graceful imitator of French elegance to appear in this period. Not only in style but also in content his work affords a great contrast to that of Hartmann and Wolfram. In place of the principles of restraint and moderation (*mâze*) and the lessons of moral earnestness and religious endeavor inculcated in their works, Gottfried's one great epic, *Tristan und Isolde,* which was left uncompleted with almost 20,000 lines, appears to countenance erotic unrestraint and lawless passion. Indeed, from the point of view of modern morality it seems nothing less than a glorification of adultery. Judged by the courtly conventions of its own time, however, it turns out to be a great *exemplum* of, as the love poems of the period are glosses on, the art of courtly love, as actually practiced in courts of love such as those established by Eleanor of Aquitaine at Poitiers and by her daughter Marie of Champagne at Troyes, and as seriously described in a treatise on the subject by the latter's chaplain, Andreas.

Many a medieval troubadour, who glorified and wooed a married lady according to style, may have been in the situation of young Tristan, who had gone to woo fair Isolde of Ireland for his old friend and uncle Mark, king of Cornwall, but who, even after her marriage to the king, could not master his own desires. A mysterious love potion was supposedly responsible for this case of adultery, which after years of conflicting bliss and guilt and unhappiness could but end in death.

Tristan und Isolde has become one of the immortal love stories in literature, a powerfully and convincingly told tale, far superior to the crude battle scenes of the early epics, far superior also to the first painstaking analysis of passion in Heinrich von Veldeke's *Eneit,* yet ethically inferior to the works of Hartmann and Wolfram.

LYRIC POETRY

Walther von der Vogelweide. Instead of dwelling on HEINRICH VON MORUNGEN, REINMAR DER ALTE, ULRICH VON LICHTENSTEIN, and other accomplished love poets in whom a skillful observation of troubadour rules gradually came to mean more than sincerity and originality of emotion, we direct attention only to Walther von der Vogelweide, the foremost minnesinger and the greatest lyric poet in German literature before Goethe. In Germany, minnesong or love poetry, mostly written to married ladies and patronesses, as its particular convention required, had a more spiritual and mystical meaning than in France. Hence the relative ease with which many German poets changed over to religious poems, addressed no longer to an earthly lady, but to the Virgin Mary. In fact, much of the medieval cult of womanhood may have been inspired by the fervor of the so-called *Marienlieder. Minne* (love), as originally conceived, could not easily maintain itself on the difficult level of unselfishness and devotion; either it rose to religious heights of sublimity, as for example in the case of HEINRICH VON MEISSEN, significantly called *Frauenlob* (praise of women), or it sank to downright physical love, to the wooing no longer of a noble and reluctant lady but of a buxom peasant girl, as in the case of NEIDHART VON REUENTHAL, who is remembered as a courtly writer of rustic poetry (*höfische Dorfpoesie*), the author of the earliest pastorals in German literature. The courts of rich aristocrats became the stimulating centers of the minnesingers, as for example the Wartburg, the court of the landgrave Hermann of Thuringia (d. 1217).

The fact that Walther von der Vogelweide was deprived by death of his protector, and consequently compelled to wander restlessly over Central Europe until Frederick II finally granted him a small fief in Austria, constituted the greatest boon to his poetic genius, for his wanderings and sufferings made him acquainted with the heights and depths of life and the joys and griefs of mankind. Had he been permanently maintained rather than temporarily entertained at a provincial court, he might have become nothing more than a fashionable minnesinger, an accomplished stylist; but through his misfortune the whole world with its many problems was opened up to his genius.

Walther's fame rests primarily upon three pillars: first, he was an ardent and sincere celebrator of love on several levels, a worshipper not only of remote and highborn ladies but also of real, warmhearted women, of whom he sang in tender and affectionate tones; second, he was an observer and admirer of natural beauty, which he perceived and reproduced with much greater insight into its meaning than did the conventional courtier and court singer, thus happily blending love and springtime in his poetry; and, third, he was, especially in his *Sprüche* or didactic and political poems, a bold battler, an ardent patriot, a staunch defender of the Emperor and of the Ghibelline cause against the insubordination of the Guelfs and the endless intrigues of the Popes. The patriotism, moral integrity, and social idealism of German knighthood found a perfect exponent in Walther von der Vogelweide; as a lover of women, as an admirer of the beauties of nature, and as a glorifier of his native German land, his poetic accomplishment is undisputed.

TRANSLATIONS

GENERAL COLLECTIONS

Bithell, J. *The Minnesingers.* New York, 1909.

Hawthorne, Julian. *The Masterpieces and the History of Literature.* New York, 1906. (Vol. I: Lamprecht's *Alexander,* Walther von der Vogelweide, etc.)

Lancaster, C. M. *Two Moods of Minnesong* (containing "The Poem of Hapless Henry" and "Tristan and Isolde"). Nashville, Tenn., 1944.

Longfellow, H. W. *The Golden Legend* (a dramatic poem blending the stories of Poor Henry and of Faust, and subsequently incorporated as the middle, medieval section of Longfellow's trilogy entitled *Christus: A Mystery*). Boston, 1851.

Nicholson, F. C. *Old German Love Songs.* London, 1907.

Richey, M. F. *Essays on the Mediaeval German Love Lyric with Translations in English Verse.* Oxford, 1943.

ANDREAS CAPELLANUS: Parry, J. J., tr. *The Art of Courtly Love, by Andreas Capellanus.* New York, 1941.

GOTTFRIED VON STRASSBURG: Weston, Jessie L., tr. *The Story of Tristan and Iseult.* London, 1910. 2 vols.

GUDRUN: Armour, Margaret, tr. *Gudrun* (prose translation). London & New York (Everyman's Library), 1932.
Nichols, Mary P., tr. *Gudrun, A Medieval Epic* (verse translation). Boston & New York, 1889.

HARTMANN VON AUE: Bell, C. H. *"Der Arme Heinrich,"* in *Peasant Life in Old German Epics.* New York, 1931.
Comfort, W. W., tr. *Arthurian Romances* (translated from the French and containing versions of *Erec and Enid* and of *Yvain*). London & New York, 1935.
Rossetti, D. G. *Henry the Leper, A Swabian Miracle-Rhyme.* Boston, 1905. 2 vols.
Schlauch, Margaret. "Heinrich the Unfortunate," in *Medieval Narrative, A Book of Translations.* New York, 1928.

NIBELUNGENLIED: Armour, Margaret. *The Nibelungenlied, A Prose Translation.* London & New York (Everyman's Library), 1939.
Needler, G. H. *The Nibelungenlied, Translated into Rhymed English Verse in the Metre of the Original.* New York, 1904.

SONG OF ROLAND: Butler, Isabel, tr. *The Song of Roland* (translated from the French). Boston, 1932.

WALTHER VON DER VOGELWEIDE: Betts, F., tr. *Songs and Sayings of Walther von der Vogelweide, Minnesaenger.* Oxford, 1918.
Colvin, I. G., tr. *I Saw the World: Sixty Poems from Walther von der Vogelweide.* London, 1938.

WOLFRAM VON ESCHENBACH: Weston, Jessie L., tr. *Parzival, A Knightly Epic of Wolfram von Eschenbach.* London, 1894. 2 vols.

22

CHAPTER IV

THE LITERATURE FROM 1300 TO 1600

GENERAL OBSERVATIONS

After the monks and in turn the knights, it was the sturdy burghers who next assumed leadership in German culture. This position they occupied from the end of the thirteenth to the beginning of the seventeenth century, i.e., to the time when the Thirty Years' War destroyed the flower of German burgherdom. Humanism and the Reformation, to be sure, introduced new and very important trends and elements into German thought, but they did not in any way replace the basically bourgeois atmosphere of these three centuries with anything new. It is, therefore, important to emphasize that, except for the Reformation, German literature immediately before and after 1500 was essentially the same. In Italy, France, and England the Renaissance had early turned against the popular literature of the preceding centuries and had advocated aristocratic exclusiveness and courtly aestheticism instead; but in Germany this did not happen until much later, early in the seventeenth century. Thus the late MHG literature of the fourteenth and fifteenth centuries and the early NHG literature of the sixteenth century are discussed together: both were essentially bourgeois and realistic.

Literature in Other Countries

In foreign literatures Dante in Italy and Chaucer in England, though in many respects heralds of the modern era, still basically embodied the values of medieval thought. Immediately after them, however, the literature of Europe veered towards the Renaissance and towards increasingly neoclassical concepts in literature, according to which scholars and courtiers rejected and despised the often uncouth realism and didacticism of the bourgeoisie, and, to a lesser extent, the shallow romanticism of knightly adventure. This trend to-

wards greater artistic refinement began in Italy in the fourteenth century with Petrarch and Boccaccio; then, with
Lorenzo de' Medici, Poliziano, Ariosto, Bembo, Machiavelli,
and Castiglione, the Italian Renaissance reached its peak in
the years between 1480 and 1530. Tasso, in the second half
of the sixteenth century, was its last great representative.
In France, the definite rupture with the Middle Ages had to
wait almost until the middle of the sixteenth century: although
the French invasion of Italy had begun to bring in Italian
influences as early as 1494, it was really only Ronsard and
du Bellay in lyric poetry, Jodelle and Garnier in the drama,
and Rabelais and Montaigne in prose literature who incarnated the spirit of the Renaissance and who consciously
imitated Greek, Latin, and Italian literary standards. The
same holds true for England: though the Oxford Humanists
like Colet and More and lyrical poets like Wyatt and Surrey
started their efforts in the days of Henry VIII, it was only
under the reign of Elizabeth, with Spenser, Sidney, and
Shakespeare, that the English Renaissance reached its full
bloom. In Spain may be noted such innovators as Nebrija and
Vives among the Humanists and Garcilaso de la Vega and
Boscán among the lyricists; but in the field of the drama and
the (picaresque) novel medieval and realistic traditions continued to an unusual degree in Spain, as in Germany.

THE HISTORICAL BACKGROUND

With the proud dynasty of the Hohenstaufens destroyed
and so many German knights degenerated into robber barons,
the hopelessly split-up Empire faced a period of painfully
slow decay which lasted for centuries and which, in 1806,
finally led to the official dissolution of the First Reich. The
Hapsburg Emperors in Vienna were really only the rulers of
Austria and Bohemia and had little more to say in the Empire
as such. Endless feudal strife between the great princes likewise contributed to the general national chaos. Through the
"Babylonian Captivity" of the Popes at Avignon in the fourteenth century and the subsequent Great Schism within the
Church between the Pope of Rome and the Pope of Avignon,
the power of the Holy See was also tremendously weakened.
In an important German law, the so-called Golden Bull of

1356, the German princes not only restricted the power of their Emperor, but also forbade the constant meddling by the Pope in the affairs of the Empire. The only Emperor who was of any cultural or political importance during this time was Charles IV (1347–1378) of the House of Luxemburg: he tried to reassert his power in Italy, encouraged Humanism, and built up Prague as his capital. But, even so, the gradual breaking away from the Reich of little Switzerland, which started in 1291, shows clearly how impotent the Emperor had grown and how disorganized his Empire had become.

In this period of decline the German burghers were the only really vital element of the German population. Their cities grew and their trade flourished, making them rich and envied. In numerous skirmishes their armed convoys managed to defend themselves valiantly against the robber barons and the greedy princes. Of all the prosperous city leagues, the most famous was the Hansa, a union of enterprising trading cities centering on the Baltic Sea with the Capital at Lübeck and offices and dealings extending from Spain and England to Sweden and Russia. The Hansa flourished particularly in the fourteenth century: together with the Teutonic Knights, a valiant religious order of warriors, these burghers Christianized, colonized, and Germanized the Baltic States deep into Russia. The Teutonic Knights were utterly defeated by the Poles and the Lithuanians in 1410, and the discovery of America and the gradual shifting of international trade to Spain and England finally brought about the disintegration of the Hansa also.

The increasing impoverishment of the lower German aristocracy led to a rebellion of the knights in 1522, and the ruthless exploitation of the serfs led to the bloody Peasant War in 1524 and 1525. But in spite of this utter disorganization of the Empire the Hapsburg dynasty early in the sixteenth century blossomed as never before or afterward in history. Through a series of advantageous marriages the Hapsburgs acquired Burgundy, Spain with all her colonies overseas, and Hungary, and so the greatest Hapsburg ruler, Charles V (1519–1556), indeed ruled over many lands besides his German-Austrian-Italian possessions. But it was a hollow splendor: his claims to Burgundy involved him in what later

25

became a century-long struggle against France; in the southeast the Turks, after the conquest of Constantinople (1453), advanced to the very gates of Vienna; the Swiss refused to give up their independence; the princes remained arrogant, the knights and peasants remained rebellious; and the beginning of Luther's Reformation plunged Germany into even greater chaos. Discouraged, Charles V in 1556 again dissolved his mighty but incohesive Empire: to his brother, Ferdinand, he gave the German-Austrian-Italian imperial crown and to his son, Philip II, he gave Spain, the Netherlands, southern Italy, and the colonies.

After these false dreams of greatness had vanished, the old Holy Roman Empire of the German Nation appeared more moribund than ever. The kings of France and England had been shrewd realists and had built up small but absolutely united and compact states; the German colossus, however, had overreached itself, and its rulers had paid more heed to their imperial dream of a well-nigh impossible German-Italian amalgamation than to a sound national policy. England and France in the sixteenth century were ready for great action and expansion; Germany, on the other hand, was doomed to ever greater disintegration.

THREE CENTURIES OF BOURGEOIS REALISM

Religious and Dramatic Literature

Scholastic Literature. At the peak of papal power and of knightly culture the official philosophy of the Church was Scholasticism. ALBERTUS MAGNUS (1193–1280) of Cologne was one of the greatest German representatives of this system of thought, which tried, often by hairsplitting arguments, to harmonize Reason and Faith. Thomas Aquinas in Italy and Duns Scotus in England were other great Scholastic thinkers of the time.

German Mystics. With the gradual disintegration of political and social standards, however, there occurred a departure from the rigid formalism and the sterile, empty arguments of Scholasticism in the direction of a simpler and warmer way to God. The German mystics were the first forerunners of the Reformation: neither books, nor dogmas, nor priests were of use to them; like Parzival, they had to find their way to God alone. MEISTER ECKHART (1260–1327) was the greatest German mystic; others were HEINRICH SEUSE (or Suso), JOHANNES TAULER, and THOMAS À KEMPIS (1380–1471), the latter the author of the most significant book of mysticism, the *De Imitatione Christi*. In literature the mystics deserve a special place because in their endeavor to express the ultimately inexpressible experience of correspondence and actual union with God, they contributed to the wealth of the German language and to the development of German prose style.

Religious Plays. Out of the Bible recitations in church— for example, the story of Christ's resurrection on Easter morning—there gradually developed, as early as the beginning of the eleventh century, the religious drama. Various parts were read by individual priests, longer sentences were substituted for the ones found in the Bible, entire new scenes were made up and interpolated, German was slowly introduced to take the place of Latin, and the whole play was performed outside the church rather than within it, and, finally, it was put on in the market place. Most striking is the gradual secularization of these plays: as the clergy and the patricians withdrew, the sturdy citizenry took hold of them, and realistic, earthy, and even obscene scenes eventually overshadowed the originally religious theme. Among the scores of religious dramas which have been preserved, Easter Plays are far more numerous than Christmas Plays. By assimilating new biblical material the erstwhile short Easter Plays, relating originally only the story of the resurrection, gradually grew into the *Passionsspiele* (Passion Plays), which, in turn, finally encompassed the whole story of Christ's life—indeed, the whole of the Bible from the Creation to the Savior's death. Performances often lasted several days (Frankfurt, Heidelberg, Lucerne); each guild of burghers, given a special task, tried to outdo the others in pomp and showmanship. The bourgeois love of mixing religious exaltation with coarseness and good-natured laughter was particularly well demonstrated in these dramas, and one of the favorite characters in them was Mary Magdalene, a great saint who had once been an even greater sinner. One of these Passion Plays, which came to be performed regularly at Oberammergau from the seventeenth century on, is popular even today; but in its modern version it is of course purely religious, having been cleansed of all its earthy elements.

The *Redentiner Osterspiel* (Redentin Easter Play) of 1464 is an especially fine example of this type of literature. In mighty words it tells of Christ's resurrection and of his descent to hell, where he liberates all the anxiously waiting souls; with sly humor it then describes the devils' wrath at seeing themselves deprived of their victims and depicts how they manage to find more than enough sinners to fill their hell again by checking up on the evil doings of the inhabitants of the neighboring city of Lübeck.

Didactic and Satirical Works

Compared with the noble romanticism of the preceding age, the literature of the burghers was realistic and sober. Art for art's sake was no longer cultivated; instead, literature had to teach, to educate, or to satirize human weaknesses and vices. Consequently the language lost its beauty, the rimes lost their fluency, and numerous local dialects destroyed whatever linguistic uniformity had existed in MHG literature. New life broke forth everywhere; the growing restlessness and rebelliousness announced the dawn of the modern era. Political, social, religious, and literary forms and conventions were swept away by this new vitality. In literature the cultivated standards of knighthood vanished, and although the poetic formulas and metric rules were carefully and stubbornly adhered to, the poetic spirit was gone and poetry became wooden and coarse. But beneath these superficial defects there was tremendous strength, the strength of men who were about to break the yoke of medieval tradition and dogma.

Freidank. In the first half of the thirteenth century Freidank's *Bescheidenheit* (Sagacity), in a more sober fashion than some of Walther's poems, continued to expound patriotic and anti-Roman sentiments. Under the pen name of Freidank, or Freethinker, the author was one of the first representatives of the new bourgeois mentality.

Wernher. The important and interesting epic *Meier*

Helmbrecht by Wernher the Gardener tells the story of a young peasant fop who imitated the criminal escapades and arrogant behavior of the robber barons and who came to an evil end. While it ostentatiously preaches bourgeois modesty and acceptance of a lowly position in society, this epic affords valuable glimpses into the moral and physical decay of knighthood.

Volksbücher. From the large group of works often called *Volksbücher vom sterbenden Rittertum* (Folk Books about Dying Knighthood) may be mentioned such examples as *Das Buch von Troja* (The Book about Troy), by HANS MAIR of Nördlingen, and *Hug Schapeler* (Hugo Capet), by the Countess ELISABETH VON NASSAU-SAARBRÜCKEN. These long-winded and—in spite of their fantastic subject matter —drily sober prose renderings of old tales of war and chivalry cannot compare with the epic stateliness of *Le Roman de Troie* (The Tale of Troy) by Benoît de Sainte-Maure in France or with such romantic compilations as the *Amadis de Gaula* by Lobeira in Portugal and Montalvo in Spain, and the *Morte d'Arthur* by Thomas Malory in England; for the German works emphatically express the burghers' utter distaste for militarism and foolish adventurousness. Even aristocrats like the Countess Elisabeth gradually came to accept the bourgeois viewpoint that no criminal wars or mad expeditions should be permitted to interfere with trade and civic progress. Both native themes, such as *The Tale of the Horn-Skinned Seyfrid,* and Renaissance tales from abroad, such as *The Tale of the Beautiful Magellone,* were in general well represented among these chapbooks.

Heinrich von Wittenweiler. The greatest peasant epic is *Der Ring* (The Ring), written in Switzerland by Heinrich von Wittenweiler early in the fifteenth century. It is an endless and grotesque tale about churlish peasants, a book full of didacticism and eroticism which ends in a gigantic war between hostile clans and villages. It also demonstrates how much the new realists liked to burlesque the formerly great traditions of knighthood and minnesong.

Shrovetide Plays. The fifteenth century likewise witnessed the peak of the Shrovetide Plays—coarse, short, and mostly improvised comedies about sex and other personal problems, in which the vices of men, particularly of monks, and of women were not always good-naturedly ridiculed. Also political and social problems were occasionally pilloried. Since these comedies were mostly played during the carnivals early in spring, however, they primarily dealt with biological fermentations caused by the return of spring.

Fables. Fables were particularly popular with these new middle-class poets because under the convenient guise of animals (the cunning of the fox, the stupidity of the bear, the lasciviousness of the she-wolf, the greed of the lioness, etc.) they could easily satirize human foibles and teach a practical lesson. Most famous is the story of *Reineke Fuchs* (Reynard the Fox), a beast epic which originated in Flanders and which tells how the tricky fox, instead of being punished for his depredations, finally even became chancellor of the Reich. HEINRICH VON ALKMAR was one of the poets to treat this story (*c.* 1487), which has been given currency in modern times through the translation made by Goethe.

Brant. *Das Narrenschiff* (The Ship of Fools) by Sebastian Brant, published in 1494, is another example of didactic and satirical literature, in which the author undertook to poke fun at all sorts of fools by classifying them, having them embark on a ship, and sending them off to *Narragonien,* the land of fools. A Latin version of this text, made by the Humanist JAKOB LOCHER, was promptly translated into English by the Scotch poet Alexander Barclay (1509).

Till Eulenspiegel. The peasants' revenge for being ridiculed as particularly ignorant by the burghers of the towns can be seen in the stories connected with the name of Till Eulenspiegel, for in this book of gay pranks the smart young peasant Till could easily outwit any magistrates or gullible townsmen. The name of the author who, early in the sixteenth century, collected and published these roguish, picaresque tales is not known. The so-called *Schildbürger* stories, in which the stupidity of small townsfolk is pilloried in many an unforgettable episode, have the same purpose.

Dedekind. Much coarser is a work by Friedrich Dedekind, *Grobianus* (1549), a description of the most ill-mannered and ill-bred fellow imaginable, carrying the didactic implication, of course, that the reader should avoid all these crudities.

The originally Latin text of this satire was translated into German by KASPAR SCHEIT in 1551.

Pauli and Wickram. Since collections of short moralizing stories were particularly popular among the honest burghers, men like Johannes Pauli in *Schimpf und Ernst* (Jesting and Serious Tales) and Jörg Wickram in *Das Rollwagenbüchlein* (Travelers' Book) supplied that need. The latter author, an Alsatian, deserves special mention for having been among the first writers of novels in the history of German literature. His books (e.g., *Der Goldfaden,* 1557) mark the transition from the medieval verse epic to the social prose novels of later centuries.

Faust. One of the many folk books that was to become especially famous was *Die Historia von Dr. Johann Faust,* published anonymously in Frankfurt in 1587, which tells of a magician so ambitious that he sold his soul to the devil in order to secure the latter's services. A few years later Christopher Marlowe used this text for his well-known Faustus tragedy. Later generations of German poets were influenced by new versions of this *Volksbuch,* by the popular puppet plays on this theme, and by Marlowe's tragedy, which was brought back to Germany by wayfaring English Comedians.

Lyric Poetry

Meistersong. In the fifteenth and sixteenth centuries sincere burghers, masters of guilds rather than masters of poetry, attempted to imitate the glories of MHG literature by forcing their simple and homespun thoughts into the very elaborate system of versification derived from the minnesingers. The difference between minnesong and meistersong is the difference between real inspiration and mechanical imitation. Busily these butchers, bakers, and candlestick makers studied their great models, sincere in their regrets that poetry since the days of Walther should thus have declined, sincere also in their effort to create again good and great literature. They knew the rules and believed that this was all that was needed; but, alas, they completely lacked genius. Today the meistersong is dead and forgotten; but, even so, it represents a pathetic effort of German burghers to revive the literary greatness that once had been.

Folk Songs. One of the few types of literature which flourished luxuriantly during these fermenting centuries is the German folk song. Composed anonymously and preserved in several different versions and simple melodies, these folk songs are a true mirror of the soul of the German people. Tender and unsophisticated in their language and rapid in their build-up of situations, they speak of love and jealousy, of grief and separation, of work and pleasure, of farewells and returns, of paradise and hell-fire, of hope and despair, of travels and political problems—of all the things that really move the hearts of men and women. The fifteenth and sixteenth centuries witnessed the richest production of these beautiful and sincere compositions. Through wars, crises, and revolutions they have preserved their popularity up to this day, and in the course of the centuries have repeatedly influenced and inspired the more contrived and artful forms of poetry.

A Typical Burgher Writer

Hans Sachs (1494–1576). The best embodiment of the bourgeois culture of these centuries is Hans Sachs, the shoemaker of Nürnberg, a sober and homespun poet, an ardent supporter of Luther, a man who completely typifies the virtues and limitations of German burgherdom. Several thousand miscellaneous works of his are preserved: his meistersongs are justly forgotten; his farces and Shrovetide Plays (*The Children of Eve, The Excision of Fools, The Wandering Scholar*), although didactic, are interesting and quite superior to the comedies of the preceding century; his verse tales and legends are wholesome and well worth reading (*Saint Peter and the Goat*); his religious plays and poems show his Protestant ardor (*The Nightingale of Wittenberg*). Sachs's literature is not great art; but it is clean and edifying, and it embodies the bourgeois virtues of thrift, piety, and forthrightness which made him so popular with the lower middle class and which induced Richard Wagner to glorify him in his *Die Meistersinger von Nürnberg*.

HUMANISM (1480–1530)

In this bourgeois atmosphere, in this literature which produced lasting values really in only two types, the satire and the folk song, two new trends appeared: Humanism and the Reformation. Humanism tried to contribute to the great European movement of the Renaissance by delving into the literature, history, and philosophy of ancient Greece and Rome and by attempting to create from this rich cultural inheritance a new ideal of humanity and of learning. Hence its slogan: "Back to the sources!" The Reformation tried to contribute to this great European rebirth by going back to the genuine teachings of Christ and of the early Church Fathers and by doing away with so much that later centuries had deemed it necessary to introduce. The Turkish conquest of Constantinople in 1453 and the resulting flight of Greek scholars into Italy and other western European countries encouraged the ardent study of Greek antiquity, while Johannes Gutenberg's invention of printing at about the same time enabled the Humanists to attract for their works a truly international reading public of intellectuals. The cosmopolitan figure of Erasmus of Rotterdam, the friend of monarchs and Popes, the universally acknowledged leader of all European scholars, illustrates best the international character of Humanism.

The earliest influences of the Italian Humanism of Petrarch, Boccaccio, and the political visionary, Cola di Rienzi, made themselves felt at Prague, at that time the capital of the Reich. Emperor Charles IV, aided by his Humanist chancellor, JOHANN VON NEUMARKT, established at Prague the first German university in 1348; Vienna followed in 1365 and Heidelberg in 1386. The best known work of this earliest German Humanism, the so-called Bohemian Humanism, is *Der Ackermann aus Böhmen* (The Plowman from Bohemia), written in 1400 by JOHANNES VON SAAZ, a dialogue between a lowly plowman and Death, in which man for the first time dares to rebel against the omnipotence of death and to assert a new pride and a new dignity in man. These first beginnings of Humanism in the Empire were then destroyed by the riots and the religious war which followed in the wake of the

33

burning of the Bohemian reformer, JOHANNES HUS, in the year 1415.

Later, during the latter part of the fifteenth century, a second Humanistic movement started in the lands of the southwest: the Swabian HEINRICH STEINHÖWEL, the Swiss NICHOLAS VON WYLE, and the Franconian ALBRECHT VON EYB distinguished themselves in doing preliminary spade work by translating sundry works of Italian Humanists (Petrarch, Boccaccio, Aeneas Silvius Piccolomini) and Latin comedies by Plautus and Terence.

The Humanists were enlighteners, rationalists, and cosmopolites in the best sense; but in spite of their moral and scholarly integrity, their movement suffered from various disadvantages:

a. They wrote their original works in Latin and Greek rather than in German.

b. Their movement was therefore represented and supported exclusively by intellectuals, relatively few in number; it never took root among the masses.

c. In the question of religious reforms they were timidly and tolerantly in favor of compromises only, and were therefore swept away by the tremendous avalanche started by Luther who, writing and speaking in the language of the people, had the support of the broad masses.

One great achievement may be accredited to the Humanists, however: gradually they penetrated and thoroughly reformed the German universities, which, up to 1500, had been dominated by narrow-minded and bigoted supporters of Scholasticism. The Humanists, mainly under the leadership of JAKOB WIMPFELING, an Alsatian scholar, introduced new curricula of studies which disregarded sterile dialectics and which emphasized a broad and truly Humanistic culture.

In Humanists like Sebastian Brant, Jakob Wimpfeling, and CONRAD CELTIS is to be observed also their staunchly German patriotism and their love for medieval German culture: Brant left the important cultural center of Basel after that city had decided to join the Swiss Confederation (1501); Wimpfeling wrote what may be called the first history of Germany (*Epitoma rerum Germanicarum usque ad nostra tempora*, 1505); and Celtis was, among other things, the first to edit

Tacitus' *Germania* and the forgotten plays of Roswitha of Gandersheim.

The German Humanists achieved great beauty and elegance in their lyrical, epic, and dramatic works; in style, though not necessarily in thought, their Latin books were superior to the often crude German works of that bourgeois era. EOBANUS HESSUS and PETRUS LOTICHIUS were the greatest neo-Latin poets among the German Humanists. In this connection it should be emphasized that neoclassical principles such as stylistic perfection, metaphorical embellishments, and courtly wit and polish, which characterize Renaissance literature in other lands, are to be found in Germany only among these neo-Latin poets. Neoclassical poems written in German did not appear until early in the seventeenth century.

Johannes Reuchlin (1454–1522). Reuchlin, the first outstanding scholar of Hebrew in modern Europe, became involved in an ugly anti-Semitic quarrel in which the Scholastic universities sought a last chance to discredit the Humanists in general and Reuchlin in particular. However, all famous men of contemporary Europe rushed to his help, and Reuchlin, by publishing their complimentary letters under the title of *Epistolae clarorum virorum* (Letters of Famous Men, 1514) was vindicated in his Hebrew studies, even though the Pope finally sided with his Scholastic and anti-Semitic enemies. Ulrich von Hutten and others also intervened in this greatest quarrel between modern Humanism and antiquated Scholasticism by ridiculing Reuchlin's enemies in a bitter satire, the *Epistolae obscurorum virorum* (Letters of Obscure Men), published anonymously in 1517. Reuchlin was responsible for a clear and scholarly re-establishment of the ancient Hebrew text of the Old Testament, a text which Luther later used for his translation of the Bible into German. Besides tending to their critical, scholarly work, most Humanists endeavored also to create new literary works of their own, as Wimpfeling in his *Stylpho* (1470), the earliest Humanistic comedy in Germany, and as Reuchlin in his farce *Henno* (1498).

Desiderius Erasmus von Rotterdam (1466–1536). Born in Holland, widely traveled in Germany, France, England, and Italy, yet living mostly in Basel, Switzerland, Erasmus, without doubt the greatest Humanist and the first true European, is usually included in histories of German literature. Besides his innumerable letters in excellent Latin, his *Adages* (a collection of wise sayings of antiquity), his well-observed *Colloquies* about the people and customs of his time, and his faultless re-establishment of the correct Greek text of the New Testament, Erasmus wrote two particularly famous works:

a. *The Praise of Folly* (1508), a book of good-natured satire against human weaknesses, in the manner of Sebastian Brant and of Hans Sachs, in which he singled out for bitter attacks his special enemies, the clerics.

b. *The Handbook of a Christian Soldier* (1509), in which, very much in the manner of Luther, he endeavored to lead Catholicism back to the true teachings and the simplicity of the gospel and in which he also gave the reader a fine outline of the education of a Christian leader.

In spite of so many points on which Erasmus agreed with Luther, he, the scholar and diplomat, was in favor of slow evolution rather than of sudden revolution. Afraid of mob violence and of Luther's lack of restraint, he, almost against his will, sided ever more with his friends, the Popes and the Cardinals, because he had a horror of Luther's fanatical frontal attacks. Humanism and Reformation, personified in Erasmus and Luther, might have been brothers-at-arms because they both abhorred the demoralization of Rome; yet they ended by being enemies. They held similar goals, but proposed different methods; theirs was an enmity not of kind, but of degree. Indeed, Erasmus may well have died of a broken heart when he saw Luther's mighty avalanche sweep away all his fine compromises. Erasmus is one of the greatest rationalists and enlighteners of all times; but what his time thought it needed was not half-hearted compromises, but total and radical solutions.

Ulrich von Hutten (1488–1523). Hutten and Melanchthon were the only Humanists to support Luther's cause. A valiant struggler, one of the most admirable fighters in German literature, a bitter enemy of Rome, Hutten joined Luther for political rather than for religious reasons, because he wished above all to free Germany from all foreign religious

and political influences. The fact that the German Emperor
Charles V was a Spaniard rather than a German was a great
tragedy for the Reich in general and for Hutten in particular,
because thus, in its greatest hour of need, the Empire was
ruled by a foreigner and a Catholic, by the secret powers of
Rome and Madrid, rather than by men of strong German
convictions. As a friend of the Humanists, Hutten defended
Reuchlin and admired Erasmus; later, however, when the
latter split with Luther, Hutten scolded and cursed Erasmus
for his lack of courage and conviction, and died a bitter and
early death in exile in Switzerland, where Zwingli had
granted him shelter. His *Gesprächbüchlein* (Book of Dialogues, 1521) contains acid dialogues condemning Roman
greed and immorality; especially *Vadiscus* represents one of
the most vitriolic attacks against the Catholic Church digni-
taries and the Pope. Aware of the fact that it was more important to reach the broad masses than the relatively few
Humanists of Germany, Hutten, in a decision which was
quite symbolic of the ultimate outcome of the great struggle
between Humanism and Reformation, hastened to translate
many of his early polemical works from Latin into German.

Philip Melanchthon (1497–1560). Melanchthon, a fine
scholar, professor of Greek at Wittenberg, the Protestant
stronghold, and bound to Luther through an everlasting
friendship, was really the diplomat of the Reformation.
Luther was the battler; Melanchthon, however, was the
brain behind the movement, the man who formulated the
Protestant Creed (1530) and who kept in touch with the
chanceries of Europe. The quarrels between Luther and
Erasmus, between Luther and Hutten, and finally even between Luther and Zwingli (in the Religious Dispute of
Marburg, 1527) must have grieved Melanchthon greatly;
yet he remained loyal to his fearless friend. On account of
his excellent scholarly textbooks and his efforts for educational reforms Melanchthon is often called the *praeceptor
Germaniae.*

THE GERMAN REFORMATION

The German mystics, the teachings of Johannes Hus, and
the critical work of the Humanists had already prepared the

great rebellion of northern Europe against Rome, of which Martin Luther in Germany and Huldreich Zwingli and John Calvin in Switzerland were the outstanding leaders.

Martin Luther (1483–1546). Luther, an Augustinian monk, began the conflict with the Church of Rome through his ninety-five theses attacking the sale of indulgences (1517). Various discussions failed to induce him to retract, and at the Imperial Diet of Worms in 1521 there occurred the irreparable rupture between Luther on the one hand and Pope and Emperor on the other hand, a rupture that might perhaps have been avoided if Erasmus had cared to speak up. As it was, Charles V for imperial reasons decided against Protestantism, and Germany, in her hour of need, thus found herself with a ruler who did not really understand her. Excommunicated and outlawed, Luther for some time found a refuge on the Wartburg in Thuringia, while his friends continued his work at Wittenberg. About two-thirds of Germany gradually became Lutheran, with the Rhineland, Bavaria, and Austria remaining the chief Catholic strongholds.

The bold call for a new freedom broke off somewhat abruptly when Luther saw in the Peasants' War of 1524–1525 to what excesses his message could lead, and from then on he tended to become rather conservative and dictatorial, as was shown by his unpleasant quarrel with Zwingli on account of the latter's liberal interpretation of transubstantiation. In 1530 the proclamation, at Augsburg, of the Protestant Creed, the work of Luther and Melanchthon, guided the Protestant movement into definite channels.

In spite of his stubborn and belligerent attitude, however, Luther managed to avoid the outbreak of a religious war, partly, to be sure, because the Emperor also, in view of the French and Turkish invasions, could not afford such a conflict. The first religious war, the so-called *Schmalkalden* War (1546–1555), started only after Luther's death and ended in a draw, a truce, rather than a real peace (the Peace of Augsburg), in which both sides were compelled to acknowledge each other's strength and right to exist.

Of Luther's works may be mentioned:
a. Various pamphlets of fundamental importance in which he attacked Rome and defended his new Protestant ideas:

An den christlichen Adel deutscher Nation (To the Christian Nobility of the German Nation); *Von der babylonischen Gefangenschaft der Kirche* (On the Babylonian Captivity of the Church); *Von der Freiheit eines Christenmenschen* (On the Liberty of a Christian), all three published in 1520.

b. The German translation of the Bible (1522–1534), a masterpiece whose enormous distribution not only strengthened the Protestant cause but also gave Germany a literary language. Luther's German even more than the language previously cultivated at any of the governmental chanceries gradually crowded out the various dialects and finally became the generally accepted written language of the whole country.

c. Pamphlets like *An die Bürgermeister und Ratsherren* (To the Mayors and Councilors) in which Luther proposed a general education of the people and advocated state-supported elementary schools; and *Wider die mörderischen Rotten der Bauern* (Against the Murderous Gangs of the Peasants) in which he turned violently against the very masses which, in the name of the new Christian freedom he had proclaimed, had rebelled against serfdom.

d. His beautiful *Geistliche Lieder* (Religious Songs) of the type of *Ein' feste Burg ist unser Gott* (A Mighty Fortress Is Our God), German hymns which henceforth took the place of the Catholic Latin church songs, eliciting imitations even in Catholic countries and gaining general currency in distant times and climes.

Thomas Murner. Murner, a Franciscan monk of Alsace, was one of the earliest and most inveterate enemies of Luther. His satirical vein was much more unbridled than Sebastian Brant's, by which it was influenced. Among his early works may be mentioned *Die Geuchmatt* (The Fools' Meadow), a harsh and merciless condemnation of the fools of love in which the misogynous monk lashed out at all strata of society, including his own class of ecclesiastics. Most renowned was his venomous, coarse, and often quite obscene satire *Von dem grossen lutherischen Narren* (On the Great Lutheran Fool, 1522), in which his vituperation against the imagined

39

viciousness of Luther and of the Reformation reached grotesque, yet in spots witty and brilliant, expression.

Hans Sachs, Ulrich von Hutten, and Philip Melanchthon have already been mentioned as supporters of Luther; to them can be added the names of the greatest German painters of all times, Albrecht Dürer and Hans Holbein the Younger.

Protestant Comedy. The new Renaissance comedy had first been subjected to the influence of Plautus and Terence, especially by the Humanists Wimpfeling and Reuchlin. Subsequently Protestant authors of the sixteenth century, whose comedies were written sometimes in Latin, sometimes in German, endeavored not only to do away with the long-winded bulkiness of medieval dramas but also to inject a note of greater moral earnestness into their imitations of Latin models—just as Roswitha had tried to do, centuries before. Attacks against Catholicism and themes borrowed from the Old Testament were particularly frequent in these short, scholarly, and somewhat dry Protestant comedies. As examples can be mentioned *Vom Papst und seiner Priesterschaft* (On the Pope and His Hierarchy) and especially *Der Ablasskrämer* (The Seller of Indulgences), by the Swiss Zwinglian, Nikolaus Manuel; *Die Parabel vom verlorenen Sohn* (The Parable of the Prodigal Son), written in Low German by Burkard Waldis; and *Susanna,* by Paul Rebhun, an Austrian friend of Luther. The last two themes are typical of the Protestant faith and, serving as demonstrations of the new dogma, were highly popular: not necessarily good deeds, but faith alone brought about the salvation of the Prodigal Son; and Susanna was seen as the symbol of the true Christian dogma which was attacked and defiled by judges and priests. Outstanding among those who followed the Humanists in writing comedies mostly in Latin was the ardent Protestant Philip Nikodemus Frischlin, who glorified heroines taken either from the Bible or from German history (*Susanna, Rebecca, Ruth, Hildegardis magna, Wendelgard,* etc.). In *Julius Caesar Redivivus* (1584), the great Roman, having been brought back to life, is shown as marveling at the high level of learning, culture, and mechanical advancement, as in the invention of gunpowder and of printing, among those very Germans whom he had once fought as barbarians; and he is shocked by the national and moral decline of Catholic Italy, whose population now deserved to be called barbarian indeed. Many of the plays of this period were written as recital exercises for the students of the Humanist Latin Schools; hence the name *Humanistisches Schuldrama* (Humanist School Drama).

Fischart. Johann Fischart, another Alsatian—and Alsace was indeed the most fertile region in sixteenth century German literature—was the author of the pleasant epic *Das glückhafte Schiff von Zürich* (The Good Ship from Zurich, 1576), one of the few works of that age which sustained a continuous action without falling into constant episodic digressions. It is a poem which describes the loyal friendship between the two cities of Zurich and Strassburg and tells how swiftly the Swiss meant to rush to the help of their Alsatian ally. Fischart is, however, especially famous as an unrelenting enemy of Catholicism, particularly of the Jesuits; his bitter satire *Das Jesuitenhütlein* (The Jesuits' Cap, 1580) gives ample proof of the power of his wrath. Important as the first indication of new foreign influences, which were to become so typical for the seventeenth century, are Fischart's adaptation of Rabelais' grotesque tales of *Gargantua* and *Pantagruel* under the title of *Geschichtsklitterung,* in which he displayed the most bombastic exaggerations of style and thought and an almost paranoiac dissolution of form and language; and his translation, in 1572, of various chapters of a French version of the famous Spanish romance *Amadis de Gaula.*

Rollenhagen. Georg Rollenhagen, realizing the rich possibilities of the beast epic for the purpose of satirical and polemical writings, in 1595 published his mock-heroic *Der Froschmeuseler* (The Battle between Frogs and Mice) in which he ridiculed the feud between Protestants and Catholics, very much to the discredit of the latter.

TRANSLATIONS

Special attention is called to B. Q. Morgan's fundamentally important *Critical Bibliography of German Literature in English Translation, 1481-1927* (Stanford University Press, 1938), from which most items in the following lists of translations have been gleaned.

41

HISTORY OF GERMAN LITERATURE

GENERAL COLLECTION

Hawthorne, Julian. *The Masterpieces and the History of Literature.* New York, 1906. (Vol. III: *Reynard the Fox, Tyll Eulenspiegel, Hans Sachs,* etc. Vol. VI: Brant, Hutten, Luther, etc.).

INDIVIDUAL WORKS AND AUTHORS

BRANT: Zeydel, E. H., tr. *The Ship of Fools.* New York, 1944.

EPISTOLAE OBSCURORUM VIRORUM: Stokes, F. G., tr. *Epistolae Obscurorum Virorum; The Latin Text with an English Rendering, Notes, and an Historical Introduction.* New Haven, 1925.

ERASMUS: Born, L. K., tr. *The Education of a Christian Prince.* New York, 1936.
Hudson, H. H., tr. *The Praise of Folly.* Princeton, 1941.
Johnson, Rev. E., ed. *The Colloquies Concerning Men, Manners, and Things.* London, 1900.

FAUST: Rose, William, ed. *The History of the Damnable Life and Deserved Death of Doctor John Faustus, 1592.* London (Broadway Translations), 1925.

LUTHER: Lambert, J. F., tr. *Luther's Hymns.* United Lutheran Publications, 1917
Ninety-Five Theses; Address to the German Nobility; Concerning Christian Liberty. New York (Harvard Classics, XXXVI), 1910.
Smith, Preserved, and H. P. Gallinger, tr. *Luther's Conversations.* Boston, 1915.
Wace, H., and C. A. Buchheim. *Luther's Primary Works.* London, 1896.

MEISTER ECKHART: Blakney, R. B. *Meister Eckhart, A Modern Translation.* New York, 1941.

RELIGIOUS PLAYS: *The Passion Play at Oberammergau: The Complete German Text of the Play with English Translation Printed Side by Side.* London, 1900.
Zucker, A. E., tr. *The Redentin Easter Play, Translated from the Low German of the Fifteenth Century.* New York, 1941.

REYNARD THE FOX: Dole, Nathan H., ed. "Reynard the Fox" (Goethe's version translated), in *The Works of J. W. von Goethe,* I. New York, 1902.

SACHS: Leighton, W., tr. *Merry Tales and Three Shrovetide Plays* (English verse). London, 1910.
Ouless, E. U., tr. *Seven Shrovetide Plays.* London, 1930.

THOMAS À KEMPIS: *The Imitation of Christ.* New York (Everyman's Library), 1932.

TILL EULENSPIEGEL: Mackenzie, K. R. H. *Master Tyll Owlglass, His Marvellous Adventures and Rare Conceits.* London & New York (Broadway Translations), 1923.

CHAPTER V

BAROQUE AND PSEUDOCLASSICISM, 1600–1750

THE HISTORICAL BACKGROUND

Baroque literature stands under the sign of the Counter Reformation. This counterattack of the new orthodoxy, both Catholic and Protestant, on the proud individualism of Luther's century gathered momentum at the Council of Trent (1545–1563) and led to its first holocaust in the Netherlands, whose inhabitants, after the execution of Count Egmont in 1568, engaged in a bitter war against the Catholic Inquisition and Spanish oppression, a war of Dutch liberation which was to last fully eighty years.

It was in Germany, however, that the greatest religious struggle, the Thirty Years' War (1618–1648), was fought. Only in its beginning was this a war between Protestant Europe (central and northern Germany, Holland, Denmark, Sweden, for a short while England also) and Catholic Europe (Emperor and Pope, i.e. Southern Germany, Austria, Italy, Spain); later it degenerated into a free-for-all fight for the spoils of the moribund Holy Roman Empire, as the intervention of Catholic France on the Protestant side clearly indicates. From a religious point of view the war was again a draw, with the principle of mutual toleration as enunciated in the Augsburg Treaty of 1555 acknowledged anew; from a political and cultural point of view, however, the war and the ensuing Westphalian Peace of Münster and of Osnabrück were the greatest disasters in German history. The flower of the German bourgeoisie was now completely annihilated, with the population of the country cut down through war, plagues, and starvation from 18 to 6 millions. France in the southwest and Sweden in the northeast conquered large sections, and the Emperor was reduced to a more impotent state than ever. Petty German princes, most of them bribed by France and aping the splendor of Louis XIV, now became all-powerful and were even permitted to ally themselves with foreign monarchs, although not against their own Emperor—a ruling which, however, was soon enough broken. The population was hardworking, pious, and impoverished; the princes were more absolute and unbridled than ever.

Even after the Westphalian Treaty of Peace of 1648 matters went from bad to worse for the Hapsburg Emperors, for they could put up no united German front against the ever increasing French encroachments in Flanders, Alsace, and the Palatinate. The bloody War of the Spanish Succession (1701–1714) deprived the Emperor also of Spain's support, because after the death of the last Spanish Hapsburg ruler a French Bourbon king instead of an Austrian Hapsburg was placed on the throne of Spain. Only in one undertaking were the Emperor's armies at last successful: in driving the Turks out of Hungary and in thus freeing the Empire from a danger that had threatened over the southeast for two and a half centuries.

While the Empire under Hapsburg-Austrian-Catholic leadership fell more and more to pieces, a new state, the nucleus of future greatness, gradually grew in the north of Germany: Prussia, under Hohenzollern-Protestant leadership. Frederick William (1640–1688), the Great Elector of Brandenburg, was able to regain for his own crown some of the lands lost by the Reich to Sweden and Poland, and under his successors the electorate of Brandenburg was raised to a kingdom, the kingdom of Prussia (1701). After decades of defeat and centuries of disintegration there thus emerged a new state with an excellent army, a disciplined administration, and a patriotic spirit of service and sacrifice, which, especially under Frederick II, or the Great (1740–1786), and subsequently, was to achieve true greatness. Henceforth the history of Germany was double-tracked: it was not only the history of the dying First Reich but, within that First Reich, also the history of the young and energetic kingdom of Prussia, the nucleus of the coming Second Reich. Officially the king of Prussia was still a vassal of the Holy Roman Emperor in Vienna; actually, however, this fact did not prevent Berlin from gradually equaling and then over-shadowing Vienna in political importance.

GENERAL OBSERVATIONS

The universal devastations of the Thirty Years' War and the absolute hegemony of France in western Europe help us to understand why politically and culturally Germany reached, around 1650, perhaps the lowest point in her history, and why France became the undisputed arbiter of manners and literature alike. During the Baroque Period, i.e. up to about 1680, the influence of early French Classicism with its increasing emphasis on rules, decorum, conciseness, and verisimilitude could not prevent the persistence of certain German literary irregularities and crudities that had been typical of the age of Hans Sachs; only later, in the early eighteenth century, when Boileau's and Racine's influence increased the prestige and pressure of classical literature, did Germany slowly and unwillingly submit to a pale and bloodless imitation of French rules of literary etiquette. The exuberant strength and earthiness of the German burghers of the fifteenth and sixteenth centuries were now harnessed; the result was that free literary inspiration was almost completely stifled. It was not burghers who were essentially the representatives of this increasingly pseudoclassical literature, but learned, gallant, and polished court poets. The Thirty Years' War had destroyed the power of the German cities; instead of sober burghers, elegant and Gallicized aristocrats now reigned supreme in German literary taste.

Literature in Other Countries

Foreign literature showed a similar unwillingness to bow to the standards prescribed by Paris—with the difference, however, that the Baroque Age, notably in Spain and England, produced a much greater literary wealth than was the case in chaotic Germany. Italy was the only country to follow Germany into a period of literary decline; between Tasso at the end of the sixteenth and Metastasio early in the eighteenth century this unhappy and subjected country produced no works of lasting value. Whereas Italian, French, and English letters had reached their loftiest peak during the

Renaissance, two new countries now experienced their Golden Age during the century of the Counter Reformation: Spain and Holland. The *Siglo de Oro* of Spanish culture and literature may be said to have begun with the birth of Cervantes in 1547 and to have ended with the death of Lope de Vega in 1635 or, at the latest, with the death of Calderón de la Barca in 1681. Colorful, irregular *comedias* on historical themes, saints' lives, love, intrigue, seduction (*capa y espada*—"cloak and dagger"), and the keen Spanish sense of honor (Lope, Tirso de Molina, Guillén de Castro, Calderón), and realistic novels about the empty dreams (Cervantes) and the rapid demoralization of Spanish society (Alemán, Espinel, Quevedo, Luis de Guevara) contributed most to the value of Spanish literature. The Dutch experienced the Golden Age of their culture in the first half of the seventeenth century in the midst of their heroic War of Liberation; the dramatist Joost van den Vondel, artists like Franz Hals and Rembrandt, scholars like Hugo Grotius represent the flower of their cultural life. In England the Renaissance aestheticism of Sidney and Spenser gave way to the greater realism and the emotional upheaval of the Baroque Age; although Ben Jonson tried to uphold neoclassical ideals, the dramatists around and after him became ever more naturalistic and unrestrained in their crude Senecan presentations of intrigues and crimes. The Cavalier Poets (Suckling, Carew) were the last representatives of sensual Renaissance hedonism; among English as among Spanish writers, the increasing religious orthodoxy tended ever more to destroy the inner harmony which the Renaissance had tried to achieve in mankind (Donne). Milton's thoroughly classical education prevented *Paradise Lost,* the finest symbol of the religious ardor of the seventeenth century, from being written in the naturalistic, dynamic, and cacophonic style customary among Baroque authors. Spanish and Italian Jesuits, French Huguenots, English Puritans, and increasingly bigoted German Lutherans shared alike in the mighty surge of the new orthodoxy, which endeavored to obliterate the "godless" Renaissance trend towards man's inner emancipation. In the New England colonies Puritan orthodoxy established a particularly merciless theocracy: the three generations of the

Mather "dynasty" in Massachusetts and, as late as the first half of the eighteenth century, the name of Jonathan Edwards in Connecticut gave ample evidence of the weight of religious pressure upon man's mind.

The Growth of French Classicism

Against the elemental outbreaks of man's passions and fears which were caused by the tremendous pressure of the diametrically opposed trends of the Renaissance and the Counter Reformation, there now arose ever more pointedly the Classicism of France. Opposed at least theoretically to the immorality of the libertine age, it tried to blend the aestheticism of the sixteenth with the new ethical earnestness of the seventeenth century. It emphasized dignity, decorum, and verisimilitude in literature and therefore condemned the Baroque trends towards didactic bulkiness noticeable e.g. in du Bartas, or towards stylistic irregularities such as could be found e.g. in Cyrano de Bergerac. Scaliger around 1560 and Malherbe around 1620 had been among the first to advocate rules and dignity in literature, and to combat the "crude" mixtures of comedy and tragedy, of loftiness and obscenity, which abounded in France, and also abroad in the dramas of Shakespeare and of Lope de Vega. With the founding of the *Académie Française* by Richelieu in 1633, and with the coming of Corneille and, especially, of Racine, Molière, Boileau, and La Fontaine (*L'École de 1660*), classical stateliness and purity then definitely won out in France. Reason, dignity, and minute psychological probings into the souls of men and women constituted the chief aspect of this literature of the age of Louis XIV (1643–1715), its emphasis on propriety doing away with the naturalism, gore, and horror of the Baroque stage. After the fall of the Puritan Commonwealth and the return of the Stuarts to London, England too, from Dryden up to Pope, fell under the spell of French classical perfection and wit—although, to be sure, the notorious Restoration comedies were far below the moral earnestness of Corneille and Molière. Like England and Germany, so also Italy (Goldoni, Alfieri), Spain (Luzán, Moratín), and America (Franklin) in the eighteenth century were to be in great need of tempering French influences in order to overcome the cumbersome heaviness and painful lack of balance of the Baroque century.

BAROQUE LITERATURE (1600–1680)

Stages of Development

At the beginning of the century the wholesome bourgeois realism and optimism of the preceding age clashed with both the fanatical ardor of the new orthodoxy and the insinuating gallantry of libertines and court poets. Realism and fanaticism, intensified by the horrors of the Thirty Years' War, at first seemed to present an insurmountable front against the spreading of the rules of French Classicism. This Baroque Age of violent trends and countertrends hence produced a literature tortured by doubts and crises: its dramas and poems were constantly oscillating between heaven and hell, between the spiritual and the sensual. It was a *fortissimo* literature in which all words, metaphors, and superlatives seemed to fail to give adequate expression to what was moving the poet's soul. French rules of restraint and decorum were as yet of no avail and were usually broken; the vanity of life drove the poets either into religious ecstasy or into coarsest eroticism. Hence the meaning of the word "baroque": bombastic, dynamic, superlative, inflated, unbalanced, antithetical. The groping for a firm hold in a strife-torn world where all faiths and traditions seemed to have lost their former values filled the breasts of Protestants and Catholics alike.

After 1650 the religious ardor was exhausted and subsided; but eroticism and rationalism continued to increase within the framework of French-inspired Pseudoclassicism. The last Baroque authors in Germany, devoid of the religious earnestness of the earlier generation, therefore dealt in horror and eroticism for their own sake. They embodied all the defects and none of the virtues of that unhappy literary period.

After 1680 the bombast of the Baroque language also died of its own excesses and gave way to a very dry and rationalistic style. Though Baroque literature around 1640 may have been guilty of many aesthetic crimes, it had at least presented real problems and conflicts beneath its bulkiness, and thus was surely superior to the shallowness of thought and the dull regularity of form which dominated under Pseudoclassicism from 1680 to about 1750.

Literary Critics and Associations

Together with French, Italian, and Spanish troops, French, Italian, and Spanish literary forces also invaded Germany. It was only now that a "Renaissance" of German literature began, if by that term is meant an observation of classic principles, of rules which were now to be superimposed upon the fermenting mass of German thought.

Martin Opitz (1597–1639). Opitz, though a mediocre poet, was of great importance in this connection, because he became the lawgiver of the new era. He opened the dikes of foreign influence, translating tragedies from Seneca (*The Trojan Women*) and Sophocles (*Antigone*), introducing into Germany the first Italian opera (*Dafne*), and rendering into German John Barclay's state novel *Argenis* and Philip Sidney's pastoral romance *Arcadia*. His important *Buch von der deutschen Poeterei* (Book on German Poetry, 1624) for a century remained the lawbook of all imitative, neoclassical German poets. Opitz was also responsible for introducing into German literature the classical French Alexandrine meter of twelve syllables, which superseded the shorter couplets of the meistersingers and which, for better or for worse, dominated the form of German verse dramas until the days of Lessing. From the time of Opitz on, the simple folk element of the sixteenth century gradually disappeared from literature, giving way to a stilted, scholarly, courtly, and insincere type of poetry. For more than a century and a half the practice of bold and free creation was abandoned in favor of the principle of timid and fussy imitation of foreign models and rules: Roman comedies, French tragedies, Italian epics, Spanish picaresque novels, English pastorals. Hence the bad connotation of the words "Neoclassicism" or "Pseudoclassicism."

By a strange paradox the Baroque poets, who were so fond of aping foreign models, were at the same time mili-

tantly patriotic and antiforeign. Resenting the superiority of
foreign literature, they resolved to equal and surpass their
models, to cleanse their vocabulary of the horrible medley
of foreign words that had crept in during the Thirty Years'
War, and to establish academies for the advancement of culture and Germanism which, like the *Accademia della Crusca*
at Florence and later the *Académie Française* in Paris, would
foster this process of national purification. Hence the founding, in 1617, of the *Fruchtbringende Gesellschaft* by Prince
Ludwig of Anhalt, to be followed by Philipp von Zesen's
Rosenorden and Johann Rist's *Elbschwanenorden,* both in
Hamburg, and by Georg Philipp Harsdörffer's *Gekrönter
Blumenorden* of the Pegnitz Shepherds in Nürnberg.

Among later lawgivers of the seventeenth century may be
mentioned the well-known grammarian JUSTUS GEORG SCHOT-
TELIUS, whose *Ausführliche Arbeit von der deutschen Haupt-
sprache* (Detailed Treatise on Standard German) of 1663
established the norm for all writers; and DANIEL GEORG
MORHOF, whose *Unterricht von der deutschen Sprache und
Poesie* (Instruction on the German Language and Poetry,
1682) at last began to substitute the influence of Boileau's
theories for the inferior brand of earlier Neoclassicism.

Lyric Poetry

Baroque superlativeness is noticeable in both the religious
poems of the burghers and the erotic poems of the courtiers
of that time; but whereas the latter became ever more shallow and stilted, the former, in spite of all despondent words
and cacophonic effects, showed great strength and character.

ANDREAS GRYPHIUS (1616–1664), PAUL GERHARDT, AN-
GELUS SILESIUS (Johann Scheffler), PAUL FLEMING, FRIED-
RICH VON SPEE, and others are outstanding representatives
of Baroque religious poetry, in which the horrors, the fears,
and the hopes of the masses during the great war were mirrored. Especially Gerhardt's mighty hymns are impressive
and popular even today. Angelus Silesius was one of the
foremost mystics of the century; like the leading mystic
prose writer of the period, JAKOB BÖHME, a humble cobbler
in Breslau, he wanted to bridge the fearful abyss between
Catholics and Protestants by eliminating hate-provoking

dogmas and by seeking his own way to God. But the greatest poetic force of the German Baroque is undoubtedly Gryphius, whose poems—among them the *Sonn- und Feiertagssonette* (Sunday and Holiday Sonnets)—express powerfully the emotional tension, the passionate religious fervor, and the agonizing despair in the face of a shaken and senseless world, all of them so characteristic for this period. Both in depth of thought and in intensity of expression, Gryphius can be compared to John Donne. Broad-minded and compassionate to an unusual degree was the Jesuit poet Friedrich von Spee, who, while professor at Würzburg, within two years had to prepare in this district alone more than 200 witches for death—a horrible task in this century of fanaticism and superstition, which left a deep imprint upon his poetry.

To the gloomy motto of the *Vanitas, vanitatum vanitas* of these pious poets the elegant courtier poets opposed their eager motto *carpe diem:* gather ye rosebuds while ye may. CHRISTIAN HOFMANN VON HOFMANNSWALDAU and DANIEL KASPER VON LOHENSTEIN are two notorious examples of bombastic, exotic, and erotic poets; their works are usually referred to as *Schwulstliteratur* (overladen, inflated, literally tumorous literature).

The Novel

In the novel also may be noted the same struggle between the spirit and the flesh in the soul of the Baroque poets, and its unfortunate consequences for beauty of style.

Grimmelshausen. Hans Jakob Christoffel von Grimmelshausen's *Simplicius Simplicissimus* (1669) is undoubtedly the greatest novel of the seventeenth century. It is an apprenticeship novel and shows a young man who like Parzival sets out into a world full of sin and temptation in order to find his philosophy of life and his peace. But where Parzival had moved in a romantic world of medieval knighthood, Simplicissimus is pictured against the gruesome background of the Thirty Years' War, and it is shown how he becomes a soldier, a robber, a killer, and a dissipated fellow before he realizes the vanity of all human ambitions and becomes a hermit in order to repent and to serve God. The Spanish *picaro* (or rogues') novels had served as models for this book and had furnished some of the naturalistic and unsavory background (Alemán), with Grimmelshausen adding the strongly religious and exhortatory elements. In view of the great success of the book, Grimmelshausen, a few years later, wrote a continuation in which the former hermit—several decades ahead of the publication of Defoe's *Robinson Crusoe* —was shipwrecked and spent his last years on a small tropical island.

Ziegler and Braunschweig-Wolfenbüttel. Among the other Baroque novels, which lack Grimmelshausen's ethical purpose and which revel in bombast, gore, lust, and pathological crimes for their own sake, may be mentioned Heinrich Anselm von Ziegler's *Asiatische Banise oder blutiges doch mutiges Pegu* (Banise, an Asiatic Princess, or the Siege of Bloody yet Courageous Pegu, 1688), a tale of pompous state affairs and spectacular crimes in Burma, in the best Oriental fashion. To this same type belongs *Octavia* (1685) by the Duke Anton Ulrich zu Braunschweig-Wolfenbüttel: it is an endless and minute canvas of Roman intrigues, concupiscence, and conspiracies.

Zesen. Only Philipp von Zesen (1619–1689) seemed able to strike a happy balance; though he copied erotic and exotic tales from French models (e.g. *Ibrahim Bassa* and *Die afrikanische Sophonisbe,* both imitated from the works of Mlle. de Scudéry), he managed in his best and shortest novel *Adriatische Rosemund* (Rosemund, from Venice on the Adriatic Sea, 1645) to write the first German novel of unhappy love and death. Not Oriental princes and unspeakable crimes form the background of this novel; rather, like Jörg Wickram before him, Zesen portrayed contemporary middle-class characters—the love of a young German for an Italian girl, and the unhappiness caused by religious obstacles which blocked the marriage between a Protestant and a Catholic. Although no masterpiece, *Die Adriatische Rosemund* marks nevertheless a great step forward in the history of the German novel. Baroque in its simultaneous emphasis on religion and sensualism, on pure love and sinful passion, on courtly splendor and paternalistic statesmanship is Zesen's last great novel *Assenat,* 1670—"The Holy State-, Love-, and Life-

Story of Assenat," daughter of Potiphar and ultimately wife of Joseph in Egypt.

Lohenstein. Lohenstein's *Arminius* (1689), an immense, involved, and unfinished novel of more than 3,000 pages treating old Germanic tribal history, valor, and virtues and Roman imperialistic intrigues and vices, indicates clearly that the patriotic love for Germany's national past, which had grown under the Humanists and which was to reach its apex with the Storm and Stress movement and Romanticism, existed even in the seventeenth century of foreign influences and scholarly pedantry. A glorification of early German and Bohemian tribes is found also in the novel *Herkules und Valiska* by ANDREAS HEINRICH BUCHOLTZ.

Satirical Writers. A prose work of special character is *Die Gesichte Philanders von Sittewald* (The Visions of Philander von Sittewald, 1642) by HANS MICHAEL MOSCHEROSCH, a scathing attack upon the immorality and foppery of Germans during the great war. This work Moscherosch adapted from *Los Sueños* of the Spaniard Quevedo, who in turn had been influenced by Dante's *Inferno*. The Augustine monk and preacher ABRAHAM A SANTA CLARA likewise stands out as a particularly vigorous satirist during the postwar era. As a third writer of that type should be named FRIEDRICH VON LOGAU, the finest and sharpest epigrammatist of the seventeenth century and one of the foremost of all ages and lands. Of different character is CHRISTIAN REUTER's satirical novel *Schelmuffsky* (1696), a forerunner of the braggart romances and the tall stories and adventures of Baron Münchhausen.

The Drama

Jesuits and English Comedians. The stark contrast between the spiritual and the sensual trends of that century can best be seen if we compare the strongly didactic Latin plays which the proselyting Jesuits wrote and performed with the crude and increasingly obscene plays which the so-called English Comedians peddled from village fair to village fair. What these Englishmen brought with them was the Elizabethan theater emasculated for an audience craving for nothing but action and low humor and unable to understand the language in which the plays were written and performed. Even before 1600 HEINRICH JULIUS, Duke of Braunschweig, was among the first to welcome these English traveling actors at his court; in his own plays the Duke indeed even imitated their realistic, swift, and crude technique. JAKOB AYRER of Nürnberg, the successor of Hans Sachs, was also distinctly influenced by the dramatic style of the English Comedians; his plays mark the transition from the static Renaissance drama to the dynamic Baroque drama. The comic person—called Pickelhering, Harlekin, Johan Bouset, or Hanswurst, and originally taken over from the Italian *commedia dell' arte* (improvised comedy)—inclined in the course of the seventeenth century increasingly to dominate the stage and to drag the dramatic presentations down into the low sphere of coarse jokes and gross gestures.

Gryphius and Lohenstein. Andreas Gryphius, the greatest German dramatist of the seventeenth century, wrote three good comedies: *Die geliebte Dornrose* (The Beloved Briar Rose, 1660), which pokes fun at the amorous adventures of peasants; *Peter Squentz,* a good-natured satire against the clumsy theatrical ambitions of craftsmen, in whose performance of the story of Pyramus and Thisbe can be perceived an indirect influence of Shakespeare's *Midsummer Night's Dream;* and *Horribilicribrifax,* an imitation of Plautus' *Miles Gloriosus,* a comedy written in a medley of "stylish" languages, which attacks a particularly obnoxious type of man: the bragging soldier, the "hero" of a dozen bloody battles and amorous affairs.

The contrast between what was formerly called the First Silesian School and the Second Silesian School, i.e. between the first religious and the second rationalistic and erotic generation of Baroque poets (most of them hailing from Silesia, the center of seventeenth century German culture), is nowhere better marked than in the tragedies of Andreas Gryphius and of Daniel Kasper von Lohenstein. Gryphius' tragedies *Katharina von Georgien, Felicitas, Carolus Stuardus,* and others, through tortures, killings, and gruesomeness, inculcate steadfastness, courage, faith in God, and a religious exaltation to which Gryphius himself had attained after the bitter experiences and miseries of the war. Lohenstein used similar tales of crimes but was entirely devoid of Gryphius' ethical background. In *Cleopatra, Sophonisbe,* or *Agrippina* he shows how his heroines intrigue, fight, and murder until, enmeshed in their own sins, they at last fall victims of their own crimes. Lohenstein's tragedies are infinitely more dramatic than Gryphius' monotonous reiterations of virtue, but beautiful or edifying literature they are not. The butcheries of the war and the hothouse eroticism of courtly gallantry had left too deep an imprint on German literature, as is clearly seen in the writings of Lohenstein no less than in those of Ziegler or of Hofmannswaldau. Still to be mentioned among Gryphius' works is *Cardenio und Celinde* (1648), sometimes called the first bourgeois drama in German literature, the story of a passion that does not shrink from a nocturnal exhumation, a ghastly spectacle dear to the feverish minds of a Baroque audience.

PSEUDOCLASSICISM (1680–1750)

After the excesses of religious exaltation, the excesses of Baroque adornment and bombast also gradually disappeared. The neoclassic rules of restraint and verisimilitude, introduced by Opitz and strengthened through the influence not only of Boileau and Racine but also of the rationalistic philosophy of Bacon in England, Descartes in France, and Gottfried Wilhelm Leibniz (1646–1716) in Germany, finally achieved supremacy also in German literature. Religious ardor persisted during these decades only as an undercurrent, in the words and deeds of God-fearing Pietists of the type of Philipp Jakob Spener and of Count Nikolaus Ludwig von Zinzendorf, the latter the founder of the sect of Moravian Brethren. The same held true in England, where the strongly religious works of John Milton and John Bunyan were completely neglected by the fashionable crowd at the court of the last Stuarts. Strong religious exaltation, in the German genius, subsisted, above all, in the great music of Johann Sebastian Bach and of Georg Friedrich Händel (the latter in the service of the House of Hanover both in Germany and in England).

Wasserpoeten. True lyrical and imaginative poetry was impossible during this age when rationalism reigned supreme.

The poetasters of the neoclassic period were hence mere verse makers who imitated French models and produced occasional verse, obediently glorifying the births, weddings, garden parties, and deaths of the princes at whose courts and for whose glory they lived. Friedrich Rudolf von Canitz and Benjamin Neukirch may be named as representatives of these court poets, who on account of their shallowness of thought and their dullness of style are frequently called *Wasserpoeten*. One important fact must be stated in their favor, however: they were determined enemies of the stylistic excesses of the Second Silesian School and they strove to cleanse literature of Lohenstein's and Hofmannswaldau's unbelievable bombast.

Weise. In the field of the drama Christian Weise, a schoolmaster from Zittau on the Bohemian border, marks well the transition from the floweriness of the seventeenth to the dry didacticism of the early eighteenth century. Best known among his plays, written to be performed by his pupils, is the tragedy about the Neapolitan fisherman, *Masaniello* (1682), who, but a few years before, had led a rebellion against the Spanish viceroy. Weise's *Comödie von der bösen Catharina* (Comedy of Wicked Catherine) represents a German version of *The Taming of the Shrew,* though here again the authorship of Shakespeare was not actually known. The comedy *Vom niederländischen Bauer* (The Peasant from the Lowlands) is reminiscent of Calderón's masterpiece *La vida es sueño,* because here, too, Weise wanted to teach that life and its foolish ambitions are mere dreams.

Johann Christoph Gottsched (1700–1766). The last and quite pathetic representative of Pseudoclassicism imported into Germany from France was Professor Gottsched of Leipzig, for a while the literary dictator of Germany. He simplified and cleansed the German language from many unsavory excesses and dialectal irregularities; he also fought the naturalism and obscenity of the German drama. His special enemies were the English Comedians and their native successors who had toured Germany for more than a century, because he opposed their mixture of the English Baroque bombast with the German crudities of the type of "Hanswurst." Instead, Gottsched praised the dignity and

noble restraint of the French tragedies and therefore translated countless French masterpieces into wooden German
Alexandrine verses. German depth of thought, blended with
French elegance of form, had produced in Hartmann, Wolfram, and Gottfried the immortal masterpieces of MHG literature. In Gottsched, however, any genius, any depth of
thought, was completely missing. What he saw in the French
works was not their hidden fire, their stirring psychological
crises, but only their outward rules and regularity—and these
alone he imitated and transplanted. Hence the mediocrity of
his own tragedy *Der sterbende Cato* (Dying Cato) which
he copied largely from English (Addison) and French
models; hence also the scorn with which the irrational and
impetuous geniuses of the later Storm and Stress generation ridiculed his *Versuch einer kritischen Dichtkunst* (Attempt at a Critical Art of Poetry, 1730), an uninspiring
book in which Gottsched tried to explain in a didactic and
dry manner how one ought to proceed in order to write great
"classical" literature. In spite of this, Gottsched held sway
in German literature all during the 1730's, until his pedantic
bigotry was attacked by the Milton-enthusiast Bodmer early
in the 1740's and by the Shakespeare-enthusiast Lessing late
in the 1750's.

Christian Fürchtegott Gellert (1715–1769). Gellert is
a typically transitional figure in whom a timid Pseudoclassicism of form and an increasingly sentimental Preromanticism
of thought are strangely intermixed. He was the outstanding
didactic and rationalistic author of that age, the Dorothy Dix
of eighteenth century Germany, a kindly and helpful man, a
tremendous letter writer, famous above all for his gently
moralizing *Fabeln und Erzählungen* (Fables and Tales,
1746), in which the pseudoclassical preoccupation with didacticism could best express itself. Gellert's homespun philosophy of life resembled greatly that of Hans Sachs, the people's
poet of the sixteenth century. In his dramatic productions—
Die Betschwester (The Hypocrite), *Das Los in der Lotterie*
(The Lottery Ticket), *Die zärtlichen Schwestern* (The Affectionate Sisters)—Gellert followed closely the narrow and
sentimental pattern of the so-called "Tearful Comedy"
(*comédie larmoyante*) as represented by Nivelle de la

Chaussée, Diderot, and other Frenchmen, with their *petit bourgeois* moralism, their confusions and mistaken identities, their social satires, and their happy denouements under easily and profusely flowing tears. Best known of Gellert's prose works is his *Leben der schwedischen Gräfin von G* (Life of the Swedish Countess G., 1747–1748), a sentimental, moral, and yet slightly lascivious tale written under the influence of Richardson's novels. Gellert's *Geistliche Oden und Lieder* (Religious Odes and Songs, 1757) betray the strong pietistic undercurrent that refused to be entirely suppressed by the Age of Rationalism.

TRANSLATIONS

GENERAL COLLECTIONS

Translated poems by Angelus Silesius, Fleming, Gellert, Gerhardt, Gryphius, Günther, Logau, Luther, Opitz, Rist, Sachs, Spee, and others are contained in the following collections:

Dunn, Catherine. *Hymns from the German.* London, 1861.

Mills, H. *Horae Germanicae, A Version of German Hymns.* New York, 1856.

Winkworth, Catherine. *Christian Singers of Germany.* London, 1869.

———. *Lyra Germanica* (two series). London, 1855 & 1858.

INDIVIDUAL AUTHORS

BOHME: Bax, C., tr. *The Signature of All Things.* London & New York (Everyman's Library), 1934.

Earle, J. R., tr. *Six Theosophic Points and Other Writings.* New York, 1919.

Palmer, W. S., ed. *Confessions* (with Introduction by Evelyn Underhill). New York, 1920.

GELLERT: *History of the Swedish Countess of Guildenstern* (translator anonymous). London, 1752.

Nuske, J. A., tr. *Fables.* London, 1850.

GERHARDT: Kelly, John. *Paul Gerhardt's Spiritual Songs.* London, 1867.

GRIMMELSHAUSEN: Goodrick, A. T. S., tr. *The Adventurous Simplicissimus.* London & New York (Broadway Translations), 1924.

CHAPTER VI

GERMAN ENLIGHTENMENT, 1730–1780

GENERAL OBSERVATIONS

The lifetime of Goethe (1749–1832) encompasses the second Golden Age of German literature. This period can be subdivided into the following trends, with typical representatives:

a. Enlightenment: Wieland, Lessing.
b. Storm and Stress: Klopstock, Herder, young Goethe, young Schiller.
c. Classicism: Goethe, Schiller.
d. Romanticism: Kleist, Novalis, Tieck, Eichendorff, Grillparzer, etc.

Often Wieland, Lessing, Klopstock, and Herder are also classed together under the name of preclassicists.

French Influence

French influences in Germany during the eighteenth century were of three varieties:

a. The influence of pseudoclassical rules and etiquette, which from Opitz up to Gottsched had shown such poor results. Of this influence no more need be said.
b. The influence of French gracefulness of style and frivolity of thought, commonly called Rococo, which was characteristic of the courtly refinement of the *ancien régime:* Wieland.
c. The influence of French enlightening philosophers who advocated religious tolerance and greater political freedom: Lessing.

Philosophy and Science

Philosophy in most European countries in the first half of the eighteenth century was largely under the influence of France. This was the Age of Enlightenment (*Aufklärung*), when progressive thinkers and writers, all of them still neo-classicists at heart, were beginning to assail the haughty absolutism of the state (Louis XIV and XV) and the bigoted orthodoxy of the Church. The rationalistic philosophers of the seventeenth century had prepared the ground: just as the men of the Renaissance had freed themselves from the yoke of medieval restrictions, so the enlighteners of the eighteenth century now rejected the reactionary and Baroque conception of state and Church. What Descartes had started in seventeenth century France was more fully developed by the men around the *Encyclopédie* one hundred years later; from Leibniz in seventeenth century Germany the line led to Christian Wolff, Lessing, and Immanuel Kant; in England Bacon was to become the spiritual father of men like Hobbes and Locke who grappled with the problems of man's rights and justified the popular uprisings of 1649 and 1688 against unbearable royal absolutism; in America fearless thinkers from Roger Williams up to Benjamin Franklin and Thomas Jefferson were resolved to repudiate the presumptuousness of royal (or, in the case of Williams, of theocratic) absolutism. Seventeenth century scientists contributed to this trend towards man's emancipation: Galileo in Italy, Newton in England; religious thinkers added their share to break the stranglehold of orthodoxy: Bruno in Italy, Böhme in Germany, Spinoza in Holland. Decades of slow preparatory work by these enlightened thinkers then led to the two greatest deeds of liberation in the eighteenth century: the American and the French Revolutions.

Literature in Other Countries

Although in philosophy the enlighteners, especially of England, chronologically preceded those of France, in literature it was the French writers who dominated European thought: Montesquieu, Voltaire, Diderot. Novelists like Lesage in his *Le Diable boîteux* (The Limping Devil) and his *Gil Blas de Santillane* reverted to Spanish themes (Luis de Guevara), especially to picaresque stories (Espinel), in order to show the corruption of the *ancien régime* and to applaud the highly symptomatic success of shrewd and lowly-born heroes in equaling and perhaps even usurping the power of the aristocrats; Beaumarchais followed this line in his comedies. Acid criticism of contemporary society also appeared in the picaresque novels of Defoe (*Moll Flanders*) and Fielding (*Jonathan Wild*); eighteenth century England was, indeed, characterized by the gradual rise of the lower bourgeoisie, which then imposed its tastes and opinions on literature. In Italy Parini in his *Il Giorno* (The Day) wrote the most mordant satire against the parasitic life of decadent aristocrats; Alfieri in his rhetorical tragedies declared war on all forms of despotism, past and present, and through his unrelenting hatred of the Austrian oppressors he became one of the first heralds of the later Italian *Risorgimento*. In Spain Francisco de Isla in his *Fray Gerundio* ridiculed the grandiloquent orthodoxy of the Baroque century; towards the end of the eighteenth century, the poet, statesman, and reformer Jovellanos, who was greatly influenced by the French enlighteners, spent a lifetime working at the gigantic task of Spanish progress and liberalism. Among the orators who, before and during the great revolutionary storms, tried to whip public opinion into shape must be named Burke in England, Patrick Henry in America, Mirabeau in France. As with Lessing, so also with many other enlighteners the problem of religious tolerance was fully as important as the problem of political freedom; reference may be made to Locke's and Voltaire's treatises on tolerance; to English deists like Shaftesbury, Bolingbroke, Pope, and Hume; in America to Thomas Paine, a fierce battler for both political and religious liberation; and—tinged with the warmheartedness and irrationalism of Preromanticism—to the religious viewpoints of Rousseau in Switzerland and of Kant in Germany.

THE HISTORICAL BACKGROUND

The evident weakness of the Empire and the latent rivalry between Austria and Prussia within the Empire came to a head when, in 1740, a woman, Maria Theresa, became Empress at Vienna at the same time that the greatest Hohenzollern, Frederick II or the Great (1740–1786), became king of Prussia. Frederick's successful conquest of Silesia led a few years later to a great European war in which the big powers, rather than attacking the Empire as usual, for the first time helped the Empire fight back against the dangerously increasing might of Prussia: it was the Seven Years' War (1756–1763), in which Frederick held out against an overwhelming number of enemies (France, Saxony, Poland, Russia, and the Hapsburgs of Austria), while England, officially allied to Prussia, in the meantime calmly pocketed the great French empire in India and America. Saved almost by a miracle and victorious in the end, Prussia was permitted to keep Silesia and through this war earned for herself an honored place among the great powers of Europe. From this time to his death, Frederick was busily engaged in building up an ever increasing power in the family of German states and in restricting the rule of the Austrian Hapsburgs more and more to their immediate Austrian, Hungarian, and Bohemian possessions.

Frederick II, the personal friend of Voltaire, and Emperor Joseph II, the son of Maria Theresa, are the best representatives of enlightened German rulers. Individual princes in petty states may still have persisted in aping the parasitic French system of impoverishing and exasperating the masses (for Voltaire's warnings bore no fruit in France), a policy which finally led to the great Revolution of 1789; Frederick and Joseph, however, ruled wisely and benevolently, abolishing many injustices, introducing fairer taxes, better commercial facilities, greater religious tolerance. Under this benevolent absolutism they considered themselves merely the first servants of the state and acted generously because it was their pleasure to do so. Democracy and parliamentary system were as yet unknown in Germany; but Joseph II certainly performed one of the most liberal deeds of history when he freed the peasantry from the serfdom to which they had been subjected ever since the feudal Middle Ages.

THE ROCOCO

The graceful culture of aristocratic courts, in which the crude eroticism of the previous century had been replaced by playful naughtiness, is well epitomized in many beautiful compositions by Christoph Willibald von Gluck, Franz

Joseph Haydn, and Wolfgang Amadeus Mozart. The operas of Metastasio in Italy, several light and graceful comedies by Marivaux and the paintings by Watteau in France, and Pope's *Rape of the Lock,* a masterpiece of trifling stateliness in England, embody best the charm and elegance of the Rococo; and the fine porcelain figures of Sèvres, Meissen, and Dresden typify beautifully the delicacy of its culture.

Anacreontic Poets. In German literature, the Rococo was represented especially by the so-called Anacreontic Poets—men like FRIEDRICH VON HAGEDORN, JOHANN PETER UZ, JOHANN WILHELM LUDWIG GLEIM, or EWALD VON KLEIST, who like the old Greek poet Anacreon sang of wine, women, and song. They also imitated such Roman poets as Ovid and Horace. Their amorous heroines were all imaginary Daphnises, Phyllises, and Chloes; their lyric poems were artificial and light, though graceful. In the history of German versification the Anacreontic Poets deserve a place for having contributed to render the German verses—so long dominated by the heaviness of Gottsched's Alexandrine meter—more fluent and nimble. After having run the whole galaxy of noble shepherds and shepherdesses, and after having become the confidant of the whole Rococo Parnassus by his immense and tearfully sentimental correspondence with his literary friends, Gleim in his *Preussische Kriegslieder von einem Grenadier* (Prussian War Songs of a Soldier, 1758) became one of the first to express the strong patriotic feeling stimulated by the exploits of Frederick the Great.

Young Goethe (I).* While a student at the university of Leipzig (1765–1768), young Goethe began his literary career in the era of the Rococo. His earliest poems contained in *Annette* and *Das Leipziger Liederbuch* (The Leipzig Song Book) include little masterpieces like *Mit einem gemalten Bande* (With an Embroidered Ribbon). Best known among these early works is *Die Laune des Verliebten* (The Wayward Lover, 1768), a pastoral in Alexandrine meter thoroughly in keeping with the Rococo atmosphere, with shepherds, shepherdesses, and problems of love playing the main role. Yet the chief character of the playlet, the quarrelsome and melancholy lover, points already towards Goethe's dis-

* See also pp. 83–86.

satisfaction with the elegant but artificial Rococo emotions and manners.

Christoph Martin Wieland (1733–1813) (I).* In spite of his pagan sensualism Wieland was also essentially an enlightener. Not political or religious enlightenment was his chief concern but the problems of human happiness, of the harmony between the spirit and the flesh, of the aesthetic education of man. Together with Gottfried von Strassburg he is the best German imitator of French fluency and beauty of style; yet beneath his polished naughtiness there is the serious intention of a smiling philosopher and a broad-minded cosmopolitan to free his fellow men from age-worn inhibitions and false taboos. Wieland was not an original poet, because he gladly borrowed his themes from France, Italy, England, Spain, and Greece; but the beauty of his language and the beauty of his message make him a great poet nevertheless. After centuries of mental struggles and awkward didacticism in German literature, he was the first fluent and graceful author whose language was polished and refined as it had not been since the days of Barbarossa. Especially through his love of Greece, Wieland prepared the ground for the masterpieces of German Classicism which were to follow later through Goethe and Schiller. In his mentality Wieland was still entirely a rationalist, in his art still entirely a neoclassicist; but his first translation of twenty-two of Shakespeare's dramas into German (1762–1766) indicated that the future wave of Germanic irrationalism had already reached him, however slightly it touched him.

Wieland's first novel, *Der Sieg der Natur über die Schwärmerei, oder die Abenteuer des Don Silvio von Rosalva* (The Victory of Common Sense over Exaltation, or the Adventures of Don Silvio of Rosalva, 1764), is important for two reasons: in its imitation of Cervantes' *Don Quixote* it indicates Wieland's love for Mediterranean literatures (which we find also in his *Der neue Amadis*); and in the autobiographical narrative about Don Silvio it shows that Wieland, early in his life, managed to rid himself of the religious fervor which an acquaintance with Bodmer and Klopstock had momentarily

* See also pp. 66–67.

aroused in him. Instead, he prefers to become a man of the world, elegant, witty, graceful, and sceptical, a poet especially deeply influenced by the hedonism of Shaftesbury and the whimsical style of Sterne.

Agathon (1766), one of the great German novels of the eighteenth century, is a novel of apprenticeship in which, however, the aesthetic rather than the religious education of the young hero is emphasized. Fine psychological analyses of Agathon and of the ideal Danae, two lovable Greek epicureans of the fourth century B.C., have here replaced the many outward events that had hitherto usually formed the substance of the German novel. The background of this Greek seeker of a philosophy of life is utterly different from the romantic and medieval haze which had prevailed in *Parzival,* or from the gruesomely naturalistic atmosphere obtaining in *Simplicissimus.*

Musarion, oder die Philosophie der Grazien (Musarion, or The Philosophy of the Graces, 1768), a short and graceful epic about a Greek youth who foolishly sought happiness in philosophy rather than in a woman's love, contains in a nutshell Wieland's cheerful message of hedonism and epicurean sensualism. After the oppressive age of the Counter Reformation with its constant emphasis on hell-fire, damnation, and despair, such a message was bitterly needed and appreciated indeed.

Die Abderiten (1774) is a novel in which Wieland, under the guise of an attack upon the often ridiculed burghers of the ancient Greek city of Abdera, good-naturedly pokes fun at the philistinism and narrow morality of the people of the town of Biberach where he, the elegant cosmopolitan, had spent a few unhappy and boring years (1760–1769).

Oberon (1780) is a colorful medieval fairy tale about the king of the elves, relating how he helped Huon of Bordeaux to perform wondrous deeds in the Orient. It is a fine example of how Wieland replaced the dull sobriety of the age of Gottsched by a beautiful language, smooth rimes, and a colorful imagination, even though fairy tales of course were just another thing this sceptical philosopher did not believe in. The influence of Shakespeare's *Midsummer Night's Dream* and

65

of Ariosto's *Orlando Furioso* is especially marked in this epic; indeed, on account of his wit and scepticism Wieland has often been called the German Ariosto or the German Voltaire.

THE ENLIGHTENMENT

In fighting against the despotism and corruption of individual princes, continental enlighteners more and more extolled England, whose moderate and constitutional monarchy became an ideal for all oppressed peoples. Most enlighteners were still neoclassicists at heart and hence utterly opposed to the irregularities of English literature, in spite of their preference for the English political system (Voltaire); decades later, however, after the Storm and Stress had driven out the last traces of French-inspired Pseudoclassicism in Germany, the influence also of English literature became ever more important among the preromanticists. Especially the English moral weeklies, which were emulated in great numbers on the continent, helped to spread and to popularize the ideas of the leading European enlighteners.

Graviseth and Haller. *Heutelia* (1658), the critical account of a trip through Switzerland by the liberal thinker Jakob von Graviseth, constituted one of the earliest works of Enlightenment, in which much-needed reforms were discussed and demanded; but much more important than this early forerunner was Albrecht von Haller, another Swiss. Haller, a poet and scientist from Bern, agreed with Montesquieu's idea that climate exerts great influence on the form of government: hot climates making for despotism, cold climates for greater freedom. Hence Haller's three state novels: *Usong* (1771), the study of despotism in Persia; *Alfred, König der Angelsachsen* (Alfred, King of the Anglo-Saxons, 1773), a study of constitutional government in early England; and *Fabius und Cato* (1774), a study of the Roman republic, such as Haller, the Swiss, naturally would glorify it. Haller's famous poem *Die Alpen* (The Alps, 1729) also contains many utopian descriptions of true democracy and freedom amidst the Swiss Alps.

Wieland (II).* Wieland likewise meditated about an ideal, utopian form of government and about a better education and

* See also pp. 64–66.

preparation of young princes. His outstanding state novel *Der goldene Spiegel* (The Golden Mirror, 1772), which combined a high seriousness of purpose with occasional irony and flippancy, met with great approval, notably that of the duchess-mother Amalia of Sachsen-Weimar, who at once sent for Wieland and made him the tutor of her sons Karl August and Konstantin. Thus Wieland was the first of the great German writers to enter Weimar, the town which a few years later, under Goethe, was to become the capital of German literature.

Gotthold Ephraim Lessing (1729–1781). Together with Luther and Schiller, Lessing belongs among the manliest German battlers for human freedom. In spite of his dislike of France he too, almost as much as Wieland, still belonged to the rationalistic, neoclassical, French-inspired camp of literature; in many of his ideas (e.g. in his love of Sophocles and of Shakespeare), however, he clearly shared in the new movements that were in the making—movements which in the case of Lessing were to lead up not so much to the Storm and Stress (of whose irrational excesses he, the rationalist, never approved), but to Goethe's and Schiller's great Greek-inspired Classicism.

LESSING AS A LITERARY CRITIC. First of all Lessing was a literary critic, a man clear, just, and merciless, who castigated the German poetasters around Gottsched and who upheld higher ideals. Classicism there must be—not the timid, fussy French brand of Pseudoclassicism, but genuine Greek Classicism instead. The French, he insisted, had misinterpreted Aristotle and had perverted the Greek ideal of literature: hence the necessity for a return to the Greeks directly in order to know what great literature really is. Concerning the sacred three unities of time, place, and action, as scrupulously observed in the French drama, Lessing insisted that Aristotle had never put them up as rigid rules, but only as valuable pieces of advice which were to be followed only when feasible. Lessing therefore endeavored to make the neoclassical drama more flexible and to grant it more freedom. Nor did he approve of the mistaken pseudoclassical restriction which said that tragedies were concerned with great princes and heroes alone, dealing with big events and state actions

67

(*Haupt- und Staatsaktionen*) only, as Opitz and Gottsched had falsely maintained, and that comedies were only for lowly-born characters and trivial incidents. Here Lessing again liberated the drama from stifling French fetters and, within certain limitations of Neoclassicism, he left as much as possible to the author's discretion.

Especially in his *Kritische Briefe, die neueste deutsche Literatur betreffend* (Critical Letters on the Most Recent German Literature, 1759 ff.) and also in his *Hamburgische Dramaturgie* (Dramatic Notes from Hamburg, 1767 ff.) Lessing elucidated his anti-French and pro-Greek classical ideas. In the former work he was ably assisted by two of his three best friends, the philosopher Moses Mendelssohn and the bookdealer Friedrich Nicolai. In both publications he bitterly condemned Corneille, Racine, Boileau, Voltaire, and their cheap imitators in Germany such as Gottsched; French tragedies, he maintained, had degenerated into endless monologues and analyses, in which really powerful action was completely lacking. Thereupon he extolled Shakespeare, as the greatest modern dramatist of all countries, the genius who may not have known the French rules, but who certainly succeeded in creating mighty dramatic conflicts. Lessing therefore advised the Germans that instead of following in the footsteps of Gottsched (whom he ridiculed especially in the seventeenth *Letter on Literature*) they should try to blend the gigantic characters and mighty conflicts of Shakespeare with the restrained, lucid, and really classical form of Sophocles in order to create a perfect drama. In suggesting to his readers native themes worthy of dramatic treatment, Lessing quoted one scene from his *Faust*—a tragedy the manuscript of which was unfortunately lost.

In another critical essay, *Laokoon* (1766), Lessing fought against the long-established fashion of mixing painting and poetry. A painting or a piece of sculpture (as e.g. Agesander's statue of Laocoön) represents that which is simultaneous— it is static; and a poem (as e.g. Virgil's description of Laocoön's struggle against the serpents in his *Aeneid*) represents that which is successive—it is dynamic. A poet thus should always show action; he should never paint with words, as the Baroque poets had so absurdly done in their descriptions. And, showing a succession of actions, a poet may well be allowed to show occasional climaxes, e.g. the yelling of Laocoön from pain—whereas the sculptor or the painter, showing one moment alone, should choose the most fertile rather than the most climactic moment, a Laocoön merely groaning, with a half-opened mouth.

LESSING AS A DRAMATIST. Lessing's second claim to fame lies in his dramas. He wrote plays in order to advance his ideas and in order to illustrate the points he made in his literary criticism. His literary career in Berlin, his activity as a secretary to a Prussian general during the Seven Years' War and, finally, his position as director of the new National Theater in Hamburg gave him the necessary experiences for his important dramatic productions.

Miss Sara Sampson (1755), the first full-grown bourgeois drama in German literature, demonstrates that the tragedy of ill-fated love, murder, and suicide is possible also among middle-class people and not only among royal families, as Gottsched had maintained. In this trend to portray in literature the slowly rising bourgeois class Lessing followed the example not so much of Gryphius in *Cardenio und Celinde*, but of Lillo in England (*The London Merchant, or the History of George Barnwell,* 1731).

Philotas (1759), a one-act tragedy of Spartan patriotism and manliness, served as an indirect rebuke to the prevalent French fashion of showing amorous, effeminate characters only. It tells of a young Greek prince who, rather than give his enemies a chance to exploit the fact that he had been captured in battle, resolved to commit suicide. Written during the Seven Years' War, the theme echoes Frederick the Great's firm determination never to let his enemies take him alive.

Minna von Barnhelm (1767) can be called a comedy because of several excellently drawn minor characters and also because it shows how resolutely Minna goes about getting her man; but it is even more an earnest portrayal of a Prussian officer, Major von Tellheim, and of his keen sense of honor which seems to forbid him to marry Minna. This first truly modern German comedy also served a patriotic purpose, because its representation of the marriage of a Prussian officer with a Saxon noblewoman was to teach the Germans to forget the animosities of the Seven Years' War and to live in unity. One of Lessing's best friends, Ewald von Kleist, to whom he had already addressed his *Letters on Literature,* served as the prototype for Major von Tellheim; for the first time a soldier was represented as a man of honor rather than as a bragging fool, as most European dramas had portrayed him before Lessing's time.

Emilia Galotti (1772) is a violent protest against the immorality of princes, a tale of seduction and death resembling the melodramas of the Storm and Stress, yet written in an absolutely classical, concise, and epigrammatic style. It is one of the best built of all German tragedies, from a technical point of view a real masterpiece; but it also betrays the shortcomings of Lessing, because he, the rationalist, could not become really convincing and lyrical in his description of passion. The tragedy tries to combine Shakespearean might with Sophoclean restraint; but it is not a complete success.

Lessing as a Religious Enlightener. As an enlightener Lessing inculcated national unity (*Minna von Barnhelm*) and patriotic sacrifice (*Philotas*), and attacked seduction and immorality (*Miss Sara Sampson, Emilia Galotti*); but it was in the field of religious enlightenment that he achieved his greatest glory. An ardent Protestant, he was inclined towards Deism, i.e. so-called natural religion, which retained most of the fundamental tenets of Christianity but which eliminated the many embellishments that had been added by the medieval Church and by modern sects. In a different way from Wieland he envisaged a happy future unoppressed by fanatic priests, bigotry, and petty intolerance. During the last years of his life, while he was librarian at Wolfenbüttel, Lessing clashed with orthodox Lutherans, especially with one Pastor Goeze from Hamburg, who suspected heresy and treason behind Lessing's proreligious but antiecclesiastical attitude. Of the many works resulting from this quarrel with Goeze, the following two are especially significant.

Nathan der Weise (Nathan the Wise, 1779), a fine dramatic poem, shows both Lessing's noble spirit of tolerance and his free and un-French dramatic construction. The parable of the three rings borrowed from Boccaccio's *Decameron* and ennobled in this drama contains one of the most beautiful messages in German literature. An actual comparison of the characters shows that the Jew and the Mohammedan are at least as noble as the Christian, in fact far superior to such a despicable fanatic as the Patriarch, the prototype of Goeze. This greatest drama of religious enlightenment, depicting the clash of three religions at the time of the Crusades, is also important because Lessing, disliking the French Alexandrine meter and hence having hitherto written all his plays in prose, now for the first time used Shakespearean blank verse—a relatively unknown meter in Germany which after *Nathan* was to become the classical meter of German dramatic literature. From a technical viewpoint one may discover several flaws in this drama, but it is its spirit, its idealism, which make it an immortal work in the history of German thought.

Die Erziehung des Menschengeschlechts (The Education of the Human Race, 1780) is an inspiring essay which explains the imperfections of our world by the thesis that adolescent mankind has thus far had only two "primers" to learn from: the revelation of the Father (the teachings of Moses) and the revelation of the Son (the teachings of Christ). Only after the third lesson, the revelation of the Holy Ghost, which is still to come, will man's soul be truly blessed, tolerant, and worthy of God. Only then will mankind enter the Millennium, the beginning of which the earnest God-seeker Lessing so ardently hoped for.

TRANSLATIONS

GENERAL COLLECTION

Pontes, L. Davésiès de. *Poets and Poetry of Germany* (containing poems by Gellert, Gleim, Hagedorn, Haller, E. v. Kleist, and others). London, 1858.

INDIVIDUAL AUTHORS

HALLER: *The Moderate Monarchy; or, The Principles of the British Constitution, Described in a Narrative of the Life and Maxims of Alfred the Great and His Counsellors* (translator anonymous). London, 1849.

Usong, An Eastern Narrative (translator anonymous). London, 1772.

LESSING: Beasley, E. C., and H. Zimmern, tr. *Selected Prose Works* (containing "Laocoön," "Dramatic Notes," "How the Ancients Represented Death"). London, 1890.

Bell, E., ed. *The Dramatic Works* (containing—besides translations of Lessing's earliest plays like "Die Juden," "Der junge Gelehrte,"

"Die alte Jungfer," "Der Misogyn," "Der Freigeist," "Der Schatz"
—"Miss Sara Sampson," "Philotas," "Minna von Barnhelm,"
"Emilia Galotti," "Nathan der Weise"). London, 1895. 2 vols.

Robertson, F. W., tr. *The Education of the Human Race.* New York
(Harvard Classics, XXXII), 1909.

Steele, W. A., tr. *Laocoon, Nathan the Wise, and Minna von Barnhelm.*
New York (Everyman's Library), 1930.

WIELAND: Adams, John Quincy, tr. *Oberon, A Poetical Romance
in Twelve Books,* edited by A. B. Faust. New York, 1940.

The Adventures of Don Sylvio de Rosalva, with an introduction by
E. A. Baker. London & New York, 1904.

Christmas, H., tr. *The Republic of Fools, Being the History of the
State and People of Abdera, in Thrace.* London, 1861.

"The Golden Mirror; or, The Kings of Scheschian" (translator anonymous), *Hibernian Magazine,* 1798.

The Graces, A Classical Allegory (translator anonymous). London,
1823.

The History of Agathon (translator anonymous). London, 1773.
4 vols.

Sotheby, William, tr. *Oberon, A Poem.* London, 1798. 2 vols.

CHAPTER VII

THE STORM AND STRESS, 1760–1785

GENERAL OBSERVATIONS

Against French scepticism bordering on atheism, against Wieland's elegant frivolity, against Gottsched's dull preaching of rules and imitation, there now arose a powerful Germanic reaction which clamored for nature instead of civilization, originality instead of imitation, religion instead of irony, passion instead of convention, lyricism instead of didacticism. The enlighteners, too, in their subtle ways, had fought against the moral corruption of the *ancien régime;* but now came the more powerful wave of the Storm and Stress which flooded the country and buried all compromises in very much the same way as Luther's Reformation had buried the subtle compromises of the Humanists. The *Sturm und Drang* provided the rebellious poets of the era with an opportunity to give vent to their repressed emotions, so that in the critical years after 1789 internecine bloodshed could be avoided. Wise princes like Frederick II of Prussia and Joseph II of Austria had already improved social and political conditions in Germany to such an extent that an open revolution after the French model did not become necessary there.

Literature in England

In part simultaneously with Germany the poets and writers of England, Switzerland, and, later, Italy and Spain, also began their struggle against the yoke of French-inspired Classicism. England produced a rich group of preromanticists: with Addison's moral weeklies Milton began to be justly appreciated and his fame was spread on the Continent; Defoe's *Robinson Crusoe* advocated simple life away from the temptations of European civilization; Thomson's poems at last began again to describe and glorify the beauties of nature; the emphasis, in Shaftesbury's philosophy, upon tenderness and sentiment started to thaw the ice of French etiquette; Lillo in his bourgeois dramas and Richardson in his bourgeois novels replaced the stiltedness of princely problems by a domestic atmosphere and everyday crises and catastrophes; Edward Young not only brought into English literature the mood of gentle melancholy and nocturnal meditations, but also, through his *Conjectures on Original Composition,* commenced a belated but full appreciation of Shakespeare's great and original genius; Thomas Gray, through his *Elegy Written in a Country Churchyard,* gave memorable expression to the funereal meditations of a whole group of churchyard poets and also wrote in praise of the common man; Bishop Percy through his *Reliques of Ancient English Poetry* extolled the poetic merits of old popular ballads, which he considered far superior to the artificial and shallow sentiments of modern court poets; James Macpherson, in his versions of the (forged) songs of Ossian, evoked the worshipful memory of an old Celtic past, of an ancient northern culture infinitely more noble and more tender than the Graeco-Roman culture upon which France had based her intellectual hegemony; Sterne, in his irrational and rambling novels, disregarded the rules of compactness previously demanded by the French; Goldsmith in his *Vicar of Wakefield* turned to idyllic, rustic scenes; and Robert Burns, after generations of stifling Neoclassicism, proved at last to be another real people's poet.

Literature in France and Switzerland

The great significance of the German-Swiss poets will be discussed later in this chapter; here must be mentioned the most important French-Swiss author, the "father of French Romanticism," Jean Jacques Rousseau of Geneva, who, while in Paris, was a Swiss among Frenchmen, a republican among monarchists, a Calvinist among Catholics, a bourgeois among courtiers, and who thus was destined to play a truly revolutionary role in the intellectual life of France. This is proved by his startling political book *Le Contrat Social* (The Social Contract, 1762), by his *Julie, ou la Nouvelle Héloïse* (Julie, or the New Heloise), a novel which blended the tearful sentimentality of the new age with the ever increasing love for

rustic simplicity, and by his *Émile,* an anti-intellectual book
on education whose radical theories were soon to be amended
by Heinrich Pestalozzi, the best known educator of Switzerland and one of the greatest pedagogues of all times. Indeed,
if considered in connection with the German-Swiss authors
from Zurich and Bern, the literature of Switzerland in the
eighteenth century appears so important that it might well be
said that Romanticism properly speaking did not originate
in Germany and in England but in the two mountainous
countries of Switzerland (Haller, Bodmer, Gessner, Rousseau) and Scotland (Macpherson, Burns, and, to a lesser
extent, Percy and Gray). Whereas the continental enlighteners had idolized English political institutions but had mostly
disregarded English literature, the poets of the Storm and
Stress now admired and copied also the depth of thought and
irregularity of form of English poets—and Swiss cities like
Zurich now became one of the main centers of Anglophiles on
the Continent.

Literature in Italy and Spain

Italy, too, produced an increasing number of thinkers and
writers who reacted against the stranglehold of French Classicism; and, as in England the genius of Shakespeare and
Milton had served as a ram against the power of Voltaire,
so in Italy the religious ardor and irrational visions of Dante
Alighieri were at last appreciated again and defended against
the sneers of neoclassicists of the type of Bettinelli. Muratori,
the friend of the Swiss preromanticist Bodmer, was the first
to turn towards a study of the Middle Ages, which the neo-
classicists had despised as barbaric and Gothic; Vico, comparable to Herder in Germany, evolved a deep and original
philosophy of history. Baretti, long a resident of England,
imitated Addison's moral weeklies and lashed out against the
false taste and presumptuousness of France. The Abbé Cesa-
rotti, in 1763, produced one of the best translations of Ossian
to any foreign tongue. Ugo Foscolo in his *Le ultime lettere
di Jacopo Ortis* betrayed the influence of Goethe's *Werther,*
and his *I Sepolcri* reflected the moods of the English churchyard poets. The same influence of Young and Gray is also
observed in Pindemonte's *Alla melancolia* and *I Cimiteri.* In

75

Spain attention is called to Juan Meléndez Valdés and his contemporaries, upon whom the influence of Milton, Thomson, Young, and Ossian, and of Rousseau and Gessner, was most effective—as is indicated by Meléndez Valdés' imitation of Young entitled *La noche y la soledad* (Night and Solitude).

The Growing Importance of German Literature

After centuries of relative isolation and passive receptivity, German literature, from the middle of the eighteenth century on, assumed an ever more important role in the concert of European letters. The international fame of Haller, Gessner, Klopstock, and Lessing prepared the ground for Goethe, whose *Sorrows of Young Werther,* with one stroke, established firmly the popularity and thereby the prestige of German literature abroad—a prestige which steadily grew in importance until, by 1800, the influence of German thinkers and poets in the intellectual life of Europe and America became supremely important.

FORERUNNERS OF THE STORM AND STRESS

Günther. Johann Christian Günther (d. 1723), a vagabond poet whose short life is deeply tragic, showed great lyric power in the expressions of his religious crises and of his erotic experiences. But he was born too soon and, temperamentally unrestrained, he found little scope for his poetic gift or appreciation for his productions in the frigid world around Gottsched. Günther is often called the last great Silesian poet of that age and the connecting link between Baroque and Storm and Stress. The life of this outcast youth, because of its wretchedness and restlessness, has often been compared to the life of the late medieval French poet François Villon.

Haller.* The Bernese patrician Albrecht von Haller in his famous poem *Die Alpen* (The Alps, 1729) for the first time visualized nature not as a dainty screen, as the neoclassicist shepherds had done, but as a powerful and awe-inspiring panorama of God's creation. He also contrasted effectively the virtues and industriousness of Swiss mountain-dwellers with the vices and luxury of corrupt courts and cities. His

* See also p. 66.

Alpen is contained also in a later collection of verse called *Versuch schweizerischer Gedichte* (Experiments in Swiss Poems, 1732), in which the influence of Alexander Pope is particularly marked.

Schnabel and Wyss. Johann Gottfried Schnabel's *Die Insel Felsenburg* (Island Felsenburg, 1731) is the earliest and best German imitation of Defoe's *Robinson Crusoe*. In this story of a German youth, an English bride, a Belgian bridegroom, and a French captain (the latter two being killed after a shipwreck because of the captain's lust), Schnabel mingles enlightened cosmopolitanism, bourgeois pietism, pre-romantic sentimentality, and utopian planning, all in an exotic setting. Most famous among the continental imitations of Defoe is *Der schweizerische Robinson* (The Swiss Family Robinson, 1813) by Johann Rudolf Wyss from Bern; written during the chaos of the Napoleonic Wars, it expresses the same desire to turn away from man-made civilization and to revert to the peace and simplicity of nature.

Brockes and Ewald von Kleist. Barthold Heinrich Brockes and Ewald von Kleist, early descriptive nature poets and imitators of Thomson's *Seasons,* contributed greatly to the rebirth of German lyric poetry. Brockes, a poet from Hamburg (a second gateway, besides Zurich, through which English influences entered German literature), is known for his collection of poems *Irdisches Vergnügen in Gott* (Earthly Delight in God) ; Ewald von Kleist, an officer in the Prussian army mortally wounded in the Seven Years' War, left behind him a fragmentary elegiac poem on the seasons, called *Frühling* (Spring).

Bodmer. Johann Jakob Bodmer (1698–1783), the head of the Zurich group of poets, the translator of Milton's *Paradise Lost* (1732) and the author of another biblical epic, *Noah* (1750), was an enthusiastic defender of irrational and religious poetry. He was the greatest enemy of Gottsched, whose dull and rationalistic theories of literature he wanted to overcome by allotting imagination and fantasy an important place in any work of art. Hence the important literary quarrel between the two, often called the quarrel between Zurich and Leipzig, or between the Swiss and Gottsched, in many respects comparable to the quarrel, in France and England, between

77

the "Moderns" and the "Ancients," which ended in the former's victory. Other English works which Bodmer translated and adapted in order to use them as missiles against his enemies and as examples for his partisans are Dryden's *MacFlecknoe,* Pope's *Dunciad,* and Butler's *Hudibras*—the latter aimed by Bodmer especially against the orthodox clergy of Zurich. Bodmer also deserves full credit for being one of the first modern authors to care for medieval German literature and to study and edit many of the epic and lyric poems of the Hohenstaufen era. Hence also his interest in Ossian and in Percy's *Reliques of Ancient English Poetry,* many of whose pages he translated into German. Much less deserving are the repeated Shakespeare imitations contained in his various historical dramas. In keeping with his love for Milton, Bodmer was also the first poet in German-speaking lands to hail Dante Alighieri as the inspired author of the *Divina Commedia,* rather than to acclaim him only as the pro-Ghibelline and antipopish writer of *De Monarchia,* as the German Protestants during the sixteenth century had been wont to do. A close friend and associate of Bodmer's was JOHANN JAKOB BREITINGER, who helped him in the editing of the journal *Die Discourse der Mahlern* (The Discourses of the Painters, 1721 ff.) and in the writing of such great anti-Gottschedian essays as *Kritische Abhandlung über das Wunderbare in der Poesie* (Critical Treatise on the Miraculous in Poetry, 1740) and *Betrachtungen über die poetischen Gemälde der Dichter* (Reflections on the Poetic Portraits of Authors, 1741).

Gessner. Salomon Gessner, like Bodmer a Swiss from Zurich, wrote his *Idyllen* (1756) in poetic prose which, in spite of the Rococo-like daintiness of style, is full of religious feeling, tenderness, and tearfulness. The eagerly desired Golden Age of Innocence, which Haller thought he had found among the Swiss Alps, Gessner visualized only in a distant era of biblical times when Cain had not yet slain Abel—as evidenced, for instance, in Gessner's best known work, *Der Tod Abels* (The Death of Abel, 1758). Chronologically Gessner and Haller were the first poets in German-speaking lands in the modern age to become internationally famous and to be emulated by foreign authors. Gessner also achieved considerable importance as a painter and as the leading book publisher of Zurich, who, among other things, inspired and printed and adorned with vignettes of his own Wieland's translation of Shakespeare.

Periodicals

One of the most influential vehicles to spread and popularize the ideas both of the Enlightenment and of Preromanticism were the moral weeklies with their preaching of common sense and civic virtues and their fight against absolutism and for the improvement of social institutions, civil manners, and literary taste. Written in fluent and simple language, and catering to the taste also of women, these periodicals by popularizing the thoughts of great thinkers and poets began to bridge the abyss which ever since the age of Humanism had separated the small intelligentsia of the nation from the vast masses of burghers. All of them conscious imitations of Addison's and Steele's *Tatler* (1709) and *Spectator,* they exerted a great influence also in the era of the Storm and Stress and beyond. One of the earliest was the Swiss *Die Discourse der Mahlern* (The Discourses of the Painters, 1721), followed in Hamburg by *Der Patriot* (1724) and by the two weeklies edited by Gottsched, *Die vernünftigen Tadlerinnen* (The Reasonable Female Critics, 1725) and *Der Biedermann* (The Honest Bourgeois). Among the leading periodicals in the later eighteenth century, mention must be made of *Die Bremer Beiträge* (The Bremen Contributions), largely supported by JOHANN ELIAS SCHLEGEL, an early admirer of Shakespeare, who, in 1741, wrote a *Vergleichung Shakespears und Andreas Gryphs* (A Comparison between Shakespeare and Andreas Gryphius). *Der nordische Aufseher* (The Nordic Spectator) was especially important because in it men like HEINRICH WILHELM VON GERSTENBERG, a Dane by birth, a German by language, popularized the knowledge of Scandinavian mythology and literature. Some periodicals that were connected with the greatest names of the age were *Der teutsche Merkur* (The German Mercury), edited by Wieland from 1773 on; *Die Blätter von deutscher Art und Kunst* (Pages about German Mind and Art), the leading periodical of the Storm and Stress, edited by Herder, with young Goethe as a contributor;

Die Horen (The Hours), edited by Schiller, the periodical of the classical age of German literature; *Das Athenaeum,* the periodical of the Romantic School, edited, from 1798 on, by August Wilhelm Schlegel and Friedrich Schlegel.

THE STORM AND STRESS

Friedrich Gottlieb Klopstock (1724–1803). Klopstock, sometimes called the German Milton, was the reawakener of religious poetry, the herald of a great Nordic Renaissance, the liberator of German lyrical poetry from the yoke of French neoclassicist restrictions, a forerunner rather than a representative of the German Storm and Stress.

Der Messias (The Messiah, 1748 ff.) is an ambitious religious epic, the appearance of which really marked the end of the French-inspired period of Neoclassicism and the beginning of new greatness in German literature. In an ecstatic and rhapsodic fashion and a language that is at times too abstract and ethereal Klopstock represented the life, sufferings, and resurrection of Christ. Exalted pietism, which ever since the end of the Baroque Age had been an undercurrent only, now broke forth again in full vigor.

Klopstock's *Oden* (Odes), glorifying religion, friendship, and nature, likewise restored emotionalism and irrationalism to their proper place in the realm of poetic creation. In the history of German versification these *Oden* are remarkable, too, because of the rich variety of metrical forms in which Klopstock now tried his hand.

Der Tod Adams (The Death of Adam, 1757), an exceedingly sentimental religious drama about the death of the first man, is a lyrical effusion in which Adam bewails the sins, miseries, and mortality which he has brought to mankind. In keeping with the irrational and irregular trends of the time, it is not at all a tragedy in the concise and customary meaning of the word.

Die Hermannsschlacht (The Battle of Hermann, 1769) and other bardic dramas about the heroic chieftain who had defeated the Roman legions in the Teutoburg Forest show Klopstock's love for the Germanic past. This renaissance and new appreciation of northern antiquities was enhanced through Klopstock's long stay in Denmark (1751–1770). The courage, virtues, and manly simplicity of the old Germanic tribes, as reported already in Tacitus' *Germania,* now served to underscore the worthlessness of the modern (French) civilization of the eighteenth century. Besides the *Germania,* the ancient Germanic tales contained in the Icelandic *Edda* now also became widely popular and were acclaimed—by Gerstenberg in *Gedichte eines Skalden* (Poems of a Norse Bard, 1766) and others—as welcome allies in the fight against Roman-French standards. Of considerable European influence was also the *Histoire du Danemark* (1755 ff.) written by the French-Swiss scholar Paul Henri Mallet, who stayed at Copenhagen at the same time Klopstock did.

Johann Gottfried Herder (1744–1803). Like Klopstock originally a theologian, Herder is the great philosophical leader of the Storm and Stress, the center and propagator of all new irrational and anticlassicist trends, the leading folklorist of his age, the German representative of Rousseau's return-to-nature movement, an essayist and a teacher rather than a creative poet. Of chief importance among the men who influenced Herder is JOHANN GEORG HAMANN, a profound thinker on language, literature, and religion, one of the most fertile and irrational minds of the century, whose aphoristic and fragmentary works Herder endeavored to digest and clarify.

HERDER AND LESSING. Herder's *Fragmente über die neuere deutsche Literatur* (Fragments on Recent German Literature, 1766), like all his other literary interpretations inspiring and enthusiastic, though fragmentary, contrast sharply with Lessing's rational and coolly analytical *Literaturbriefe* (Letters on Literature) to which publication they served as supplements. Likewise his *Kritische Wälder* (Critical Forests, 1769) form a complement, and even more a dynamic contrast, to Lessing's calm literary elucidations in his *Laokoon.*

In his important essay on *Shakespeare* (1773) Herder continued Lessing's glorification of the great Englishman, extolling him as the greatest dramatist since the age of Pericles, an original genius who may not have known the petty rules of French Classicism, but, Herder agreed with Lessing, whose works tower far above anything Corneille, Racine, and Voltaire may have written. Shakespeare is represented as a titan, an eruptive genius, who obeys no laws except those of his own divine inspiration.

URPOESIE. *Ossian und die Lieder alter Völker* (Ossian and the Songs of Old Nations, 1773) and *Stimmen der Völker in Liedern* (Voices of Nations in Songs, 1778) show Herder's everlasting quest of *Urpoesie*—not poetry made by witty poetasters and courtiers or even conscious artists of modern civilization, but old and genuine poetry originating among the people and reflecting the innermost soul of a nation. Herder mistook Macpherson's heroic and sentimental tales about the old Celtic bard Ossian for such *Urpoesie* and hence glorified them; but besides these he also included folk songs of all ages and all nations in his collection. Every people should remain faithful to and should give expression to its own inborn genius and should never stoop so low as to ape foreign rules and standards: that was the message Herder wanted to convey to the newly awakening national consciousness of Germany.

PHILOSOPHY OF HISTORY. Herder's *Ideen zur Philosophie der Geschichte der Menschheit* (Ideas on the Philosophy of the History of Mankind, 1784) and his *Briefe zur Beförderung der Humanität* (Letters on the Advancement of Humanism, 1793) contributed greatly to the Golden Age of German Idealism, because to Wieland's happy hedonism and to Lessing's broad tolerance, Herder, in dreaming about a future better world, now added his touch of religious and emotional ardor. The "organic" interpretation of history and culture which was to culminate in Goethe and the representatives of the "Historical School" (Savigny, Grimm, Ranke) found its earliest and most brilliant advocate in Herder. For him historical periods and cultural cycles develop like organisms, from birth to maturity to decay. But each cycle is a step forward in man's approach toward the perfect humanity. In this progress of humanity, poets, according to Herder, should be leaders, priests, and prophets and thus fundamentally different from the courtiers and poetasters prevailing during the neoclassical age.

POETRY. Herder created one real work of poetry in *Der Cid* (published posthumously in 1805) by translating and coordinating into a stately epic the many ballads existing in

Spanish literature about the Spanish national hero Rodrigo
Díaz de Bivar, commonly called El Cid Campeador, who in
the eleventh century had been the great leader of the Spaniards
in their battles against the Moors. As in all his translations
of foreign folklore Herder displayed a fine intuitive understanding of the ideals and mentalities of other nations and
other ages.

Young Goethe (II).* Johann Wolfgang von Goethe
(1749–1832), the son of a wealthy patrician family of Frankfurt, began his literary career in the fashion of the Rococo
while studying law at the University of Leipzig (1765–
1768), the residence of Gottsched and Gellert. Later, during his studies at Strassburg (1770–1771), he met Herder
and, inspired by him, became the chief representative of the
Storm and Stress. After his return to Frankfurt he spent
a few months at Wetzlar (1772) and in 1775 he moved
to Weimar, as the friend and adviser of the young Duke
Karl August of Sachsen-Weimar, where manifold influences
gradually contributed to turn him from the restlessness of
the Storm and Stress to a truly classical conception of literature.

LYRIC POETRY. Sincerity and simplicity, warmth of
thought, and beauty of expression contributed to make
young Goethe the greatest lyric poet in German literature.

a. His love poems to Friederike Brion of Sesenheim near
Strassburg are ardent and genuine and succeed admirably in blending his moods with the varying aspects of
nature. Examples: *Willkommen und Abschied* (Welcome
and Departure); *Mailied* (May Song).

b. In his simple folk poems Goethe, under the influence of
Herder, succeeded beautifully in emulating the naive and
tender language of folk songs. Example: *Das Heiden-
röslein* (Rose among the Heather).

c. In his ballads the love of the Storm and Stress for irra-
tional and mysterious events is well expressed. Examples:
Der Erlkönig (The King of the Elves); *Der Fischer* (The
Fisherman).

d. Goethe's hymns express not only the rebellious restlessness of the young generation (*Prometheus*), but also its

* See also pp. 63–64.

titanic power and aspirations (*Mahomet*), and its pantheistic yearning for union with God (*Ganymed*). During
the first years at Weimar, the note of fervent pantheism
and obedient humility before God supplanted the previous
unrestraint, as evidenced in the *Gesang der Geister über
den Wassern* (Song of the Spirits over the Waters), or
Die Grenzen der Menschheit (The Limits of Man).

e. His *Lieder an Lili* (Songs to Lili) contain the love poems
addressed to Elisabeth Schönemann of Frankfurt, for a
few months his fiancée.

EARLY WORKS. The tragedy *Götz von Berlichingen* (1773)
reveals in its loose and kaleidoscopic construction the anti-
French and anticlassical influences of Herder and, through
him, of Shakespeare. Love of late medieval knighthood; the
bold courage of Götz to rebel singlehanded against a whole
world of sycophants; his return to and intimacy with nature
and with simple folk, the source of his strength; finally the
defeat of Götz in his unequal struggle against corrupt civilization—all these were favorite themes of the Storm and
Stress.

The essay *Von deutscher Baukunst* (On German Architecture, 1773), a glorification of Gothic architecture, especially of the Strassburg Cathedral and its architect, Erwin
von Steinbach, demonstrates further the pro-Germanic, pro-
medieval, anticlassical and anti-French taste of young Goethe.
To this period belongs also Goethe's *Rede zum Shakespeare
Tag* (Address for the Shakespeare Anniversary), in which
he, in contrast to Herder, eulogized not only the creative
power but also the consciously shaping artistic will of the
great Englishman.

Die Leiden des jungen Werthers (The Sorrows of Young
Werther, 1774), a novel in epistolary form which at once was
to become world-famous, released the sentimentality of men
and women whose warmer emotions had for decades been
dammed up and starved by the rigid rules of French etiquette. Richardson and Rousseau exerted a certain influence
upon this lyrical and tearful tale of unhappy love and suicide; but in the main it is based upon Goethe's passion for
Charlotte Buff while at Wetzlar. Like Götz, like Prometheus,

Werther is a "titan"—a titan of feeling. He must die, not essentially because his love remains unanswered, but because no reconciliation is possible between the rigid demands of reality and the super-sensibility, the emotional richness of his heart. The novel made its author famous overnight; indeed, it was the first European book to be translated into Chinese. It called forth not only translations, but also adaptations and imitations in most European literatures.

Götter, Helden und Wieland (Gods, Heroes, and Wieland) is a farce in which Goethe, in the titanism of his youth, ridiculed the hedonistic and effeminate characters in Wieland's Greek works; but another farce, *Satyros,* directed against the crude and Rousseauistic primitivism of Herder and his circle (of which Goethe himself had been the most promising member), on the other hand indicates clearly that he had already passed the peak of his Storm and Stress eruptiveness.

Clavigo (1774), a tragedy treating the theme of man's ruthlessness and of woman's loyalty, in which Goethe chastised himself for his own cruel desertion of Friederike Brion, is stylistically remarkable because its compactness indicates that the preromantic excesses of *Götz* were past and that Goethe was gradually veering towards a calmer and more classical style. Like Werther, so also Clavigo was a weak superman who could not reconcile his soaring ambition with his love for Marie.

Stella (1775) is again a tragedy in which Goethe subjected his own impetuous love-life to merciless scrutiny. In view of the bitter attacks of the young generation against man-made laws and restrictions it is not to be wondered at that Fernando, the weak hero of this drama, the lover of Cäcilia (Friederike Brion) and of Stella (Elisabeth Schönemann), even advocates the desirability of bigamy. But stylistically *Stella* is even more regular and compact than *Clavigo.*

Egmont (published in 1787) is also still essentially a Storm and Stress drama, again the tragedy of a titanic hero who dares to challenge a whole world of enemies and who, like Götz, is finally defeated and killed. With his increasingly classical taste Goethe considerably reduced the originally planned broad folk scenes; it became the tragedy not so much of the Dutch people in their fight against Spain as of one overoptimistic titan only, whose self-confidence, in 1568, led him to death.

Finally, the first form of *Faust,* too, is essentially a Storm and Stress drama combining two themes so dear to the Storm and Stress rebels: the story of the superhumanly ambitious Faust, whose avid intellect acknowledges no limitations of human knowledge and who because of his burning desire for universal experience concludes a pact with Mephistopheles in order to pierce the walls of human ignorance with the devil's help—and the story of the seduction and desertion of Margaret, a theme which Goethe had already treated in *Götz, Clavigo,* and *Stella.* It is essentially a drama in Faust's own soul, describing his struggle for his own individual salvation; yet when reading the (subsequently added) *Prolog im Himmel* (Prologue in Heaven) we become aware of the fact, too, that in its larger meaning it is a struggle raging in the breast of man between the Lord and Satan—and we feel in the very beginning that God is right in believing that Faust, in spite of all his errors and sins, will never become Mephistopheles' victim, but that he will always be aware of the right path ("des rechten Weges wohl bewusst") and that he will sooner or later revert to it.

Minor Storm and Stress Writers. The tenor of the Storm and Stress literature is essentially lyrical. Lyric poetry hence prevails, and even the many dramas of protests and rebelliousness have a lyrical ring. The lyrical element is pronounced, if not predominant, in the novel also, for we might indeed consider every letter in Goethe's *Werther* as a lyrical outburst in prose.

Lyric Poetry

Many of the impassioned and fervent poets of the Storm and Stress, acknowledging Klopstock as their revered master, united into the pronouncedly Germanic *Göttinger Hainbund* (Göttingen Grove League) and published their verses in the *Göttinger Musenalmanach.* Their poems were tenderly sentimental, religious, irrational, Ossianic, and enthusiastically patriotic.

CHRISTIAN SCHUBART, the most ardent poet of political

liberty, was for ten years cruelly incarcerated (1777–1787) by the duke of Württemberg, on account of his rebellious convictions.

GOTTFRIED AUGUST BÜRGER, a lover of folk poetry, the creator of the modern German ballad, and an admirer of Bishop Percy's *Reliques of Ancient English Poetry*, is remembered especially for such ballads as *Lenore* (1773), a very dramatic and gruesome poem on the death of a soldier's bride—a theme encountered again in Washington Irving's *The Spectre Bridegroom*. Bürger is also important for having been the first really to popularize the stories and pranks of the pleasant liar, Baron Karl von Münchhausen. Some tales had first appeared in a German periodical in 1781 and these relatively unknown stories one RUDOLPH RASPE, a German residing in England, completed, translated into English, and published in Oxford in 1785–1786. Bürger translated Raspe's collected edition into German and published it in 1786 and, in a new augmented edition, in 1788.

JOHANN HEINRICH VOSS, together with HEINRICH CHRISTIAN BOIE and LUDWIG HÖLTY one of the mainstays of the *Göttinger Hainbund,* was widely acclaimed as the author of the idyllic epic *Luise* (1783), an important predecessor of Goethe's *Hermann und Dorothea*. In this age which extolled Greek originality and condemned the Roman and French spirit of neoclassic imitation, Voss also produced what still today is the best German translation of Homer's *Odyssey* (1781) and *Iliad* (1793).

MATTHIAS CLAUDIUS with his simplicity of form and piety of thought is one of the beloved poets of the German people even in our own age. He combined a childlike naiveté with a rare depth and purity of feeling, which gave some of his poems the true ring of a folk song—as, for instance, *Abendlied* (Evening Song).

CHRISTIAN and FRIEDRICH LEOPOLD ZU STOLBERG, friends of Goethe, in their lyric poems followers of Klopstock, translated Homer, Aeschylus, Sophocles, and Ossian. Friedrich was one of the first poets to follow the typically romantic trend of embracing Catholicism.

JOHANN KASPAR LAVATER, whom Goethe repeatedly visited in Zurich, was a fervently patriotic and, above all, a religious poet of the type of Bodmer and Klopstock, and in his *Schweizerlieder* (Swiss Songs) a fiery defender of Swiss independence against the French invaders (1798). He is best known for his pseudoscientific work *Physiognomische Fragmente zur Beförderung der Menschenkenntnis und Menschenliebe* (Physiognomical Fragments for the Advancement of the Knowledge and Love of Man, 1775 ff.), to which Goethe contributed some phrenological analyses.

Dramatic Writing

Minor dramatic works consisted of naturalistic and vigorous dramas of revolt against political, social, or literary fetters and traditions. Rather than by authors, these tragedies might be arranged by topics:

Hatred between brothers, the supreme proof of the corruption of modern civilization: Schiller's *Die Räuber* (The Robbers), MAXIMILIAN KLINGER's *Die Zwillinge* (The Twins), and JOHANN ANTON LEISEWITZ' *Julius von Tarent.*

Social inequality and moral corruption: JAKOB MICHAEL REINHOLD LENZ's *Der Hofmeister* (The Tutor) and *Die Soldaten* (The Soldiers), Klinger's *Sturm und Drang* (which drama gave the whole movement its name), and Schiller's *Kabale und Liebe* (Intrigue and Love). (Cf. also the influence of Lessing's *Emilia Galotti.*)

Wronged and forsaken women: Klinger's *Das leidende Weib* (The Suffering Woman), HEINRICH LEOPOLD WAGNER's *Die Kindermörderin* (The Infanticide); and, in Goethe, Gretchen in *Faust,* Maria in *Götz,* Marie in *Clavigo,* Stella and Cäcilia in *Stella.* (Cf. also the influence of Lessing's *Miss Sara Sampson.*)

Superhuman aspiration and presumptuous self-confidence: Faust in Goethe's, Klinger's and FRIEDRICH MÜLLER's versions, Goethe's Götz and Egmont (cf. also his poems on Prometheus and on Mahomet), Karl Moor in Schiller's *Die Räuber.* Weak supermen: Goethe's Clavigo (and also his Werther).

Rebellion against moral restrictions: Adelheid in Goethe's *Götz von Berlichingen,* and Fernando in *Stella.*

Struggle against political injustice and tyranny: Goethe's Götz and Egmont; Schiller's *Die Verschwörung des Fiesko*

in Genua (The Conspiracy of Fiesko in Genoa), and Marquis
Posa in Schiller's *Don Carlos.*

To these dramatists who admired Shakespeare's gigantic
characters and conflicts may be added the name of Heinrich
Wilhelm von Gerstenberg. Like Klopstock he was an ardent
advocate of old Nordic literature, and like Herder, Goethe,
Schiller, and others enthusiastic about Shakespeare. As well
as for his *Briefe über Merkwürdigkeiten der Literatur* (Letters on Noteworthy Things in Literature, 1766 ff.) Gerstenberg is famous, above all, for his tragedy *Ugolino* (1768).
This story of how a father and his sons were revengefully
starved to death claimed to be Shakespearian by emphasizing
character sketches more than action; at the same time it
betrays the slowly growing preromantic love for Dante, for
Gerstenberg was the first German poet to adapt a famous
incident from the first canticle of the *Divina Commedia.*

Young Schiller. Friedrich Schiller (1759–1805), born
at Marbach, Württemberg, son of an army officer, began his
literary activity while unhappy and oppressed at the military
academy of the duke of Württemberg called the *Karlsschule,*
where he studied law and later medicine instead of theology,
his own early choice. Rousseau's works increased his rebellious restlessness; Shakespeare inspired him to his own dramatic creations. After deserting the duke's services in 1782,
he found for a short while a livelihood at the theater of
Mannheim; later, overcome by sickness and poverty, he was
offered a shelter at Leipzig and Dresden by Christian Körner,
father of the poet Theodor Körner.

Die Räuber (The Robbers, 1781) is a powerful naturalistic tragedy, the immediate success of which caused Schiller
to supplant Goethe as the leading representative of the Storm
and Stress, after the latter had outgrown the movement.
It is a drama of fraternal hatred and of injustice which makes
the hero curse society and civilization and causes him to
doubt his family and even God. At the head of a band of
robbers he dares to defy God and man—only to atone willingly for his crimes as soon as he realizes that his accusations
have been baseless and that a lawless rebellion is no remedy
for the ills of a world out of joint.

Die Verschwörung des Fiesko in Genua (The Conspiracy of

HISTORY OF GERMAN LITERATURE

Fiesko in Genoa, 1782) was the first of Schiller's many historical and political tragedies. It describes the Genoese dream of a republican democracy, which, however, fails because Fiesko, after a successful revolution against the patrician oligarchs of the city, breaks the pledges he has given to his supporters and turns out to be an even worse tyrant. After his assassination in 1547 the discouraged Geneose call back their former patrician masters: a sad admission that for them the hour for democracy has not yet come.

Kabale und Liebe (Intrigue and Love, 1783), a bourgeois tragedy, is an acid condemnation of the corruption and aristocratic conceit of the *ancien régime* which made it impossible for a young nobleman to marry a commoner. Intrigue proves to be stronger than love; and suicide presents the only way out for Ferdinand and Luise.

Don Carlos (1787), describing the hatred of the young prince of Spain for his father, King Philip II, also begins in the accusing and naturalistic fashion of the Storm and Stress. As Schiller, however, gradually started to veer towards Classicism, he neglected the personal woes of Don Carlos and shifted the emphasis of the drama to Marquis Posa and the much greater and finer problem of human freedom and dignity in general.

TRANSLATIONS

Note: For translations of Goethe and Schiller, see pp. 109–110.

GENERAL COLLECTIONS

Hawthorne, Julian. *The Masterpieces and the History of Literature.* New York, 1906. (Vol. VIII contains poems by Bürger, Hagedorn, Gellert, Gleim, Goethe, Klopstock, Lessing, Schiller, Voss, Wieland, "The Stormsters.")

Knortz, K. *Representative German Poems, Ballad and Lyrical* (containing poems by Bürger, Claudius, Goethe, Haller, Herder, Schiller, Schubart, Stolberg, Voss, Wieland, etc.). New York, 1885.

INDIVIDUAL AUTHORS

BODMER: Collyer, J. *Bodmer's Noah.* London, 1767.

BÜRGER: Rose W., ed. *The Travels of Baron Münchhausen.* New York (Broadway Translations), 1923.

Scott, Sir Walter, adaptor. *The Chase* (Der wilde Jäger) and *William and Helen* (Lenore). Edinburgh, 1796.

90

THE STORM AND STRESS

GESSNER: Collyer, Mrs. M., tr. *Gessner's Death of Abel*. London, 1761.

The Works of S. Gessner (translator anonymous), with a "Life of the Author" by F. Schoberl. London, 1805.

HALLER: Howorth, Mrs. J., tr. *The Poems of Baron Haller*. London, 1794.

HERDER: Churchill, T., tr. *Outlines of a Philosophy of the History of Man*. London, 1800.

The Cid (translator anonymous). London, 1828.

Marsh, J., tr. *The Spirit of Hebrew Poetry*. Burlington, Vt., 1833.

Treatise upon the Origin of Language (translator anonymous). London, 1827.

KLEIST, Ewald von: Egestorff, G. H., tr. *Kleist's Vernal Season*. London, 1814.

KLINGER: Borrow, G., tr. *Faustus; His Life, Death, and Descent into Hell*. London, 1825.

KLOPSTOCK: Egestorff, G. H., tr. *Messias, A Poem in Twenty Cantos*. Hamburg, 1821.

Lloyd, R., tr. *The Death of Adam, A Tragedy in Three Acts*. London, 1763.

Nind, W., tr. *Odes*. London, 1848.

LAVATER: Fuseli, J. H., tr. *Aphorisms on Man*. London, 1788.

Remonstrance . . . to the . . . Directory of the French Republic, against the Invasion of Switzerland (translator anonymous). London, 1798.

LEISEWITZ: Will, P., tr. "Julius of Tarentum, A Tragedy," *German Museum* (London), 1800.

VOSS: Cochrane, J., tr. *Louisa, A Poem*. Edinburgh, 1852.

WYSS: *The Swiss Family Robinson*. New York (Everyman's Library), 1910.

CHAPTER VIII

GERMAN CLASSICISM, 1785–1805

GOETHE AND SCHILLER COMPARED

The two men who from 1794 to Schiller's death in 1805 formed the most important friendship in German literature were in many respects strikingly different, though they both, independently of each other, gradually abandoned their Storm and Stress impetuosity for the restraint and sublimity of classical literature.

Goethe was handsome, rich, a patrician, an elegant man of the world, an extensive traveler. Schiller was sick and poor all his life, a man who never had a chance to see Switzerland, Italy, and France, as Goethe had.

Goethe was a great lover of women and was inspired by them, as was proved by Friederike Brion (*Faust*), Charlotte Buff (*Werther*), Lili Schönemann (*Stella*), Frau von Stein (*Iphigenie*), Christiane Vulpius (*The Roman Elegies*), Minna Herzlieb (*The Elective Affinities*), Marianne von Willemer (*The West-Eastern Divan*), Ulrike von Levetzow (*The Marienbad Elegy*), and others. Schiller, with the exception of his unhappy passion for Charlotte von Kalb, was a one-woman man and happily married to Charlotte von Lengefeld.

Goethe was a universal genius, a truly great man with an astounding number of interests. Besides being Germany's greatest poet he was a painter, a lawyer, a statesman and high administrative official, a scientist interested particularly in botany, geology, anatomy, and the theory of colors, an actor, and a theater director. Schiller, besides being a poet, was interested "only" in history and philosophy.

In their poetic productivity, too, Goethe was more universal and Schiller more restricted. Schiller excelled only in three types of literature: tragedies (in which he is superior to Goethe), ballads (he is the most famous ballad writer in

German literature), and aesthetic and philosophical essays. Goethe, however, a man of truly exceptional literary talents, produced love lyrics, ballads, philosophical poems, novels, epics, tragedies, philosophical dramas, satires, short stories, pastorals, and operettas.

The Naive and the Sentimental Poet

Goethe was a natural poet, concrete, plastic, realistic, to whom writing came easily, and who used his rich life as a background and his many experiences and conflicts as themes for his many works, all of which are basically autobiographical. He was inductive, ascending from daily experiences and concrete facts to the idea behind experience and fact. Schiller was much more abstract, an idealist, a thinker and a seer, who often had difficulty in giving shape to his thoughts; he was a deductive poet who descended from the postulated thought to actual facts. Or, as Schiller himself put it in his essay *Über naive und sentimentalische Dichtung* (On Naive and Sentimental Poetry): Goethe was a "naive" poet, one with nature, essentially classic; he, Schiller himself, however, was a "sentimental" poet who had lost this intimate contact with nature. Hence Schiller sentimentally and romantically yearned for that innate unity and natural simplicity, as do most modern poets (in contrast with the ancient naive poets). Schiller was also the greatest poet of freedom in German literature, a bold prophet of a better future, always guided by a lofty abstract ideal rather than by actual earthly experience, as Goethe was.

Influence of Spinoza and of Kant

Another striking difference between Goethe and Schiller can be seen in the fact that the former was essentially influenced by the philosophy of Spinoza, the latter by the philosophy of Immanuel Kant. Spinoza's philosophy was pantheistic; he taught that God was in His works, in flowers, in sunsets, rather than in books—and Goethe's entire life indeed consisted of a happy and beautiful unity with God and nature. Kant, however, who did not believe in such Godlike simplicity in man, formulated strong ethical laws, categorical imperatives, which should guide man in the face of all temptations. Schiller accepted these stern teachings, though he softened Kant's hard Prussian sense of duty with Shaftesbury's gentler sense of beauty, and thus preached goodness for beauty's rather than for duty's sake. By declaring, furthermore, that beyond the world of actual sensual experience there exists also a world of pure thought which surely exists, even though it transcends actual proof and demonstration, Kant also—as Schiller understood him—split man's world into a real, physical half, and an abstract and transcendental half—a theory which the unity-loving Goethe rejected, though Schiller, sick and poor in this world, ardently believed in this promising vision of another, an ideal world.

REASONS CONTRIBUTING TO GOETHE'S EVOLUTION TOWARDS CLASSICISM

Political Activity

First should be mentioned Goethe's strenuous political activity at the court of his friend, Duke Karl August of Sachsen-Weimar. Instead of a few weeks only, as he had planned, Goethe stayed in Weimar for the rest of his life (1775–1832). As an enlightened administrator he was early put in charge of the finances and then of the interior affairs of the duchy, soon became privy councilor, then was granted the title of nobility, and finally became what might be called the Prime Minister of the little country. Hard work and Weimar's dangerous position between the hostile powers of Prussia and Austria taught him restraint and discipline. Not revolution, as he thought during his Storm and Stress years, but evolution alone, he came to believe, could permanently improve the fate of men and nations.

Charlotte von Stein

Of immense influence upon the development of Goethe's character was also his hopeless passion for Frau Charlotte von Stein, wife of a courtier of Weimar, probably the most important woman in his life. She was a very cultured and inspiring lady who in spite of her love for Goethe insisted on the proprieties of society. Numerous poems prove how he, overburdened with work, and depressed by the hopelessness of his love, struggled on until he learned to control himself:

Wanderers Nachtlied I & II (Wanderer's Night Song I &
II), *Das Göttliche* (The Godlike), *Die Grenzen der Menschheit* (The Limits of Man). The Promethean exuberance of
former years, useful though it may have been, was over now
(*Ilmenau*); what remained was work, self-control, manliness, responsibility.

Work in Science

Goethe's scientific work in botany and anatomy convinced
him that nature grows organically and shapes beautifully—
that it does not grow in leaps and bounds, but that it evolves
slowly, step by step. Literature, too, should be like that, he
began to think: not wild soapbox oratory, dwelling on individual passions and idiosyncrasies, but calm, composed, organic, dealing only with eternally true and universally valid
themes. In his geological studies Goethe quite logically upheld the theory that wind and water through slow erosion,
rather than sudden catastrophes through violent quakes, had
given shape to the earth. In nature also, then, he perceived
evolution, not revolution. Goethe's most significant scientific
work was his *Farbenlehre* (Theory of Colors, 1810).

Study of the Classics

Another factor contributing to Goethe's evolution to Classicism was his growing love of Greek and Latin literature. He
came under the influence of JOHANN JOACHIM WINCKEL-
MANN (1717–1768), the foremost Hellenist and archeol-
ogist of the century, whose *Gedanken über die Nachahmung
der griechischen Werke* (Thoughts on the Imitation of
Greek Works, 1754) and *Geschichte der Kunst des Altertums* (History of the Art of Antiquity, 1764) extolled
Greek originality and perfection as compared with modern
French imitation and German irregularity. Winckelmann's
words, that Greek art is characterized by *edle Einfalt und
stille Grösse* (noble simplicity and quiet grandeur), Goethe
now applied also to his own new writings in classical temper,
and his readings in Homer, Pindar, and Sophocles only con-
firmed him in his conviction. Lessing, likewise a follower of
Winckelmann, had felt similarly, but he had been too rationalistic and too submissive to the neoclassic principle of imi-

tation, and hence his works had been *Klassizismus* or Pseudo-classicism only. Goethe, however, now wanted to vie with the Greeks rather than imitate them; furthermore, his tempestuous Storm and Stress youth had given him a warmth and vitality which the cool rationalist and dry imitator Gottsched had lacked. Goethe's works hence are real *Klassik,* or Classicism in the best sense of the word.

Italian Influence

His journey to and stay in Italy (Venice, Rome, Sicily) from 1786 to 1788 was perhaps the most important single event in his life. Escaping the burden of tiresome administrative work, the increasingly exasperating relationship with Frau von Stein, and the menacing literary sterility implicit in such a life, Goethe found new youth, new ardor, and new inspiration in Rome. With his own eyes he now saw what the *edle Einfalt und stille Grösse* of ancient culture really meant. His break with the past and his affirmation of strictly classical ideals now became definite. After years of asceticism he also found in Italy new love and new inspiration through women.

REASONS CONTRIBUTING TO SCHILLER'S EVOLUTION TOWARDS CLASSICISM

Philosophical Studies

Mention has already been made of Schiller's preoccupation with philosophy. As he grew older, he realized that Kant's stern ethical teachings seemed to be directed not against tyrants only, whom Schiller had gladly condemned in his earliest dramatic works, but also against reckless rebels such as certain Storm and Stress titans who were too eager to play with fire and whose radical oratory endangered the cause of freedom and decency as much as the cruelty of tyrants did at the other extreme. Hence a certain moderation of Schiller's rebelliousness became noticeable in his classical period: he henceforth upheld rebellion only as the last resort when all means of conciliation had failed. Schiller did not become a conservative and an aristocrat, as Goethe had; but his concept of freedom nonetheless underwent certain modifications.

Historical Studies

His historical studies tended further to restrain and mature him. In 1789 he became professor of history at the University of Jena, and two books, *Der Abfall der Niederlande* (The Revolt of the Netherlands, 1788), and *Die Geschichte des dreissigjährigen Krieges* (The History of the Thirty Years' War, 1802), represented the result of his ceaseless historical studies. Through them he came to see that Divine Providence, guiding mankind on its slow but steady march towards ever greater freedom, condemns not only tyrants, who try to retard or stop that divinely ordained trend, but condemns also shortsighted and immature rebels who try to accelerate the work of God and who endeavor to find foolish short cuts. This idea tended to make Schiller more careful in his advocacy of man's eternal right to revolution—for first it would have to be ascertained whether such a revolution were just. What man needs, in order to thwart tyrants and reckless rebels alike, is faith in God and in human progress; and Schiller tried to instill that faith by showing that even such dark episodes as the Spanish oppression of the Dutch and the horrible Thirty Years' War between Catholics and Protestants ended by contributing to man's progress and enlightenment. The cruel failure of the French Revolution proved that man should never strive for shallow outer freedom as long as he does not possess inner freedom, i.e. the will power to restrain and discipline himself. Without such ethical fortitude and restraint in every individual, even the most successful outer revolution against governments and laws is doomed to bloodshed and to failure. The concept of inner freedom thus became more important than the concept of outer freedom; men must first reform themselves, before they start reforming governments.

Literary Studies

Schiller's study of Greek, Latin, and French literature made him desist from writing any more dramas between 1787 and 1799, until he had mastered the classical style. He translated parts of Euripides' *Trojan Women* and of Virgil's

Aeneid; likewise he translated Racine's great tragedy *Phèdre* into German blank verse in order to train himself still further in classical expression; indeed, in order to test his craftsmanship, he also rendered Shakespeare's Baroque drama *Macbeth* into classical German form.

Friendship with Goethe

Another factor contributing to Schiller's evolution towards Classicism was his friendship with Goethe from 1794 on—a friendship which had been impossible as long as Schiller's Storm and Stress dramas had irritated the increasingly classical Goethe and which was possible only when Schiller's classical ideals at last caught up with Goethe's. During eleven years there now took place an extremely fruitful and stimulating interchange of opinions and influences between the scientist and the philosopher, the realist and the idealist, the naive and the sentimental poet.

GREEK CLASSICISM IN OTHER COUNTRIES

The appearance, with Goethe and Schiller, at the very end of the classical period, in fact in the midst of the preromantic revolt, of a purified Greek brand of Classicism in place of the outmoded French brand was an almost unique occurrence in European literature. Besides pointing to Wieland, Lessing, Goethe, and Schiller, mention can be made also of the Hellenistic inspiration of André de Chénier in France and of Ugo Foscolo in Italy—both poets, quite significantly, having been born in Eastern Mediterranean lands, close to the source of ancient Greek culture. In England, where Shaftesbury had prepared the ground, there appeared, in the midst of the Romantic Period, Walter Savage Landor and, above all, the plastic restraint and the truly Greek perfection of form many critics find in the poems of John Keats. Not to be confounded with this renewed worship of the Greek ideal of classical beauty are the romanticists' passionate outbursts in behalf of the political liberation of modern Greece from the yoke of the Turks (Hölderlin, Shelley, Byron, and others), for in that political phase the Greeks were simply one of the many oppressed nations (Poland, Italy, etc.) which enlightened European opinion supported.

GOETHE'S CLASSICAL PERIOD (1787–1805)

The last scenes of *Egmont* (begun in 1775, finished in 1787) show the broader conceptions of classical influence on Goethe. Egmont does not die uselessly and futilely as Götz and Werther had died, for he realizes the deeper meaning and implications of his death: that he is the victor, not the vanquished; that he is one of the liberators of Holland, a harbinger of new freedom; that the end of his life signifies at the same time the dawn of Dutch independence. In Egmont, Goethe had depicted an optimistic, serene, and lovable character like himself; his decision to face the approaching Spanish danger is not due to overconfidence, but to Egmont's (and Goethe's) firm belief in destiny, in the *daimon,* the divine mission which is in man and which he must fulfill no matter what dangers have to be faced, if he wants to remain true to himself and to his calling.

Iphigenie (1787), one of the truly great dramas in German literature, was Goethe's first work written in blank verse, a masterpiece in which the yearned-for synthesis between ancient Greece and modern Germany, between paganism and Christianity, between Athens and Weimar, was perfectly accomplished. The story may resemble Euripides' play; but in this Greek setting Iphigenia is an absolutely Christian character who achieves her goal, not through deception as in Euripides, but through truthfulness and purity. Nor is Orestes saved through a purely mechanical device only, as in the Greek play, but through the love of a saintly sister and through the modern Christian conception of repentance and faith. Woman's purifying and ennobling influence on despairing man has seldom been so beautifully extolled as in this tragedy; it is Goethe's immortal monument of gratitude to Frau von Stein.

Torquato Tasso was finished in 1790, after Goethe had broken with Frau von Stein. It is an exceedingly autobiographical play which reflects well Goethe's loneliness after he had returned from Italy to his estranged friends at Weimar— a loneliness which was even more increased because many ostracized him on account of his taking pretty but insignificant Christiane Vulpius into his house as his common-law wife.

Torquato Tasso, the story of the famous Italian poet of the late Renaissance, describes the tragedy of being a supersensitive poet. He is a second Werther, ill at ease at the court of Ferrara (Weimar), driven to despair and insanity through his hopeless love for Princess Leonore (Frau von Stein). But besides the mentally unbalanced poet there gradually grows in importance the figure of Antonio, the realistic man of the world, the shrewd diplomat, the elegant courtier—and with him rather than with Tasso Goethe comes to identify himself at the end. For he is much too sane and strong a character to end as miserably as Werther and Tasso have ended; he can overcome the crisis and readjust himself. The play is a masterpiece, a real jewel of a psychological classical tragedy, though it is almost devoid of outward action.

Reineke Fuchs (Reynard the Fox, 1793) is a beautiful classical reproduction of the late medieval animal story, an amusing and satirical epic strongly influenced by Homer's stately epic style. Goethe wrote it partly in order to give vent to his anger against the follies and vices of the leaders and the mob of the French Revolution, most of them smart and deceitful like Reineke.

Römische Elegien (Roman Elegies, 1795) are outspokenly pagan and sensual poems referring in restrained language not so much to Goethe's amorous adventures while in Italy as to his passionate love-life with Christiane Vulpius.

Wilhelm Meisters Lehrjahre (Wilhelm Meister's Apprenticeship, 1795) is one of the great apprenticeship novels in German literature. It describes first the aesthetic education of the hero, who starts out as an actor and a Shakespeare enthusiast; later, through his contact with the "Beautiful Soul," with Lothario, Therese, and Nathalie, his ethical education begins. The background and style of this novel may already be slightly romantic; but Wilhelm, after the aimlessness of his Storm and Stress youth, becomes increasingly realistic, classical, restrained, and purposeful.

Die Xenien (1796), literally "the gifts of hospitality," written in collaboration with Schiller, is a collection of short and acid poems in sharp condemnation of all political (i.e. revolutionary), literary (i.e. drily rationalistic), and religious (i.e. bigoted) enemies of Goethe, and, to a lesser extent, of Schiller.

Hermann und Dorothea (1797) belongs, with *Iphigenie* and *Faust,* to Goethe's finest works. It is a perfect idyllic epic contrasting peace and revolution, telling the story of a refugee girl who is wooed and won by a noble youth. The rumblings of the French Revolution far away serve only to emphasize the quiet industriousness and moral decency of the little German town where Hermann lives. Hermann and Dorothea, two truly "beautiful souls," are perfect embodiments of Kant's moral law—without becoming bloodless and boring. This work is one of the finest and most inspiring idyls in world literature.

The "ballad year 1797" in which Goethe and Schiller wrote some of their finest classical ballads, witnessed the composition of such works as:

a. *Die Braut von Korinth* (The Bride of Corinth)—in which the sane sensualism of Greece is preferred to life-killing Christian asceticism;

b. *Der Gott und die Bajadere* (The God and the Bayadere) —a poem showing that even lowly-born sinners may be worthy and may be saved by God;

c. *Der Schatzgräber* (The Treasure Seeker)—which illustrates that there is no short cut to success and wisdom;

d. *Der Zauberlehrling* (The Sorcerer's Apprentice)—the famous ballad about the presumptuousness of a young fool who can start things but not stop them.

In various minor dramas, from *Der Grosskophta* (The Great Magician, 1792) to *Die natürliche Tochter* (The Illegitimate Daughter, 1803), Goethe tried vainly to deal directly and successfully with the distasteful problem of the French Revolution.

SCHILLER'S CLASSICAL PERIOD (1787–1805)

The second half of *Don Carlos* (1787) was already distinctly classical, with the noble Marquis Posa and his lofty fight for the principle of human freedom in general supplanting Carlos' egotistical quarrel with his father. *Don Carlos* was also Schiller's first drama in blank verse. In spite

101

of its sudden shift of emphasis and its resulting lack of unity, it is an important tragedy because it best shows Schiller's gradual transition from the Storm and Stress to Classicism.

In his philosophical essays *Über Anmut und Würde* (On Gracefulness and Dignity) and *Über die ästhetische Erziehung des Menschen* (On the Aesthetic Education of Man, 1793) Schiller sought to define his challenging ideal of a "beautiful soul"—a soul, namely, in whom Kant's concept of duty and Shaftesbury's concept of beauty are harmoniously united. Goethe created such "beautiful souls" in his *Iphigenie,* in his *Hermann und Dorothea,* and in his *Wilhelm Meister;* Schiller now wrote abstract essays about the same subject—a difference of treatment between the poet and the philosopher that may indeed be called typical. Wieland, Lessing, Herder, Kant, Goethe, and Schiller all dreamed about a better aesthetic and ethical education of man; together, these authors represent the finest peak of German Idealism.

Then there followed philosophical poems such as *Der Künstler* (The Artist), *Der Spaziergang* (The Promenade), and especially the famous *Lied von der Glocke* (Song of the Bell), to which, in the ballad year 1797, there must be added masterful ballads like *Der Taucher* (The Diver), *Der Handschuh* (The Glove), *Der Ring des Polykrates* (The Ring of Polycrates), and *Die Kraniche des Ibykus* (The Cranes of Ibycus), and later *Die Bürgschaft* (The Pledge), *Der Kampf mit dem Drachen* (The Struggle with the Dragon).

After twelve years of interruption, of intensive studies in history, philosophy, and Greek literature, Schiller from 1799 on composed his great historical dramas in quick succession. *Wallenstein* (1799), his most ambitious work, is a trilogy in eleven acts: *Wallensteins Lager* (Wallenstein's Camp), *Die Piccolomini* (The Piccolominis), and *Wallensteins Tod* (Wallenstein's Death)—an enormous historical canvas. Wallenstein's conspiracy against his own emperor during the Thirty Years' War, his fatal addiction to astrology, and his ultimate assassination are squeezed into one single tragedy; and the frame of historical events (which Schiller treated in detail in his *History of the Thirty Years' War*) was so great that the poet often had to use types rather than individuals in order to tell his tale. Particularly moving is the conflict in the breast of Max Piccolomini: he was an ardent admirer of Wallenstein and the lover of his daughter, yet at the same time the son of the one treacherous friend of Wallenstein who ultimately brought about the general's downfall.

Maria Stuart (1800) is another historical tragedy in which the clash between two great characters (so beautifully developed already in *Don Carlos* in the interview between King Philip and Marquis Posa) is worked out to perfection. Schiller's sympathies lay with Mary rather than with Elizabeth; her valiant yet hopeless struggle against her impending doom is stirring and pathetic.

Die Jungfrau von Orleans (The Maid of Orleans, 1801) is a romantic rather than a classical drama, colorful, ardent, irrational. It shows Schiller's great admiration for Joan of Arc, her unquestioning patriotism and piety, and her struggle against the powers of darkness. The end, when Joan in spite of chains and dungeon walls ascends to heaven, is very poetic, though not in accord with historical fact. Interesting also is Joan's tragic guilt: she wants to atone and die, not because the ungrateful mob accuses her of witchcraft, but because she thinks she has failed in her divine mission by falling in love with an English enemy. Her death was really an act of freedom, similar to Mary Stuart's positive acceptance of her fate.

Die Braut von Messina (The Bride of Messina, 1803), the most Hellenistic play in Schiller's career, is a fate tragedy exceedingly stern, strict, and classical, and strongly influenced by Sophocles' *Oedipus*. It tells of a prophecy that Beatrice will be criminally loved by her own two brothers and that she will bring about the extinction of the ruling family of Messina; and nothing the frantic parents may or may not do about this sinister oracle can prevent the incestuous passion and the downfall of the princely dynasty. It is essentially a drama of fraternal hatred as *Die Räuber* had been—yet immensely more sublimated and classical. The impression of venerable dignity and classical artistry is enhanced by the fact that Schiller here has reintroduced the ancient Greek chorus of wise men, which gives the play a distinctly religious and philosophical background. The character and the noble function of the chorus Schiller discussed in a prefixed essay, *Über den Gebrauch des Chors in der Tragödie* (On the Use of the Chorus in Tragedy).

After oscillating between the romantic irrationalism of *Die Jungfrau von Orleans* and the stern classical compactness of *Die Braut von Messina,* Schiller, in his *Wilhelm Tell* (1804), found the perfect synthesis of Classicism and Romanticism, of Greek style and Germanic theme. This beautiful patriotic drama about early Swiss history describes a rebellion which is no longer light-hearted and reckless, as the Storm and Stress poets would have advocated, but which is undertaken only with a heavy heart and after all means of conciliation with the House of Hapsburg have failed.

Demetrius, a fragment only, is the tale of a false pretender to the Russian throne who, like Karl Moor in *Die Räuber,* is willing to fight a whole world of enemies as long as he believes himself to be in the right. After having found his right path and his ideal form in *Wilhelm Tell,* Schiller would have been ready for a great future of brilliant literary activity—and his premature death in 1805 thus deprived German literature of a genius whose promise was greatest just before his passing away.

GOETHE'S OLD AGE (1805–1832)

With Wieland, Goethe, and Herder in Weimar, and with Schiller, the famous philosophers Johann Gottlieb Fichte, Friedrich Wilhelm Joseph von Schelling, and Georg Wilhelm Friedrich Hegel, the international explorer and scientist Alexander von Humboldt, and the romantic writers Wilhelm von Humboldt, August Wilhelm Schlegel, Friedrich Schlegel, Clemens Brentano, and Ludwig Tieck in nearby Jena, the Golden Age of modern German culture reached its highest peak. Schiller's death and the consequences of the disastrous battle of Jena in 1806 struck a serious blow at that magnificent epoch. The Romantic School constituted a continuation of the lofty era of German Idealism which had begun with Lessing, Herder, and Kant; yet after a few decades the cultural greatness of Weimar and Jena vanished.

As he grew older, Goethe lost the classical compactness and

the plastic qualities of his style, and he gave way to loose and often rambling constructions. Symbolical and allegorical pictures began to prevail, because the wisdom of the Patriarch of Weimar had become so profound and so extensive that symbols alone seemed adequate to express all the implications of his thought (cf. especially the second parts of *Wilhelm Meister* and of *Faust*).

The influence of Romanticism likewise tended to mellow Goethe's style and thought, to make him more irrational and his language more colorful. On the whole, however, Goethe opposed Romanticism with its irresponsible outbursts, its vagueness, its lack of stamina, its easy surrender to Catholicism; for Goethe was too much of a realist and a man of action to accept the escapism and the unbridled spirit of the younger generation.

Pandora (1808), a fragmentary dramatic poem, expresses Goethe's faith that beauty and culture will always stay with us in spite of wars and revolutions. It tells how Pandora, the first woman, the symbol of beauty, the possessor of a wondrous box containing blessings for all mankind, at last decides to return to Epimetheus, her dreamy and idealistic husband, who hitherto had appreciated her only passively. The marriage of their daughter Epimeleia to Phileros, son of the fiery activist Prometheus, then happily unites the thinker and the doer, the idealist and the realist, and a human race will spring from them that will appreciate Pandora's gifts more fully than the meditative Epimetheus ever had. Thus even the race of Prometheus, of Napoleon, of modern conquering France, can be made gentler and richer by the gifts of Pandora, of Epimeleia, of German Idealism; the mating of Epimeleia's Germany with Phileros' France will thus produce a well-nigh perfect type of man.

Die Wahlverwandtschaften (The Elective Affinities, 1809), a novel with a very important ethical message, not only depicts the clash in men and women between the natural laws of instincts (which drive Edward and Charlotte, though married, into the arms of other mates) and the social law of the holiness of matrimony; it emphasizes even more that a human being—Ottilie—must remain true to her inner calling and that any deviation from the mission, the law that is in her, will lead to disaster. Through her love affair with Edward, Ottilie is not, above all, guilty of a social misdemeanor, the crime of having become a party to adultery (though moralists may well interpret the novel this way and call it Goethe's outstanding condemnation of the moral laxity of so many romanticists); she is, in the first place, guilty of having deviated from her saintly calling. The death of Edward's and Charlotte's child convinces her of the errors of her ways; voluntarily she reverts to her calling, accepts the law that is in herself (atones for her crime, as Kant and Schiller would say), and dies as a saintly person. The miracle that even after her death she saves another child's life indicates clearly that God has forgiven her; and in view of such a noble example of moral greatness the other three characters also, in one way or another, learn to solve the conflicts in their souls and, like Egmont, to follow the *daimon,* the divine destiny, that is in them. In this book, written at the peak of the Romantic Age, Goethe formulated the most classical of all messages, the message of mental and emotional discipline.

Dichtung und Wahrheit (Fiction and Truth, 1811 ff.) is the title of Goethe's autobiography. However, it deals only with his Frankfurt, Leipzig, Strassburg, and Wetzlar days and breaks off in 1775. Rich in cultural and historical detail, it mirrors, as evidenced in its very title, Goethe's conviction of the insoluble oneness of reality and poetry in his life. Especially beautiful and famous is his description of his Sesenheim idyl with Friederike Brion. With Augustine's autobiography and Rousseau's *Confessions, Dichtung und Wahrheit* ranks among the greatest works of this type.

Des Epimenides Erwachen (The Awakening of Epimenides, 1815), a dramatic poem, represents a belated admission by Goethe that in his great admiration of Napoleon he may have misjudged the strength of the German national rebirth. During Napoleon's domination of Europe Goethe seemed quite satisfied to let the French rule militarily, as long as German culture, appreciated and encouraged by Napoleon, was permitted to rule Europe spiritually. Hence he opposed the romanticists' fierce hatred of France and the whole fanaticism of the German War of Liberation. But after Waterloo he admitted his error in having underestimated Germany's national regeneration and vowed henceforth to take a greater interest in German political life.

Der westöstliche Divan (The West-Eastern Divan, 1819) is a collection of love poems written during Goethe's friendship with Marianne von Willemer, and at the same time his outstanding literary work dealing with Oriental culture. Ever anxious to embrace and appreciate mankind's great cultural trends, Goethe, after the German Protestantism of his Storm and Stress and after the Greek paganism of his classical period, studied the Islam of the Orient and thus added Mohammed to Jesus and Apollo. Heartily in agreement with the romanticists' efforts to familiarize German readers with the works of Arabian, Persian, and Indian poets, Goethe, especially influenced by Hafiz, a Persian poet of the fourteenth century, now clothes his love for Marianne in an Oriental garb and provides the poems of the two supposedly Oriental lovers Hatem and Suleika with an Oriental atmosphere and an Oriental mentality.

Die Marienbader Elegie (The Marienbad Elegy, 1823) is Goethe's last great lyric poem, a moving document inspired by his love for the nineteen-year-old Ulrike von Levetzow and her refusal to marry him. It is a deeply touching outburst of despair in which the poet realizes that he is old and through with life and that he must hurry to finish his remaining great works.

Wilhelm Meisters Wanderjahre (Wilhelm Meister's Travels, 1829) continues the problem of the hero's education by dwelling particularly on the theme of work and renunciation. Goethe's main purpose is no longer to make Wilhelm an egocentric individual, but to make him a citizen, a useful member of society. No longer a mere aesthete, Wilhelm endeavors to combine humanitarianism with craftsmanship by becoming a surgeon. Trying to cope with two of the greatest problems of the modern age, the Industrial Revolution and international co-operation, Goethe then sketches a utopia in which Freemasons and other men of good will play an increasingly large part. Of great beauty and significance also is his outline of the Pedagogical Province, which was largely inspired by the far-sighted theories of the Swiss educator Heinrich Pestalozzi and which aimed to preserve men's souls and characters amidst the conflicts and the materialism of the modern machine age. Though written in an exasperatingly symbolical and rambling style, with too many interpolated stories interrupting the flow of the main action, the *Wanderjahre* perhaps even more than *Faust* can be considered the testament and the supreme wisdom of the Patriarch of Weimar.

Faust (the earliest sketch, the *Urfaust,* begun in Frankfurt, the first part published in 1808, the second part in 1832) is probably the greatest philosophical drama of modern Europe. No longer is it his lust for power and pleasure that induces Faust to conclude his pact with the devil (as the *Volksbuch* of 1587 had indicated), but his idealism—an earnest quest for truth and God so great that he is even willing to pay the supreme price for the fulfillment of that wish. After the seduction of Margaret and the coarseness of the German Walpurgis Night Faust has reached his lowest depth; from this point on, the influence of Mephistopheles diminishes, Faust's inherently noble character reasserts itself and, rising through the Classical Walpurgis Night, he approaches ever greater perfection and sublimation. His meeting and mating with Helen of Troy assumes a beautifully symbolical meaning which it had not had in earlier versions, for now the synthesis of paganism and Christianity, of Greece and Germany, of Helen's Classicism and Faust's Romanticism, of ancient Mediterranean culture and modern Germanic culture, is fully achieved, and their child, Euphorion (whom Goethe likened to Lord Byron), is the perfect offspring of the two great cultures of humanity. Like Wilhelm Meister, so also Faust ends as a useful citizen rather than as an egocentric individualist: adhering to the motto of *die sittliche Tat* (the humanitarian deed), he plans to irrigate large tracts of land which will nourish thousands of his fellow men. Though old and blind, he keeps on planning, dreaming, and hoping to his last day, ever ambitious and dissatisfied with himself, never a lazy and materialistic glutton as Mephistopheles had tried to make him. And when he comes to die, Faust, for the sake of his idealism and his noble aspirations, is indeed snatched away from the devil and carried to Paradise in a beautiful scene which was inspired by the end of Dante's *Divina Com-*

media—for: *"wer immer strebend sich bemüht, den können wir erlösen"* (whoever aspires unweariedly is not beyond redeeming). Like Parzival and Simplicissimus, so also Faust sought, erred, yet persevered; and at last he, too, has found his Father's mansion. Never has there been set up a more beautiful monument to man's hopes and aspirations; and never since the Bible have we been more happily assured that though we may sin and stumble we shall reach our goal if we but persevere.

In conclusion, mention must be made of JOHANN PETER ECKERMANN and his important *Gespräche mit Goethe* (Conversations with Goethe, 1837 ff.). Eckermann, a German Boswell, was Goethe's secretary and friend during the last years of his life, and there is no better book of information about the grand old man's political, social, and literary ideas than these faithfully collected notes about the daily conversations between the two men.

TRANSLATIONS
GENERAL COLLECTIONS

Francke, Kuno, editor-in-chief. *The German Classics of the Nineteenth and Twentieth Centuries.* Albany, 1913 ff. 20 vols.
> Vol. I: Goethe's Poems. Hermann and Dorothea. Iphigenia in Tauris. Faust.
> Vol. II: Goethe's Elective Affinities. Shakespeare and Again Shakespeare. Oration on Wieland. The Pedagogic Province (from Wilhelm Meister's Travels). Winckelmann and His Age. Maxims and Reflections. Conversations with Eckermann. Letters to Wilhelm von Humboldt. Correspondence with Zelter.
> Vol. III: Schiller's Poems. The Death of Wallenstein. William Tell. The Homage of the Arts. The Last Campaign of Gustavus Adolphus (from The Thirty Years' War). On the Use of the Chorus in Tragedy. Schiller-Goethe Correspondence.

Kant's Fundamental Principles of the Metaphysics of Morals (together with Lessing's Education of the Human Race, and Schiller's Letters upon the Aesthetic Education of Man). New York (Harvard Classics), 1910.

INDIVIDUAL AUTHORS

GOETHE: Bruns, F., ed. *Goethe's Poems and Aphorisms.* Edited for the Goethe-Society of America. New York, 1932.
Dole, N. H., ed. *The Works of J. W. von Goethe.* New York, 1902.
> Vol. I: Poems. Hermann and Dorothea. West-Eastern Divan. Reynard the Fox.
> Vol. II: Faust. Clavigo. Egmont. The Wayward Lover.
> Vol. III: Truth and Fiction Relating to My Life.

HISTORY OF GERMAN LITERATURE

Vol. IV: Wilhelm Meister's Apprenticeship.
Vol. V: Wilhelm Meister's Travels. The Recreations of the German Emigrants. The Sorrows of Young Werther. Elective Affinities. The Good Women. A Tale.
Vol. VI: Letters from Switzerland. Letters from Italy. Iphigenia in Tauris. Torquato Tasso. Götz von Berlichingen. The Fellow Culprits.
Vol. VII: *Life of J. W. von Goethe,* by George Henry Lewes.
Spingarn, J. E. *Goethe's Literary Essays.* New York, 1921.

KANT: *Kant's Perpetual Peace* (translator anonymous). London, 1796. (Reprinted, with an introduction by Nicholas M. Butler, New York, 1939.)
Müller, Max, tr. *I. Kant's Critique of Pure Reason,* with a historical introduction by L. Noiré. New York, 1907.

SCHILLER: Dole, N. H., ed. *The Works of Friedrich Schiller.* New York, 1902.
Vol. I: Aesthetical Letters and Essays. The Ghost-Seer. The Sport of Destiny.
Vol. II: The Maid of Orleans. The Bride of Messina. The Use of the Chorus in Tragedy. Wilhelm Tell. Demetrius. The Robbers. Fiesco, or The Genoese Conspiracy. Love and Intrigue.
Vol. III: The Piccolomini. The Death of Wallenstein. Wallenstein's Camp. Don Carlos. Mary Stuart.
Vol. IV: Poems. Semele. *The Life of Schiller,* by Duntzer.
Vol. V: The Revolt of the Netherlands. The Thirty Years' War.

CHAPTER IX

GERMAN ROMANTICISM, 1790–1830

THE HISTORICAL BACKGROUND

The Romantic Period coincided with the great political upheaval of the French Revolution and the Napoleonic Wars (1789–1815). In the endless wars between revolutionary France and the European powers allied against her, Germany was the chief sufferer, for most of the great battles were fought on her soil. Napoleon's success was also made easier by the fact that the Allies did not strike simultaneously, so that France was able to eliminate several countries (Italy, Holland, Switzerland) before the really fatal battles started.

The defeat of Austria in 1803 led to a thorough reorganization of the Empire: in the so-called *Reichsdeputationshauptschluss* (Main Decree of the Imperial Deputations) of Regensburg all the lands west of the Rhine (including Holland and Austrian Belgium) were given to France. As compensation for these losses the German princes were given the former ecclesiastical lands and free imperial cities east of the Rhine, which were abolished as political units and lumped together. Through this very important law the number of German states was reduced by more than three-fourths, and Napoleon thereby became one of the great unifiers of Germany.

The year 1806 brought new severe blows to the members of the Empire: first, it was Prussia's turn to face the French onslaught and she was defeated at Jena, completely occupied, and deprived of all her lands west of the Elbe; second, the Holy Roman Empire of the German Nation, the First Reich whose roots had reached back to Charlemagne, was dissolved; third, the *Rheinbund* was established, a conglomeration of vassals of France embracing all German states with the exception of Austria and Prussia and extending from the Rhine to the Elbe and from the Alps to the North Sea. The last

111

feeble bond of German unity thus disappeared and the Hapsburgs, instead of being German Emperors, became merely
emperors of Austria and kings of Bohemia and Hungary.

At the *Fürstentag* or princes' meeting in Erfurt in 1808
(which Goethe and Wieland also attended) Napoleon reached
the peak of his power, as four German kings and thirty-four
German princes rendered homage to the unifier of Europe—
though England, the sworn enemy of continental unity, still
opposed him. His downfall began in 1812 with the disastrous
expedition to Russia, and his defeat in the *Völkerschlacht*
near Leipzig in 1813 and the occupation of Paris in 1814
apparently put an end to his career. But he escaped from his
exile on the island of Elba, and after his return to France it
was only the Anglo-Prussian victory at Waterloo in 1815 and
Napoleon's subsequent banishment to St. Helena that finally
destroyed his titanic ambition.

The Congress of Vienna (1814–1815) tried to restore
monarchies and boundaries as they had existed before the
French explosion twenty-five years earlier. Germany could
not regain Belgium, which for a while was joined to Holland;
nor could she get back Alsace-Lorraine, which she had lost in
the seventeenth century. The internal structure of Germany
remained greatly simplified, however, because the decrees of
1803 were not revoked and the innumerable German Lilliputian states were not restored. Increasing rivalry between Austria and Prussia for the first place within the German family
of states prevented the restoration of a new Empire, a Second
Reich.

Two great problems subsequently occupied Germany
throughout the entire nineteenth century: first, the problem
of German unification, either under Prussian or under Austrian leadership; second, the problem of democracy, of a
constitutional parliamentary government. In spite of the defeat of Napoleon the slogans of *liberté* and *égalité* lingered
on among the German masses, who had not fought and suffered merely to restore the old absolutistic order. Yet for
years the establishment of the reactionary Holy Alliance
under the leadership of the Austrian foreign minister Prince
von Metternich cruelly disappointed all these fond expectations.

112

CHARACTERISTICS OF ROMANTIC LITERATURE

Romanticism was a continuation of the Storm and Stress and to a large extent also a reaction against German Classicism—although the two terms Classicism and Romanticism are often united under the name of German Idealism. By abandoning the leadership of the Storm and Stress and by re-emphasizing the necessity of restraint and other classical rules, Goethe and Schiller had greatly isolated themselves. Around them the poets and thinkers of Germany were swept on by the great wave of irrationalism and emancipation which dominated Europe at the turn of the century.

Lyricism and Freedom from Limitations

German Romanticism appears at its best in its lyrical productions. It is irrational, imaginative, colorful, and fantastic. German Classicism had been objective, calm, and restrained; Romanticism was emotional, subjective, ecstatic, and moody, wildly pouring forth its griefs and passions, its joy and despair. Classicism may be compared to a Greek statue, plastic, concrete, and lucid; Romanticism, however, is best compared to music, to melody, something endless, intangible, sonorous. Lacking the stern self-discipline of a Goethe, a romanticist's inspiration lasts only as long as his mood; hence the many fragments and torsos that result from attempts to write longer works such as novels.

Nor did the romanticists agree with Goethe or Kant that there are rules and limitations in life, literature, or morals. They wanted to be absolutely free and unfettered in their lives as well as in their works. Hence the immorality of so many romanticists; hence also the extreme variety of their works, in which a chaos of moods and inspirations sought to express itself. No harmoniously balanced characters here, but colors, melodies, fantasy, hallucinations, supreme individualism.

German Romanticism is unfinished, endless, a yearning only, if compared with the completeness and purposefulness of German Classicism. In spite of his many errors Goethe's Wilhelm Meister had at least finished his education; the romantic imitators of that novel, however, admiring its romantic form without heeding its ethical message (just as they did in the case of *Die Wahlverwandtschaften*), showed aimlessness only, the quest of something which they did not really know and which they did not ever find and possess—the chasing after a fancy, a dream, which for lack of a better name or identification they called "the Blue Flower." In the last analysis romantic apprenticeship novels do not really deserve their name, for they led nowhere and their apprenticeships remained unfinished.

The romanticists' emphasis on the holy right of subjectivity and individualism also led to increasing emancipation of women and to their ever greater participation in the literary movement of their time. Outstanding among them were Dorothea Schlegel, daughter of the philosopher Moses Mendelssohn and wife of Friedrich Schlegel; Caroline Schlegel, wife of August Wilhelm Schlegel and later married to the philosopher Schelling; Sophie and Bettina Brentano, wife and sister of Clemens Brentano, Bettina being famous for her correspondence with Goethe (*Goethe's Briefwechsel mit einem Kinde,* published in 1835) and later married to Achim von Arnim. The salons of two brilliant Jewesses, Rahel Varnhagen von Ense and Henriette Herz, formed favorite meeting places for the poets and thinkers of this age.

Weltschmerz

A typically romantic phenomenon is *Weltschmerz* (literally, world-grief), the inability of many of these unstable and eccentric geniuses to adapt themselves to the hard realities of the world. Endless conflicts, gloom, and despair resulted from such maladjustments. Goethe's Werther and also his Torquato Tasso had been among the first to suffer from the utter pessimism and disillusionment of *Weltschmerz;* but later, especially in *Wilhelm Meisters Wanderjahre,* Goethe had tried to indicate how man could preserve his soul and his rich emotional life in the midst of a restrictive and mechanized reality. Poets of *Weltschmerz* in German literature were notably Lenau and Heine; yet Hölderlin, Novalis, Kleist, and Grillparzer were also in many respects "misfits" and led deeply tragic lives. In philosophy may be mentioned Arthur Schopenhauer, for although the influence of his pessimistic ideas made itself felt only in the second half of the century, his fundamentally important book *Die Welt als Wille und Vorstellung* (The World as Will and Idea) appeared in 1819, in the midst of the Romantic Period. In music, too, appeared hopelessness and gloom, especially in *Der fliegende Holländer* (The Flying Dutchman), one of Richard Wagner's early operas; and Weber in his Faustian opera *Der Freischütz* (The Seventh Bullet) combined desperation with supernatural events. Nor was this romantic *mal du siècle* restricted to Germany alone—mention need only be made of Byron (*Manfred, Childe Harold's Pilgrimage*) in England or Hawthorne in America.

Variety and Cosmopolitanism

Goethe and Schiller had tried to create art according to eternally valid rules and to write works that would be eternally beautiful, and hence they had worshipped Greece as the great originator of truly beautiful art. Not so the romanticists: according to them there are no rules which are valid at all times and in all nations. Each century and each country is entitled to its own standards, likes, and dislikes; it is a mistake to assume that, e.g., Greece or France alone can be the lawgivers of the world's literature. Hence here again the extremely kaleidoscopic and cosmopolitan variety of the romanticists' tastes and works. They refused to be restricted to one age or to one model, just as they refused to be restricted to only one emotion, style, or theme. In the choice of their themes their interests ranged from India to America, from the age of Napoleon to the age of Pericles; and in their style they mingled prose and poetry, comedy and tragedy, sonnets and *terza rima,* blank verse and hexameter—for there was nothing their universal interest did not embrace.

Besides Greece, the Middle Ages, for instance, seemed to them just as interesting and admirable to study and to imitate. The Middle Ages, those picturesque and powerful centuries when Germany had been a great Empire and had ruled over half of Europe, indeed became the favorite period of the romanticists, and novels, dramas, and ballads alike dealt with the resplendent age of chivalry, tournaments, and minstrelsy. As opposed to Greece-inspired Classicism, Romanticism was an essentially German movement; and the study of the great Germanic past inspired the poets with new enthusiasm and patriotism. But there was a still deeper reason for the romanticists' love of the Middle Ages. Children of a highly refined intellectual age, suffering under the complexity of modern life, thrown into the maelstrom of dissolving empires and a dissolving pattern of society, the romanticists were yearning for the simplicity, spontaneity of experience, and innocence of man's lost childhood, for the great unity where man was still an integral part of an encompassing organism. All this the romanticists thought to find in the political, social, and religious order of the Middle Ages.

And the romanticists still found something else besides imperial greatness and cultural oneness in the fairy-like colorfulness of the Middle Ages: the greatness of the Catholic Church. Romanticism was an essentially Catholic movement; in that it differed profoundly from the Protestantism of the Storm and Stress and of Classicism. Denying the validity of all rules and laws in life and asserting their right to think and act as they pleased, the romanticists, shattered by the storm of life and passion, finally came to acknowledge at least one pillar to which they could cling: Catholicism. Hence the astounding number of conversions among the romanticists; hence also the fervent mysticism of these irrational geniuses who dared no more face life proudly and freely, as Goethe sternly bade them, but who found refuge only in the bosom of the Catholic Church.

Romantic Irony

One peculiarly romantic phenomenon remains to be mentioned: "romantic irony." In spite of their fervent emotions the romanticists, by willfully destroying the beautiful illusion they had created in the reader, were often anxious to show that they stood above their own poetic creations—or, for that matter, above their readers, whom they often held in scorn. Thus in some dramas—as, by the way, also in Goethe's minor play *Der Triumph der Empfindsamkeit* (The Triumph of Sentimentality), in which he poked fun at his own *Werther* —the actors suddenly stop acting their proper parts and step out of character to argue among themselves, with the spectators, the theater director, or the playwright before the show goes on again. Among the lyric poets particularly Heinrich Heine often cruelly destroys the veil of his readers' illusion in a last unexpected line, uttering sarcastic remarks which imply that we should not take him or his work any more seriously than he does himself. Caring more for their own whims than for the opinion of a dull reading public, the romanticists often did not mind ending their works in such an ironic way—or, quite as frequently, did not end them at all.

GERMAN CULTURE AT HOME AND ABROAD

This greatest age in German history, which was witnessed and enriched by Klopstock (d. 1803), Herder (d. 1803), Kant (d. 1804), Schiller (d. 1805), Wieland (d. 1813), and Goethe (d. 1832), produced, besides the romanticists proper, great thinkers like Johann Gottlieb Fichte (1762–1814), Georg Wilhelm Friedrich Hegel (1770–1831), Friedrich Schleiermacher (1768–1834), Friedrich Wilhelm Joseph von Schelling (1775–1854), and Arthur Schopenhauer (1788–1860); renowned composers like Karl Maria von Weber (1786–1826), Ludwig van Beethoven (1770–1827), and Franz Peter Schubert (1797–1828); and notable painters like Caspar David Friedrich (1774–1840) and, later, Moritz von Schwind (1804–1871). It can be contended that this is the richest period in modern European culture, superior to the Golden Age of France under Louis XIV, of Spain under Philip II, or of England under Queen Elizabeth, and comparable only to the great Age of Pericles in the fifth century B.C. With regard to the very important relationship between philosophy and literature, reference can be made to the great influence of Kant's ethics on Schiller, of Schelling's mysticism on Novalis, of Fichte's nationalism on Kleist, of Hegel's historism on Hebbel, and of Schopenhauer's pessimism on Wagner.

Switzerland

European and American romanticists, if they did not go to Germany personally (Mme. de Staël, Stendhal, Nerval, Coleridge, Scott, Irving, Longfellow, Oehlenschläger, etc.), learned about German culture mainly through Mme. de Staël of Geneva, who carried on the Swiss tradition (which Bodmer had already so beautifully fulfilled) of mediating between foreign countries. Her book *De l'Allemagne* (On Germany), one of the most important and inspiring publications of that time, appeared in 1813, a year doubly significant in the history of Germany, because it also witnessed the beginning of Napoleon's downfall. Mme. de Staël's estate at Coppet on Lake Geneva became the intellectual center of European Romanticism, the meeting ground of most European men of letters, where the Schlegel brothers expounded their new romantic theories and directly or indirectly passed them on to the poets of other lands. Not quite so fundamentally important as Mme. de Staël's elucidations on German culture and her enthusiastic analysis of German literature were the efforts of yet another Swiss, Benjamin Constant, translator of Schiller and author of an essay on the German drama. His novel *Adolphe,* the story of his unhappy love affair with Mme. de Staël, was distinctly influenced by *Werther.*

England

Among the English romanticists (all of them visitors either in Germany or at Coppet), Coleridge wrestled mainly with the problem of German philosophy; Scott was enthusiastic about, and a frequent translator of, German literature and imparted his ardor to his American friend Washington Irving. Between Goethe and Lord Byron there existed a bond of personal friendship and mutual admiration—for Byron, like Faust's Euphorion, to Goethe seemed best to represent the happy synthesis of Germanic Romanticism and Greek Classicism, of modern European progress and ancient Mediterranean culture. William Taylor of Norwich set out systematically to discuss and translate the masterpieces of German literature into English. Among the British periodicals, the *Edinburgh Review* was foremost in explaining to its readers the Golden Age of German culture. Even unworthy German writers like Kotzebue were prized in England far beyond their merits—as is proved by Sheridan's acclaimed adaptations of the dramas of this "German Shakespeare." Among the later analysts, propagators, and translators of German literature in England, Carlyle occupied a particularly prominent place: he was the author of a *History of Frederick the Great,* of a *Life of Schiller,* and of essays on Goethe, Jean Paul, and Novalis, and was the translator of Goethe's *Märchen* and *Wilhelm Meister* and of tales by La Motte-Fouqué, Hoffmann, Jean Paul, and Tieck, among others.

America

In America Washington Irving showed various German influences in his *Sketch Book* and his *Tales of a Traveller: The Spectre Bridegroom* is based on Bürger's *Lenore, The Devil and 1 om Walker* can in a small way be likened to *Faust,* and *Buckthorne* might be called an American *Wilhelm Meister;* and also for *The Legend of Sleepy Hollow* and *Rip van Winkle* interesting parallels can be found in German saga (Emperor Barbarossa sleeping in the subterranean castle of Kyffhäuser, etc.). In *Mardi,* Herman Melville blended beautifully the apprenticeship novel and the state novel of the (German) eighteenth century: Taji, in the archipelago of Mardi, sought his ideal Yillah more fervently than Parzival had ever sought the Grail or Heinrich von Ofterdingen the Blue Flower; in its symbolism and haze, too, the book reminds us of many aspects of European Romanticism. Poe in his tales of horror and grotesqueness is generally considered to have been influenced by E. T. A. Hoffmann. The American Transcendentalists in Cambridge and Concord, the "Weimar and Jena" of American literature, were imbued with the spirit of Kant, Goethe, Schleiermacher, Schelling, and Hegel—even to the extent of borrowing the word "transcendental" from Kant. Thus Emerson in his philosophy and his Goethe essay; thus *The Dial,* the periodical of Transcendentalism, which he and Margaret Fuller edited and to which especially the latter (often called the American Mme. de Staël) contributed many fine and significant essays on German literature. Margaret Fuller also translated Goethe's *Torquato Tasso* and Eckermann's *Gespräche mit Goethe* into English. But most pronounced are the German influences in Longfellow: *Hyperion,* containing fine analyses of Goethe and of Jean Paul, by its very title reminds us of Hölderlin, and by its theme of restless wandering and searching it recalls Novalis' *Heinrich von Ofterdingen* or Eichendorff's *Aus dem Leben eines Taugenichts;* it is a *Weltschmerz* novel par excellence. In *The Golden Legend,* the second part of his *Christ* trilogy, Longfellow blended in an unusual but fascinating fashion the tale of Goethe's *Faust* and that of Hartmann von Aue's *Armer Heinrich.* Longfellow also proved to be an excellent translator of many German poets from Luther up to Goethe and the German romanticists. Between his epic *Evangeline* and Goethe's *Hermann und Dorothea* many interesting parallels and borrowings have been noted; even more striking are the indisputable influences of Schiller's *Das Lied von der Glocke* upon Longfellow's *Building of a Ship.* Also Lowell, one of the earliest American critics of literature, in his lectures and essays evidences a great and lasting interest in German literature.

France

In France, Chateaubriand was the greatest immediate forerunner of Romanticism; his ardent Catholicism and revival of faith constituted a long-overdue reaction against the frigid scepticism of the *Encyclopédistes.* Chateaubriand was deeply influenced by Milton; his religious fervor makes him comparable to Novalis; his short stories *Atala* and *René* are *Weltschmerz* tales in the best Wertherian fashion. A similar *Weltschmerz* or *mal du siècle* is found in Musset's *Confessions d'un enfant du siècle,* in Sénancour's *Obermann,* and, above all, in Alfred de Vigny's dismal pessimism, an echo of Goethe's description, in *Werther* and *Tasso,* of the sufferings of sensitive men and maladjusted poets in modern society— a pessimism (especially touchingly expressed in his tragedy *Thomas Chatterton*) which is worthy of his great German contemporary, Schopenhauer. Victor Hugo, in his romantic theories and dramatic themes and technique was deeply influenced by Shakespeare and by the Germans, especially by the Schlegel brothers. Among the main translators and mediators in France were the Germanophiles Gérard de Nerval (the translator of Goethe's *Faust*), Charles Nodier, and, later, Edgar Quinet, Jules Michelet, and Ernest Renan.

Italy and Spain

The two greatest Italian romanticists, Manzoni (in his *I promessi sposi* a follower of Scott's historical novels) and the sickly and despondent *Weltschmerz* poet Leopardi, showed few direct German influences; lesser lights like Foscolo (an imitator of Goethe's *Werther* and later a refugee in England), Monti (an imitator of Klopstock and an important friend of Mme. de Staël), and Bertòla (in his *Idea della bella letteratura alemanna,* 1784) displayed greater evidence of them. In Espronceda, the greatest romanticist of Spain, are found echoes of Ossian and Byron and, in his most ambitious work, *El diablo mundo,* the distinct influence of Goethe's *Faust.* Besides Goethe, also Gessner, Schiller, Kotzebue, the Schlegel brothers, Humboldt, and Heine quickly became known among Spanish men of letters (Böhl von Faber, Solís, Hartzenbusch, Gertrudis Gómez de Avellaneda, and others).

Scandinavia

Modern Scandinavian literature, after having undergone the influence of French Enlightenment, achieved some of its best works partly through the inspiration received during the Golden Age of German literature. In Norway, Wergeland, in his religious epic poetry, was greatly indebted to Klopstock. Among the Danish preromanticists Ewald was likewise influenced by Klopstock, and Baggesen, a friend of most German poets of note, by Swiss pastoral poetry of the type of Gessner's *Idyllen.* German influences were supreme in the greatest Danish romanticist, Oehlenschläger, a frequent traveler in Germany and a visitor of Mme. de Staël's at Coppet. The Swedish preromanticist Thorild combated the Scandinavian disciples of Voltaire with the aid of Ossian, Rousseau, Klopstock, and Schiller; during the apogee of Romanticism, Atterbom became the leader of the so-called Fosforists, the admirers of the Schlegels, Tieck, and Novalis. Stagnelius was the unhappiest among the Scandinavian purveyors of *Weltschmerz;* Tegnér, the greatest Swedish romanticist, owed much to Goethe, Byron, and Oehlenschläger. Thus Germany repaid Scandinavia amply for the stimulating influences received from the Nordic Renaissance around 1750.

Russia and Poland

German influences are notable in the two great Russian romanticists Pushkin and Lermontov; but in their poetry, their passionate lives, and their premature deaths they resemble Byron most. In Poland can be mentioned Brodzinski, an admirer of Herder and Schiller; Slowacki, a poet bitter and desperate in his *Weltschmerz;* and, the greatest among the Polish romanticists, Mickiewicz, a Lithuanian by birth, in many of his works a pupil of Goethe and Byron.

TWO FORERUNNERS OF ROMANTICISM

In order to take into consideration the many varieties and the shifting emphases of German Romanticism, the treatment of the period under discussion is subdivided into four sections:

a. Two Forerunners of Romanticism: Hölderlin, Jean Paul.
b. Early Romanticism: Novalis, Tieck, the Schlegel brothers, etc.
c. Patriotic Romanticism: Kleist, Arndt, Körner, Uhland, etc.
d. Late Romanticism: Eichendorff, Lenau, Grillparzer, Heine, etc.

The older romanticists were mostly centered in Jena (the Schlegel brothers, Tieck); but the younger romanticists were scattered all over Germany, from Berlin (Kleist, Chamisso, Hoffmann) to Heidelberg (Brentano, Arnim, Görres), and from Swabia (Hölderlin, Uhland, Hauff) to Austria (Grillparzer) and Silesia (Eichendorff).

Friedrich Hölderlin (1770–1843). In his lyric poems (*An die Parzen, Sonnenuntergang, Brot und Wein, Der Rhein, Heidelberg, Patmos,* etc.) Hölderlin revealed himself as a deeply tragic poet, one of the great and dynamic lyricists of Germany, whose intense subjectivity and pessimism finally drove him to insanity (1802). Being a great lover of ancient Greece, he is significant for his new and different interpretation of the Greek mentality: to him Greek literature appeared irrational, emotional, romantic, and not, as Goethe had insisted, calm, sublimated, classical. Apollo, the god of beauty and art, Hölderlin held, may here and there have restrained Greek poets and made them sublimate their sufferings; fundamentally, however, Dionysos, the Asiatic god of romantic ecstasy and wild orgies, was much stronger among them. Thus after Wieland had represented the Greeks as elegant epicureans, Lessing as stern Spartans, young Goethe as super-human titans, and old Goethe as calm and restrained humanists, Hölderlin represented them as romantic, unbalanced, tragic individuals. Hölderlin's hymnic and elegiac odes, of great beauty and rare depth of thought, are not readily comprehensible to the superficial reader and were therefore appreciated only by a handful of connoisseurs during his lifetime. It was not until early in the present century that Hölderlin was "discovered" as one of the greatest and loftiest poets in German literature.

Hölderlin's great novel *Hyperion* (1797) is an apprenticeship novel which, in contrast to *Wilhelm Meister,* ends in disillusionment and death. It tells of a noble youth, a modern Greek, who wants to restore the greatness of his fatherland and to fight against the Turkish yoke and who, after the death of his noble friends Diotima and Alabanda, finding his faith and ideals cruelly shattered, turns away from this world to become a hermit. It is the pathetic story of many of Hölderlin's own problems and frustrations.

Der Tod des Empedokles (The Death of Empedocles), a dramatic fragment, represents a great philosopher, a Faustian character, a darling of the gods, a new Messiah whose divine message is doubted by the people and who therefore commits suicide by plunging into the abyss of Mount Etna in a last desperate attempt to prove his godlike character and to rally the nation around his new religion. Like *Hyperion,* the drama may be a glorification of an idealist whose disillusionment can end only in death.

Jean Paul (1763–1825). (Jean Paul Friedrich Richter). Fantastic and grotesque elements prevail in Jean Paul's novels. His typically romantic effusions, which more often than not border on inverisimilitude, were written in a colorful, incoherent, and arabesque style that offered a striking contrast to the classical compactness of the preceding age. His heroes are all emotion and sensation; they think, talk, and dream incessantly, but do not really act. Bold imagination and colorful visions are more important than normal everyday problems; hence the fairy-like unreality of so many of Jean Paul's works. Rationalism and realism are of little consequence, for the poet can spread a magic veil of beauty over the most trifling incidents and objects. Fantastic descriptions rather than normally constructed tales are found in his two apprenticeship novels, *Die unsichtbare Loge* (The Invisible Lodge, 1793) and *Hesperus* (1795), and in his most ambitious work, *Titan* (1800 ff.), a bizarre tale of love and romantic yearning in which may be heard echoes of Faust and Don Juan.

Much better are *Siebenkäs* (The Married Life, Death, and Wedding of the Advocate of the Poor, Firmian Siebenkäs, 1796) and his shorter novels like *Das Leben des vergnügten Schulmeisterlein Maria Wuz in Auental* (The Life of the Happy Schoolmaster Maria Wuz in Auental, 1793—originally part of *Die Unsichtbare Loge*) and *Das Leben des Quintus Fixlein* (The Life of Quintus Fixlein, 1796), for in them Jean Paul, in addition to revealing his rich imagination and giving marvelous descriptions of nature, shows his kindliness and gentle humor. In contrast to the mythological figures and mighty potentates that had figured so prominently in the works of Goethe and Schiller, Jean Paul humbly and lovingly dwelt on little people and little problems and described the joys, the worries, and the absurd flights into imagination of meek little men and women. Jean Paul is often compared to two English novelists, his kindly humor suggesting Charles Dickens and his rambling and blurred style Laurence Sterne, who undoubtedly exerted a considerable influence upon him. Only in his last works such as his unfinished *Flegeljahre* (Walt and Vult, or The Twins, 1804) and his significant educational treatise *Levana* (Levana, or The Doctrine of Education, 1807) did Jean Paul endeavor to become more concise and purposeful in his presentations. But even so, in style as well as in thought, he afforded a striking contrast to the prevailing Classicism of Weimar.

EARLY ROMANTICISM

Of the three periods to be considered hereafter, this is the most subjective and recklessly individualistic. Acknowledging no laws and traditions, the author, as a man and as a poet, became a law unto himself and indulged in unrestrained emotionalism. Fairy tales became particularly popular among many of these writers because they represent the purest form of fantasy. Compared with later romanticists these early poets were not excessively productive, because they were still largely preoccupied in establishing a romantic *Weltanschauung,* a system of thought on life, religion, and literary criticism.

August Wilhelm Schlegel (1767—1845) and Friedrich Schlegel (1772–1829). The Schlegel brothers can be considered among the leaders of this Romantic School. Their periodical *Das Athenaeum* (1798–1800) became important and instrumental in spreading their significant critical and philosophical ideas.

August Wilhelm, having like Herder a vast and intuitive understanding of foreign nations and literatures, achieved international fame among the European romanticists through his fine literary criticism (e.g. *Berlin Lectures on Literature and Art,* 1801, and *Vienna Lectures on Dramatic Art and Literature,* 1808), in which, in an effort to break the literary hegemony of France, he paid loving attention especially to England and to the irrational and Catholic authors of Italy and Spain. Together with his brother he became one of the chief theorists of European Romanticism.

Friedrich's outstanding literary work is his rhapsodic and fragmentary *Lucinde* (1799), a glorification of free love and supreme emotionalism. It portrays a recklessly irrational, passionate, and individualistic attitude which, as Goethe was to warn in his *Wahlverwandtschaften,* is apt to undermine state and society.

Novalis (1772–1801) (Friedrich von Hardenberg). Novalis is the greatest lyric poet among the early romanticists. His melancholy *Hymnen an die Nacht* (Hymns to the Night), inspired by the death of his young bride (and to some extent influenced by Young's *Night Thoughts*), expresses his intense desire to follow her in death. Besides this morbid grief which hails night and death as friends who deliver mortals from their sufferings, there are also to be found in these poems intense religious fervor and mysticism. Especially beautiful are his hymns addressed to Christ (*Wenn ich ihn nur habe*) and to the Virgin Mary in which the poet tries to sublimate his sorrows.

125

The same Catholic ardor glows in his *Die Christenheit oder Europa* (Christianity or Europe), a treatise in praise of the Middle Ages when religion had really been the source and center of all things. Novalis was deeply impressed by Schleiermacher's outstanding book *Über die Religion; Reden an die Gebildeten unter ihren Verächtern* (On Religion; Speeches to Its Cultured Despisers); and by comparing these two works with, e.g., *Le Génie du Christianisme* (The Genius of Christianity) by the famous French Catholic Chateaubriand it may be observed how completely Romanticism is imbued with religion.

Heinrich von Ofterdingen (1799), a fragment, is an apprenticeship novel, an imitation of *Wilhelm Meister,* the romantic tale of a young poet who sought the Blue Flower, in whose chalice he had seen the countenance of Matilde. How he found her and lost her again through death and how he wandered on into the realm of the supernatural, of visions, metaphysics, and fairy tales, is depicted against a rich medieval background of emperors, poets, knights, and crusades. Imagination and fantasy are praised as the finest attributes of life and poetry; and, as in the case of so many other *Weltschmerz* poets, sweet sadness and tender melancholy pervade this tale of Heinrich's endless pilgrimage and yearning.

Wilhelm Heinrich Wackenroder (1773–1798). Like Novalis, Wackenroder was a sensitive and poetic youth who died prematurely. His *Herzensergiessungen eines kunstliebenden Klosterbruders* (Outpourings of an Art-loving Monastic, 1797) reveals his fine appreciation of art and music and in its time contributed much to enhance the romanticists' enthusiasm for medieval German art and culture. Art to him was a divine revelation, and by extolling, for instance, the intrinsic beauties and values of Albrecht Dürer, Wackenroder helped to lead German inspiration away from the Hellenism of Weimar, back to Germany's own cultural inheritance.

Ludwig Tieck (1773–1853). In 1796 Tieck, a very close friend, traveling companion, and collaborator of Wackenroder, wrote a particularly striking example of a reckless and amoral romantic story, *Die Geschichte des Herrn William Lovell* (The Story of Mr. William Lovell). In its nihilism this adventurer's tale was inspired by the writings of the rather notorious French author Restif de la Bretonne, and its hero seems to have been entirely unaware of the necessity of moral discipline such as was extolled by most other German thinkers during this Golden Age of German Idealism.

Der gestiefelte Kater (Puss in Boots, 1797), a charming example of a romantic comedy, is a fairy drama full of wit and fantasy in which romantic irony and a complete disregard of the accepted dramatic rules prevail. The story of Gottlieb and his astounding tomcat Hinze also gave Tieck an opportunity to ridicule the dull rationalism of some of his contemporaries. *Ritter Blaubart* (Knight Bluebeard) and *Prinz Zerbino* are other examples of *Märchendramen* in which comedy and tragedy, satire and grotesqueness are intermingled.

Franz Sternbalds Wanderungen (The Wanderings of Franz Sternbald, 1799) is an apprenticeship novel, again a glorification of the Middle Ages, the dreamland of all romanticists. Under the influence of his friend Wackenroder, Tieck endeavored to replace his former fantastic playfulness with greater coherence and purposefulness, as evidenced, for instance, in Sternbald's interview with Albrecht Dürer, or in his wanderings to the Rhineland and the Netherlands; later, however, the novel becomes confused and kaleidoscopic, with Sternbald's romantic and artistic yearning and Tieck's unfathomable fantasy and visions going beyond the bearable.

Leben und Tod der heiligen Genoveva (Life and Death of Saint Genevieve, 1799) is a tragedy typically romantic in its portrayal of a Catholic medieval legend. This tale of a husband's cruel arrogance and an outcast wife's long and patient sufferings is also particularly noteworthy because in it Tieck used and intermixed with true poetic license all possible forms of style and meter.

Heinrich von Kleist (1777–1811) (I).* *Robert Guiskard,* a mighty drama about a famous Norman duke who on the eve of his victory before the gates of Constantinople was destroyed by the plague, may well serve as a symbol of Kleist's deeply tragic life. Unhappy in love, snubbed by Goethe, despairing of his genius, and consumed by the titanic ambition to create, on the first attempt, an enduring masterpiece which would place him beside the immortals of Weimar

* See also pp. 132–133.

and Jena, Kleist, in 1803, in utter hopelessness, burned his *Guiskard,* the tragedy in which he had tried to blend Shakespeare's powerful conflicts with Sophocles' dramatic art. The few scenes which he later rewrote in calmer moments may be only a faint echo of what was to have been his greatest work.

Penthesilea is a tragedy about the searing passion of the queen of the Amazons for Achilles, a passion which ends in disillusionment and rage, during which she kills and utterly disfigures the Greek hero. There is no better way of comparing Classicism with Romanticism than to contrast Goethe's pure and noble Iphigenia with Kleist's passionate and bloodcrazed Penthesilea; the one is Apollonian, the other Dionysian, art at its most typical.

Das Käthchen von Heilbronn (Catherine of Heilbronn) is a medieval drama with all its romantic paraphernalia of emperors, knights, secret courts, visions, dreams, and angels. The mysterious, humble, and patient love of Käthchen for her hero is described against the picturesque background of old Swabia.

Among Kleist's novels may be mentioned *Die Marquise von O . . . ,* a masterful presentation of an absurd sexual theme, and *Das Erdbeben auf Chili* (The Earthquake in Chili), *Die Verlobung in San Domingo* (The Betrothal in San Domingo), and *Der Findling* (The Foundling), three tales containing elements of violence and mysteriousness. Kleist's themes may be romantic, but his style, rich and sonorous, though somewhat involved, tends towards realistic principles.

Kotzebue and Iffland. In absolute contrast to Kleist's ambitious striving were August von Kotzebue and August Wilhelm Iffland, whose sentimental and tearful bourgeois dramas are mentioned less for their literary value than for the astounding popularity they enjoyed in Germany and, in the case of the former, even more in England. Kotzebue's *Menschenhass und Reue* (The Stranger, or Misanthropy and Repentance), *Die Spanier in Peru* (The Spaniards in Peru, or Rolla's Death), and *Das Kind der Liebe* (Lover's Vows, or The Child of Love), and Iffland's *Verbrechen aus Ehrsucht* (Crime from Ambition) and *Der Spieler* (The Gambler), entertained and moved undiscriminating crowds which, in spite of Goethe's and Schiller's mockery in the *Xenien,* preferred such fare to *Iphigenie* or *Die Braut von Messina.*

Kunstmärchen

A characteristic feature particularly of this early group of romanticists is the development of the *Kunstmärchen,* or artistic fairy tale, a type of literature in which colorful imagination and extravagant fantasy can best express themselves.

Goethe had been among the first to cultivate this type with his *Das Märchen* (The Fairy Tale), a symbolical representation not only of the decay, but also of a possible inner rebirth, of the German Empire.

Tieck's fairy tales, misleadingly called *Volksmärchen* (Popular Fairy Tales, 1797), include besides the *Geschichte von den Haymonskindern* (Story of the Haymon Children) and the *Wundersame Liebesgeschichte der schönen Magelone* (Wondrous Love Story of the Beautiful Magelone) especially *Der blonde Eckbert* (Fair Eckbert), one of his best and at the same time most mysterious tales.

Of Clemens Brentano may be mentioned his pretty *Märchen von Gockel, Hinkel, und Gakeleia* (The Wondrous Tale of Cocky, Clucky, and Cackle)—and in this connection perhaps also his touching and tragic *Geschichte vom braven Kasperl und dem schönen Annerl* (Story of Honest Caspar and Beautiful Annie, 1817).

Of FRIEDRICH DE LA MOTTE-FOUQUÉ's works *Undine* (1811), the tale of a forsaken mermaid and a faithless knight, is the only one which has remained really popular.

Faust-like in its implications is Adelbert von Chamisso's *Peter Schlemihls wundersame Geschichte* (The Wondrous History of Peter Schlemihl, 1814), the romantic tale of a man who sells his shadow and who then is so haunted among men that he seeks peace and solitude in nature.

Among the works of Ernst Theodor Amadeus Hoffmann especially *Der goldene Topf* (The Golden Pot) and *Nussknacker und Mausekönig* (Nutcracker and Mouse-King) belong to this group of fairy tales.

Wilhelm Hauff's fairy tales contained in his two frame-stories *Das Wirtshaus im Spessart* (The Inn in the Spessart) and *Die Karawane* (The Caravan) are still popular today. Among them may be mentioned *Zwerg Nase* (Nosey, the Dwarf), *Das kalte Herz* (The Cold Heart), and *Die Geschichte von Kalif Storch* (The Story of the Caliph Stork).

Cosmopolitanism

One of the finest features of Romanticism, especially of the early period—and one with which Goethe was in full agreement, as his *Der westöstliche Divan* shows—is the trend to ever wider literary cosmopolitanism. In their universal urge to inspire themselves by the cultural beauties of all nations and all ages, the romanticists, with great linguistic skill and fine intuition, appreciated and translated the literary masterpieces not only of England, Italy, and Spain, but also of Persia, India, and the Far East. In this they were true disciples of Herder and Goethe, and German literature owes them a great debt of gratitude for having thus enriched Germany's intellectual wealth.

Among earlier examples are to be mentioned Goethe's translation of Voltaire's dramas *Mahomet* and *Tancred,* and of the autobiography of the famous Italian Renaissance artist, Benvenuto Cellini; Schiller's translation of Racine's *Phèdre,* Shakespeare's *Macbeth,* and Gozzi's *Turandot;* and Voss's translation of Homer's *Iliad* and *Odyssey.* Kleist's adaptation of Plautus' and Molière's *Amphitryon* should also be included here, though it became a masterpiece in its own right and is only loosely related to the Latin and French models.

Of monumental importance is the great Shakespeare translation (1797 ff.) jointly undertaken by August Wilhelm Schlegel, Ludwig Tieck, and the latter's daughter Dorothea —a most excellent work which makes Shakespeare to this day one of the leading classics of the German stage. Tieck also furthered the study of English literature in his *Altenglisches Theater* (Old English Theater, 1811).

The fervent Catholicism of Italian and Spanish authors inspired Karl Streckfuss to do a translation of Dante's *Divina Commedia* and of Torquato Tasso's *Gerusalemme liberata* (1822). From the Spanish literature some of Calderón's religious dramas were translated by August Wilhelm

Schlegel (1803) ; and the greatest Spanish novel, Cervantes'
Don Quixote, was rendered into German by Tieck (1799).
At about this time also appeared Herder's posthumously
published *Der Cid* (1805). Friedrich Schlegel was one of
the first Europeans to rediscover the great beauties of the
Portuguese national epic of the Renaissance, the *Lusiads*
by Camoëns.

It was, however, the knowledge of Oriental literature
which assumed special significance during this period. Path-
breaking was Friedrich Schlegel with his studies *Über die
Sprache und Weisheit der Inder* (On the Language and
Wisdom of the East Indians, 1808) ; from 1818 on, his
brother August Wilhelm was the first professor of San-
skrit at the University of Bonn. Hammer-Purgstall's translation of the medieval Persian poet Hafiz (1812) inspired
Goethe to his *Westöstlicher Divan* (1819). August Graf von
Platen in his *Ghaselen* (1821) and in his epic *Die Abassiden*
(1834) imitated the Orient in form and in thought. Among
the later poets and scholars influenced by the Orient, mention
may be made of Friedrich Rückert, a facile translator, for
his *Die Weisheit des Brahmanen* (The Wisdom of the
Brahmin, 1836), and especially of Friedrich Bodenstedt
for his *Lieder des Mirza-Schaffy* (Songs of Mirza-Schaffy,
1851). Ferdinand Freiligrath can also be named in this connection, although his exotic poems deal with Africa and
America as well as with the Orient.

PATRIOTIC ROMANTICISM

With the shattering defeat of Prussia and the dissolution
of the Holy Roman Empire, even the most egocentric romanticists came to realize that unrestrained individualism
had tended to undermine state and society, and that hard
work, patriotism, and unselfish sacrifice must inspire all
Germans if their country was ever to become free again.
Hence, from the defeat at Jena in 1806 to the final victory
at Waterloo in 1815 a new and different period of Romanticism began to take shape, the militant period of the *Deutsch-
romantik,* which was devoid of the earlier daydreaming, its
disciplined poets becoming leaders in the fight against France
and proud preservers of the German national past.

Heinrich von Kleist (II).* Kleist's drama *Prinz Friedrich von Homburg* became the finest expression of this changed mentality. It tells of a young prince who is a typical romanticist, a dreamer, a somnambulist, an ardent lover, who, after the battle of Fehrbellin in 1675, has been condemned to death on a technical charge of insubordination. But in jail he matures and becomes a man and realizes at last that obedience, discipline, and unquestioning loyalty to one's fatherland mean more than personal whims and idiosyncrasies. Other critics hold that it is not military discipline which is inculcated in the prince, but a sense of responsibility, so that he becomes not the prototype of the subservient subject, but a model of the intelligent, self-reliant, and reliable citizen who should constitute the ideal state. Thus the conflict between freedom and compulsion is resolved and, in Schiller's words, duty becomes inclination. This drama of Prussian self-discipline is so clear and well built that we again feel that Kleist is more closely related to the conciseness of the realists than to the formlessness of so many romanticists.

Fiercest in its blood-curdling hatred of the enemy is Kleist's tragedy *Die Hermannsschlacht* (The Battle of Hermann). Forbidden to write against the French Emperor, in this work he hailed the valor and patriotism of the old Germanic tribes which in their days, in the Teutoburg Forest, had utterly routed another invader from beyond the Rhine; and he appeared to pray that yet another Hermann might arise who would free modern Germany from the yoke of a foreign conqueror.

Also in his lyrics (e.g. *Germania an ihre Kinder*) Kleist summoned his fellow countrymen to the coming great battle of annihilation.

Among his novels pertaining to this disciplined phase must be mentioned *Michael Kohlhaas,* a realistic and famous historical tale of the sixteenth century. It tells us of an honest and law-abiding citizen who, embittered by wrongs endured, through his highly developed sense of justice turns into a fierce avenger of his cause, a scourge of his time. Michael Kohlhaas reminds the reader of Götz von Ber-

* See also pp. 127–128.

lichingen: though both men stand convicted in the eyes of the law, they know that their motives have been good and unselfish. And, like the Prince of Homburg, so also Kohlhaas in his last days comes to acknowledge the necessity and the supremacy of the state and willingly submits to its laws, though they demand his death.

Thoroughly German in its earthy atmosphere is *Der zerbrochene Krug* (The Broken Pitcher), one of the few really good comedies of this age, an amusing picture of a village tyrant, the cunning and tricky judge Adam, who finally gets caught in his own net of lies. Kleist, it is apparent, is not only a romanticist, as such works of his as *Käthchen* indicate; in his excellent and accurate character sketches, which betray a fine observer, he is even more a forerunner of the later school of Realism.

Despairing of his literary success and grief-stricken by the continued French occupation and humiliation of Germany, Kleist, in 1811, committed suicide. Most of the works of this great and tragic poet were not published until 1821, by Ludwig Tieck.

Ernst Moritz Arndt (1769–1860). Arndt is one of the most militant poets of his time, urging the Germans in his poems and songs to keep ready, not to despair, but to fight and die for their independence from France (*Lied der Rache, Vaterlandslied, Schlachtgesang, Was ist des Deutschen Vaterland?*).

Theodor Körner (1791–1813). Körner, too, was in the fullest sense a poet of the German War of Liberation, for he died on the battlefield. His poems are still popular today with the German people (*Gebet während der Schlacht, Aufruf, Lützows wilde, verwegene Jagd*).

Also his drama *Zriny,* a historical tragedy written in the manner of Schiller, serves to admonish and encourage his people, for it shows the desperate defense of Hungary against the Turkish invaders in the sixteenth century, and it ends in a grand finale with the Hungarians preferring certain death to surrender.

Friedrich Rückert (1788–1866). In his *Deutsche Gedichte* —among them the *Geharnischte Sonette* (Sonnets in Armor) —Rückert was likewise a battler for the cause of German liberation. Especially well-known is his poem *Barbarossa,* a tribute to the great German Emperor of the Middle Ages who, the legend states, will some day return to save his people from distress.

Fichte. In connection with this militant attitude must be mentioned also the philosopher Johann Gottlieb Fichte, who, in his inspiring *Reden an die deutsche Nation* (Addresses to the German Nation, 1808) exhorted German youth to stand by and to be ever mindful of the great past and the important future of their country.

Görres. Joseph Görres, later an outstanding leader of German Catholicism, made his *Rheinischer Merkur* (1814 ff.) the leading political journal of the time, the mouthpiece of the fermenting national and liberal movement. His valuable publications of *Die deutschen Volksbücher* (German Chapbooks, 1807) for the first time shed light on the sober late-medieval prose renderings of the great heroic epics.

Interest in the German Past

Of special importance during this period of national defeat and humiliation were the efforts of many romanticists to revive the greatness of the German cultural and literary past and thus to inspire new confidence and new pride among their readers. Whereas the early romanticists had endeavored to make the German public familiar with foreign literatures, this second group of romanticists endeavored to make its readers familiar with the greatness of their own history and the treasures of their own literature. Here, too, Herder served as a pathbreaker.

Arnim and Brentano. Achim von Arnim and Clemens Brentano, in 1805, published *Des Knaben Wunderhorn* (The Youth's Cornucopia), the most important collection of German folk songs. Not only have these songs of past centuries been thus collected, recorded, and preserved for posterity, but their simple beauty and their straightforward language have continued to inspire German poets to this day and to keep them from the pitfalls of artificiality and insincerity. Of Arnim's other works *Die Kronenwächter* (The Guardians of the Crown, 1817), a historical novel, and *Halle und Jerusalem,* an adaptation of Gryphius' *Cardenio und Celinde,* are particularly noteworthy. Among Brentano's other collections may be mentioned his *Rheinmärchen* (Fairy Tales of the Rhine). His *Godwi* is another apprenticeship novel, full of titanic strivings and incoherent episodes. Brentano, one of the most imaginative romantic poets, showed his strong Catholic leanings especially in his *Romanzen vom Rosenkranz* (Romances of the Rosary).

The Brothers Grimm. Of equally great significance with *Des Knaben Wunderhorn* is the collection of fairy tales made by the famed scholars Jakob and Wilhelm Grimm and published under the title of *Kinder- und Hausmärchen* (1812 ff.) —a rich contribution to German folklore which only the romanticists' enthusiasm for the Germanic past could have collected so painstakingly. In these fairy tales for children and home we find the real soul, the imagination, and the beliefs of the people through the centuries—something that the earlier romanticists, in spite of all their efforts, could but rarely achieve in their skillful *Kunstmärchen.* Jakob Grimm (1785–1863), commonly hailed as the real founder of the science of Germanic philology, later also published his *Deutsche Grammatik* (1819 ff.) and his *Geschichte der deutschen Sprache* (History of the German Language, 1848). In 1829 Wilhelm Grimm (1786–1859) published his *Die deutsche Heldensage* (The German Heroic Saga) and, together with his brother, the *Deutsche Sagen* (German Sagas).

Tieck and Others. Ludwig Tieck added his share in this discovery of the German past by modernizing medieval love poems in his *Minnelieder* (1803). He also republished Ulrich von Lichtenstein's *Frauendienst* (Chivalrous Love, 1812) and, in his *Deutsches Theater* (1817), edited dramas of the sixteenth and seventeenth centuries. Finally Tieck also deserves special credit for publishing the works of his tragic fellow romanticists Wackenroder, Novalis, and Kleist.

KARL SIMROCK was the most prolific among later translators of medieval German literature. His modern versions of the *Nibelungenlied* (1827), Walther von der Vogelweide, Wolfram von Eschenbach, Gottfried von Strassburg, the *Heliand,* etc. are excellent.

KARL LACHMANN, like Jakob Grimm a "grand old man" of Germanic philology, continued the ever increasing trend

135

towards a better exploration of the German Middle Ages through his painstaking publications of the critical texts of the *Nibelungenlied,* Walther von der Vogelweide, Hartmann's *Iwein,* Wolfram's *Parzival* (1833), etc.

German Historians. Concurrent with this literary exploration of the German past is also the purely historical investigation of early centuries. In 1819 German scholars began the publication of the impressive *Monumenta Germaniae historica,* an extensive collection of source material of inestimable value; and a generation later German historians of the caliber of LEOPOLD VON RANKE (born in 1795), THEODOR MOMMSEN (born in 1817), and HEINRICH VON TREITSCHKE (born in 1834) reached the same high degree of scholarship and eminence throughout the Western World as did the German philologists before them.

Ludwig Uhland (1787–1862). One of the most lovable of the Swabian romanticists, a man renowned both as a poet and as a professor of literature, Uhland can be mentioned here for his elucidation of *Walther von der Vogelweide* (1822) and for his collection of *Alte hoch- und niederdeutsche Volkslieder* (Old High and Low German Folk Songs). Besides this, Uhland was one of the best creative poets dealing with the Middle Ages, certainly the best ballad writer in German literature after Schiller, as evidenced in *Des Sängers Fluch* (The Curse of the Minstrel), *Schwäbische Kunde* (Swabian Tale), *Bertran de Born, Taillefer,* and other poems. He is also noteworthy for his historical dramas, e.g. *Herzog Ernst von Schwaben* (Duke Ernest of Swabia); and his simple and sincere soldiers' song *Der gute Kamerad* (The Good Comrade) is popular to this day.

Adelbert von Chamisso (1781–1838). Chamisso, too, composed excellent ballads which dealt either with medieval history (The Women of Weinsberg), simple folk themes (The Old Washerwoman), or exotic topics suggested by his extensive travels (*Salas y Gomez*). *Das Schloss Boncourt* (The Castle of Boncourt) expresses beautifully his nostalgia for France, for Chamisso was the son of French aristocrats who had fled to Germany before the horrors of the Revolution.

136

Hebel. Johann Peter Hebel, the author of many homespun poems and simple anecdotes, was, in his very popular works, an early forerunner of the *Heimat* poets of a later generation. He wrote in the Swabian-Swiss dialect prevalent around Basel. Among his best known works are his *Alemannische Gedichte* (Alemannic Poems) and *Das Schatzkästlein* (The Treasure Box).

Wagner. Richard Wagner's operas glorify the greatness of the German Middle Ages to such an extent that he may well be called "the last romanticist"; but chronologically he belongs to the realistic group of poets. See pp. 162–165.

LATE ROMANTICISM

After 1815, when victory brought back princely despotism instead of liberalism and democracy, the vigorous strength and the patriotic eagerness for discipline and sacrifice of the *Deutschromantiker* gave way to bitter disillusionment. Prince von Metternich and the reactionary Holy Alliance now reigned supreme; anxious to wipe out the last vestiges of *liberté* and *égalité,* they suppressed freedom of speech and of assembly and crowded the jails with protesting patriots. From this resulted an atmosphere of fearfulness and of frustration; the last romanticists were obliged to write escape literature in order not to clash with Metternich's police. Somewhat like the first romanticists, they escaped into the realm of pure fantasy, at times ending up in weirdness and grotesqueness; or, more often, they escaped into the beauties of nature and wrote touchingly and perfectly as never before about the sweet sadness of autumn and the serene anticipation of death. This passivity and *Weltschmerz* lasted only a few years, however; after 1830 a vigorous and angry reaction against Metternich's policy was bound to come.

Joseph von Eichendorff (1788–1857). Eichendorff is one of the finest poets in the history of German literature, whose melodious poems deal almost exclusively with the beauties of nature and with his romantic yearning for peace in the fold of nature (*Sehnsucht, Morgengebet, Der frohe Wandersmann, Mondnacht*). There is beauty and music in the very words "Waldeinsamkeit," "Mondesschimmer," "Wander-

lust" which Eichendorff and Uhland ("Regenbogenglanz"),
Heine ("Abendsonnenschein"), and other romanticists use
in their poetry. Like Goethe at Strassburg, Eichendorff had
the felicitous gift of expressing his tender emotions simply
and sincerely, so that many of his poems have become real
folk songs (*Das zerbrochene Ringlein*). And just as Goethe's
lyric poems had appealed to composers like Schubert and
Hugo Wolf, so Eichendorff's (and Heine's) lyrics inspired
Schumann to some of his best compositions (*Liederkreis*).

Among his prose works may be mentioned the well-known
Aus dem Leben eines Taugenichts (From the Life of a
Good-for-Nothing, 1826), a humorous and yet aimless little
tale with the stress more on colorful descriptions of detail
and melodious romantic moods than on compact thought and
construction.

Eichendorff is noteworthy also as the translator of some
of Calderón's religious dramas and as the author of a
treatise on German literature viewed from a strictly Catholic
angle. Also in his lyric poetry can be noted the tendency, so
common among many romanticists, to revert to Catholic
Spanish and Italian poets, themes, and landscapes as a
source of inspiration.

Müller. More positive and joyous than the dreamy Eichendorff is Wilhelm Müller (1794–1827), whose fine lieder and
nature poems are deservedly famous among all classes of
the German people (*Im Krug zum grünen Kranze, Am
Brunnen vor dem Tore, Ich schnitt' es gern in alle Rinden
ein, Frühlingseinzug, Das Wandern ist des Müllers Lust*).
These poems, together with others, constitute two of
Schubert's best known cycles of songs, *Die Winterreise* (The
Winter Journey) and *Die schöne Müllerin* (The Fair Maid
of the Mill).

Nikolaus Lenau (1802–1850). A Hungarian by birth,
Lenau was one of the loneliest and saddest of men, a
Weltschmerz poet who in his desperate search for idyllic
peace and happiness even traveled to the American Middle
West, only to return a bitterly disillusioned man and to end,
like Hölderlin, in insanity. The pleasure of sadness and the
poetry of pessimism are especially well expressed by him in
such poems as *Frühlings Tod, Herbstklage, Bitte, Wald-*

lieder, Schilflieder; and *Die drei Zigeuner* (The Three Gyp-
sies) tells of the futility of all hope and ambition.

His epic poems and dramatic attempts deal with equally
restless and unhappy characters who are eternally dissatisfied and disillusioned in their desperate quest of the absolute:
Faust, Don Juan, Ahasver—surely the three unhappiest seekers and wanderers in world literature. Lenau's poems treating
historical topics also portray man's everlasting groping for
truth: *Savonarola, Johannes Ziska, Die Albigenser.*

Heinrich Heine (1797–1856) (I).* Heine is one of the
great lyric poets among the late romanticists, though much
of his later work proves him to be an essentially political
and satirical poet of the Young German group of writers.
His influence was considerable, not only in Germany, but in
most countries of the Western World—as attested by the
scores of translations, imitations, and critical discussions of
his works abroad. Heine's *Buch der Lieder* (Book of Songs,
1827) and his later and more mature *Romanzero* (1851) contain many poems of exquisite beauty, although his talent
is often marred by his sarcasm and witticisms. Byron's *Weltschmerz* had a considerable influence upon him; and his own
unstable and hybrid character only helped to emphasize his
feelings of loneliness and bitterness. Born a Jew, he was
converted to Christianity; born a German, he soon preferred
to live in France; a marvelously gifted lyric poet, he tended
ever more to become a political polemicist; a theoretical,
parlor revolutionary, he had a horror of the masses; veering
towards atheism, he experienced his religious crises—and all
these conflicts and contradictions naturally tended to make
him unhappy and to distort his undoubtedly great genius.
Among the finest of Heine's poems, not marred by his irony,
may be mentioned *Leise zieht durch mein Gemüt, Im wun-
derschönen Monat Mai, Du bist wie eine Blume, Ein Fichten-
baum steht einsam, Auf Flügeln des Gesanges, Wo?, Ich
hatte einst ein schönes Vaterland;* and among his ballads *Die
Lorelei, Asra, Balsazar, Die Grenadiere, Die Wallfahrt nach
Kevlaar* are especially famous.

Ernst Theodor Amadeus Hoffmann (1776–1822). Hoffmann is one of the great masters of the fantastic novel, an

* See also pp. 155–156.

author who escapes into the realm of pure imagination and who often ends up in weirdness and horror. Titles like *Fantasiestücke* (Fantastic Tales, 1814) and *Nachtstücke* (Weird Tales, 1817) are significant, for spooks animate his tales, reality and hallucination are closely intertwined, color and melody enrich his style. The congeniality of his temperament with Edgar Allan Poe's and the similarity of their subjects and style are noteworthy; both writers succeeded in blending weird romanticism with an almost scientific realism, in tempering the wild flights of their imagination with an exact and realistic style. Hoffmann, a lawyer by profession, was also an accomplished musician and an admirer of Mozart; his sketches *Ritter Gluck* and *Don Juan,* and his opera *Undine* (1816), illustrate this predilection.

Best known among Hoffmann's works are *Die Elixiere des Teufels* (The Devil's Elixir), a tale resembling in theme the Jekyll and Hyde story, in which the desires, crimes, and insanity of a monk are emphasized more than his ultimate atonement; *Das Majorat* (The Entail), a novel of greed and murder in a storm-swept castle, which in its representation of a deadly hatred between two brothers somewhat resembles Schiller's *Räuber;* and *Das Fräulein von Scuderi* (Mlle. de Scudéri), the thrilling solving of a series of murders in seventeenth century Paris.

Fate Tragedies. Romantic gruesomeness is found also in the opera—for instance, the popular theme of a pact with the devil as represented in Weber's *Der Freischütz*. But it is in the so-called fate tragedies that the element of horror appears most distinctly. In them the romanticists in a rather convenient manner ascribed to a cruel and merciless fate whatever mishap chanced to befall their unruly heroes. Schiller's *Braut von Messina* had treated such a delicate topic in a classical and restrained manner. Among the romanticists who delved into this field Ludwig Tieck should be mentioned first, for his bloody *Karl von Berneck* constituted the first romantic fate tragedy.

ZACHARIAS WERNER, a man of little integrity, but for a while a protégé of Goethe's, placed the scene of his *Der 24. Februar* (1810) high up in the storm-beaten Alps of Switzerland. It showed how crimes and curses, including the murder of a son by his own parents, took place on the same fatal day as the years passed by—and, of course, with the same deadly weapon.

ADOLF MÜLLNER's *Der 29. Februar,* a tale of incest, carried this device to the point of absurdity, as the very title indicates.

Grillparzer, a greater figure by far than the authors of fate tragedies already mentioned, also began his career with this type of drama. His *Die Ahnfrau* (The Ancestress, 1817) is a horrifying, though well-done, tragedy dealing with robbers, patricide, incest, and insanity—not to speak of all the other paraphernalia of Gothic workmanship.

Among the successful parodies which put an end to these fate tragedies Platen's *Die verhängnisvolle Gabel* (The Fatal Fork, 1826) deserves first place.

Franz Grillparzer (1791–1872) (I).* Grillparzer is the foremost dramatist of Austria, and he and Kleist are the two greatest dramatists of the Romantic Age. Unhappy in his private life, worn down by a mediocre career as a minor civil official, in which position he was never properly encouraged, and embittered by the complete failure of one of his plays, Grillparzer became increasingly passive and pessimistic, and after 1838, suffocated by the censorship and the reactionary system of Metternich's regime, he no longer even bothered to publish his works.

König Ottokars Glück und Ende (King Ottokar, His Rise and Fall, 1825) is a historical tragedy of the thirteenth century and describes the successful campaign of the first Hapsburg ruler, Rudolf I, against his intriguing and presumptuous vassals of the type of Ottokar of Bohemia.

Der Traum ein Leben (The Dream, a Life, 1834) is a beautiful and significant drama which reminds the reader of Calderón's masterpiece, *La vida es sueño,* and which consists mostly of a long dream. It expresses well the utter passivity of dying Romanticism, because the hero, Rustan, only dreams that he sets out into the world in order to achieve big things, but when he wakes up, he prefers to stay at home after all, rather than face the dangers of greatness. Rustan has often been called the Austrian Faust, and his

* See also pp. 158-159.

wicked adviser Zanga is Mephistophelian indeed; but the differences between Goethe urging a life of action and Grillparzer advocating escape and passivity are too striking to be overlooked.

Weh dem der lügt (Thou Shalt Not Lie, 1838), a historical comedy about the seventh century, is an amusing play with an earnest undertone, telling about a humble yet witty kitchen boy who, through his inflexible truthfulness, was capable of freeing his master's nephew from captivity among the barbarians. The signal failure of this play at its first performance only added to Grillparzer's discouragement and bitterness.

Ein Bruderzwist in Habsburg (Family Strife in Hapsburg)—like *Libussa* and *Die Jüdin von Toledo* (The Jewess of Toledo) published only after the author's death—the tale of the events leading ultimately to the outbreak of the Thirty Years' War, may not be a perfect drama, but it again illustrates magnificently the fearful passivity of certain men during the age of Metternich, the conviction that activism is the greatest of all evils and that human ambition can lead only to disaster. Grillparzer, not really writing for the stage any more, put his own philosophical (and undramatic) ideas into this representation of the lives of two Austrian Emperors, Rudolf II and Matthias.

Libussa, a romantic tragedy mixing legend with a deep philosophical message and culminating in the melancholy conclusion that gods and men cannot ever unite and be happy, tells of a princess of ancient Bohemia who is endowed with magic powers. In order to strengthen her state and to become part of this world, she renounces her supernatural gifts and marries Primislaus, a sturdy peasant full of practical wisdom. But she cannot really bridge the gulf between herself and man; she dies, and only her child, representing a synthesis between deity and humanity, is destined to bring about the future greatness of Bohemia which she, Libussa, had striven for.

As a writer of short stories Grillparzer distinguished himself in his markedly autobiographical *Der arme Spielmann* (The Poor Musician), and in *Das Kloster bei Sendomir*

(The Monastery of Sendomir), a romantic tale of passion
and murder which Gerhart Hauptmann later adapted in his
drama *Elga*.

Wiener Volksstück. In connection with Grillparzer
should be mentioned a typically Viennese literary product,
das Wiener Volksstück (the Viennese Popular Play), to
which Grillparzer at points is unconsciously indebted. The
Wiener Volksstück is the heir of the Italian *commedia del-
l'arte,* which thrived mostly on the improvisations of the
comic actors (the roguish jester, the coquettish chamber-
maid, etc.), who amused an unpretentious audience with
their drastic and down-to-earth humor. In the early eighteenth century it developed into the most popular theater entertainment in the hands of such great comedians as Joseph
Stranitzky and Gottfried Prehauser. The tradition was continued in Vienna by the *Zauberpossen* (burlesque fairy tales),
one of which, Schikaneder's *Zauberflöte* (Magic Flute),
made its way into the repertoires of all theaters thanks to
Mozart's music. In the early nineteenth century the *Zauber-
posse* found its supreme master in the Viennese actor and
playwright FERDINAND RAIMUND (1790–1836), who managed to blend the plain popular humor and the fantastic
fairy-tale elements into charming and whimsical musical comedies. His plays *Der Barometermacher auf der Zauberinsel*
(The Barometer Maker on the Magic Island), *Der Alpen-
könig und der Menschenfeind* (The King of the Alps and
the Misanthropist), *Der Bauer als Millionär* (The Peasant
as a Millionaire), and, above all, his masterpiece, *Der Verschwender* (The Spendthrift) are still favorites with the
theater audience, which is captivated by the sentimental humor, the sly moralizing, and the naive imaginative plots.
Raimund found a dangerous competitor in the Viennese actor
and playwright JOHANNES NESTROY, whose comedies *Lumpa-
zivagabundus, Zu ebener Erde und im ersten Stock* (On the
Main Floor and on the First Floor), and *Einen Jux will er
sich machen* (Out on a Spree He Goes) are characterized by
a much more critical humor with distinct social and political
undertones; but they lack the melancholy gentleness of
Raimund.

143

HISTORY OF GERMAN LITERATURE

TRANSLATIONS

GENERAL COLLECTIONS

Francke, Kuno, editor-in-chief. *The German Classics of the Nineteenth and Twentieth Centuries.* Albany, 1913 ff. 20 vols.

Vol. IV: Jean Paul: Selections from *The Life of Quintus Fixlein, Titan, The Flegeljahre.*
Wilhelm von Humboldt: *Schiller.*
A. W. Schlegel: *Lectures on Dramatic Art.*
F. Schlegel: *Lucinda,* Aphorisms.
Novalis: Selections, Aphorisms, Poems.
Hölderlin: Poems.
Tieck: *Puss in Boots, Fair Eckbert, The Elves.*
Kleist: *Michael Kohlhaas, The Prince of Homburg.*

Vol. V: Schleiermacher: *On the Social Element in Religion.*
Fichte: *The Destiny of Man,* Addresses VIII and XIV of the *Addresses to the German Nation.*
Schelling: *On the Relation of the Plastic Arts to Nature.*
Arnim and Brentano: From *The Boy's Magic Horn.*
J. and W. Grimm: From the *Fairy Tales.*
Arndt, Körner, Schenkendorf, Uhland, Eichendorff: Poems.
Eichendorff: From *The Life of a Good-for-Nothing.*
Chamisso: Poems, *The Wonderful History of Peter Schlemihl.*
Hoffmann: *The Golden Pot.*
La Motte-Fouqué: Selections from *Undine.*
Hauff, Rückert, Platen: Poems.

Vol. VI: Heine: Poems, *The Journey to the Harz, Boyhood Days, English Fragments, Lafayette, The Romantic School, The Rabbi of Bacharach.*
Grillparzer: *Medea, The Jewess of Toledo, The Poor Musician, My Journey to Weimar.*
Beethoven: Letters.

Vol. VII: Hegel: *Introduction to the Philosophy of History, The Philosophy of Law, Introduction to the Philosophy of Art.*
Bettina von Arnim: *Goethe's Correspondence with a Child.*

Longfellow, H. W. *The Poets and Poetry of Europe* (containing poems by Arndt, Bodmer, Bürger, Chamisso, Claudius, Freiligrath, Gellert, Gessner, Gleim, Goethe, Hagedorn, Haller, Heine, Herder, Herwegh, Hoffmann von Fallersleben, E. von Kleist, Klopstock, Körner, Kotzebue, Lessing, Müller, Platen, Rückert, Schiller, C. and L. Stolberg, Tieck, Uhland, Voss, Wieland). Philadelphia, 1845.

Pierce, F. E., and C. F. Schreiber. *Fiction and Fantasy of German Romance* (containing Kleist's *Käthchen von Heilbronn,* extracts from Hölderlin's *Hyperion,* prose selections from Wackenroder, poems by Hölderlin, Novalis, Uhland, Chamisso, etc.). New York, 1927.

Smith, R. M. *Types of Historical Drama* (containing Schiller's *William Tell,* Kleist's *The Prince of Homburg,* Hebbel's *Agnes Bernauer*). New York, 1928.

———. *Types of Romantic Drama* (containing Grillparzer's *Sappho*). New York, 1928.

Warner, C. D., ed. *The Library of the World's Best Literature, Ancient and Modern* (containing translations from Arndt, Beethoven,

144

GERMAN ROMANTICISM

Brentano, Bürger, Chamisso, Claudius, Eichendorff, Fichte, Freiligrath, Goethe, Grillparzer, Hauff, Hegel, Heine, Herder, Hoffmann, A. von Humboldt, Kant, Kleist, Klopstock, Körner, La Motte-Fouqué, Lessing, Mörike, Müller, Novalis, Platen, Richter, Schiller, A. and W. Schlegel, Schopenhauer, Tieck, Uhland, Wieland). New York, 1917.

Individual Authors

BODENSTEDT: Gibson, J. Y., tr. *The Songs of Mirza Schaffy.* London, 1887.

BRENTANO: Krocker, K., tr. *New Fairy Tales.* London, 1902.

FICHTE: Jones, R. F., and G. H. Turnbull, tr. *Addresses to the German Nation.* Chicago, 1922.

GRILLPARZER: Burkhard, A., tr. *The Argonauts.* Yarmouth Port, Mass., 1942.

———, tr. *A Faithful Servant of His Master.* Yarmouth Port, Mass., 1941.

———, tr. *Family Strife in Hapsburg.* Yarmouth Port, Mass., 1940.

———, tr. *The Guest-Friend.* Yarmouth Port, Mass., 1942.

———, tr. *Medea.* Yarmouth Port, Mass., 1941.

Stevens, H. H., tr. *Hero and Leander.* Yarmouth Port, Mass., 1938.

———, tr. *King Ottocar, His Rise and Fall.* Yarmouth Port, Mass., 1938.

———, tr. *Libussa.* Yarmouth Port, Mass., 1941.

———, tr. *Thou Shalt Not Lie.* Yarmouth Port, Mass., 1939.

GRIMM: Beeson, Ernest, tr. *Fairy Tales.* London, 1924.

Crane, Lucy, tr. *Household Stories.* New York, 1926.

Stallybrass, J. S., tr. *Teutonic Mythology.* London, 1882.

HAUFF: Stowell, E., tr. *Tales of the Caravan, Inn, and Palace.* Chicago, 1882.

HEINE: Armour, Margaret, *et al.,* tr. *Poetical Works.* London, 1917.

Ashton, E. B., tr.; H. Kesten, ed. *Works of Prose.* New York, 1943.

Leland, C. G., *et al.,* tr. *Works.* London, 1891 ff. 12 vols.

Rhys, Ernest, ed. *Prose and Poetry.* New York (Everyman's Library), 1935.

Salinger, H., tr. *Germany, A Winter's Tale.* New York, 1946.

Webb, P. G. L., tr. *Poems.* London, 1927.

HÖLDERLIN: Hamburger, M., tr. *Poems of Hölderlin.* London, 1943.

Prokosch, Frederic, tr. *Some Poems of Friedrich Hölderlin.* Norfolk, Conn., 1943.

HOFFMANN: Bealby, J. T., tr. *Weird Tales.* New York, 1923.

KÖRNER: Richardson, G. F., tr. *Zriny.* Contained in *The Life of Carl Theodor Körner, with Selections from His Poems, Tales, and Dramas,* written by his Father. London, 1845.

KOTZEBUE: Smith, C., tr. *The Dramatic Works.* New York, 1800. 3 vols.

LA MOTTE-FOUQUÉ: Gosse, E., tr. *Undine.* London, 1886.

NOVALIS: Dalton, J., tr. *Christianity or Europe*. London, 1844.
Henry of Ofterdingen (translator anonymous), with Tieck's "Life of Novalis." Cambridge, Mass., 1842.

RÜCKERT: Martin, E. M., tr. *The Brahman's Wisdom*. London, 1910.

SCHLEGEL, A. W.: Morrison, J. W., ed. *A Course of Lectures on Dramatic Art and Literature*. London, 1902.

SCHLEGEL, F.: Millington, E. J., tr. *The Aesthetic and Miscellaneous Works of F. von Schlegel*. London, 1889.
Robertson, J. B., tr. *The Philosophy of History*. London, 1888.

SCHLEIERMACHER: Oman, J., tr. *On Religion: Speeches to Its Cultured Despisers*. London, 1892.

SCHOPENHAUER: Edman, I., ed. *The Philosophy of Schopenhauer*. New York, 1928.
Haldane, R. B., and J. Kemp, tr. *The World as Will and Idea*. London, 1896.

TIECK: *Tales of Fairyland* (translator anonymous). London, 1879.

UHLAND: Skeat, W. W., tr. *The Songs and Ballads of Uhland*. London, 1864.

WERNER: Riley, E., tr. *The 24th of February*. London, 1844.

CHAPTER X

REALISM, 1830–1890

THE HISTORICAL BACKGROUND

Against the Holy Alliance of most European monarchs the pressing popular wish for the establishment of democratic institutions could make but little headway, and only individual princes, e.g. Karl August, the grand duke of Sachsen-Weimar, were ready to grant their peoples a constitution and parliamentary representation. The hope that the Revolution of 1830 in Paris might give the signal for the oppressed peoples of Central Europe to rise up against their autocratic rulers was not fulfilled; and even the Revolution of 1848 for a time threatened to end in failure. But many events encouraged the growing movement of political liberalism: the Latin American nations won their independence from Spain; the Greeks won their freedom from the Turks; the Italian people were fretting against the yoke of Austria; the Poles were increasingly restless under their Russian conquerors. After bitter fighting, the Austrians in 1848 at last succeeded in forcing the dismissal of Metternich; and in 1850 the king of Prussia granted his people a constitution. This partial success of democracy was, however, soon overshadowed and relegated to the background by the second great problem which occupied German history in the nineteenth century: the problem of the reunification of the German Reich.

After having absorbed Silesia and Posen in the eighteenth century, and Westphalia and the Rhineland in 1815, the growing and energetic state of Prussia was not willing to see the unity of the Empire restored under Hapsburg-Austrian leadership. Hence the delay in establishing the Second Reich: the rivalry between Berlin and Vienna and the unwillingness of many lesser German princes to accept a new overlord had to be dealt with first. Prussia had the advantage in this race:

with the rich industrial regions of the Rhineland and Silesia making her the most industrialized and progressive nation on the continent, she established, in 1834, the German *Zollverein* (Customs Union), which united all the German states except Austria into a compact commercial block. At the first German *Nationalversammlung* at Frankfurt in 1848 the *Kleindeutsche Partei,* which wished to unite Germany under Prussia's leadership, won out over the *Grossdeutsche Partei,* which insisted that Austria-Hungary-Bohemia should be included and the Hapsburgs restored to their supreme Emperorship; but the king of Prussia, fearing Austria's displeasure, did not yet consider it opportune to accept the imperial crown offered to him.

With Prince Otto von Bismarck becoming prime minister of Prussia, the plan for Prussia's unification of Germany was systematically advanced. In the Prussian-Austrian war of 1866 Austria was quickly defeated and, though no humiliating peace was imposed upon her, she had to promise not to interfere any more with Prussia's plans of unification. In the same year Prussia also absorbed Schleswig-Holstein, Hannover, and Hessia, thus further diminishing the dwindling number of independent German states. France, whose rulers had for centuries striven to destroy the unity of the First Reich, remained as a last enemy to oppose the founding of a Second Reich, which if established would automatically reduce her to the second place in western Europe; yet France, too, was defeated in the Franco-German war of 1870–1871. Now at last the Second Reich could be established, with the king of Prussia, William I of Hohenzollern, becoming Emperor of Germany and with Bismarck becoming the chancellor of the new Empire. Unification, a centuries-old dream of the German people, was now fulfilled—not, however, as the best Germans had hoped and striven for, on the foundation of political liberalism, but on the foundation of war and power politics.

GENERAL OBSERVATIONS

Many factors contributed to the gradual decline of Romanticism. Kleist had early used a realistic style and had reintroduced conciseness into his dramatic construction; Heine's bitter irony had done much to pierce the veil of romantic fantasy and to destroy the last vestiges of its colorful illusions. Hegel's philosophy, by introducing logic and necessity into man's conception of history, built up a rationalistic system in which romantic individualism and idiosyncrasy had no place. Science made tremendous progress; what in Herder's days had been mere visions now became reality and was reduced to hard, proved facts. The political struggle against Metternich and the burning social problems which followed in the wake of the Industrial Revolution compelled the intellectual leaders to cease their romantic dreams and to turn to contemporary events. The subjectivity of the preceding generation gave place to an objectivity in which man was considered from a social, scientific, and political point of view. Amidst the turmoil of the new time, which Goethe had so accurately forecast in the second part of his *Wilhelm Meister,* a poet preserved his poetic aloofness often only with difficulty; and many a poet became a mere propagandist and journalist, fighting for immediate and concrete objectives only. The first volume of Karl Marx's *Das Kapital* appeared in 1867—and with the new socialistic movement, with the increasing class struggle and the ever widening influence of science, scepticism, and materialism, a pessimistic attitude, which had been well prepared by Schopenhauer's philosophy, took hold of many of the best minds. Others preferred aggressiveness to inactive pessimism; hence so many excesses of the subsequent Age of Naturalism. A new era had begun, an era different from Goethe's sublimated Classicism and Tieck's colorful Romanticism, an era of factories and proletarians, of scientific progress and commercial imperialism. Political and literary radicalism and the shallow sentimentality and dangerous nationalism of the rising bourgeoisie were equally inimical to the concept of either classical or romantic literature.

Subdivisions of Realism

The Age of Realism can conveniently be subdivided into three groups of poets:

a. Young Germany (1830–1850). In contrast to the passive acquiescence of the late romanticists, the Young German

149

poets turned actively and bitterly against Metternich's system. Theirs was a political realism.

b. The Epigones (1830–1850). Adverse both to the vagueness of the romanticists and to the often artless pamphleteering of the Young Germans, some poets turned to greater realism than the former and to greater artistic perfection than the latter. Theirs was a classical realism, a wish to resemble Goethe and Schiller and their Greek models as much as possible. Hence their nostalgic name "The Epigones": they were the late-born ones, born a generation too late to share in the greatness of Weimar and Jena.

c. Out of these two preparatory tendencies, the greater emphasis on contemporary German affairs of the Young Germans and the finer, almost classical, stylistic efforts of the Epigones, there developed, from 1850 to 1890, the age of what we can best call Artistic Realism, which achieved its best works especially in the novel and which culminated in men like Raabe, Storm, and Fontane in Germany, Stifter in Austria, and Keller and Meyer in Switzerland.

German Culture in the Nineteenth Century

German culture continued to flourish during the nineteenth century. German music continued its Golden Age: Felix Mendelssohn-Bartholdy (1809–1847), still a romanticist, in whom resounded echoes of Ossian, Shakespeare, Goethe, and Jean Paul; Robert Schumann (1810–1856), who, like Hölderlin, ended in insanity and who set to music poems by Heine, Körner, Eichendorff, Rückert, and Chamisso; Jakob Meyerbeer (1791–1864), like Heine a self-exiled Jew in Paris, whose operas were influenced by the French romanticists; Franz Liszt (1811–1886), like Lenau half Hungarian, half German; the great Richard Wagner (1813–1883); the Austrian Anton Bruckner (1824–1896); Johannes Brahms (1833–1897), simpler, more manly and more restrained than the romanticists; Hugo Wolf (1860–1903), the song composer and interpreter of Mörike, Goethe, and Eichendorff; the immortal Viennese waltzes by Johann Strauss the Elder

(1804–1849) and the Younger (1825–1899); the operettas by Jakob Offenbach (1819–1880).

In art, Romanticism continued in Peter Cornelius (1783–1867) and in the religious painter Friedrich Overbeck (1789–1869), while Ludwig Richter (1803–1884) revealed the naive simplicity of the *Biedermeier* bourgeoisie. The same simple and humorous realism appears also in Karl Spitzweg (1808–1885). *Biedermeier,* characterized by passivity as opposed to activism, existed at the same time as Young Germany. Each of these two tendencies represented one of the two possible reactions in the disillusionment following after 1815: resistance and aggressiveness, or acceptance with recourse to simplicity, domestic joys, and a quiet life of bourgeois thrift. Hence the peaceful and homespun atmosphere of *Biedermeier* art and literature.

Among the religious thinkers David Friedrich Strauss (1808–1874) in *Das Leben Jesu* (The Life of Jesus, 1835) and Ludwig Feuerbach (1804–1872) in *Das Wesen des Christentums* (The Nature of Christianity, 1841) both rejected traditional dogma and veered towards a daringly unorthodox liberalism. Bismarck's later *Kulturkampf* against the Catholic Church, partly provoked by the declaration of the infallibility of the Pope in 1870, revealed a similarly anticlerical trend.

In philosophy Schopenhauer's pessimism and his attempt to suppress man's restless will, the source of all his misery, was soon to be supplanted by Friedrich Nietzsche with his stirring new message of vigorous activity and man's ever increasing will to perfection.

The nineteenth century was also the Golden Age of German science, among whose foremost representatives should be mentioned names like Gauss, Ohm, Schwamm, Wöhler, Mayer, Liebig, Bunsen, Kirchhoff, Koch.

Literature in Other Countries

Political, social, and religious crises caused other countries also to veer ever more towards Realism. The growing rebelliousness against the Holy Alliance accelerated this trend; the years between 1830 and 1848 were charged with smouldering discontent. France, while granting a shelter to such exiled poets as Heine, Slowacki, and Mickiewicz, fought against reactionary Bourbons and Bonapartists alike; the popular political songs of Béranger and, above all, the intransigent attitude of Victor Hugo, who preferred exile to acquiescence in the dictatorial regime of Napoleon III, best characterize French liberalism and idealism. The Czech Kollár glorified Bohemia, resuscitated Pan-Slavism, and cursed the Germanic oppressors of his fellow countrymen, while Petőfi, the greatest poet of Hungary, died in battle defending his land against the Russian allies of Metternich. Among the Italians who strove for and at last achieved the political independence of their country from Austria were Gioberti, a priest, Niccolini, a dramatist, Guerrazzi, an author of patriotic historical novels, and Silvio Pellico, himself for years a prisoner of the Austrian regime; but the greatest among the poets of the Italian *Risorgimento* was Giosuè Carducci. In America, Transcendentalism and Romanticism were rudely swept aside by the hatreds caused by the Civil War; the antislavery poems of Whittier and the mighty calls to freedom of Walt Whitman were indicative of the new trend. The fermentation caused by religious doubts and crises also added to the turmoil of the time when political and social revolutions seemed to break down the barriers of old faiths and traditions; both Renan in France and Kierkegaard, the greatest thinker of Denmark, profoundly Christian, yet utterly anticlerical, should be mentioned in this connection.

But even apart from these political and social considerations the time was ripe for a turning away from the often hazy dreaminess of Romanticism. In France, Théophile Gautier preached art for art's sake and advocated a return to more classical poetry; he was followed in that move by a whole group of so-called Parnassians. George Sand began as a romantic novelist; but her tales tended, to an ever greater degree, to emphasize social problems and the question of woman's emancipation. Honoré de Balzac was the greatest novelist of French Realism; beside him are to be named Stendhal, Gustave Flaubert, Alphonse Daudet, and, later in the century, Anatole France, Pierre Loti, and Paul Bourget. English poetry was dominated by the great names of Tennyson and the two Brownings; a distinct return to classical principles of style was noticeable in Swinburne. The rich field of the Victorian novel was best represented by Thackeray and, above all, by Charles Dickens; the latter mingled with his kindly humor an earnest striving for social reforms. Among women novelists Jane Austen, Charlotte and Emily Brontë, and George Eliot were especially noteworthy. Towards the end of the century Meredith, Stevenson, Hardy, and Galsworthy remained the great representatives of English Realism, while with the novels of Disraeli and Gissing social problems and bitterness seemed to become ever more accentuated. American post-bellum literature, under the influence of Whitman, turned away from Europe-inspired Romanticism to distinctly American, regional works, and discovered the vast possibilities of American landscapes and of American themes: Mark Twain from Missouri, Bret Harte from California, George Washington Cable from Louisiana, the poet Sidney Lanier from Georgia, Edward Eggleston from Indiana; and in the midst of this new life of Realism and Americanism only a few men like William D. Howells and Henry James persevered in striving for poise, restraint, and classicism. In Spain, the romantic dramas of Hartzenbusch and Zorrilla were followed by realistic portrayals of manners in Eguilaz and Ayala. Innate Spanish Realism emerged especially in the field of the novel: Juan Valera, Pérez Galdós, Palacio Valdés were leaders in the field of analytical, historical, and regional novels. In Poland, the influence of Walter Scott's historical novels (an influence so distinct in Germany and Switzerland and also in Hugo, Vigny, Dumas, Manzoni, Guerrazzi, Galdós, Cooper, and Hawthorne) produced real masterpieces in the works of Sienkiewicz.

Growth of Naturalism

As the social conflicts grew in bitterness and the new socialistic ideas took hold of the writers, Realism changed into Naturalism, and literature was often used as just another weapon in the battle for man's economic rights. Art for art's sake did not exist any longer; like the poets who had fought Metternich in 1830 and 1848, so also the poets of the very last decades of the nineteenth century became polemicists who wrote pamphlets, novels, and dramas in order to show the injustice of the system, the misery of the proletarians, the arrogance and gluttony of the capitalists, the inescapability of scientific facts, the brutality of life, the tragedy of sex. Thus the novels of Zola, Maupassant, and Margueritte in France, for whom Victor Hugo's *Les Misérables* had prepared the ground, and the plays of Becque and Bernstein; thus the powerful and impressive novels by Dostoevski, Tolstoi, and Gorki in Russia, which spread a veil of mysticism over human misery; thus the sensational and hard-hitting plays of Ibsen in Norway, the naturalistic dramas of Rovetta in Italy, the novels of Butler and Moore and the plays of Shaw in England; thus Jack London, Upton Sinclair, Theodore Dreiser, and their whole tribe of "muckrakers" in America. In vain did there arise against all this a *fin de siècle* group of aesthetes and symbolists: Mallarmé in France, Maeterlinck in Belgium, Wilde in England, d'Annunzio in Italy, Hofmannsthal in Austria, Stefan George in Germany —the bulk of European literature at the turn of the century was and remained grossly naturalistic.

YOUNG GERMANY

German Romanticism, including so many aristocrats (Novalis, Arnim, Kleist, Eichendorff, Lenau, de la Motte-Fouqué, Chamisso) and Catholics among its poets, had, after Metternich's assumption of power, often tended to become reactionary itself; hence now the vigorous counterdrive, the new and bitter breeze which set in with the Young Germans. Their literature centered around, and culminated in, the two revolutions of 1830 and 1848. In their aggressive attempts to reform the political and social conditions of their time, these men are reminiscent of the poets of the Storm and Stress; and in both cases the public's interest in their works vanished as soon as these disputed conditions changed or disappeared. Most Young Germans had no cohesion as a school, nor were they bound to one another through personal relationships; but they were given an apparent unity as a school by an official governmental decree in 1835 which suppressed their writings. Several Young Germans emigrated early and went to France (Heine, Börne); others, after the events of 1848, fled to Switzerland (Wagner, Herwegh) or to England (Freiligrath). In spite of the doubtful value of many of their works, the Young Germans deserve a great deal of credit for having accelerated the development of German prose style.

Typical of these poets' militantly political attitude are the many poems written in behalf of the suppressed Greeks and Poles: Wilhelm Müller's *Lieder der Griechen* (Songs of the Greeks), Chamisso's *Lord Byrons letzte Liebe* (Lord Byron's Last Love), Platen's *Polenlieder* (Polish Songs), JULIUS MOSEN's *Die letzten zehn vom vierten Regiment* (The Last Ten of the Fourth Regiment). Mosen deserves to be mentioned also because of his epic *Ahasver,* his drama *Cola Rienzi,* and his novel about the Greek revolt, *Der Kongress zu Verona* (The Congress at Verona, 1842).

Heinrich Heine (II).* Of Heine's works belonging here are to be mentioned *Atta Troll,* a romantic satire against Romanticism, often quite grotesque in its description of a bear hunt; and *Deutschland,* a witty and amusing poem with many serious undertones, often absurd in its debunking criticism of Germany, a merciless presentation of German national vices, and a violent attack against the readiness of most Teutons to display political immaturity and to acquiesce in the suppression of personal liberties.

Heine's merits as a prose writer—which are perhaps not generally appreciated—shine forth in his *Reisebilder* (Pictures of Travel), especially in his *Harzreise* (Trip to the Harz). Though they occasionally do dwell on the beauties of nature, the *Reisebilder* are mainly social satire, in which Heine reveals himself to be an unsurpassed master of German prose, an elegant *causeur,* a sarcastic cosmopolitan. Heine was the first to blend literature with journalism; he is indeed to be called the father of the German *feuilleton* style. Also in *Salon,* sketches on French art, he shows himself a fluent prose writer and a real connoisseur and fine observer of art. His *Die romantische Schule* (The Romantic School) is the earliest history of Romanticism by one who termed himself its last representative; it is an essay which mingled

* See also p. 139.

profound remarks with cheap witticisms and vile attacks (e.g., on August Wilhelm Schlegel).

Börne. Ludwig Börne, like Heine Jewish and an exile in France, is important especially for his earnest *Briefe aus Paris* (Letters from Paris, 1831 ff.). These letters are models of German prose, written by a man whose sincere democratic convictions and strong sympathy for the underprivileged classes cried out against the political reaction and the injustices in his fatherland.

Grün. Anastasius Grün (Alexander Graf von Auersperg), an Austrian, formulated his revolutionary ideas in his *Spaziergänge eines Wiener Poeten* (Promenades of a Viennese Poet, 1831).

Laube. Heinrich Laube, together with Gutzkow the leader of the Young German movement, was the editor of the *Zeitung für die elegante Welt* (Magazine for the Elegant World) and as a theater director in Vienna he was known for his support of Grillparzer. Among his prose works may be named *Das junge Europa* (Young Europe, 1833), whose call for political and moral emancipation netted him a jail sentence, and among his dramas especially his sensational *Die Karlsschüler* (The Pupils of the Karl Academy, 1847), which was prohibited in most German lands because it tried to portray the sufferings of young Schiller at the hands of a reactionary, absolutistic prince.

Karl Gutzkow (1811–1878). Gutzkow's *Wally die Zweiflerin* (Doubting Wally, 1835), a novel which took many of its cues from Schlegel's *Lucinde,* is, on the whole, of slight moral and artistic value. It is important mainly because, during this era of growing liberalism, it pleaded for the emancipation of yet another group, namely for the complete moral emancipation of women. (A finer assertion of the ideals of modern womanhood was given in a Young German version of the old *Griseldis* theme by Friedrich Halm (1834), in which the heroine for the first time refused to accept unnecessary sufferings and humiliations at the hands of a brutal husband and spoke up in behalf of dignity and decency in the relationship between man and wife.)

Zopf und Schwert (Sword and Queue, 1843) is a historical comedy of intrigue at the time of Frederick the Great.

Das Urbild des Tartüffe (The Premiere of *Tartuffe*, 1847)
is a comedy which by indirection bitterly attacks the censorship of the age of Metternich. It shows against what stupidity and pettiness the great Frenchman Molière had had to
fight before his great play against religious hypocrisy could
be performed.

Uriel Acosta (1847), a tragedy, is perhaps the finest work
of the entire Young German era. It is a plea for religious
tolerance second only to Lessing's *Nathan der Weise,* for the
play depicts the martyrdom of a young liberal Jew of Amsterdam whose great ideas did not agree with and were cruelly
condemned by the leading orthodox Jews of the city.

Die Ritter vom Geist (The Knights of the Spirit, 1850)
and *Der Zauberer von Rom* (The Sorcerer of Rome) are
Gutzkow's most ambitious works, in which he wanted to establish himself as the founder of a new type of realistic and
social novel which emphasized the milieu rather than the plot.
On account of their utter confusion in presenting the reactionary postwar conditions and the atmosphere of Papal
Rome they are, however, usually considered failures—
though it must be admitted that because of their new technique Gutzkow is often called a pioneer of the modern German novel.

Herwegh. Georg Herwegh was one of the most radical
poets of his time, a fire-eater and Metternich-hater whose
revolutionary *Gedichte eines Lebendigen* (Poems of a Live
Man, 1841) are particularly noteworthy (*Aufruf, Das Lied
vom Hasse, Reiterlied,* etc.). Because of his radicalism and
his uncompromising stubbornness he was repeatedly exiled
and spent much of his life in Switzerland and also in France.

Ferdinand Freiligrath (1810–1876). This lover of exotic
romances and translator of French, English, and American
poetry was also drawn into the political strife of his time. His
political creed is found in *Ça ira;* in his *Neuere politische
und soziale Gedichte* (New Political and Social Poems) he
urged action upon a Germany which, like Hamlet, did not
seem able to make up her mind; in his *Die Toten an die
Lebendigen* (The Dead to the Living) the men who have
died in the struggles of 1848 addressed bitter and revolutionary words to their fellow countrymen.

Patriotic Songs. A threatening war against France and the continued passivity of reactionary German governments, which refused to keep in step with the new times that were in the making, released a new wave of popular restlessness and enthusiasm which found expression in:

a. NIKOLAUS BECKER's *Rheinlied* (Rhine Song): *Sie sollen ihn nicht haben, den freien deutschen Rhein!* (They shall not have it, the free German Rhine!)—sarcastically answered by Alfred de Musset in his *Nous l'avons eu, votre Rhin allemand!* (We have had it, your German Rhine!)

b. MAX SCHNECKENBURGER's *Die Wacht am Rhein* (The Watch on the Rhine, 1840), still a favorite anthem.

c. HEINRICH HOFFMANN VON FALLERSLEBEN's *Deutschlandlied* (*Deutschland über alles,* 1841). Hoffmann von Fallersleben is also renowned for his *Unpolitische Lieder* (Nonpolitical Songs, 1840), in which he attacked the unwise attitude of the German rulers, and which resulted in his dismissal from his professorship at the University of Breslau.

THE EPIGONES

Franz Grillparzer (II).* Of Grillparzer's works belonging to this group may be mentioned the following dramas, all of them visible proofs that he really wanted "to stand where Goethe and Schiller stood."

Sappho (1818) shows the tragic life of the great Greek poetess whom immortal fame cannot make happy so long as she cannot share the love of man. Unable to win the affection of Phaon, she commits suicide. Poets, like gods and great leaders, are destined to be lonely in their greatness; both Sappho and Grillparzer had to learn that bitter truth.

Das goldene Vlies (The Golden Fleece, 1821), a trilogy consisting of *Der Gastfreund* (The Guest-Friend), *Die Argonauten,* and *Medea,* tells of a treasure, the Golden Fleece, which like the hoard of the Nibelungen brings misfortune to him who possesses it. Against the struggle for the possession of this treasure Grillparzer portrays the passionate love of the barbarian Medea for the adventurous and civilized

* See also pp. 141–143.

Greek Jason—a marriage which for many reasons was bound to end in utter tragedy. In this his most ambitious dramatic achievement, Grillparzer reiterated as in all his other plays the gospel of resignation, the dangerous futility of self-assertion and of every human attempt to overstep one's bounds.

Des Meeres und der Liebe Wellen (The Waves of the Sea and of Love, 1831), one of the great masterpieces of German literature, treats in a beautiful fashion and with a lucid and classical style the immortal story of Hero and Leander. Especially exquisite is Grillparzer's delicate gift for portraying the fine psychological changes in Hero as she grows from a priestess and a virgin to full womanhood, a mature character whose passion and grief are so great that she dies of a broken heart over the corpse of her lover.

Die Jüdin von Toledo (The Jewess of Toledo) is a tragedy which, to be sure, does not deal with a Greek theme, but which nonetheless contains a message of restraint and discipline that is alien to romantic self-indulgence. As he was inspired in his *Der Traum ein Leben* by Lope de Vega and Calderón, so Grillparzer here was inspired by an often treated Spanish tale of King Alfonso who, enflamed by the bewitching beauty of the Jewess Rahel, neglected both his cold English wife and his urgent affairs of state. This conflict in him between passion and duty, between sensualism and manly responsibility, is solved by the death of Rahel, who is murdered at the behest of the queen and the royal councilors; Alfonso realizes the gravity of his aberrations and, strengthened in his character, returns to his duties.

August Graf von Platen (1796–1835). Platen is one of the great artists of German literature, whose lyric poems, in the perfection and lucidity of their style and construction, are in sharp contrast to the soft vagueness of Romanticism. An embittered enemy of the Young Germans of the type of Heine and an ardent admirer of the Greek way of living and of Pindar, the famous lyric and patriotic poet of ancient Greece, Platen, in disgust over the political and cultural conditions in Germany, spent the last ten years of his life in Italy.

Ghaselen (1821) is a collection of lyric poems in an Oriental metric form. Even more than his friend Rückert, Platen possessed the fine intuitive gift of adapting, translating, and imitating Oriental poetry. *Die Abassiden* (1835), a short epic, gives further evidence of his great love for the Orient, especially for Mohammedan culture.

His *Sonette aus Venedig* (Sonnets from Venice, 1825) show Platen as a great admirer and skillful imitator of Italian metric forms, and his *Gedichte* (Poems, 1829) also contain Greek and Roman forms, odes, eclogues, and hymns in the manner of Pindar, Theocritus, and Horace. In the latter collection are also included such well-known ballads and romances as his *Das Grab im Busento* (The Grave in the Busento River), *Der Pilgrim von St. Just,* etc.

Die verhängnisvolle Gabel (The Fatal Fork, 1826), a satirical comedy in the manner of Aristophanes, was written against the excessive popularity of fate tragedies.

Karl Leberecht Immermann (1796–1840). Hailing from northwestern Germany and firmly rooted in the soil of his native Westphalia, this manly and vigorous author was equally opposed to the escapism and shiftlessness of the romanticists and to the artless journalism and mental shallowness of the Young Germans.

Merlin (1832), a drama suggestive of the Janus-faced Faust, because the magician Merlin was the son of Satan and of the noble virgin Candida, portrays man's own eternal conflicts and his fruitless efforts to adjust himself to the good and evil powers that rage in him.

Die Epigonen (1836), a novel which has given its name to the whole group of postclassical writers, is a work which recalls Wilhelm Meister's efforts to master the social and industrial revolution of the nineteenth century and to adjust men to the new trends in the making. Immermann's was an unhappy age of transition, an age in which old and proved standards were vanishing and in which men were becoming mere "epigones." This novel with its somewhat fantastic plot is not only a satire against these conditions; it also indicates that salvation for the new generations could come only from the soil and from the peasantry in which dwells the strength of every nation.

Münchhausen (1839) is again a novel against the artificiality, the eccentricity, and the mediocrity of Immermann's time. But it is not this negative part of the novel, of which the old liar Baron von Münchhausen forms the fitting center, that constitutes the glory of the book; rather it is the positive part, *Der Oberhof,* an interpolated peasant tale of West-phalia, which deserves the reader's full attention. *Der Ober-hof,* detached from the rest of the book, is one of the best novels in German literature, beautiful both in its love story of Lisbeth and Oswald and in its glorification of the sturdi-ness and respectability of the old and proud peasant families of northwestern Germany. With this book Immermann turned away from the romanticists and the Young Germans, as well as from the Greek themes of Grillparzer and Platen; his *Der Oberhof* is an important harbinger of the coming great age of the *Heimatliteratur.*

ARTISTIC REALISM

This vast and comprehensive chapter cannot readily be sub-divided into the customary groupings of lyric poetry, drama, and novel, because so many authors excelled in several genres of literature and for that reason do not lend themselves to treatment by types. Roughly speaking it might, however, be stated that Storm, Reuter, Raabe, Fontane, Stifter, Gotthelf, Keller, and Meyer are the great novelists of this age, Mörike and Droste-Hülshoff the outstanding lyric poets, and Hebbel the supreme representative of the drama. Besides these writers Wagner and Nietzsche occupy a lofty place apart.

Early Lyric Poetry

Annette von Droste-Hülshoff (1797–1848). Annette von Droste-Hülshoff is the greatest lyric poetess in the history of German literature, a woman of great earnestness, realistic observation, and a deep psychological insight, like Immermann a Westphalian, firmly rooted in the land and among the people of her province (*Gedichte,* 1838). In her religious poems contained in *Das geistliche Jahr* (The Spiritual Year, 1852) she revealed her ardent Catholicism, though grievous religious crises and doubts were not alien to her. Especially marked was her love for English literature (Byron).

Die Judenbuche (The Jew's Beech Tree, 1842) is her best novel, one of the finest narratives of the mid-century, a tragic

161

village tale of ignorance, crime, and racial prejudice in which the sins of the fathers are visited upon their sons.

Eduard Mörike (1804–1875). Mörike is a sensitive, meditative poet, a Swabian by birth, a clergyman by profession, a man whose poems, serene and yet at the same time melancholy, are unexcelled in the nineteenth century (*Gedichte*, 1838). His simple and warmhearted language often approaches the style of folk songs (*Früh wenn die Hähne krähen*); his verses are beautiful, melodious, sincere, subjective, and a real inspiration to song composers like Hugo Wolf. Mörike was also well acquainted with ancient Greek and Roman poets of idyls and elegies (*Klassische Anthologie*, 1840); yet he was essentially a Swabian *Heimat* poet, a lover of nature and of simple joys. After Uhland, Kerner, and Hauff, to whom he was superior as a genuine poet, he was the last great representative of the *Schwäbische Dichterschule*, the Swabian School of Poets.

Maler Nolten (Painter Nolten, 1832), a novel written under the influence of *Wilhelm Meister*, shows in its tragic and often fantastic theme and in its arbitrary construction the continuing influence of Romanticism; but in its realistic descriptions and psychological analyses it has progressed far beyond the romantic principles.

Mozart auf der Reise nach Prag (Mozart on His Journey to Prague, 1856) is a masterful and charming, though inconclusive, sketch of a single day in Mozart's life shortly before the performance of his opera *Don Giovanni*. Its allusion to the early death of the young genius casts a tragic shadow over this portrait.

The Opera and the Drama

Richard Wagner (1813–1883). The bulk of Wagner's work belongs to this period of Realism, though in his art he was really a romanticist and in his political convictions a Young German. He is one of the great geniuses of German culture, although at times misled by prejudices, a visionary who in his *Das Kunstwerk der Zukunft* (The Work of Art of the Future, 1850) dreamed of future grandiose spectacles in which all arts should be united into one harmonious and perfect form. Within such a vast frame poetry was to assume a place which, if not inferior, was at least not superior to the role assigned to music, to drama, to the fine arts. Wagner's operas are masterpieces of dramatic concentration; yet the requirements of music often prescribed a style which tends to become obscure, and a dramatic construction which tends to lack psychological depth. On account of his participation in the upheaval of 1848 and also on account of his later international fame, Wagner spent years in Switzerland (Zurich, Geneva, Lucerne), Paris, London, and St. Petersburg before he, through the help of King Ludwig II of Bavaria, was able to establish his own great theater at Bayreuth (1876). In contrast to many Young German poets whose negative criticism consisted of tearing down the existing order, Wagner, in a positive way, thought that he could do nothing better to help bring about the rebirth of a Second Reich than to glorify the greatness, the power, the romanticism, and the colorfulness that had characterized the best years of the First Reich. And, with very few exceptions, his operas indeed deal with the German Middle Ages, their legends, their mysticism, and their prestige.

Der fliegende Holländer (The Flying Dutchman, 1841) tells the romantic story of a tragic hero who is cursed to lead a restless and unhappy life until the love of a Norwegian girl, Senta, frees him from that curse. In his character and his sad fate the Flying Dutchman resembles other restless wanderers and eternal seekers of the type of Faust, Ahasuerus, or Don Juan.

Tannhäuser und der Sängerkrieg auf der Wartburg (Tannhäuser and the Minstrels' Competition on the Wartburg, 1845) presents the stirring tale of the sinner Tannhäuser, who, after his stay in the Venusberg, finds neither peace nor forgiveness among men until the love, prayers, and death of Elisabeth finally lift the curse which the Pope had hurled against him. The beautiful minstrels' competition on the Wartburg of the landgrave Hermann of Thuringia is also interesting because, besides Tannhäuser, singers like Wolfram von Eschenbach and Walther von der Vogelweide participate.

Lohengrin (1848) deals with Elsa von Brabant, a girl slandered and pursued by her enemies, and her love for Lohengrin, the son of Parzival and the king of the Grail, who in his quest for the love of woman has hastened to her defense. The failure of their marriage reminds us of the unhappiness of Schiller's Joan of Arc, of Kleist's Penthesilea, and of Grillparzer's Sappho and Libussa: the divine and the human are not destined to mingle and be happy together; the former must remain aloof and lonely in their greatness, for human happiness is not meant for them.

Der Ring des Nibelungen (1853) is a mighty tetralogy consisting of *Das Rheingold, Die Walküre* (The Valkyries), *Siegfried,* and *Die Götterdämmerung* (The Twilight of the Gods). The operas are based mostly upon the old Scandinavian mythological versions of the bitter struggle of dwarfs (Alberich), giants (Fafner), and Wotan for the possession of the accursed treasure of the Nibelungen; only the last opera represents in a modified form the story, well known from the old German version of the *Nibelungenlied,* of Brunhilde, Gutrune (i.e. Kriemhilde), Siegfried, Gunther, and Hagen.

A comparison of Wagner's famous *Tristan und Isolde* (1859) with Gottfried von Strassburg's long epic shows best how masterfully Wagner was able to condense and dramatize his libretto. In contrast to what amounts almost to an open glorification of adultery in the medieval text, Wagner emphasized the deep feeling of guilt of his hero, who finally succeeded in his various attempts to commit suicide. The music of the second act (Tristan and Isolde's Love-Death) with its passionate yearning for deliverance from the fetters of earthly existence and for a blissful submerging into death, is one of the most gripping and powerful passages of all musical literature and seems like a musical transcription of Schopenhauer's pessimistic philosophy, which deeply impressed Wagner.

Die Meistersinger (1867), Wagner's only comic opera, is a glorification of Hans Sachs and the meistersingers of Nürnberg. The love of Walter and Eva and the help Hans Sachs gives them against the disagreeable suitor and city clerk Beckmesser supply the plot of this colorful opera.

Parsifal (1882) is mainly based upon Wolfram von Eschenbach's *Parzival*—with the exception of the magician Klingsor, who, in his wicked plans against Amfortas, Parsifal, and the other knights of the Grail, assumes an important role in Wagner's opera.

Büchner. Among the forerunners of the realistic drama may be mentioned, besides Kleist, two gifted though undisciplined authors, both of whom died in early manhood: Büchner and Grabbe.

As a result of his revolutionary pamphlet *Der hessische Landbote* (Messenger to the Hessian Peasants), Georg Büchner was hunted by the political authorities until, shortly before his untimely death, he found refuge in Switzerland. Büchner's most important work is *Dantons Tod* (Danton's Death, 1835), a play depicting the last days of the great French "People's Tribune" who, in Büchner's interpretation, becomes a victim of his own recklessness rather than of the scheming of his enemies. His unfinished second tragedy *Woyzek* depicts the life of a simple soldier who, tortured by his superiors and cheated by the girl he loved, becomes a murderer and a suicide. It is the misery and forlornness of the dumb defenseless creature which Büchner wanted to emphasize in the fast and gloomy sequence of short, abrupt scenes. Equally unfinished is his tale about *Lenz,* the poet of the Storm and Stress Period to whom, no doubt, he felt attracted because of the irrationality and unstability of his own character. In his comedy *Leonce und Lena* Büchner showed that the tender and fairy-like whimsicality of the romanticists was not alien to him.

Grabbe. Deeply depressing also is the tragic ending and the utter failure of Christian Dietrich Grabbe, the author, above all, of *Don Juan und Faust* (1829), in which the legends of two restless adventurers—the seeker of the flesh and the seeker of the spirit—are fascinatingly blended. Following in the footsteps of Schiller and Kleist, Grabbe also tried his hand at great historical dramas (*Hannibal, Die Hermannsschlacht, Kaiser Friedrich Barbarossa, Heinrich VI*); the best among them is *Napoleon oder die hundert Tage* (Napoleon, or the Hundred Days, 1831).

Friedrich Hebbel (1813–1863). In spite of his early struggles against poverty and misfortune which often drove him to despair (cf. his diaries), Hebbel gradually developed into the great master of the realistic drama. The pessimism of man powerless in the face of a heartless and tremendous universe (Hegel's influence) pervaded most of his dramas; the conflicts are mostly based, not upon any individual guilt, but upon the fact that the heroic character is out of step with his time and hence crushed by it. As backgrounds for his tragedies Hebbel preferably chose an age of transition in which an old culture has not yet died and in which a new and better culture is not yet born; and between these two forces the hero or the heroine is crushed.

Judith (1840) is a powerful tragedy which deals with the well-known biblical tale of Judith's struggle against the superhuman and atavistic barbarian Holofernes. In succumbing to this man's brutal desires the fanatical Jewess who had set out to liberate her people from its worst enemy seems to have failed in her mission; but her offended womanhood rather than her racial or religious ardor finally urges her on to slay him.

Genoveva (1841) gives new shape to a legend already treated by Tieck. In this tragedy Golo, who slanders Genoveva and causes her banishment, seems to be the main character, for in him Hebbel portrayed much of his own passion, frustration, and despair.

Maria Magdalena (1844) is one of the great bourgeois tragedies of German literature, a gloomy drama of seduction and meanness which drive the girl to suicide. Perhaps even more responsible for the sufferings and death of the girl than her seducer and the petty moral standards of contemporary society is Anton, the girl's father, a stern man of the old school, whose rigid and horrifying sense of honor intensifies his daughter's despair.

Herodes und Mariamne (1848) portrays, like *Judith,* not only the battle between two cultures, but the battle of the sexes, between a man suspicious and brutal, and a woman proud and sensitive. And again the woman is victorious—not, as in *Judith,* by slaying the man, but rather by choosing death for herself, which she prefers to a continuation of her ignoble marriage. The news of the birth of Christ symbolically indicates to the defeated "victor" that his age of ruthless cruelty has come to an end.

166

Gyges und sein Ring (Gyges and His Ring, 1854) shows
in its portrayal of the chaste and sensitive Asiatic queen
Rhodope how perfect an analyzer of female psychology
Hebbel has become. Like Judith and Mariamne, Rhodope has
been deeply hurt in her womanly dignity, and suicide seems
the only way out of a humiliating dilemma in which her in-
discreetly boastful husband Kandaules and the passionate
Greek youth Gyges have placed her by means of the latter's
magic ring.

Agnes Bernauer (1855), a historical tragedy of fifteenth
century Bavaria, deals with a beautiful and bold burgher's
daughter in advance of her time who dares to marry young
Duke Albrecht and who consequently must suffer assassination for reasons of state. Particularly impressive is the end
of the drama when the old duke, in noble and sincere words,
tries to soothe his enraged son and to explain why he, the
father, has had to order Agnes' death.

Die Nibelungen (1862), a trilogy consisting of *Der ge-
hörnte Siegfried* (Horn-Skinned Siegfried), *Siegfrieds Tod*
(Siegfried's Death), and *Kriemhilds Rache* (Kriemhilde's
Revenge), is based upon the medieval German epic and shows
anew Hebbel's delicate gift of portraying the souls of women
(Brunhilde and Kriemhilde), who clash in their fierce struggle
for the love of Siegfried. After despair has driven Kriemhilde to the last atrocities of her cruel revenge, there is again
indicated the end of an age and the dawn of a new culture,
for Dietrich von Bern now takes over Etzel's rule "in the
name of Him who perished on the cross."

In his *Gedichte* (Poems, 1842) Hebbel revealed himself to
be a very great lyric poet of impressive power and depth.
It is to be regretted that the fame of his dramas overshadows
so completely the high qualities of his poems (*Gebet, Nachtlied, Abendgefühl*, etc.)

Like Schiller, Hebbel at the time of his death was working
on a drama about Demetrius. Like Schiller's, it remains a
fragment.

Otto Ludwig (1813–1865). His endless analyses of Shakespeare's plays and technique (*Shakespeare-Studien,* 1871)
discouraged rather than encouraged Ludwig in his dramatic
activities, and fortunately this discouragement at last made

him turn to the writing of prose tales, which are superior to his many dramatic attempts.

Der Erbförster (The Hereditary Forester, 1850) is a tragedy showing the unjustifiable hatred between two former friends whose animosity ends in murder and suicide. The play is famous particularly for its rustic background and its strong and earthy characters. It is unfortunate, however, that this *Heimat* drama about foresters, game wardens, and poachers is spoiled by many melodramatic elements, which are reminiscent of some of the faults of the romantic fate tragedies.

Die Makkabäer (The Maccabeans, 1854) is an imperfect tragedy full of lofty inspiration: it describes the bitter and fanatical struggle of Judas and his strong-willed and proud mother Leah against Roman imperialism. The struggle in defense of their beloved Jewish religion shows clearly that mother and son even in their most exalted moments are humble and fervent servants of Jehovah.

Die Heiterethei (1854) is an excellent village tale full of humor, warmth, and colorfulness about two young people who finally find each other in spite of their own stubbornness and their gossiping neighbors.

Zwischen Himmel und Erde (Between Heaven and Earth, 1856), Ludwig's outstanding work, is a tale of powerful conflicts and realistic descriptions in which the enmity between two brothers is analyzed. Against the background of their dangerous profession as roofers we see how Fritz hates, slanders, robs, and humiliates Apollonius, only to fall to death from the church steeple from which he had planned to plunge his brother. But even then Apollonius, inhibited by his years of suffering and by his own severely honorable character, does not dare to rejoice, to rebuild his life, or to marry his brother's widow, his own former fiancée.

The Historical Novel

Of the two great types of realistic novels which flourished for several decades, the historical novel and the regional or provincial novel, the former will be discussed first.

Hauff. Among the earliest German authors to show the significant influence of Sir Walter Scott's "Waverley Novels" is Wilhelm Hauff, whose *Lichtenstein* (1826) is a fascinating and picturesque tale of Swabia in Ulrich von Hutten's time.

Alexis. Willibald Alexis (Wilhelm Häring) wrote novels dealing with the early history of Brandenburg-Prussia: *Roland von Berlin, Der falsche Woldemar* (The Wrong Woldemar), *Der Werwolf* (The Werewolf), etc. Especially noted is his *Die Hosen des Herrn von Bredow* (The Hose of Mr. von Bredow, 1846), a humorous tale in which Alexis' interest in sixteenth century history and his love for the North German plains and heaths are intimately linked.

Gustav Freytag (1816–1895). Freytag's *Die Journalisten* (1852) is one of the few comedies of this age worth mentioning. His *Soll und Haben* (Debit and Credit, 1855) is a well-known though lengthy novel in which he praises the enterprising spirit and perseverance of sturdy North German merchants. This novel deserves full attention because, in glorifying the growing power of the German bourgeoisie and the strength and honesty of the German upper middle class, Freytag has given an interesting picture of the culture of the early nineteenth century.

Bilder aus der deutschen Vergangenheit (Pictures from the German Past, 1862) was Freytag's first contribution to historical literature. At a time when Germany was busily working towards the establishment of a Second Reich, he endeavored to collect historical and literary monuments of past centuries and to publish them with a running explanatory text.

Die Ahnen (The Ancestors, 1880), a series of eight rather mediocre historical tales, demonstrated anew that Freytag wanted to be a painter of the German people, their culture, and their history, not only in the present (as in *Soll und Haben*), but also in the past.

Joseph Viktor von Scheffel (1826–1886). *Der Trompeter von Säckingen* (The Trumpeter of Säckingen, 1854) is a mediocre yet popular epic in which a romantic love story, the historical background of seventeenth century culture, love of the Black Forest, and the wisdom of Hiddigeigei, the tomcat, are blended into an amusing picture.

Ekkehard (1857) is one of the outstanding historical novels of German literature. It paints a vivid and interesting picture of the people and the history of the districts around Lake

Constance in the tenth century. Aside from the touching love story of the duchess Hadwig of Swabia for the monk Ekkehard of the monastery of St. Gall, interest attaches especially to the figure of the monk, actually a composite portrait of three monks of the same name, two of them the original author and the later redactor of the *Waltharilied,* which is reproduced in full in modern German translation together with a fictionalized account of its origin.

As a lyrical poet Scheffel is famous above all for his *Gaudeamus* (1868), a collection of very popular German student songs of the type of *Alt Heidelberg, du feine.*

Dahn. Felix Dahn is remembered for his thrilling historical novel *Der Kampf um Rom* (The Struggle for Rome, 1876), the tale of the last desperate battles of the East Goths in Italy in the sixth century, a novel which combines instruction and entertainment in an ideal fashion. His other novels deal with the Huns (*Attila*), the Vandals (*Gelimer*), the Romans (*Bissula*), and the Migrations in general (*Felicitas*).

Conrad Ferdinand Meyer (1825–1898). Hailing from Zurich, Switzerland, Meyer is one of the greatest masters of nineteenth century realistic prose, and famous especially for his historical tales. His language is of a clarity and a smoothness which betray French influences. In her new appreciation and interpretation of Italy, particularly of the culture and history of the Italian Renaissance, Switzerland, after the Anglophile Bodmer and the Germanophile Mme. de Staël, now for the third time played the noble role of a mediator among nations. Following in the footsteps of JEAN DE SISMONDI of Geneva, author of the *Histoire des républiques italiennes du moyen âge* (1807) and the *Littérature du midi de l'Europe* (1813), and in those of the greatest Swiss historian, JAKOB BURCKHARDT of Basel, author of *Die Kultur der Renaissance* (1860), Meyer also in many of his tales discovered and described the greatness and colorfulness of the Italian Renaissance.

Among his works dealing with German history may be mentioned *Huttens letzte Tage* (Hutten's Last Days, 1871), a verse tale about the sad death of Ulrich von Hutten, one of the bravest battlers of the German sixteenth century; and

Gustav Adolfs Page (The Page of Gustavus Adolphus), a short story dealing with the Thirty Years' War.

France is depicted in *Das Amulet* (1873), a narrative about the Huguenot Wars and the terrors of the St. Bartholomew's Massacre in Paris—a background which is found also in Meyer's masterful ballad *Die Füsse im Feuer* (Feet in the Fire) ; it is depicted also in *Die Leiden eines Knaben* (The Sufferings of a Boy), a moving tale of hardships caused by the Jesuits in the days of Louis XIV.

Swiss history is represented in *Jürg Jenatsch* (1874), Meyer's longest historical novel, dealing with the repercussions of the Thirty Years' War in southeastern Switzerland and northern Italy, a grandiose and heroic tale of battles and intrigues; *Der Schuss von der Kanzel* (The Shot from the Pulpit) and *Plautus im Nonnenkloster* (Plautus in the Nunnery), the only humorous works among Meyer's short stories —the latter dealing with Humanists and nuns in the fifteenth century; *Die Richterin* (The Woman Judge), the portrait of tragic conflicts in the soul of a woman in the days of Charlemagne.

In *Der Heilige* (The Saint, 1880) Meyer selected a bold and fascinating chapter of the history of England : the adventurous life and the power of Thomas à Becket, Archbishop of Canterbury, his deadly feud with King Henry II, and his banishment and subsequent assassination.

The greatness of Italy is mirrored in *Die Hochzeit des Mönches* (The Monk's Wedding, 1884), a tale supposedly told by Dante, dealing with a delicate theme described against the background of medieval Verona; *Die Versuchung des Pescara* (The Temptation of Pescara), which uncovers, amidst the broad and picturesque canvas of the Italian Renaissance, the intrigues between Emperor, Pope, and Italian princes after the fateful battle of Pavia; *Angela Borgia,* which again gives a vivid picture of customs and manners, of crimes and immoralities, at the small Italian courts of the sixteenth century.

Meyer's poems (*Gedichte,* 1882) also show the great artist, his crystal-clear style, his condensed language, his supreme craftsmanship, and—on the negative side of the ledger—his

171

impenetrable aloofness (*Der römische Brunnen, Eingelegte Ruder, Abendwolke, Requiem,* etc.).

Wildenbruch. In the field of the historical drama attention may be called to the patriotic tragedies of Ernst von Wildenbruch: *Die Karolinger* (The Carolingians, 1881), *Väter und Söhne* (Fathers and Sons—about the War of Liberation), *Die Quitzows* (about the early Hohenzollern rulers of Brandenburg), and *Heinrich und Heinrichs Geschlecht* (Henry and Henry's Dynasty—about Canossa and the Emperor's struggles against the Popes). Wildenbruch also treated English themes in *Harold* and *Christoph Marlow*—although these dramas, like most of his works, are great and effective only in spots, but otherwise artificial and faulty in construction. Among his short stories, *Das edle Blut* (Of Noble Blood, 1892), a tale of boys in a military academy, deserves special mention. Wildenbruch was greatly favored by the rulers of the newly established Second Reich; today he occupies a far less conspicuous place in the realm of German letters.

The Regional Novel

Jeremias Gotthelf (1797–1854) (Albert Bitzius). Turning now to a brief outline of the rustic *Heimat* novels, mention may be made first of Jeremias Gotthelf, one of the great epic authors of the century, because in chronology as well as in quality he ranks among the very first authors of the regional type of literature. This clergyman turned out to be a first-class observer and moralist; never yet have the Swiss landscape, the well-to-do villages of the canton of Bern, and the virtues and faults of the sturdy peasants been described so realistically and humorously as in his works. Among his novels may be mentioned *Uli der Knecht* (Ulrich the Farm Hand, 1841), *Uli der Pächter* (Ulrich the Tenant), *Geld und Geist* (Wealth and Welfare), and *Käthi die Grossmutter* (Katie the Grandmother, 1847); they provide excellent character sketches, scenes of a warm and homespun quality, and sentences full of deep peasant wisdom. The world at large might be a turmoil of wars, greeds, and revolutions; in Gotthelf's Switzerland, however, life was stable, sober, and industrious.

Adalbert Stifter (1805–1868). Stifter is the regional poet of the Sudetenland, a man who glorified less the men, deeds, and history of his province, and more the majestic forests, blue hills, and fertile valleys of his native Bohemia. He is remembered especially for his *Der Hochwald* (The Tall Forest, 1844), a pathetic story of the time of the Thirty Years' War, and *Der Nachsommer* (The Indian Summer, 1857), a novel written in a truly classical and plastic style, a tale of duty, work, and resignation, with happiness only belatedly embellishing the Indian summer in the lives of two lovers. Stifter's landscapes are animated as in fairy tales; to describe their fragrance means more to him than to dwell on village folk and to contrast these, as Immermann and Gotthelf occasionally did by implication, with city people. Stifter's undisputed greatness lies also in his descriptions of the deep and genuine unity which exists between man and nature. All his stories are told in a calm, low voice, and even human tragedies as in *Abdias* or *Der Waldgänger* (The Walker in the Woods) are memorable rather through their intensity than through loud effectiveness. His pious devotion to God and men is expressed in the lovely Christmas tale *Der Bergkristall* (The Rock Crystal) from the collection *Bunte Steine* (Stones of Many Colors). In his last work, *Witiko,* an ambitious historical novel of the Middle Ages, the attempted and not always felicitous monumentality distracts somewhat from the beauty and simplicity of the folk scenes.

Berthold Auerbach (1812–1882). A fellow countryman of Scheffel, Auerbach is the *Heimat* poet of the Black Forest, celebrated especially for his *Schwarzwälder Dorfgeschichten* (Village Tales from the Black Forest, 1843 ff.). He was deeply influenced by Jean Paul, and like him he tried to derive poetry from, and to spread poetry among, the laboring classes of Germany. Like so many of his contemporaries he hoped for a new return to nature; for in the soil and in hard work alone could be found, he thought, a cure for modern ills. Being Jewish, Auerbach also worked for the emancipation of his race; thus his early novel *Spinoza* (1837) really belongs to the militant literature of the Young Germans rather than to regional literature.

Fritz Reuter (1810–1874). Born in Mecklenburg, Reuter deserves attention not only because of his homespun realism and his kindly humor, but because he wrote in the Low German dialect. An outstanding representative of the regionalist literature of northeastern Germany, he thus was one of the first poets to elevate the long-neglected *Plattdeutsch* to literary dignity again. For his patriotic activities he was cruelly incarcerated by the reactionary government of Prussia (1833–1840); with his academic future and his health ruined, only sturdy farm life could finally restore strength and faith in him.

Kein Hüsung (Homeless, 1858) is a bitter tale of serfdom, only recently abolished in Mecklenburg, and of two unhappy lovers whose marriage the lord of their estate had a right to forbid. The girl becomes insane and dies; but the man, after having killed the brutal squire, sets out with his child to find a better future in America.

Ut de Franzosentid (During the Time of the French Conquest, 1859), a novel reflecting incidents of Reuter's earliest youth, proved that he could overcome all bitterness and that gentle humor and understanding pervade his *Weltanschauung*. The influence of Charles Dickens is noticeable in him; the characters, in spite of the many anxieties and heartaches of the age of Napoleon, are humorous, alive, realistic, well drawn.

Ut mine Festungstid (During the Time of My Incarceration, 1860) was again strongly autobiographical, for it dealt with Reuter's unhappy years in prison; yet even here he was serene and wrote without rancor.

Ut mine Stromtid (During My Apprenticeship, 1864), finally, is a novel which deals indirectly with Reuter's experiences as a farmer. It is a book about honest people and about scoundrels, a tale in which he masterfully described the landscape, the problems, and the stubborn and industrious peasants of his beloved north German plains.

Groth. Besides the naive, straightforward, and humorous folk author Reuter, mention may be made also of Klaus Groth as a leading representative of Low German language and literature. More earnest, more sensitive, more of an artist than Reuter, he was a novelist as well as a lyric poet. His book of poems *Quickborn* (1853) made him at once famous in all Low German lands, from the Baltic Provinces as far as Holland and Flanders.

Theodor Storm (1817–1888). Like Hebbel and Groth, Storm hailed from Schleswig-Holstein. He was one of the greatest writers of the Age of Realism; the tenderness and melancholy of his own character and the strength and sturdiness of the wind-swept north German coast are strangely blended in him.

Storm's lyric poems (*Gedichte,* 1852) at first betrayed the romantic influence of Eichendorff and of the folk song; later, however, they became more realistic, manly, and restrained. Besides his beautiful love poems (*Gebet, Trost, Einer Toten*) and his descriptive or contemplative nature poems (*Herbstklage, Die Stadt, Meeresstrand, Sturmnacht, Waldweg*) may be mentioned also his vigorous political poems *Gräber an der Küste* (Graves on the Coast) written against Denmark and in favor of a German occupation of the contested provinces of Schleswig and Holstein.

Immensee (1852), one of his early tales, betrays well the lyricism, the melancholy, and the resignation prevalent among many late romanticists. Here, as elsewhere, Storm showed a nostalgic love for the past: its beauty and greatness, its joy and griefs, seemed dearer to him than those of the present age.

But even as he turned to ever greater realism he was seldom capable of humorous stories and happy endings—*Von jenseit des Meeres* (From beyond the Seas), *Die Söhne des Senators* (The Sons of the Senator), *Schweigen* (Silence), *Pole Poppenspäler;* mostly his earnest and pathetic short stories end in tragedy and death—*Auf dem Staatshof* (On the Staatshof), *Auf der Universität* (At the University), *Carsten Curator, Waldwinkel* (Forest Retreat), *Ein Bekenntnis* (A Confession), *Der Herr Etatsrat.*

Among his masterpieces are *Aquis submersus* (1875) and *Renate* (1878), both tales of unhappy love, with harsh relatives in the former and superstition in the latter destroying the hopes of two young people. Melodramatic and gruesome, worthy of an E. T. A. Hoffmann, is *Eekenhof* (1879), the tale of a bitter conflict between father and son, a tale also of potential murder and incest. An equally dark and weird background is found in *Ein Fest auf Haderslevhus* (A Festival at Haderslevhus, 1884), a story of passion, murder, adultery, and suicide. In spite of the greatness of his art and the intensity of passions evoked, Storm never tried his hand at a long novel or at a drama; he is at his best in beautifully written and psychologically well-motivated short stories.

Der Schimmelreiter (The Rider of the White Horse, 1888) is Storm's best work, an excellent *Heimat* tale about the hardened folk along the Frisian coast and their eternal struggle against the ravages of the sea. In this story of the dyke-grave Hauke Haien, too, appear pathos and tragedy, tenderness and powerful nature descriptions, as the hero battles valiantly against the enmity of the elements and the superstitions of the people; yet he loses in spite of all his efforts.

Gottfried Keller (1819–1890). Keller, the greatest literary figure of German-speaking Switzerland, is beloved by his compatriots not only because of his *Heimat* tales, his warm and kindly poems, his gentle humor, and his popular inspiration, but also because he, today more than ever, is the best representative of Swiss democracy, of tolerance, liberalism, and moderation. Like Meyer, Keller hailed from Zurich; though the former may be a more impeccable artist, the latter has more generally captured the hearts of his people. Like Meyer also, Keller found himself and his literary calling relatively late in his life; after years of trying to become a painter (Munich, 1840 ff.), then a dramatist (Heidelberg and Berlin, 1848 ff.), he finally managed to earn a livelihood by becoming the chief clerk of the canton of Zurich (1861–1876).

Der grüne Heinrich (Green Henry, 1855 and 1880) is an apprenticeship novel, an autobiographical tale strongly influenced by Goethe, Jean Paul, and Mörike. It dwells on the hero's youth, his cruel expulsion from school, his hope of becoming an artist, his trip to Germany, his failures, doubts, and gropings, his return to Switzerland, and the death of his mother. Like Wilhelm Meister, he endeavors to find a philosophy and a purpose in life; as is true of most Swiss authors, responsible citizenship gradually comes to mean more to Keller than artistic idiosyncrasies.

Die Leute von Seldwyla (The People of Seldwyla, 1856 and 1873) is a collection of short stories which contains some of Keller's finest masterpieces. Seldwyla is an imaginary Swiss town populated by gay and carefree, also lazy and shiftless, people who love to argue, to talk politics, and to enjoy themselves. Among the gems of this collection may be mentioned *Frau Regel Amrain und ihr Jüngster* (Frau Regula Amrain and Her Youngest Son), telling of a resolutely patriotic and democratic woman; *Die drei gerechten Kammacher* (Three Decent Comb Makers), a brilliant satire on the meanness, greed, and hypocrisy of the petty bourgeoisie; *Romeo und Julia auf dem Dorfe* (A Village Romeo and Juliet), probably the finest rustic novel in German literature, deeply tragic, written in a wonderfully plastic style; *Kleider machen Leute* (Clothes Make the Man), the humorous story of a tailor who is mistaken for and feted as a count.

Die Sieben Legenden (The Seven Legends, 1872) shows well Keller's warmhearted, simple, and tolerant attitude towards religion. Especially unforgettable is *Die Jungfrau und die Nonne* (The Virgin and the Nun), which implies that God wants a woman to become a wife and mother rather than a nun. Exquisite also is *Das Tanzlegendchen* (The Dance Legend) ; even the risqué tale of *Der schlimm-heilige Vitalis* (The Wicked and Saintly Vitalis) serves a good religious purpose.

Die Zürcher Novellen (Short Stories of Zurich, 1878) contain mostly historical and patriotic short stories such as *Hadlaub*, which gives an account of the life of one of the last minnesingers in medieval Switzerland and of the origin of his famous anthology of minnesongs, sponsored by the Manesse family, the *Minneliederhandschrift*, which is preserved in Heidelberg; *Ursula*, a colorful picture of the religious upheavals of the Reformation; *Der Landvogt von Greifensee* (The Governor of Greifensee), a portrait of the *ancien régime* in eighteenth century Switzerland, in the days of Gessner and Bodmer; *Das Fähnlein der sieben Aufrechten* (The Banner of the Upright Seven), a humorous patriotic tale of the political confusion around 1848 and of old men who stay young and vigorous in their hearts.

Das Sinngedicht (1881), a collection of tales within a framework of the cyclical type, deals with a young man who sets out to find a wife and who, after having found his ideal girl, elucidates concerning his expectations by telling sundry stories about women and love; whereupon the girl, who has her own ideas about men and marriage, tells other stories to support her viewpoint. After having reached his political and religious convictions Keller expresses in this book his serene and kindly philosophy of the enjoyment of life and love.

In *Martin Salander* (1886) Keller attempted to crusade against the shallowness and the unsatisfactory political conditions of the modern age and to give expression to his faith in the stability and soundness of the Swiss democracy; but death interrupted his plans, and the work remains a fragment.

In his collected poems (*Gesammelte Gedichte*, 1883) Keller once more revealed his love of nature (*Waldlieder, Sommernacht*), his compassion (*Aroleid, Der Taugenichts, Die kleine Passion*), his optimistic philosophy of life (*Frühlingsglaube, Abendlied*), his gentle humor (*Der Narr des Grafen von Zimmern*), and his patriotic love of the Swiss democratic way of life (*Eidgenossenschaft, Gegenüber, An das Vaterland*). His style is simple, sincere, colorful, and realistic; he belongs among the most beloved writers of the German language and the best representatives of poetic Realism.

Rosegger. Among the foremost *Heimat* novelists of Austria is Peter Rosegger, celebrated for his *Geschichten aus Steiermark* (Stories from Styria, 1871), *Die Schriften des Waldschulmeisters* (The Writings of the Forest Schoolmaster, 1875), and his autobiographical *Heidepeters Gabriel*. His didactic tendency to bemoan the passing away of sound peasant life and the spreading of the modern life of industrialization, misery, and shallowness appears in *Jakob der letzte* (Jacob the Last, 1888), *Das ewige Licht* (The Eternal Light), and *Idyllen einer untergehenden Welt* (Idyls of a Vanishing World, 1899).

Ludwig Anzengruber (1839–1889). In the field of the *Heimat* drama the Austrian Anzengruber occupies a very important place. *Der Pfarrer von Kirchfeld* (The Priest of Kirchfeld, 1870) aims to be more than a drama of conflicts among villagers in the Austrian Alps; it is also a condemnation of the narrow-minded dogmatism of the Catholic Church which forces the termination of the career of a fine young priest. Perjury, greed, insanity, yet ultimate reconciliation between two conflicting families in the second generation are portrayed in the powerful tragedy *Der Meineidbauer* (The

Farmer Forsworn, 1871). Depressing and pathetic is also *Das vierte Gebot* (The Fourth Commandment, 1878), a drama not about the peasantry, but about moral corruption in Vienna.

But Anzengruber could also be picturesque and amusing in his peasant comedies—e.g. in *Die Kreuzelschreiber* (The Cross Makers, 1872), a play which, besides making a sly dig at presumptuous priests, takes up and modernizes the risqué and humorous old theme of Aristophanes' *Lysistrata;* or in *Der Doppelselbstmord* (The Double Suicide, 1875), the amusing tale of a new village Romeo and Juliet, with a gay and sensual ending.

Best known among Anzengruber's simple and impressive Austrian peasant novels are *Der Schandfleck* (The Stain, 1876) and *Der Sternsteinhof* (Sternstein Farm, 1885).

Other Novelists

Wilhelm Raabe (1831–1910). After the discussion, first of the historical, and second of the regional, novel, attention is now directed to a group of miscellaneous novelists during the Age of Realism. Foremost among them is Raabe, a quiet and retiring man, often called the German Charles Dickens, a writer whose humor mitigates the deep pessimism of his character. Like Storm, Raabe felt uncertain about the materialism and noisiness of the new age; and the energetic unification of the Second Reich tended only to increase his doubts and his nostalgic love of the past.

Among Raabe's early works may be mentioned *Nach dem grossen Kriege* (After the Great War, 1861), a tale about the general disillusionment that set in after the defeat of Napoleon and the return of the reactionary local governments; and *Unseres Herrgotts Kanzlei* (The Chancellory of Our Lord, 1862), likewise a historical novel, a glorification of the militant Lutheran city of Magdeburg and its stanch defense during the religious troubles of the sixteenth century.

Most distinguished among Raabe's works are three novels which really can be said to form a trilogy and in which the author's pessimism becomes ever more marked: *Der Hungerpastor* (1864), the tale of man's hunger for bread, success, knowledge, or love, a depressing story of small people and of insurmountable obstacles that are in their way, a novel which, at least in the case of the pastor, ends in a limited happiness; *Abu Telfan* (1868), a book about a man who after long captivity in Africa returns to Germany, yet who is so disillusioned about men and morals in greedy Europe that he prefers to go back to the Negroes where at least he will not lose the integrity of his character; and *Der Schüdderump* (The Burial Cart, 1870), a tale full of resignation in which the vanity of man's endeavors is emphasized, a novel in which even originally strong and noble heroines like Tonie Häussler can be ruined through the lies and meanness of modern life.

Yet this fundamentally pessimistic philosophy Raabe managed to sublimate, injecting courage, kindliness, and humor into his tales. This is seen particularly in his last novels such as *Alte Nester* (Old Nests, 1880), *Stopfkuchen* (Cake Eater, 1891), and *Die Akten des Vogelsangs* (The Minutes of Vogelsang Alley, 1895)—books of poetic realism and of honest efforts to make life worth while.

Friedrich Spielhagen (1829–1911). Like Gustav Freytag in his *Soll und Haben,* Spielhagen in his novels sought to mirror German culture and German problems of his time—a task which he fulfilled in an honest though somewhat prosaic fashion. Among his works may be named *In Reih und Glied* (In Rank and File, 1867), *Hammer und Amboss* (Hammer and Anvil, 1869), and *Was will werden?* (What Shall Come? 1886); they all deal with social problems, the development from liberalism to socialism, and the dangers of materialism and nihilism, as well as of reactionary Bismarckian feudalism.

Women Novelists. Among women novelists of the age, LUISE VON FRANÇOIS and MARIE VON EBNER-ESCHENBACH are particularly noteworthy. The former excelled in her historical tale about the Napoleonic Wars, *Die letzte Reckenburgerin* (The Last of the Reckenburgs, 1871); the latter is famous for her novels about Austria, its people, and its aristocrats—as evidenced in *Das Gemeindekind* (The Child of the Parish, 1887) and *Unversühnbar* (Beyond Atonement, 1890).

Exotic Novelists. Whereas Goethe, Auerbach, Reuter, Raabe, and others had only occasionally dealt with America, there now appeared authors who specialized in exotic novels about foreign lands and adventures. Among them we can name:

a. CHARLES SEALSFIELD (Karl Postl), known especially for his *Kajütenbuch* (Cabin Log, 1842) which deals mainly with Texas.

b. FRIEDRICH GERSTACKER, a writer who under the influence of James Fenimore Cooper produced novels such as *Die Flusspiraten des Mississippi* (The River Pirates on the Mississippi, 1848), *Tahiti, Die beiden Sträflinge* (The Two Convicts—about Australia), *Gold* (about California), *In Mexiko* (1871), etc. Best known among his German tales is *Germelshausen,* the weird story of an enchanted village.

c. By far the most popular author of tales of travels and adventures even among present-day German youth is KARL MAY, author of *Winnetou, Am Rio Plata, Im Lande des Mahdi, Der Schatz im Silbersee* (The Treasure in the Silver Lake), *Die Sklavenkarawane* (The Caravan of Slaves), etc. (1892 ff.).

Paul Heyse (1830–1914). In opposition to some undesirable effects of the Young German type of literature there was formed the *Münchener Dichterkreis* (1852–1883), a circle of artists in Munich who, like the preceding Epigones, wished to preserve the classical and the romantic values of the Golden Age of German literature.

Heyse was one of the foremost representatives of this group; in his novels and poems he strove to enhance the art and dignity of literature. Among his best short stories may be named *Das Mädchen von Treppi* (The Girl from Treppi), *Die Blinden, Andrea Delfin, L'Arrabiata* (1855)—the latter betraying his great love for the classical atmosphere of Italy.

His best novel is *Die Kinder der Welt* (The Children of the World, 1873), a book which on account of its artificiality and its frequently erotic atmosphere was condemned in various quarters in spite of its polished but often shallow craftsmanship and its affirmative philosophy of life.

Among Heyse's tragedies may be mentioned *Hadrian, Alcibiades,* and *Graf Königsmark,* all of which illustrate both his immaculate artistic will and his increasingly noticeable trend towards superrefinement and decadence.

Theodor Fontane (1819–1898). After having spent several years as a newspaper reporter in England, Fontane, upon his return to Berlin, became one of the great ballad writers of the nineteenth century, a poet in whom the influence of the English and Scottish popular ballads is clearly visible (*Balladen,* 1861). Ballads dealing with English themes or with German patriotic events are particularly noteworthy: *Archibald Douglas, Hastingsfeld, Barbara Allen, Die Brücke am Tay, John Maynard, Schloss Eger, Der alte Dessauer, Seydlitz.*

As a prose writer Fontane distinguished himself through his *Wanderungen durch die Mark Brandenburg* (Wanderings through the Province of Brandenburg, 1862). Becoming a novelist very late in life, he began with *Vor dem Sturm* (Before the Storm, 1878), a patriotic tale about the days before the downfall of Napoleon, a novel which was somewhat influenced by the technique and humor of Willibald Alexis.

But the apex of his literary career—and, indeed, one of the highest levels of German novelistic literature—Fontane reached with his later so-called Berlin novels: *L'Adultera* (1882), *Cecile, Irrungen und Wirrungen* (Trials and Tribulations), *Stine, Effi Briest* (1895), in which the old gentleman in a calm and artistic, yet sympathetic, fashion deals with matrimonial problems, lovers, and the hardships of the strict and often cruel caste system of the German aristocracy. *Effi Briest* in particular is one of the great masterpieces of the European psychological novel, the story of a German Madame Bovary, of a stern Prussian official's young wife who falls in love with a handsome, carefree lieutenant. The boredom of the little provincial town, the loneliness of the vivacious young woman, and her hesitant venturing into the dangerous affair are described by a great artist whose warm heart can be felt underneath the detached attitude of an accomplished storyteller and whose masterly craft can build an exciting story out of trivial, everyday events. A gay satire against the pretentious and shallow rich bourgeois of the new Empire is found in *Frau Jenny Treibel* (1892), while in *Die Poggenpuhls* (1896) and in *Der Stechlin* (1899) Fontane mourned the passing away of doughty old aristocratic leaders—though the thought of the new world and the new ideals in the making did not fill him with any mis-givings. *Der Stechlin* especially shows Fontane at his very best: the perfect elegance of a great master, the fine and sensitive study of detail, the beautiful description of the landscape around Berlin, and, above all, the unforgettable characters drawn by someone who has reached the wisdom of the smiling sage, deeply attached to what was good in the old days and tolerantly open to the ideas of a new age. Fon-tane's novels can be compared to the very best works which psychological Realism has produced in Europe.

Late Lyric Poetry

Emmanuel Geibel (1815–1884). In turning from the drama and the novel to the late lyric poets of the Age of Realism, attention must be directed to Emmanuel Geibel, the head of the Munich School of poets, and like Heyse, and to an even greater extent than he, a shallow stylist rather than a deep and original thinker. His sweet and sentimental poems and his patriotic ballads were very popular; yet they illus-trate the gradual literary decline in Germany proper around 1870: *Zwölf Sonette für Schleswig-Holstein, Hoffnung* (Hope), *Der Mai ist gekommen* (May Has Come), *Des Deutschritters Ave* (The Ave Maria of the Teutonic Knight), *Der Tod des Tiberius* (The Death of Tiberius), etc. Influ-enced by the contemporary poets of the French *Parnasse,* Geibel emphasized the aesthetic aspects of literature and was thus bitterly opposed to the growing school of German Nat-uralism. In 1862 he published *Das Münchener Dichterbuch* (The Munich Book of Poetry), an anthology of the Munich poets—to which Heyse in 1882 then added a second anthol-ogy, *Das neue Münchener Dichterbuch.*

Detlev von Liliencron (1844–1909). Like Storm, Lilien-cron hailed from Schleswig-Holstein; together with Dehmel he was the outstanding lyric poet of the Second Reich. Though a typical aristocrat and as such opposed to the social-ism of the new age, Liliencron had a kindly and generous understanding for the working class and for the problems of the proletarians; indeed, he as well as Fontane approved of all but the worst excesses of the new naturalistic litera-ture. As a former officer and a manly and vigorous character

Liliencron was, however, opposed to false romanticism and to the Munich School. The wars of 1866 and 1870–1871, in which he had participated, were reflected not only in his vivacious poems (*Gesammelte Gedichte*—Collected Poems, 1897) but also in his prose tales (*Kriegsnovellen*—War Stories, 1895). Like Fontane, so also Liliencron was at his best in his ballads; they are vigorous, clear, and fluent. Liliencron's type of poetic Realism is often called Impressionism, of which school he is one of the best early representatives: rather than dwell too much on the objects seen, as the naturalists did, he described the effects or impressions which a given landscape or situation exerted upon the senses of the observing poet. His poems thus became more subjective than the naturalistic poems, yet they avoided the excessive subjectivity of the later school of Expressionism (*Krieg und Friede, König Ragnar Lodbrog, Die nächtliche Trauung, Sommernacht, Märztag, Der Maibaum, Der Viererzug*).

Ballad Writers. Among the minor ballad writers of the age may be mentioned three authors who were all more or less influenced by the English ballad literature:

a. MORITZ GRAF VON STRACHWITZ, whose *Gedichte* (Poems), appearing as early as 1850, were read and imitated by Fontane, Geibel, and Liliencron.

b. BÖRRIES VON MÜNCHHAUSEN, author of *Balladen und ritterliche Lieder* (Ballads and Knightly Songs, 1909).

c. FERDINAND AVENARIUS, enemy of the naturalists and author of a *Balladenbuch* (Book of Ballads, 1913).

Humor

Busch. As a figure apart, mention must be made of the most popular of all German humorists, Wilhelm Busch, a contributor to a well-known humorous periodical, *Die fliegenden Blätter*. Busch combined an easy, homespun, and, in a way, immortal wit with a great and hilarious skill in sketching and drawing. His best known work, *Max und Moritz,* appeared as early as 1865; later satires (e.g. *Die Fromme Helene*—Pious Helen, *Der Heilige Antonius*—Saintly Anthony) began to show an anticlerical trend. The interpretations of Wilhelm Busch will always be sure of a warm niche in the hearts of the German people.

Philosophy

Friedrich Nietzsche (1844–1900). Nietzsche is one of the great figures in modern German literature and philosophy, and his influence has been increasing ever since his death. In his love for and interpretation of Greece he greatly resembled Hölderlin; the noble dreams of both men about better and prouder generations to come exhausted their frail bodies, and both spent the last years of their sickly and unhappy lives in insanity. Among Nietzsche's friends may be mentioned the great Renaissance scholar Jakob Burckhardt, whose colleague he was at the University of Basel, and especially Richard Wagner, whose enemy he later became; and among his great models was Goethe, for, like the patriarch of Weimar, Nietzsche was a teacher of men, and like Faust a sworn enemy of complacent self-satisfaction, an ardent seeker of ever greater perfection and personal freedom. Freedom to him was a conquest of the self which could be achieved only with great difficulty. Man can elevate himself above nature only if he is strong enough to sublimate his instincts and conflicts gradually and heroically. What Schiller had called "a beautiful soul" was an aesthetic process of self-perfection, a state of serene harmony between body and soul; what Nietzsche now called "a superman" represented a much more vigorous and titanic attempt to achieve a similar ideal, for Nietzsche believed that man's will to quality could be steeled only in a constant mortal struggle against all forms of mediocrity both within us and about us.

Die Geburt der Tragödie aus dem Geiste der Musik (The Birth of Tragedy out of the Spirit of Music, 1872), written while Nietzsche was professor of classical philology in Switzerland, shows his preference for the Dionysian, ecstatic, and ardent type of life and literature as opposed to the almost unnaturally calm classicism of the Apollonian ideal. Deeply influenced by Schopenhauer's philosophy, he emphasized the fundamental pessimism and despair of the Greeks, who, however, in spite of or because of their conflicts, through sheer will power and sublimation, nevertheless managed to create truly great and pulsating literature.

At that time Richard Wagner appeared to him the greatest
renewer of the ancient Dionysian dramas, because his works,
in spite of the tragedy of life hidden in them, are proud
and heroic affirmations of that life.

In his famous philosophical writings such as *Unzeit-
gemässe Betrachtungen* (Thoughts out of Season, 1873),
Menschliches Allzumenschliches (Human, All Too Human,
1878), *Also sprach Zarathustra* (Thus Spake Zarathustra,
1883), and *Jenseits von Gut und Böse* (Beyond Good and
Evil, 1886) Nietzsche increasingly turned away from Schopenhauer, whose antipode he finally became. His was a
philosophy of vigorous activity, of Promethean pride and
defiance; his was the conviction that man in spite of all sufferings should be an emphatic and ruthless affirmer of life.
With Darwin he believed in the survival only of the fittest;
the battle of life could be won only by strong and heroic
men who dared to assert their high personality and who
towered far above the ordinary crowd of weak mortals. Having achieved this superhuman sublimation, such men might
well be permitted to become a law unto themselves, for
they surely stand beyond the petty moral concepts of good
and evil. Such men need not necessarily be "blond beasts";
rather they are *Gesamtmenschen* (as opposed to the ordinary *Teilmenschen*), universal geniuses who represent the
maximum of purity, profundity, and self-mastery. They
scorn Christianity (of which Wagner's *Parsifal* seemed so
foolishly fond), false humanitarianism, and modern socialism, because these have been merely invented by weaklings
for the benefit of weaklings. No such sentimentalities and
dogmas should restrain the genuinely strong man who is
born to rule and to exert his faculties of leadership to the
utmost. In his fervent idealism and optimism about the
steady progress of man towards greater perfection, Nietzsche
indeed proclaimed that such titans would be as far above
present-day men as men now are above apes. False religions
which teach us humility, factories which degrade our bodies,
socialism which claims that all men are equal, Victorian
morality which kills our vitality, the nefarious theories of
determinism which undermine man's will to live and fight—
they all have brought mankind to the brink of mental and

physical degeneration. Hence Nietzsche's morning-call to man's vitality and powers to reassert himself, to reject all mediocrity, to soar ever higher in ambition, achievement, and unconquerable strength, to revaluate all values in our age of base materialism, and to restore them to their former greatness. Nietzsche thus became the great rebel who dared to defy the conventions of Europe, who opposed titanism to Christianity, aristocratic individualism to organized society, and who utterly rejected mediocrity, especially that of the bourgeois way of life. Schopenhauer's pessimism, though still lingering on, was greatly modified, for it was supplanted by a vigor which resembled optimism and which asserted itself in spite of all struggles. Such activity and leadership is enough of inspiration and comfort to really great men; they do not need any other religion to bolster them up. Nietzsche's will to quality can not only be seen in his stern demand for a strict and everlasting education of the ego; it can be discerned also in the superb style of his books. They are clearcut and sonorous in expression, impeccable and lucid in style. His last works consist mostly of profound and carefully polished aphorisms which are phrased with a minimum of words and a maximum of power.

In his *Gedichte und Sprüche* (Poems and Aphorisms) Nietzsche proved to be a great lyric poet as well as a forceful thinker. Here, too, he dreamed of a human greatness that is free from all bourgeois pettiness and democratic mediocrity; here, too, he emphasized the loneliness of those who, in the eternal progress towards a higher life, have hurried ahead of their contemporaries (*Nachtlied, Vor Sonnenaufgang, Dem unbekannten Gott, Vereinsamt, Ecce homo*). He is one of the great masters of the German language, at times sublime, sharply opposed to the shallowness and carelessness of so many modern poet-journalists.

Nietzsche's *Briefe an Mutter und Schwester* (Letters to Mother and Sister, 1909) are deeply touching documents of a man who, paradoxically enough, prophesied and glorified the coming of a new age and of a new race of strong and proud human beings while his own body was progressively weakened by illness and his own intellect overcast by the shadows of insanity that were descending on him.

HISTORY OF GERMAN LITERATURE

TRANSLATIONS

GENERAL COLLECTIONS

Baskerville, A. *The Poetry of Germany* (containing poems by Arndt, Arnim, Brentano, Bürger, Chamisso, Droste-Hülshoff, Eichendorff, Freiligrath, Geibel, Gellert, Goethe, Grün, Heine, Herder, Herwegh, Hoffmann von Fallersleben, Hölderlin, Immermann, Kleist, Klopstock, Körner, Lenau, Lessing, Mörike, Mosen, Müller, Novalis, Rückert, Schiller, the Schlegel brothers, Schubart, Simrock, Stolberg, Tieck, Uhland, Voss, Wieland). Philadelphia, 1886.

D'Anvers, N. *English Echoes of German Song* (containing poems by Bodenstedt, Eichendorff, Freiligrath, Geibel, Grün, Hammer, Hebbel, Heine, Herwegh, Lenau, Rückert, Storm, Uhland). London, 1877.

Francke, Kuno, editor-in-chief. *The German Classics of the Nineteenth and Twentieth Centuries.* Albany, 1913 ff. 20 vols.

Vol. VII: Immermann: *Der Oberhof.*
Gutzkow: *Sword and Queue.*
Grün: From *Promenades of a Viennese Poet.*
Mörike: Poems, *Mozart's Journey from Vienna to Prague.*
Droste-Hülshoff: Poems, *The Jew's Beech Tree.*
Lenau, Freiligrath, Strachwitz, Herwegh, Geibel: Poems.

Vol. VIII: Auerbach: *Little Barefoot.*
Gotthelf: *Uli the Farmhand.*
Reuter: From *Ut mine Stromtid.*
Stifter: *Rock Crystal.*
Riehl: *Field and Forest,* and Other Tales.

Vol. IX: Hebbel: *Maria Magdalena, Siegfried's Death, Anna, On Theodor Körner and Heinrich von Kleist,* Review of L. Wienburg's *The Dramatists of the Present Day,* Review of Heinrich von Kleist's Play *The Prince of Homburg, Recollections of My Childhood,* Extracts from *The Journal.*
Ludwig: *The Hereditary Forester, Between Heaven and Earth.*

Vol. X: Bismarck, Moltke, Lassalle: Letters, Speeches, Essays.

Vol. XI: Spielhagen: *Storm Flood.*
Storm: *The Rider of the White Horse,* Poems.
Raabe: *The Hunger Pastor.*

Vol. XII: Freytag: *The Journalists, Doctor Luther, Frederick the Great.*
Fontane: *Effi Briest,* From *My Childhood Days,* Poems.

Vol. XIII: Heyse: *Blind, L'Arrabiata, Nino and Maso, The Spell of Rothenburg.*
Scheffel: *Ekkehard, In the Rhaetian Alps,* Poems.
Ebner-Eschenbach: *The District Doctor, Krambambuli,* Aphorisms.
Seidel: *Leberecht Hühnchen.*

Vol. XIV: Keller: *A Village Romeo and Juliet, The Governor of Greifensee, The Company of the Upright Seven, Ursula,* Poems.
Meyer: *Plautus in the Convent, The Monk's Marriage,* Poems.
Widmann: Poems.

Vol. XV: Schopenhauer: *The World as Will and Idea, Parerga and Paralipomena.*
Wagner: *Art and Revolution, Man and Art in General, The Art of Tone, The Art of Sculpture, Outlines of the Art Work of the*

188

Future, Opera and the Nature of Music, A Communication to My Friends, Beethoven, Speech at Weber's Grave.

Nietzsche: *Thus Spake Zarathustra, The Use and Abuse of History,* Aphorisms, Poems.

Emperor William II: Speeches.

Vol. XVI: Wilbrandt: *The Master of Palmyra.*

Anzengruber: *The Farmer Forsworn.*

Rosegger: *The Forest Schoolmaster,* From *Forest Home.*

Vol. XVII: Wildenbruch: *King Henry, Noble Blood.*

Vol. XVIII: Liliencron, Münchhausen: Poems.

Hedley, F. H. *Masterpieces of German Poetry* (containing poems by Bodenstedt, Freiligrath, Geibel, Goethe, Grillparzer, Grün, Halm, Heine, Herwegh, Lenau, Scheffel, Schiller, Uhland). London, 1876.

Knortz, K. *Representative German Poems, Ballad and Lyrical* (containing poems by Arndt, Bodenstedt, Brentano, Bürger, Chamisso, Claudius, Dahn, Eichendorff, Freiligrath, Geibel, Gleim, Goethe, Grün, Haller, Halm, Hauff, Hebbel, Hebel, Heine, Herder, Herwegh, Hölderlin, Körner, Lenau, Mörike, Mosen, Müller, Opitz, Platen, Rückert, Scheffel, Schiller, Schneckenburger, Schubart, Simrock, Stolberg, Strachwitz, Tieck, Uhland, Voss, Walther von der Vogelweide, Wieland). New York, 1885.

Melville, Lewis, and Reginald Hargreaves. *Great German Short Stories* (containing *Old Hildebrand,* Gottfried's *Tristan, Owleglass, Dr. Faustus,* Kleist's *The Marquise of O.,* Bürger-Raspe's *Münchhausen,* Goethe's *A Fairy Tale,* Tieck's *Auburn Egbert,* Chamisso's *Peter Schlemihl,* Hauff's *The Cold Heart,* Gerstäcker's *Germelshausen,* Storm's *Immensee,* Keller's *The Naughty Saint Vitalis,* Heyse's *L'Arrabiata;* and minor tales by Schiller, Hoffmann, La Motte-Fouqué, Arnim, the Grimm brothers, Körner, Heine, Sudermann). London, 1929.

Northcliffe, L., and S. McClure, *The World's Greatest Books* (containing selections from Auerbach, Chamisso, Goethe, Hegel, Heine, Humboldt, Jean Paul, Kant, Klopstock, Lavater, Lessing, Luther, Marx, Mommsen, Ranke, Rosegger, Schiller, Schopenhauer, Wagner). New York, 1910. 20 vols.

Individual Authors

ANZENGRUBER: Sigmann, A., tr. *The Fourth Commandment.* Pittsburgh, 1912.

AUERBACH: Taylor, M., tr. *Village Tales from the Black Forest.* London, 1846.

BÜCHNER: Dunlop, G., tr. *Plays.* New York, 1927.

BURCKHARDT: Middlemore, S., tr. *The Civilization of the Renaissance in Italy.* Oxford, 1945.

BUSCH: Brooks, C. T., tr. *Max and Maurice.* New York, 1899.

MacLush, J., tr. *Naughty Jemima* (Die fromme Helene). London, 1872.

DAHN: *Attila the Hun* (translator anonymous). New York, 1891.

Safford, M. J., tr. *Bissula.* Chicago, 1902.

———, tr. *Gelimer.* Chicago, 1903.

Wolffsohn, L., tr. *A Struggle for Rome.* London, 1878.

EBNER–ESCHENBACH: Robinson, M. A., tr. *Beyond Atonement.* New York, 1892.
———, tr. *The Child of the Parish.* New York, 1893.

FONTANE: Royce, K., tr. *Trials and Tribulations.* New York (Harvard Classics), 1917.

FRANÇOIS: Percival, J. M., tr. *The Last von Reckenburg.* Boston, 1887.

FREYTAG: Malcolm, Mrs., tr. *Debit and Credit.* New York, 1882.
———, tr. *Pictures of German Life.* London, 1862–63.

GEIBEL: Stowe, H., adaptor. *Poems.* London, 1879.

GERSTÄCKER: *Each for Himself* (Gold) (translator anonymous). London, 1893.
The Pirates of the Mississippi (translator anonymous). London, 1878.
The Two Convicts (translator anonymous). London, 1887.

GOTTHELF: Smith, L. G., tr. *Story of an Alpine Valley, or Katie the Grandmother.* London, 1896.
Wealth and Welfare (translator anonymous). New York, 1868.

GRILLPARZER: See references on p. 145.

GUTZKOW: Spicer, H., tr. *Uriel Acosta.* London, 1885.

HALM: Anstruther, Sir R. A., tr. *Griselda.* London, 1840.

HAUFF: Craig, R. J., tr. *Marie of Lichtenstein, A Tale of Love and War.* London, 1897.

HEBBEL: Goldberger, H., tr. *The Niebelungs.* London, 1903.
Allen, L. H., and B. Fairley, tr. *Three Plays* (Gyges and His Ring, Herod and Mariamne, Maria Magdalena). New York (Everyman's Library), 1914.
Pattee, L., tr. "Agnes Bernauer," *Poet Lore*, XX, 1909.
Van Doren, Carl, tr. "Judith," *Poet Lore*, XXV, 1914.

HEINE: See references on p. 145.

HEYSE: *Children of the World* (translator anonymous). New York, 1894.

KELLER: Hottinger, M. D., tr. *The People of Seldwyla, and The Seven Legends.* London, 1931.

MEYER: Bell, C., tr. *The Tempting of Pescara.* New York, 1890.
Hauch, E. F., tr. *The Saint.* New York, 1930.

NIETZSCHE: Levy, O., ed. *Complete Works.* New York, 1925. 18 vols.

PLATEN: Cooke, R. B., tr. *Sonnets.* Boston, 1923.

RAABE: Delffs, S., tr. *Abu Telfan, or The Return from the Mountains of the Moon.* London, 1881.

REUTER: Lewes, C. L., tr. *In the Year '13* (Ut de Franzosentid). New York, 1878.
Seed-Time and Harvest, or During My Apprenticeship (translator anonymous). Philadelphia, 1878.

REALISM

ROSEGGER: *The Light Eternal* (translator anonymous). London, 1907.

Skinner, F., tr. *The God-Seeker*. London, 1901.

SCHEFFEL: Beck, J., and L. Lorimer, tr. *The Trumpeter, A Romance of the Rhine*. Edinburgh, 1893.

Easson, H., tr. *Ekkehard*. New York (Everyman's Library), 1911.

Leland, C. G., tr. *Gaudeamus!* Boston, 1872.

SEALSFIELD: Mersch, C. F., tr. *The Cabin Book, or Sketches of Life in Texas*. New York, 1844.

SPIELHAGEN: Browne, W. H. *Hammer and Anvil*. New York, 1870.

In Rank and File (translator anonymous). New York, 1875.

STIFTER: Norman, M., tr. *Rural Life in Austria and Hungary* (containing *Der Hochwald* and other tales). London, 1850.

STORM: Millar, J., tr. *Aquis submersus*. Glasgow, 1910.

———, tr. *Eekenhof*. Glasgow, 1908.

———, tr. *A Festival at Haderslevhus*. Glasgow, 1909.

———, tr. *Renate*. Glasgow, 1909.

Upton, G. P., tr. *Immensee*. Chicago, 1907.

WAGNER: Altmann, W., ed. *Letters*. London, 1927.

My Life (translator anonymous). New York, 1911.

Newman, E., *et al.,* tr. *Complete Operas*. Leipzig, 1914.

WILDENBRUCH: Heller, O., tr. "Harold," *Poet Lore,* III, 1891.

CHAPTER XI

CONTEMPORARY LITERATURE, 1890–1948

THE HISTORICAL BACKGROUND

The soaring hopes and utter defeats, the illusions and disillusionments of modern German history have left deep imprints in the minds of the last two generations of German men and writers. After the somewhat legendary greatness of the First Reich, the Second Reich, from 1871 on, tried to emulate that former greatness and could not fail to antagonize its neighbors, whose unwillingness to submit to a new distribution of power in the world was still heightened by Germany's harsh and diplomatically unwise insistence on reconquering for herself "a place in the sun." When that attempt failed in 1918, the Third Reich, from 1933 on, once more set out on the same ambitious road with a more ruthless and catastrophic determination.

Other questions, too, attended the problem of a national rebirth—e.g. the problem of federalism versus centralization. Germany had achieved her finest culture in the age of Kant, Goethe, and Beethoven, when the Reich had been split up into scores of little principalities and when France had been the dominant military power of Central Europe. With the defeat of France in 1815 and again in 1871, Germany was ready to be reunited and to become again the political leader of Europe; but the big question was whether she, under the new leadership of Prussia, could equal the age of Goethe in culture and literature. Germany, it seems, could have either of the two: she could either be the cultural leader of Europe and be politically weak and disorganized, or she could be the military leader of Europe, a strongly centralized state, and through this compactness lose much that had been finest in her cultural life. Ever since the liberals of 1848, for the sake of national unification, had been willing to compromise with

Bismarck as to their democratic ideals, Germany seemed to have chosen the second possibility—for the Weimar Republic from 1918 to 1933 did not last long enough to constitute a real exception to the essentially Prussian trend towards centralization.

The danger of new European conflicts became acute when Germany, from 1884 on, began the establishment of African colonies. In the face of the attitude of France, which had not yet lived down her defeat of 1871, Bismarck had always insisted on a friendship with England and Russia. But Bismarck was retired shortly after the young Emperor William II ascended to the throne (1888); and the Emperor's ambitious program of naval, colonial, and commercial expansion gradually aroused distrust, fear, and envy in London. Nor did the Emperor, in view of the latent hostility between Austria and Russia, act wisely in allying himself ever more closely with Austria and her claims in the Balkans, for thus finally he lost the friendship of Russia. Italy, like Germany but recently united and therefore scorned and neglected by the wealthy colonial powers of Europe, in 1882 allied herself with Germany and Austria in order to make sure that she, too, would gain a more prominent place in the family of nations. In 1904 England and France, more or less openly supported by Russia, concluded the *Entente cordiale,* for they were resolved to oppose the Share-the-Wealth-and-Power program of the German-Austrian-Italian Triple Alliance.

The line-up remained essentially the same during the Great War of 1914 to 1918—except that Turkey and Bulgaria, because of grievances of their own, joined the German camp, while the Anglo-French group managed to lure the Italians over to their side through glittering promises of vast territorial concessions. With the failure at the Marne, in 1914, to smash the French army, and with the failure, in 1917, to smash the British blockade and to prevent the arrival of American supplies and troops, the fate of Germany was sealed; in spite of vast conquests in Russia and in the Balkans, the European continent was starved out and exhausted through the long-distance blockade by England, and Germany, whose armies were hopelessly locked in a war of attrition and which, in addition to the staggering casualties at the front, lost 800,000 old people and children through starvation in the winter from 1917 to 1918 alone, finally collapsed.

The Weimar Republic, so named after the new and democratic constitution which was debated and passed at Weimar, after the fall of the Second Reich tried to live up to the harsh conditions of the Treaty of Versailles; yet it was not only sabotaged by its inveterate antiliberal red, brown, and black enemies from within—i.e. the Communists, the Nazis, and the (Catholic) reactionaries—but also (and to the same degree) by enemies from without. After centuries of autocracy, the hour for democracy at long last seemed to have come also for Germany, and some of the finest men and some of the finest traits of the German people came to the fore in the Republic; yet in spite of high-sounding phrases about democracy, in spite of the League of Nations, in spite of the deceptive dream of a United States of Europe, the Allies, through indifference, ignorance, and in some cases even through vindictive ill-will, aggravated the situation of the young German Republic, which could have thrived only if effectively supported against its internal enemies—the militarists, imperialists, and industrial and agricultural magnates. Broken promises about disarmament and national self-determination, the occupation of the Ruhr, the folly of the reparation payments—all these things were sadder even than war, because they were perpetrated in the name of peace and justice. The destruction of the German middle class during the inflation of 1923 (on November 15, 1923, one dollar equalled 2,500,000,000,000 marks) and the deadly economic depression following in the wake of the catastrophe of 1929 only hastened the downfall of the unfortunate German Republic.

The rise of National Socialism, the destruction of the Republic, and Hitler's assumption of power in 1933 convinced the dullest Allied imperialist that a golden opportunity of reconciling western Europe had been missed and that the job had to be done all over again. Many of Hitler's Spartan methods and some of his political demands (e.g. that all racial Germans should be united in his Third Reich) found a more or less sympathetic echo abroad; but with the conquest of Prague in 1939 he threw off the mask of pretending to incorporate only German nationals and set out on a systematic career of conquest and imperialism which, in World War II, finally united England, America, and Russia against him. After six years of bitter warfare, Germany was defeated in 1945, and has since been under the control of the forces of occupation of the Four Powers (the United States, England, France, and Russia).

SUBDIVISIONS OF MODERN GERMAN LITERATURE

The vast and almost chaotic field of modern German literature can be subdivided according to different viewpoints.

A. According to genres:

1. Lyric poetry: Arno Holz, Richard Dehmel, Christian Morgenstern, Stefan George, Hugo von Hofmannsthal, Rainer Maria Rilke, Franz Werfel, Heinrich Lersch, etc.

2. The drama: Gerhart Hauptmann, Hermann Sudermann, Arthur Schnitzler, Frank Wedekind, Georg Kaiser, Ernst Toller, Fritz von Unruh, Hanns Johst, etc.

3. The novel: Thomas Mann, Lion Feuchtwanger, Jakob Wassermann, Franz Kafka, Alfred Döblin, Arnold Zweig, Hermann Löns, Hans Fallada, Hans Grimm, etc.

B. According to literary schools:

1. Naturalism.

2. Impressionism and the related trends of Aestheticism and Neoclassicism.

3. Expressionism.

4. Nazi authors.

The first two movements are still essentially linked up with the Realism of the nineteenth century, Naturalism being much more radical than Impressionism; the second two schools are essentially romantic and irrational, with Nazi literature considerably less lyrical than the preceding Expressionism. In a larger sense this new victory of Romanticism over Realism resembles the victory of Luther's ardent and deep-rooted Reformation over the moderate rationalism, liberalism, and intellectualism of the Humanists of the type of Erasmus; and it also resembles the bitter struggle, in the eighteenth century, waged by the mystical, impetuous, and fervently patriotic poets of the Storm and Stress against the scepticism of the cosmopolitan Enlighteners. Just as Luther and Erasmus, or Klopstock and Wieland, had, in principle, been comrades-at-arms in their opposition to the *status quo,* differing radically only in their methods of attack, so also most of our contemporary authors are comrades-at-arms in their enmity against the dangers of the excessive individualism and materialism of the bourgeois world; but they differ in the methods and even in the goal of their attacks, with the naturalists objectively and scientifically revealing the stains of our bourgeois and capitalistic system, and with the passionate neoromanticists ardently aiming at a complete inner rebirth of man and of society, either according to the communist pattern (as most expressionists advocate), or according to the fascist pattern (as the Nazi authors of race and soil would have it).

C. According to political ideas:

Among some impressionists alone are found approving or sympathetic delineators of the bourgeoisie. All other authors, of various schools and political affiliations, are opposed to the bourgeois way of life.

1. Defenders of the bourgeoisie: Thomas Mann, Ricarda Huch.
    a. The Austrian aesthetes: Arthur Schnitzler, Hugo von Hofmannsthal.
    b. Some minor *Heimat* novelists: Rudolf Herzog, Alfred Huggenberger.
2. Attackers of the bourgeoisie: Karl Marx, Friedrich Nietzsche.
    a. The naturalists: Gerhart Hauptmann, Otto Erich Hartleben, Carl Sternheim, etc.
    b. Postwar intellectuals, socialists, communists: Franz Werfel, Alfred Döblin, Jakob Wassermann, Rainer Maria Rilke, Lion Feuchtwanger, Georg Kaiser, etc.

   c. The Nietzscheans: Carl Spitteler, Stefan George, Paul Ernst, etc.

   d. The National Socialists: Hanns Johst, Ernst Jünger, Karl Bröger; with their mysticism (Erwin Guido Kolbenheyer, Hermann Stehr) and their new literature of race and soil (Gustav Frenssen, Hans Grimm, Friedrich Griese).

D. According to themes:

Germany, the heart of Europe, has become the battleground of all problems and conflicts that have to be fought out by modern man. Her poets are hence less complacent than those of most European countries; nor are they calm Olympians as Goethe once was. Instead, they have become battlers, propagandists, lawyers attacking the social iniquities, physicians examining the ills of our time, prophets announcing the dawn of a new age, soldiers fighting in the first ranks for whatever they believe to be right. Among the most frequent topics treated in our fermenting age and among the most representative authors may be named, among many more:

1. Problems of adolescence: Frank Wedekind's *The Awakening of Spring*.
2. Problems of sex: Heinrich Mann's *The Blue Angel*.
3. The conflict between father and son: Walter Hasenclever's *The Son*.
4. The man between two women: Gerhart Hauptmann's *Lonely Lives*.
5. The woman between two men: Georg Kaiser's *King Cuckold*.
6. Problems of marriage and womanhood: Clara Viebig's *The Women's Village*.
7. Decline of individuals and families: Thomas Mann's *Buddenbrooks*.
8. Problems of the artist: Hermann Hesse's *Peter Camenzind*.
9. The misery of proletarians: Alfred Döblin's *Alexander Square, Berlin*.
10. Protests against cities and machines: Ernst Toller's *The Machine Wreckers*.

11. Problems of law and justice: Arnold Zweig's *The Case of Sergeant Grischa.*
12. The First World War: Erich Maria Remarque's *All Quiet on the Western Front.*
13. Postwar problems: Lion Feuchtwanger's *Success.*
14. The struggle for the soil: Hans Grimm's *A Nation without Space.*
15. The problem of spiritual resurrection: Jakob Wassermann's *The World's Illusion.*
16. Problems of religion: Franz Kafka's *The Castle.*
17. The horrors of totalitarianism: Ernst Wiechert's *The Forest of the Dead.*

NATURALISM

Forerunners of Naturalism

Among German forerunners of Naturalism are to be mentioned Gutzkow, who had preached the emancipation of the flesh; Spielhagen, who had written socialistic novels; Fontane, who had presented such social problems as the liaison between aristocrat and working-class girl; Anzengruber, whose forceful dramas had laid bare many a stain in the morals of men, in the social order of the world, and in the concepts of the (Catholic) Church; Liliencron, who, in his poems, had taken a vital interest in problems of industrial progress and of social justice; and, in the social and political field, Karl Marx (1818–1883), Ferdinand Lassalle, and Friedrich Engels, the founders of modern socialism.

Foreign Influences

Among foreign authors who influenced the development of German Naturalism may be named:

a. The Russian novelists Fedor Dostoevski and Leo Tolstoi, whose works deal with the lowliest and humblest strata of the population, yet who combine with this often dismal background the message of man's possible spiritual regeneration.
b. The Swede August Strindberg and especially the Norwegian Henrik Ibsen, the father of the modern European drama, whose vigorous and effective plays deal with such

problems as heredity (*Ghosts*) and the question of the emancipation of woman (*A Doll's House*), striking hard blows at the complacency of contemporary society.

c. French novelists like Émile Zola, with his powerful novels of suburbs, proletarians, and prostitutes, in which he introduced real scientific methods of investigating the milieu, character, and motives of his heroes, and Guy de Maupassant, author of bitter and depressing novels and short stories written in a masterful style.

d. Anglo-Saxon thinkers and authors such as John Stuart Mill, Charles Robert Darwin, and Walt Whitman. Darwin's theory of evolution was popularized in Germany through Ernst Haeckel's *Die Welträtsel* (The Riddles of the World, 1899). The influence of socialist authors like George Bernard Shaw in England and Jack London in America came later and was less marked.

These foreign influences complete the picture of a new, restless, unmuzzled period of literature, during which Marx's socialism, Nietzsche's superindividualism, French passion, Russian mysticism, and English positivistic empiricism were interwoven into a canvas of laboring, sweating, suffering, and rebelling humanity.

Characteristics of Naturalism

Taking up the political battle for man's emancipation where the Storm and Stress poets and the Young Germans had left off, the naturalists, under the influence of German socialism, emphasized the raw and uncouth elements in life and literature. Theirs was an extreme form of Realism in which aesthetic considerations gave way to propagandistic descriptions of slums, misery, capitalistic exploitation, and social iniquity. They also dwelt on the hypocrisy of the bourgeoisie, the importance of class struggle, and the disastrous significance of heredity and environment. Naturalistic literature is hence unpoetic, militant, depressing, radical. Its language ceases to be cultivated; the authors use the often vigorous, blunt, and vulgar language of the common people. Dialects, too, are used intentionally and effectively. Long stage directions in the drama and minute and endless descriptions in the novel indicate the importance attached to man's environment, for exact documentation was one of the main purposes of the naturalists. Though social pity in one form or another is an ever recurrent theme with them, they try to be absolutely objective and to let the facts speak for themselves. Biological problems and especially sexual questions are discussed freely, for life is explained largely on a purely scientific basis. In their effort to show chunks of life the naturalists represent not growing, but fixed, characters. Definite tragic situations are sharply sketched, but with most of them no real solution seems possible. Monologues and asides are discarded as being unnatural in a drama. Milieu and heredity have prepared the catastrophe long before the first act starts. Within a few years Naturalism began to decline—not only because of the limitations of its style and the monotony of its themes, but also because even the laboring classes grew tired of reading these novels and plays which kept on reflecting the drabness of their existence.

Naturalist Authors

Among German naturalists can be counted Arno Holz, Gerhart Hauptmann, Hermann Sudermann, and, with great reservations, Frank Wedekind—though they all, in the general uncertainty and instability of style which is highly typical of our modern age, later forsook Naturalism for some other school. Clara Viebig and Richard Dehmel also began with or owed a great deal to Naturalism, though we might hesitate to call them full-fledged members of that school. The immense influence of Nietzsche, whom the naturalists at first had hailed as an ally in the battle against the bourgeoisie, gradually turned out to be as emphatically antinaturalistic and antisocialistic as it had been antibourgeois.

Minor Naturalists. Among the minor naturalists can be named:

a. The brothers HEINRICH HART and JULIUS HART, who made Berlin the center of the new school, and whose *Kritische Waffengänge* (Critical Jousts, 1882 ff.) gave expression to the new teachings. Together with Arno Holz and Johannes Schlaf they founded, in 1886, the literary club *Durch* (Smash), in which the new theories were formulated; later Gerhart Hauptmann also joined. In his tragedy *Der Sumpf* (The Swamp, 1886) Julius Hart, like many later naturalists, denounced the corruption of big-city life.

b. KARL BLEIBTREU, author of a *Byron* trilogy (1881 ff.) and of various historical novels such as *Dies Irae* (about the battle of Sedan), *Waterloo, Vivat Fridericus;* but famous especially for his programmatic essay *Die Revolution der Literatur* (1886).

c. MAX KRETZER, a proletarian, a disciple of Zola, who is gruesome yet gripping in his social novels *Die Betrogenen* (The Deceived, 1882), *Die Verkommenen* (The Degenerated, 1883), and especially in his *Meister Timpe* (1888), an accusation against the ever growing mechanization of the world. Proletarian misery, unbridled sensualism, and mystical symbolism are found in his *Das Gesicht Christi* (The Face of Christ, 1897).

d. OTTO BRAHM. Encouraged only by Detlev von Liliencron and Theodor Fontane, but disliked by the German bourgeoisie, criticized by *Der Kunstwart* (The Guardian of Art), an influential literary periodical published by Ferdinand Avenarius (1887 ff.), and scorned by the Munich School whose poets, like Paul Heyse, insisted on continuing as epicurean artists, and especially restrained and oppressed by the German censorship, the naturalists of Berlin, under the leadership of Otto Brahm, a prominent literary critic and later the most celebrated theatrical producer of Berlin, in 1889 finally opened their own private theater, *Die freie Bühne* (The Free Stage). Though this association existed only a few years, it made possible semiprivate performances of plays by Ibsen, Strindberg, Tolstoi, Anzengruber, Gerhart Hauptmann, Holz, and Schlaf, and thus it established the success of the new school of drama. In contrast to antiquity (*Die Antike*), the poets of Naturalism frequently called their movement *Die Moderne*.

e. MAX HALBE is remembered mainly for his *Jugend* (Youth, 1893), a pathetic tragedy of young love and seduction in which the naturalistic bluntness of minor characters is mitigated by the tenderness of the two lovers, Hans and Annchen. Like Sudermann, Halbe hailed from the Polish borderlands and excelled in the description of this region and its peasants—e.g. in *Mutter Erde* (Mother Earth) or in *Der Strom* (The Stream, i.e. the Vistula).

f. CARL HAUPTMANN, brother of Gerhart, may be mentioned for his naturalistic dramas (e.g. *Marianne,* 1894) and for his various novels: *Mathilde* (1902), the tale of a proletarian girl; *Einhart der Lächler* (Einhart the Smiler, 1907), an apprenticeship novel; *Ismael Friedmann* (1912), the story of the tragic life of a half-Jew who through this racial mixture and the ensuing problems and inhibitions is driven to suicide.

g. OTTO ERICH HARTLEBEN, an inveterate enemy of bourgeois morality and complacency, was at his best in his witty and rather shallow glorifications of the bacchanalian and amorous aspects of life (*Hanna Jagert,* 1893); but he was a failure as soon as he tried to deal with real tragedy, though in his *Rosenmontag* (Love's Carnival, 1900) he was bold enough to speak up against the arrogance of Prussian officers. His novels are satirical and humorous, ever on the alert against pedantry and philistinism: *Vom gastfreien Pastor* (Of the Hospitable Pastor), *Geschichten vom abgerissenen Knopf* (Stories of the Torn-off Button).

Arno Holz (1863–1929) and Johannes Schlaf (1862–1941). Holz's poems, contained in *Das Buch der Zeit* (The Book of Time, 1885) and in *Phantasus* (1898), in vocabulary, verse, and atmosphere are typical of the new trends, though the fact should be emphasized that Naturalism was far more successful in the drama and the novel than in lyric poetry. Very amusing and well done is Holz's *Dafnis, lyrisches Porträt aus dem 17. Jahrhundert* (Dafnis, a Lyrical Portrait of the Seventeenth Century, 1904), a highly clever imitation of Baroque style and mentality.

The new aims of literature Holz discussed in his two significant critical writings *Die Kunst, ihr Wesen und ihre Gesetze* (Art, Its Nature and Laws, 1891) and *Die Revolution der Lyrik* (1899).

Together with Johannes Schlaf, Holz was the earliest leading stimulator of naturalistic literature. In collaboration they published *Papa Hamlet* (1889), three short sketches in which the theory of the faithful reproduction of the minutest details of reality (*Sekundenstil*) was for the first time observed to the limit. The depressing power of this new style is visible especially in the third sketch, *Ein Tod* (Death), describing the interminable deathwatch at the bedside of a student fatally wounded in a duel. Also depressing is their drama *Die Familie Selicke* (1890), the tale of a daughter who sacrifices her happiness and her future for the sake of a drunken father and a suffering mother.

Traumulus (1904), written by Arno Holz in collaboration with Otto Jerschke, is an early example of a tragedy about school life and puberty, dealing with the tragic love of a schoolboy for an actress.

Johannes Schlaf then continued the repulsive portrayal of minute and ugly details in his drama *Meister Ölze* (1892), the description of the death of an unworthy and criminal old man.

Gerhart Hauptmann (1862–1946). Hauptmann is one of the great literary figures of modern Germany, more famous as a dramatist than as a novelist. He began during the age of Naturalism; however, like Ibsen, he soon grew beyond that and later reflected most of the great trends in contemporary German letters, though many of his later works are disappointingly inferior. Hauptmann was born in Silesia, and the landscape and dialect of his native province are frequently reproduced in his works.

NATURALISTIC WORKS. *Bahnwärter Thiel* (Flagman Thiel, 1887) is a naturalistic short story in the manner of Zola, about a lonely widower who is ruined by the meanness of his second wife and the sexual power she holds over him.

Vor Sonnenaufgang (Before Dawn, 1889), which caused a scandal at its first performance, is Hauptmann's first great naturalistic drama, and made him the head of the new school. It tells of a degenerate and alcohol-infected family whose only decent member, Helene, is driven to despair and suicide because her fearful and weak lover Alfred, albeit a social reformer and ostensibly an emancipated modern man, refuses to marry her in view of her hereditary background. Influences of Ibsen and Zola are clearly discernible here; but what makes this drama great is Hauptmann's tender compassion, the natural, ultrarealistic language, and the dramatic dialogue which his friends Holz and Schlaf had taught him.

Das Friedensfest (The Reconciliation, 1890) is reminiscent of Ibsen's *Ghosts,* for this drama about heredity and psychiatry shows a young man whom perhaps not even the love of a decent girl can free from the curse of being the offspring of a sick and corrupt family.

Einsame Menschen (Lonely Lives, 1891) tells of an undecided scholar, Johannes Vockerath, who oscillates between two women and whose duty to his good-hearted but unintellectual wife conflicts with his friendship for Anna Mahr, a brilliant and understanding woman (the latter, like the lovers in the above-mentioned two dramas, again a potential savior from outside). When Anna refuses to accept the situation, he, in despair, commits suicide. Like Goethe's Clavigo and Fernando, the neurasthenic Vockerath, in spite of his modern ideas, is not a big enough character to draw the necessary consequences from his theories. Hauptmann treats the same problems of a man's tragic inability to choose between two women in his later drama, *Gabriel Schillings Flucht* (Gabriel Schilling's Flight, 1912).

Die Weber (The Weavers, 1892), one of Hauptmann's greatest works, was hailed as the first socialistic drama in German literature, depicting, in crude Silesian dialect, the sufferings and despair of proletarian weavers and their futile rebellion in 1844 against those who exploited them. Not a single character, but the poor and abused collective masses are the real hero in this depressing and dismal picture of industrial and social iniquity. Much more than with social theories, Hauptmann, the poet of compassion, is concerned with the downtrodden people and with their poignant longing for a better fate, which drives them into a hopeless insurrection.

In *Kollege Crampton* (Colleague Crampton, 1892) and *Der Biberpelz* (The Beaver Coat, 1893) Hauptmann applied the theories of Naturalism to comedy; in the humorous and yet often tragic first play he described a lovable drunkard who may perhaps be saved; in the second play he drew an excellent sketch of a saucy and thieving washerwoman. *Der Biberpelz* is possibly the best naturalistic comedy; in many respects it is reminiscent of Kleist's *Der zerbrochene Krug*.

In *Florian Geyer* (1896) Hauptmann's Naturalism turned to the historical drama: it is a tragedy of the great Peasant War of 1524–1525 in which Florian Geyer, like Götz von Berlichingen, was a leader. The play suffers from many imperfections; nonetheless the last acts representing Geyer's tragic end are deeply stirring. As in *Die Weber*, Hauptmann here dramatized the rebellion of an entire class against unbearable oppression.

The same compassion, the same tragedy of life and of man's futile rebellion against the powers over him, is seen in *Fuhrmann Henschel* (Drayman Henschel, 1898): the hero is another Bahnwärter Thiel, who after the death of his wife and child and because of the hardness of his second wife feels as if Destiny or Satan in person had set out to destroy him. In *Rose Bernd* (1903) the tragedy is that of a healthy peasant girl who, like so many heroines of the Storm and Stress, is seduced and forsaken.

SYMBOLIST WORKS. As early as 1893 Hauptmann in *Hanneles Himmelfahrt* (The Assumption of Hannele) abandoned Naturalism, whose limitations he had early recognized, and created a symbolist drama, a dream-play in naturalistic setting. Not the sufferings of a mistreated and dying proletarian child are the main thing in this touching play, but rather her ecstatic visions, her fond dreams of her ascension to heaven, the compassion of the angels, and the kindly help of Christ.

Die versunkene Glocke (The Sunken Bell, 1896), more famous than, yet inferior to, *Hanneles Himmelfahrt,* is likewise a symbolist drama. Written under the influence of Goethe's *Faust* and of Nietzsche's new philosophy, and provided with a mixture of Greek and Germanic mythological background which is not always convincing, the drama tells us of a bell-founder who is crushed by the conflict between the duty he owes to his wife and family, and the duty he owes to himself, his art, his ambitious plans, and his love for the inspiring Rautendelein, a nymph, symbol of the irrational forces of life and nature. Yet Heinrich cannot emancipate himself, cannot follow Rautendelein, cannot achieve his masterpiece; he dies weakly as Johannes Vockerath had died.

205

Other symbolist dramas are *Der arme Heinrich* (1901), a reworking of Hartmann von Aue's medieval epic; *Elga* (1905), a dramatization of Grillparzer's gruesome novel *Das Kloster bei Sendomir;* and *Und Pippa tanzt* (And Pippa Dances, 1906), a fairy drama whose excellent qualities are marred by the confusion of the last acts. Pippa is the symbol of delicate beauty, desired and crushed by brute force, visible after her death only to dreamers and idealists.

Views on political problems, contributions to a democratic form of government and toward the solution of postwar problems in general, are embodied in *Ein Festspiel in deutschen Reimen* (Commemoration Masque, 1913), written for the one-hundredth anniversary of Napoleon's defeat at Leipzig, and in *Till Eulenspiegel* (1927), a great symbolic poem in hexameters, telling of the adventures and thoughts of a war pilot.

NOVELS. His declining dramatic power and his inability to create strong and great men (in contrast to the many fine female characters he portrayed) are greatly redeemed by the high quality of some of his novels. Foremost among them is the apocalyptic novel *Der Narr in Christo Emanuel Quint* (The Fool in Christ, Emanuel Quint, 1910), a stirring work betraying the influence of Tolstoi, a deeply symbolical tale of a humble Silesian carpenter and preacher who wants to emulate Christ. Like Christ he moves the hearts of his listeners through his teachings; disciples and supporters flock to him and surround him; but like Christ he is scorned, humbled, outcast, and dies a miserable death. Our time is not ready to welcome a new Christ; men would lock him up in an insane asylum rather than listen to him.

Hauptmann's later novels include *Atlantis* (1912)—not only the description of a shipwreck (as if he had divined the later catastrophe of the "Titanic") but also a symbolical presentation of the entire prewar bourgeois culture that was doomed to founder—again portraying a man oscillating between various women and finally saved by a healthy girl from afar; *Der Ketzer von Soana* (The Heretic of Soana, 1918), a hymn to love and the creative power of nature, dealing with a young priest who through his love for a girl offends the laws of the Church and of society, yet who is happy about and proud of the emotions and experiences he lives through; *Die Insel der grossen Mutter* (The Island of the Great Mother, 1924), a utopian novel about the establishment of a matriarchy on a South Sea island and the sexual problems that arise from the forced absence of all men save one lone youth who had survived the shipwreck with the women.

Hermann Sudermann (1857–1928). Besides being a novelist of some fame, Sudermann was above all a playwright whose exceedingly clever dramatic technique made his audience forget the essential shallowness and imperfection of his works. He is often compared with Kotzebue.

Die Ehre (Honor, 1889), a modernized bourgeois drama, is a gripping naturalistic play showing the double standard of honor in a wealthy and supposedly respectable as well as in a proletarian and degenerate family, with sound and debauched members appearing in either milieu.

Heimat (Magda, 1893), Sudermann's most celebrated drama, still very effective on the stage, shows the bitter conflict between father and daughter—between a stern Prussian colonel of the old school who reminds us of Hebbel's Meister Anton, and Magda, his proud, emancipated, realistic daughter who would rather break than bend.

Fritzchen (Freddie, 1896), perhaps Sudermann's best play, is a simple and touching officer's tragedy in one act dealing with the problem of duels and the heartless code of honor among army men.

Among his novels *Frau Sorge* (Dame Care, 1887) and *Der Katzensteg* (Regina, or The Sins of the Fathers, 1891) are the best. The former, in part a reiteration of the Romeo and Juliet theme, deals with the truly superhuman and almost pathological abnegation of a man who works, slaves, and sacrifices everything for his unworthy family; the latter, going back to the Napoleonic Age, narrates the tragedy of a man whose father had been a traitor and whose entire life is now ruined by prejudice and hatred. The problem is complicated by the son's love for his dead father's mistress. *Frau Sorge* in particular illustrates Sudermann's theory that leisure breeds vice and that work alone can save either man or society.

Viebig. Clara Viebig, outstanding among the women writers in the early twentieth century, blended the Naturalism of her Zola-inspired descriptions of the masses with the regionalism of the new *Heimat* literature. Her novels deal either with the Rhineland, where she was born, or with the Polish borderlands, where she lived. Among her works should be mentioned *Die Rheinlandstöchter* (Daughters of the Rhineland, 1896), a plea for the emancipation and regeneration of German womanhood; *Das Weiberdorf* (The Women's Village, 1900), a novel about the sexual starvation of a whole village of women whose men work far away in the mines of the Ruhr, in its theme somewhat reminiscent of Hauptmann's *Insel der grossen Mutter; Das schlafende Heer* (The Sleeping Army, 1904), a depressing tale of conflicts and social problems among the enslaved masses of Polish peasants; *Die Töchter der Hekuba* (Daughters of Hecuba, 1917), a moving war novel about the physical and mental sufferings on the home front.

Thoma. Ludwig Thoma, a Bavarian, was a contributor to the famous, humorous, and often radical periodical *Simplicissimus*. His comedy *Moral* (Morals, 1908) is an excellent take-off on philistine hypocrisy, for a police raid on the apartment of a local lady of easy virtue reveals that the very pillars of society have been among her intimate friends. *Lottchens Geburtstag* (Lottie's Birthday, 1911) might be called a parody of the tragedies of puberty, for the younger generation seems to possess much more sexual enlightenment than the good parents ever suspected. Equally amusing is Thoma's comedy on village politicians, *Die Lokalbahn* (The Branch Road, 1902); and his *Lausbubengeschichten* (Tales of a Bad Boy, 1907) are deservedly renowned.

Richard Dehmel (1863–1920). A close friend of Liliencron, Dehmel is a lyric poet heavy with thought and often tortured in style, whose character it is to grapple with the eternally present problems and conflicts of life and sex (*Erkenntnis, Selbstzucht*). In his nature poems he strongly defends the beauty and healthiness of country life against the drab monotony and degeneration of city life (*Predigt an das Grosstadtvolk*); in his personal poems he admonishes the younger generation to be true to itself and to defy the narrow traditions of its elders (*Lied an meinen Sohn*); in his poems on social themes he writes some of the best socialistic verses of the time (*Vierter Klasse, Zu eng, Bergpsalm, Der Arbeitsmann*).

But it is mainly the burning urge of man to woman that makes him forever restless; hence the unusual sexual connotations of his poems *Erlösungen* (Deliverances, 1891); hence his daring and much condemned analyses in his *Verwandlungen der Venus* (Metamorphoses of Venus); hence also the passionate ups and downs in his own private love life as partly reflected in his largely autobiographical *Weib und Welt* (The Woman and the World, 1896). His best known work is *Zwei Menschen* (Two Human Beings, 1903) an epic-like series of poems about the relationship between man and woman, the somewhat absurd plot of which is enriched by a transcendental wealth of thoughts about every human being's physical and spiritual possibilities, written very much in the vein of Schlegel's *Lucinde*. Like his revered Nietzsche, Dehmel dared to be fully himself; in spite of his somewhat erratic appearance and character he is one of the truly great poets of modern Germany.

IMPRESSIONISM

Characteristics of Impressionism

In the eternal struggle between Realism and Romanticism which early in the present century was fought under the names of Naturalism and Expressionism, Impressionism tried to occupy a moderating position. In view of the excesses of the naturalists, the impressionists, while still describing the realities of nature, emphasized not that which is seen, but the impression which the object observed makes upon him who sees. They give a mental rather than a physical picture; they are not so objective as the naturalists, but not so excessively subjective as the expressionists either; they are more irrational than the former, but closer to life and reality than the latter. In their delicate studies of the reactions of their souls to the outer world they often tend to become refined and somewhat decadent—exquisite artists in whom the will to live and to fight is lacking. Many impressionists, especially those of Austria, are hence often called aesthetes or decadents, although these terms are quite misleading, since the greatest poet of this group, Hugo von Hofmannsthal, tried to overcome the frustrating isolation of the "ivory tower" and searched for a new cultural and religious foundation which could give substance to man's existence. Because of a stylistic peculiarity of theirs, many impressionists are frequently also called symbolists. As opposed to the vigor, the militant tone, and the somewhat monotonous tendency of the naturalists to preach, to distort, and to exaggerate, the impressionists, tired of endless milieu descriptions, dwelt again on the importance of the poet, the observer; and they endeavored to record the finest fluctuations of his mood, his ego. Just as the revolutionary works of Karl Marx had formed an important basis for the era of Naturalism, so the famous psychoanalytical studies of Sigmund Freud (1856–1939) gave the inspiration for numerous impressionistic analytical investigations.

Rather than name the somewhat weakly Munich School of poets among the forerunners of Impressionism because its members objected to the often crude vigor of the Young Germans and the naturalists, we can point to the manlier and more important Detlev von Liliencron, in whose works we notice the almost imperceptible transition from Realism to Impressionism. Most modern authors are to a greater or lesser degree impressionists, from the Austrian Arthur Schnitzler to the Rhinelander Stefan George, and from Hermann Hesse in Switzerland to Thomas Mann on the Baltic Coast. The trend towards beauty and purity of form—noticeable already in the Swiss patrician Conrad Ferdinand Meyer—is seen especially in the Austrians of the type of Hugo von Hofmannsthal and Arthur Schnitzler.

Foreign Influences

Symbolism, so marked among several impressionists and really an outgrowth of German Romanticism, had, toward the end of the century, achieved great popularity among foreign poets, who in turn exerted an influence upon German literature. Among these foreign authors may be named the French poets Charles Baudelaire, Paul Verlaine, Stéphane

Mallarmé, and Arthur Rimbaud, who were translated and imitated by Stefan George, Rainer Maria Rilke, Hermann Bahr, and others; the Belgian poets Émile Verhaeren and Maurice Maeterlinck; the decadent Italian aesthete Gabriele d'Annunzio; and the English poets Algernon Charles Swinburne and Oscar Wilde—the latter important for his influence on Hugo von Hofmannsthal and others. These foreigners and their Austrian and German fellow aesthetes are typical *fin de siècle* poets, graceful in style, often rather pagan in their ethics, somewhat tired, blasé, and egocentric in their outlook on life. Symbolism also provides the meeting ground for the two great antipodes of modern German lyric poetry, Stefan George and Rainer Maria Rilke—the former essentially Nietzschean, pagan, stern, Spartan in his attitude, and aloof, the latter essentially compassionate, humanitarian, a Russia-inspired mystic, yet both of them symbolists, given to an exaggerated cult of form. With regard to the drama we can point to the great Henrik Ibsen, the lyricism and symbolism of whose *Peer Gynt* and *Brand* contrasts sharply with the naturalism of his other plays; in Germany, Hauptmann's *Hanneles Himmelfahrt* (a drama of transition) and *Die versunkene Glocke* mark the same contrast. Not the proletarian masses, but the single individual becomes again the hero of the drama; Naturalism is outmoded and subjectivity is restored to its rights. Romanticism and irrationalism, once banned by the naturalists, have thus managed to stage a comeback.

Subdivision of Impressionism

In keeping with the transitory character of Impressionism the whole school can be divided into two big groups, which, in turn, lend themselves to various subdivisions:

A. The objective delineators of human society and its weaknesses:
  a. Artistic impressionists: Thomas Mann, Ricarda Huch, Hermann Hesse.
  b. Austrian aesthetes: Arthur Schnitzler, Hugo von Hofmannsthal.
  c. Authors of biographies and historical novels: Stefan Zweig, Alfred Neumann, Lion Feuchtwanger.

B. The subjective seekers of a new and regenerated form of human existence, veering from the Nietzscheans on the right to the extreme Marxists on the left:

   a. Neoclassicism: Paul Ernst, Wilhelm von Scholz, Rudolf Binding.

   b. The will to quality: Carl Spitteler, Stefan George, Ernst Jünger.

   c. Poets veering towards Expressionism: Rainer Maria Rilke, Jakob Wassermann.

Objective Delineators of Human Society

Delving into the problems and idiosyncrasies of their own souls, the impressionists of this first group in their endless probings soon come to disregard the borderline between *Sein und Schein,* between reality and mere appearance. Hence the importance of dreams in their life; hence their uncertainty about real or merely imaginary living. The poet's constant preoccupation with himself leads to the *Künstlerroman,* the artist's novel, in which the author analyzes his own delicate self and his attitude towards and aloofness from a crude world beyond the realm of his thoughts. Thoughts of proud isolation, aesthetic refinement, vanishing physical strength, growing sensitivity, lingering death, erotic and subtle pleasures are especially frequent among some of the "decadents"; their style becomes mellow, perfect, of exquisite and delicate beauty. The picturesqueness, the soft climate, the colors, the passions, the perversities of Italy—particularly of Renaissance Italy—exert a great attraction for most impressionists; the art of living and of loving seems uniquely perfect there. Having become incapable of violent and lasting emotions, the impressionist, like a connoisseur, dissects his sensitivity to life and pleasure into small fragments, short episodes, in order to enjoy each one separately. Life—even for the many authors of biographies in this group—has thus lost its coherence; instead of a complete picture of his soul, the artist more often than not gives individual snapshots, intimate little scenes, preferably monologues, and keen analyses of his reaction to various situations and occurrences. In view of the spinelessness and the vagueness of such an atmosphere many poets, in their efforts to hold on to something definite and lasting, strive for a perfectly chiseled, lucid, almost classical style; others, allowing even their style to become ever more mellow, musical, and melting, strive, like the romanticists of yore, to find refuge and firm support in the mystery and certainty of the Catholic Church, the one pillar to which to cling, the one shelter in which to find peace after the storms of life.

Hermann Bahr (1863–1934). Bahr's hypersensitivity in the perception of new trends is most remarkable, for in his literary criticism he wrote his two essays *Zur Kritik der Moderne* (Criticism of Naturalism, 1890) and *Die Überwindung des Naturalismus* (The Displacement of Naturalism, 1891) at a time which had not even witnessed the apex of Naturalism; and though these essays were not able to prevent the excesses of the naturalists, they nevertheless initiated the new age of Impressionism and of increasing subjectivity and lyricism, in which the robustness of Naturalism was replaced by ever greater delicacy and refinement. Years later, in his essay *Expressionismus* (1914), Bahr likewise announced the dawn of yet another school of literature.

In his novels (*Die gute Schule*—The Good School, 1890) as well as in his plays (*Das Konzert*—The Concert, 1910) Bahr deals mainly with erotic adventures of eccentric artists whose nervous systems and complexes clamor for ever new and perverse thrills.

Hermann Hesse (1877–   ). Hesse, a Swabian poet who spent most of his life in Switzerland, through his fine knowledge and analyses of human souls has become one of the best representatives of Impressionism.

Peter Camenzind (1904) is a novel which tries to work out a cure for oversensitive artists: the hero of this *Künstlerroman* relinquishes his artistic calling and finds health and normalcy amidst the mountains of his native Switzerland.

Rosshalde (1914) is a fine psychological study of an estranged couple, showing how the man, the painter, for the sake of his beloved son, remains chained to an unsympathetic wife who cannot and will not help him.

Demian (1919) probes deep into the problems of adolescence, puberty, and, perhaps, incest, by portraying a delicate hero, Sinclair, oscillating between his demonic friend Demian, his *alter ego,* and Demian's mother. The fact that the mother

HISTORY OF GERMAN LITERATURE

and Demian are said to be lovers renders the situation particularly delicate, because for both youths the mother tends
ever more to become the symbol of all womanhood.

In *Der Steppenwolf* (The Wolf of the Steppes, 1927)
Hesse again studies the dual character of man and elucidates
on the frustration of an artist who finds himself among philistines and who at times feels like a wolf among sheep. Between them there can be no harmony, no compromise.

Narziss und Goldmund (Death and the Lover, 1930), a
fine novel with a late medieval background, assures us that
the ascetic as well as the epicurean voluptuary, the abbot as
well as the lover of beauty and happiness, will find their ways
to God.

Ricarda Huch (1864–1947). Like Conrad Ferdinand
Meyer, Ricarda Huch feels a great admiration for Italy,
though rather for the political Renaissance of the nineteenth
century than for the aesthetic Renaissance of the *Cinquecento*.
Like Hermann Hesse, she spent years of her life in Switzerland.

Erinnerungen von Ludolf Ursleu dem Jüngeren (Recollections of Ludolf Ursleu the Younger, 1893), written in a
lyrical and colorful style, anticipates Thomas Mann's *Buddenbrooks* by describing the decay of a patrician family in Hamburg; the hero escapes from the burden of life by seeking
peace in the famous Swiss monastery of Einsiedeln.

The same financial, physical, and moral decline is evident
in *Vita Somnium Breve* (1902); yet for the sake of his love
for his unworthy son the hero returns to his duties, his busi-
ness, and his wife. Like Hesse's *Rosshalde,* the novel shows
the power children hold over their parents.

The depressing yet finely sketched atmosphere of former
greatness is apparent also in *Aus der Triumphgasse* (The
Street of Triumph, 1902): an old patrician mansion in Trieste
now serves as an abode for beggars, criminals, prostitutes,
and cripples—all of them very human characters, as the
author shows them to be, in spite of their defects.

In addition to her *Erzählungen* (Tales, 1919), in which
she emulates the ironical treatment of bigotry in Gottfried
Keller's stories and legends, Ricarda Huch is especially cele-

214

brated also for her Italian and German historical works, in which she blends most beautifully the power of her imaginative narration with solid historical research: *Die Geschichten von Garibaldi* (Tales of Garibaldi, 1907), *Menschen und Schicksale aus dem Risorgimento* (Men and Destinies during the *Risorgimento*, 1908) and *Der grosse Krieg in Deutschland* (i.e. the Thirty Years' War, 1914).

Among her strictly scholarly and critical works (she took her Ph.D. at Zurich) may be named: *Die Blütezeit der Romantik* (The Golden Age of Romanticism, 1899), *Gottfried Keller* (1904), *Luthers Glaube* (Luther's Faith, 1916), *Das Römische Reich deutscher Nation* (The Roman Empire of the German Nation, 1934). Ricarda Huch is unquestionably the greatest woman writer in modern German literature.

Minor Women Writers. Minor women writers of the present century include GABRIELE REUTER, an outstanding champion of modern womanhood, author of *Aus guter Familie* (From Good Stock, 1895), *Ellen von der Weiden* (1900), *Das Tränenhaus* (The House of Tears, 1909), and the autobiographical *Vom Kinde zum Menschen* (From Childhood to Maturity, 1922); ISOLDE KURZ, like Meyer and Ricarda Huch a lover of Italy, author of *Florentiner Novellen* (Tales from Florence, 1890), *Italienische Erzählungen* (Italian Stories, 1895), and *Nächte von Fondi* (Nights in Fondi, 1922); ENRICA VON HANDEL-MAZZETTI, an Austrian whose novels dwell austerely on the painful conflicts between Catholicism and Protestantism at the time of the Counter Reformation: *Jesse und Maria* (1906), *Die arme Margaret* (Poor Margaret, 1910), *Das Rosenwunder* (The Miracle of Roses, 1924); VICKI BAUM, also an Austrian, best known for her *Menschen im Hotel* (Grand Hotel, 1929) and her *Helene Willfüer, B.S.,* the tale of an unwedded mother in a small German university town.

Among the predominately lyric poetesses are AGNES MIEGEL, who hails from East Prussia (*Balladen und Lieder,* 1907), LULU VON STRAUSS UND TORNEY, a Westphalian, whose collected ballads and poems are contained in *Reif steht die Saat* (Ripe Are the Fields, 1926), and INA SEIDEL (*Gedichte,* 1914 and 1927), who is famous also for her glorification of the Prussian spirit of sacrifice in her novel *Das Wunschkind* (The Wish Child, 1930).

Heinrich Mann (1871–1950). Born of old patrician stock in the Hanseatic city of Lübeck, with a strong element of South American blood in his veins from his mother's side, Heinrich Mann, in contrast to his younger brother Thomas, is more acid and passionate in his analyses and criticisms of society than the latter.

Die Göttinnen oder die drei Romane der Herzogin von Assy (The Goddesses, or The Three Novels of the Duchess of Assy, 1903) reverts to Jakob Burckhardt's and Conrad Ferdinand Meyer's love of Italy, adding a violent and frenzied atmosphere of lust, sadism, and Lesbianism to the colorful Italian picture of unreal supermen.

Professor Unrat (1905), famous through its film version *The Blue Angel,* is a study of the powerful sexual attraction of a demimondaine not only for adolescents, but even more for their professor, who falls into her snares until he, formerly an average decent individual, is completely ruined by her.

In keeping with his emphasis on eroticism, Heinrich Mann in *Die kleine Stadt* (The Small Town, 1910) shows the complete moral disintegration of the citizens of an Italian town caused by the arrival and influences of a troup of traveling actors and actresses.

Das Kaiserreich (The Empire, 1914–1925), a trilogy, is a daring attack on and a bitter denunciation of Germany under Kaiser William II, in which in turn the officials, the proletarians, and finally the heads of government (the Emperor, Bülow, Krupp, etc.) are described and pilloried. The vitriolic hatred for the German political vices—especially for the German's lack of "civil courage" which is brutally unmasked in the first volume of the series, *Der Untertan* (Little Superman)—makes this trilogy one of the most devastating satires of our time. Not less scathing is his denunciation of the shallow and cheap intellectual ambitiousness of the rich bourgeoisie in *Im Schlaraffenland* (Fool's Paradise, 1900) and of the hypocritical attitude of the same bourgeoisie in matters of sex and love in *Jagd nach Liebe* (Hunting for Love, 1904). However, the overemphasis on sexual excesses

216

makes this author's books at times as repulsive as the moral, political, and social deformities of Germany against which he levels his attacks.

After Hitler's advent to power, Heinrich Mann became one of the most vigorous and ardent fighters against Germany's relapse into darkness. His collection of essays *Der Hass* (Hatred, 1934) is one of the most significant political books of a German exile. He has also turned to biography and historical works in which he extols the gradual victory of humaneness over the evil powers of tyranny, as in *Die Jugend des Königs Henri Quatre* (The Youth of King Henry IV) with its extremely impressive canvas of the St. Bartholomew Massacre of 1572, and *Die Vollendung des Königs Henri Quatre* (The Maturity of King Henry IV, 1940).

Kraus. In connection with Heinrich Mann may be mentioned the powerful Austrian satirist Karl Kraus, who in his one-man periodical *Die Fackel* (The Torch, 1899 ff.) lashed out against yellow journalism, war profiteering, corrupt politicians, and their literary sycophants. Unafraid of the powers that be, he voiced his aggressive pacifism in the midst of World War I, and created in his gigantic play *Die letzten Tage der Menschheit* (Mankind's Last Days) one of the bluntest and most impressive indictments of warmongers of all brands.

Thomas Mann (1875–1955). Thomas Mann, the greatest of all living German authors, started his literary career with penetrating analytical novels which, in a masterful style, deal mainly with the decline of the modern bourgeoisie. His early heroes are cultured, tolerant, cosmopolitan, but superrefined and decadent, lacking in stamina and in a strong will to fight. His works are thus to a certain extent symbolical of the greatness, the individualism, and the blind carelessness of the democracies before 1939.

Buddenbrooks (1901) is the most famous illustration in modern literature of cultural refinement and the ensuing physical decay. It deals with a proud and formerly strong and energetic patrician family of merchants whose last scion is a highly gifted and artistic weakling. The minute description of life and manners in the old Hansa city, done in a perfectly impeccable and beautiful style, is somewhat reminiscent of the milieu technique of Naturalism.

Tonio Kröger (1903) and *Der Tod in Venedig* (Death in Venice, 1913) resume the problem, so dear to Thomas Mann and so frequent in his writings, of an artist unhappy and yet at the same time envious in a bourgeois and realistic world of normal and healthy men and women—a problem already treated in Goethe's *Werther* and *Tasso*. Tonio Kröger, son of a German father and an Italian mother, and thus sober and systematic and yet passionate and temperamental at the same time, greatly resembles the author himself. In *Der Tod in Venedig,* perhaps the loftiest and most polished piece of modern German prose, the conflict in the hero's breast between the severe and life-consuming devotion to the service of artistic creation and the vital and spontaneous yearning for the happiness of a normal existence is complicated by the discreetly homosexual motif of the tale. The problematic existence of the artist and his estrangement from the simple and unproblematic world of the healthy and normal burgher is given a burlesque turn in the delightful fragment *Bekenntnisse des Hochstaplers Felix Krull* (Confessions of the Adventurer Felix Krull, 1911 and 1937), the fictitious diary of an international cheat who, while playing the game of bourgeois society, proudly and ironically maintains his superior aloofness.

Yet not only the artist—the whole modern bourgeois civilization appears doomed in *Der Zauberberg* (The Magic Mountain, 1924). The physical and mental ills of our times are keenly investigated in this picture of life in a fashionable Swiss sanatorium. Love-making, luxurious living, and long discussions seem to be the only enjoyments and efforts of the men and women around Hans Castorp. In these discussions the spiritual heritage of western man is laid bare, and the dangers of the one-sided acceptance of a barren and optimistic rationalism on the one hand, and of an atavistic and totalitarian irrationalism on the other, are elucidated. Hans Castorp finally escapes from the hothouse atmosphere of these refined idlers, but in an inconclusive ending somewhat reminiscent of Goethe's *Torquato Tasso* he will probably meet his doom in World War I. In spite of this, the novel ends with a ray of hope, for Thomas Mann seems to have conquered his playful yearning for death; regardless of what the war may bring to Castorp, the modern European, he had at least enough strength to leave the magic Mountain of Death and to return to the hardships of real life. The hero thus undergoes a definite development of character and mind. After having experienced the seductive appeal of death, nihilism, and ideological and philosophical extremes, he who started out as a naive and unquestioning tourist finally finds a plan and vocation in the world of reality. *Der Zauberberg* is one of the highest achievements within the tradition of the German apprenticeship novel and one of the finest masterpieces of the novelistic literature of Europe.

Shortly after the publication of this monumental work, Mann delighted his readers by *Unordnung und frühes Leid* (Disorder and Early Sorrow, 1925), a thinly veiled presentation of the poet's own family life, centering around the games in the nursery, the eccentricities of the younger generation, the privations during the inflation, and the sudden and unhappy love of his little daughter for a blasé young beau.

Of Thomas Mann's minor works may be mentioned *Der kleine Herr Friedemann, Tristan,* and *Fiorenza* (1905)—the latter a drama about Girolamo Savonarola and Lorenzo de' Medici. *Königliche Hoheit* (Royal Highness, 1909) is rather exceptional among his works, for in that novel a prince saves his country through sacrifice. Its emphasis on altruism, common service, and civic spirit foreshadows Mann's later stand for democratic ideals and for everybody's responsibility for the common weal.

Among Mann's most recent novels is *Joseph und seine Brüder* (Joseph and His Brothers, 1933–1944), a tetralogy (*Die Geschichten Jakobs, Der junge Joseph, Joseph in Ägypten,* and *Joseph der Ernährer*), not only a vivid and colorful reproduction of the famed biblical theme, but also a novel valuable for its spiritual message, its delving into ancient myths, its emphasis on the growing and increasingly ennobled conception of Deity and of the position of man among Jews. Out of the old myth's dialectical and philosophical analysis, which betrays the influence of Freudian theories about the manifestations of the subconscious, Mann weaves

a monumental narrative which leads us not only to the bottom
of time, but to the bottom of the human soul as well, and
which pleads the cause of a "Third Humanism," of man's
faithfulness to the invisible God and to the demands of this
world.

Among Thomas Mann's political and historical works can
be named *Friedrich der Grosse und die grosse Koalition*
(1914), a eulogy of Frederick the Great, the great Prussian;
Betrachtungen eines Unpolitischen (Reflections of a Nonpolitical Observer, 1918), in defense of the German character
and its intrinsically apolitical, nondemocratic attitude; and,
later, *Von deutscher Republik* (On the German Republic,
1923), *Die Forderung des Tages* (The Order of the Day,
1930), *Vom zukünftigen Sieg der Demokratie* (The Coming
Victory of Democracy, 1938), *Dieser Friede* (This Peace,
1938), *Dieser Krieg* (This War, 1940), and *Was ist Deutsch?*
(What Is German, 1944), expressions of his faith in the
Weimar Republic and in universal democracy which alone
can save the world from future disasters. After the advent
of National Socialism Thomas Mann became a voluntary
exile, first in Switzerland, later in America.

Recent literary essays and interpretations include *Goethe
und Tolstoi* (1923), *Leiden und Grösse der Meister* (Past
Masters, 1935), essays which deal with Goethe, Platen,
Wagner, Storm, and others, and *Freud und die Zukunft*
(Freud and the Future, 1936). His recent novel *Lotte in
Weimar* (The Beloved Returns, 1939) is likewise a keen
analysis of the genius of Goethe: it describes a later and not
very successful meeting of the heroine of *Werther* with the
patriarch of Weimar. The novel is not only a masterful dis-
section of the great genius, but it also shows Goethe's over-
powering influence on his surroundings, and the sacrifices of
life and happiness which living near a great man involves.
The historical setting of the novel (the War of Liberation)
gives Thomas Mann occasion to muse over the political conditions and dangers of our own time.

Likewise designed for the living, with its message of unity
and harmony embracing beauty and both body and soul, life
and art, is Mann's recent literary production, an adaptation of

an ancient Hindu legend, entitled *Die vertauschten Köpfe*
(The Transposed Heads, 1940).

Minor German Impressionists.

a. EMIL STRAUSS in his novel *Freund Hein* (Death the Comforter, 1902) uses a theme dear to the naturalists: it is an
accusation of the heartless and nondiscriminating school
system of Germany, a pathetic tale of a young genius, a
musician, whom father and teachers drive to suicide—a
Künstlerroman quite different from Hesse's more robust
Peter Camenzind.

b. GEORG HERMANN in his novel *Jettchen Gebert* (1906)
presents skillfully the deep contrasts that separate certain
patrician Jews of Berlin from the unkempt and unscrupulous Jewish immigrants from the East.

c. WALDEMAR BONSELS is best known for his thinly disguised
animal stories of the type of *Die Biene Maja und ihre
Abenteuer* (Adventures of Maya, the Bee, 1912) and
Mario und die Tiere (Adventures of Mario, 1927). As a
globe-trotter he achieved fame with his *Indienfahrt* (Indian
Journey, 1916).

d. EDUARD VON KEYSERLING, like Theodor Fontane a delineator of North German aristocracy, describes in a nervously
refined style the *Junkers* of Prussia and of the Baltic
Provinces, some of them full of primitive vitality and
instincts, others neurotic dreamers and decadents: *Beate
und Mareile* (1903), *Schwüle Tage* (Muggy Days, 1906),
Abendliche Häuser (Houses in the Evening, 1913).

e. An extensive traveler and an impressionistic lyricist
(*Gesammelte Gedichte,* 1931) is MAX DAUTHENDEY,
whose love of exotic atmosphere reminds one of Freiligrath, and whose abundance of colors makes him a forerunner of the expressionistic style. *Raubmenschen* (Men
of Prey, 1911) deals with Mexico; *Lingam* (1910) portrays life and sex in the Orient. Dauthendey died in internment in Java in 1918.

Hugo von Hofmannsthal (1874–1929). Hofmannsthal is
the greatest representative of Austrian aestheticism, much
more feminine than the north German Thomas Mann, a perfect stylist, colorful, romantic, and (especially in his youthful

works) morbid. Of Austrian and Italian-Jewish parentage, living in Vienna, a city where German and Italian, Slav and Hebrew influences meet, Hofmannsthal is essentially a lyric poet (*Gesammelte Gedichte,* 1907), for even his many famous dramas betray a sensitive and quivering lyrical quality.

The refinement of the Italian Renaissance, represented already in *Gestern* (Yesterday, 1892), a playlet about a super-refined and perverse youth, is pictured even more in *Der Tod des Tizian* (The Death of Titian, 1892). This play introduces a new note indicating Hofmannsthal's ultimate victory over aesthetic morbidity, for Titian, in spite of his being a wor-shiper of beauty, is no decadent, but to his very last moment a man of action.

Der Tor und der Tod (Death and the Fool, 1893), a mas-terpiece by the nineteen-year-old Hofmannsthal written in an enamel-like, rich, and sonorous language, portrays a character typical of all these pagan and epicurean aesthetes—for when Death approaches the egotistical, blasé, and tired Claudio he discovers that he has not really lived and that in his ivory tower he has not ever really learned what friendship, love, and grief are.

In *Der Abenteurer und die Sängerin* (The Adventurer and the Singer, 1899) we meet the ever recurrent type of Casanova, the irresistible lover of women, the appreciator of fine pleasures; but whereas life holds no great new pleasures in store for him, his passing love for Vittoria has made her a truly great human being, a divine singer.

Possibly to overcome the decadent fatigue of his spirits, Hofmannsthal subsequently undertook to modernize vigorous older dramas—thus Euripides' *Alkestis,* which presents again the problem of death, and *Elektra* (1903), a work which deals with sexual repression and ensuing vampire-like fury, and in this greatly resembles Oscar Wilde's *Salome;* thus also Sophocles' *Ödipus und die Sphinx* (the study of incest seems to fascinate all Freudians), and *Das gerettete Venedig* (1905), a modernization of Otway's *Venice Preserved.*

In his quest for firm ground upon which to stand and in his wish to give up the unreal existence of an uprooted and decadent aesthete, Hofmannsthal then turned to the solid dogma, the picturesque pageantry, and the mysticism of the

Catholic Church. Thus *Jedermann* (1912), a mystery play adapted from the medieval *Everyman,* and gorgeously staged by Max Reinhardt in front of the Salzburg Cathedral; thus also *Das Salzburger Grosse Welttheater* (1922), an adaptation of Calderón's famed auto-da-fé or mystery play *El gran teatro del mundo,* in which the beggar foolishly protests against the role God has assigned him on the stage of life. In further contrast to the epicurean paganism of his earlier works he then also adapted Calderón's *La dama duende* (*Dame Kobold,* or The Ghost Lady, 1919) and his famous *La vida es sueño* (*Der Turm*—Life Is a Dream, 1925), thus demonstrating anew the Austrians' old predilection for Spanish literature. This latter play also states Hofmannsthal's postwar views on politics: Sigismund, the legitimate heir to the throne, having grown up in jail and seclusion, is pure in spirit and can thus prevail over greedy demagogues and unscrupulous politicians, for the spirit alone, ennobled by years of sufferings, will conquer. Heavy with profound symbolism, written in a transparently clear and noble language, this political testament of Hofmannsthal propagandizes for the regeneration of European culture through a "conservative revolution."

Of his many comedies, all of them lacking in the usual comical ingredients but abounding in unequaled elegance of expression and graceful disentanglements of psychological complications, may be mentioned *Der Schwierige* (The Difficult Gentleman), the exquisitely drawn portrait of an elderly gentleman who is so wrapped up in inhibitions, scruples, and doubts about his own value that he does not dare to propose to the girl he has loved for years.

The highly lyrical and musical qualities of his talent equipped Hofmannsthal ideally to write various librettos which Richard Strauss then used for his operas. Thus *Ariadne auf Naxos, Der Rosenkavalier* (The Rose Bearer, 1911), *Die Frau ohne Schatten* (The Woman without a Shadow, 1919—based on one of his own novels, another study in sex and childlessness), and *Die ägyptische Helena* (Helen in Egypt, 1928). Best known among them is *Der Rosenkavalier:* it is the tale of an eighteenth century gigolo who turns away from his aging mistress in order to marry a charming young girl and to protect her against the crude attentions of an old suitor.

Arthur Schnitzler (1862–1931). With Hofmannsthal and Schnitzler and the other Austrians of their circle, literature reached a new degree of subtlety and refined sensualism. The influence of Sigmund Freud's psychoanalysis is of course especially notable among the Viennese. In the writings of Schnitzler, a Jewish physician who skillfully laid bare the nerves and hidden thoughts of his characters, the overripe and tired culture of Hapsburg Austria is represented particularly by penetrating studies of officers and actors, and of the sweet working-class girls with whom they play.

While Schnitzler's exquisite talent was not quite able to fill a full-length novel with life and breath, it excelled in short stories like *Spiel im Morgengrauen* (Daybreak), *Traumnovelle* (Rhapsody), *Frau Beate und ihr Sohn* (Beatrice), and others.

Anatol (1893), a cycle of seven one-act plays, introduces quite a famous Schnitzlerian character: a promiscuous and expert lover, moody, often even melancholy in spite of his pleasures, a man enjoying his complexes, one to whom life offers few new thrills besides the daily routine of love-making. This somewhat melancholy eroticism distinguishes the decadence of the Viennese sharply from the manlier decadence of Thomas Mann's north Germans or Stefan George's west Germans.

Liebelei (Light o' Love, 1895) is a tragic demonstration that not all Schnitzler's characters are flirts and that some of them suffer greatly from their passionate affairs, for the "sweet girl" commits suicide after she hears that her lover has been killed in a duel because he had but shortly before had an affair with a married woman. Of a similar tenor is the tragic tale of love told in *Blumen* (Flowers).

Der grüne Kakadu (The Green Cockatoo, 1899) reverses Grillparzer's and Calderón's dictum that life is a dream, a mere illusion, because in this seething play about French actors shortly before the French Revolution what had been considered mere play-acting now suddenly becomes stark reality, i.e. a rebellion against aristocracy.

Reigen (Hands Around, 1900), Schnitzler's most notorious

work, which gained for him the title of the Austrian Boccaccio, is a chain of ten analyses of the impulse leading to cohabitation.

Similar probings into the problems of sex are found in *Paracelsus,* which deals with theoretical adultery; *Zwischenspiel* (Intermezzo), a subtle analysis of matrimonial boredom and the wife's repressed yearnings; *Die Schwestern, oder Casanova in Spa* (The Sisters), a flippant comedy about mixed-up bedrooms, and *Casanova's Heimfahrt* (Casanova's Homecoming, 1918), a tragicomic novel about the great lover's old age and impotence. Noteworthy also is *Therese* (1928), the sordid and almost naturalistic tale of the unsavory old age of a former "sweet girl" who is robbed and killed by her own illegitimate son.

Among Schnitzler's full-length plays of historical character may be named *Der Schleier der Beatrice* (The Veil of Beatrice, 1899), treating the licentious Italian Renaissance and the death-dealing Cesare Borgia; and *Der junge Medardus* (Young Medardus, 1910), a rather weak drama of Vienna during the age of Napoleon.

Of more serious bearing are *Der einsame Weg* (The Lonely Way, 1903), a drama in which an illegitimate son refuses to acknowledge and to be a comfort to his hitherto selfish real father; *Der Ehrentag* (The Hour of Fame), a short story about the tragic end of a ham actor; *Professor Bernhardi* (1912), a play which deals with a Jewish physician and ever recurrent evidences of anti-Semitism in Vienna. *Der Weg ins Freie* (The Road to the Open, 1908), Schnitzler's longest novel, also contains many discussions of the Jewish problem.

Monologue novels that are exceedingly well done are *Leutnant Gustl* (None but the Brave, 1901), revealing the tragicomic problems of a charming representative of old imperial Vienna; and *Fräulein Else* (1925), the tragic tale of a young girl in the clutches of an indecent financier.

Other Austrians. To the circle around Hofmannsthal and Schnitzler belong:

a. RICHARD BEER-HOFMANN, author of the famous *Schlaflied für Miriam* (Lullaby for Miriam, 1898), of *Der Graf von Charolais* (The Count of Charolais, 1904), an adapta-

tion of Massinger and Ford's *The Fatal Dowry,* and of the
two impressive biblical plays *Jaakobs Traum* (Jacob's
Dream, 1918) and *Der junge David* (Young David, 1933),
both beautifully lyrical hymns to Israel.

b. MAX MELL, a sincere Catholic who, in his poetic miracle
play *Das Apostelspiel* (The Play of the Apostles, 1923),
stresses the regenerating and redeeming function of faith,
because two lost vagabonds return to the ways of God
after meeting a child who, in her unshakable faith, had
believed them to be two apostles.

c. KARL SCHÖNHERR, like Schnitzler a physician in Vienna,
was like Anzengruber a delineator of Austrian peasantry
and thus racier than his Austrian fellow aesthetes. He
should be remembered for *Erde* (Mother Earth, 1908),
the comedy of an old man's stubborn refusal to die, though
the son would be glad to take over the farm and to get
married. His *Glaube und Heimat* (Faith and Fireside,
1910) is a play about the Counter Reformation with an
anti-Catholic bias typical of quite a few Austrians.

Stefan Zweig (1881–1942). Zweig, a Jewish author from
Vienna, wrote highly sensitive short stories—*Amok* (1923),
Verwirrung der Gefühle (Conflicts, 1926), and especially the
unforgettable *Die unsichtbare Sammlung* (The Invisible Collection)—and biographies and historical sketches of great
lucidity which contrast sharply with the nationalism and
mysticism of modern Nazi biographers. His autobiography,
Die Welt von Gestern (The World of Yesterday, 1943),
published after his suicide in Brazil, reveals best the sensitivity of his character and the deep tragedy of his life and
his Vienna.

Drei Meister (Three Masters, 1919) deals with Balzac,
Dickens, and Dostoevski; *Der Kampf mit dem Dämon* (The
Struggle with the Demon, 1925) analyzes Hölderlin, Kleist,
and Nietzsche; *Drei Dichter ihres Lebens* (Adepts in Self-
Portraiture, 1928) studies Casanova, Stendhal, and Tolstoi;
Sternstunden der Menschheit (Fateful Hours of Humanity,
1928), five historical miniatures, includes a fine study of
Goethe's *Marienbader Elegie;* and *Die Heilung durch den
Geist* (Mental Healers) interprets renowned persons like
Franz Mesmer, Mary Baker Eddy, and Sigmund Freud.

Among Zweig's full-length analyses are his books on *Verlaine* (1905), *Verhaeren* (1910), and *Romain Rolland* (1921), on *Marie Antoinette* and *Joseph Fouché*. In *Triumph und Tragik des Erasmus von Rotterdam* (1935) the gigantic struggle between Erasmus and Luther is particularly well worked out, though to the disadvantage of Luther, in whom the Erasmian Zweig seems to see another Hitler. His *Maria Stuart* (1935) continues Schiller's condemnation of the psychologically well-analyzed Queen Elizabeth. Among Zweig's last works are *Castellio gegen Calvin* (The Right to Heresy: Castellio against Calvin, 1936), *Magellan, der Mann und seine Tat* (Conqueror of the Seas: the Story of Magellan, 1938), and *Brasilien, ein Land der Zukunft* (Brazil, Land of the Future, 1941).

More important than *Tersites* (1907), Zweig's first drama, is his *Jeremias* (1917), a fearless denunciation of war. Following Beer-Hofmann's and Hofmannsthal's predilection for the English drama of the seventeenth century, he also wrote a German adaptation of Ben Jonson's *Volpone*.

Lion Feuchtwanger (1884–1958). *Jud Süss* (Power, 1925) unfolds a broad canvas of the moral corruption at a small absolutistic court in eighteenth century Germany, and thus serves as an excellent introduction to the cultural history of the *ancien régime*. Several incidents of the main plot are somewhat reminiscent of C. F. Meyer's *Der Heilige;* but even so, the character of the unscrupulous Jewish financier and his revenge on the duke of Württemberg are very well described.

Erfolg (Success, 1931) is a daring and debunking tale of postwar Germany during the height of the miseries of the inflation. In spite of his acid criticism Feuchtwanger must have loved Bavaria greatly. The hatred of the south Germans against the Prussians and of the atavistic Agrarians against the postwar Marxists of Berlin is vividly illustrated. His merciless account of Hitler's beer-cellar *Putsch* explains why Feuchtwanger was one of the first to flee Germany when the Nazis came to power, and why, after the fall of France in 1940, he had again to flee for his life (*The Devil in France*).

Other works of Feuchtwanger's include *Die hässliche Herzogin* (The Ugly Duchess, 1923), a historical novel about medieval Tyrol, and *Die Geschwister Oppenheim* (The Oppermanns, 1935), an excellently told story of a highly cultured German-Jewish family which is suddenly faced with the torrential outburst of race hatred in their country. A work of an entirely different type is Feuchtwanger's trilogy about *Josephus,* the Romanized historian of the Jewish Wars.

Among his dramatic compositions may be mentioned colonial plays like *Die Kriegsgefangenen* (Prisoners of War) and *Der holländische Kaufmann* (The Dutch Merchant), and his so-called Anglo-Saxon plays like *Die Petroleuminseln* (The Oil Islands, 1927) and *Kalkutta, 4. Mai* (Warren Hastings). His imitations of the Greek drama are also worth noting: *Die Perser des Aischylos* (The Persians, 1915), and *Friede nach Aristophanes* (Peace, 1918).

Minor Authors of Historical Novels and Biographies.

a. BRUNO FRANK writes about Prussia in the eighteenth century in *Die Tage des Königs* (The Days of the King, 1925) and in *Trenck, Roman eines Günstlings* (Trenck, Love Story of a Favorite, 1928). His drama *Zwölftausend* (Twelve Thousand, 1927) also deals with that period and presents the tragedy of German mercenaries sold to England in order to fight against the American colonies—a theme early touched upon in Schiller's *Kabale und Liebe.* Frank's account of *Cervantes* (1935) is an extremely sensitive fictional reconstruction of the tragic life of the great Spanish writer.

b. ALFRED NEUMANN is the author of historical novels which contain a good deal of macabre criminology and Freudian eroticism, e.g. *Der Teufel* (The Devil, 1926), a tale about devilish wickedness in fifteenth century France; *Königin Christine von Schweden* (Life of Christina of Sweden, 1935), a presentation of the love-life of the daughter of the great Gustavus Adolphus; *Rebellion* (1929), an account of the Italian *Risorgimento; Neuer Caesar* (Another Caesar, 1934), the story of Napoleon III. His last work, *Es waren ihrer sechs* (Six of Them, 1945), is a moving account of an abortive rebellion of six professors and students at the University of Munich against the Nazi regime. The best known among Neumann's plays is *Der Patriot* (1925).

c. EMIL LUDWIG is a prolific author of biographies, many of them competent, some of them slight, beginning in 1913 with *Wagner* and continuing with *Dehmel, Goethe, Rembrandt, Napoleon, Kaiser Wilhelm II, Bismarck, Christus (Der Menschensohn), Hindenburg, Simon Bolivar, Lincoln, Michelangelo, Schliemann, Beethoven.* Among his plays are to be named *Die Borgia, Tristan und Isolde, Friedrich Kronprinz von Preussen, Versailles,* and a trilogy on *Bismarck.* His most recent works include *Conversations with Mussolini,* a biography of *Roosevelt,* and, an interesting innovation, "biographies" of *The Nile* and *The Mediterranean.*

Subjective Seekers of a New and Regenerated Form of Human Existence

Among this group of impressionists appeared harbingers of a new gospel, who fought against the individualism and egotism of nineteenth century bourgeoisie, which seemed doomed after 1914. In his *Deutsche Schriften* (1878) PAUL DE LAGARDE had been one of the first to attack the smugness and the nefarious class distinctions of the old order and to strive for a real unity of the German nation, in which all strata, including labor, would be equally represented. Marxism, which, because of its being more or less suppressed, had tended to become antinational, was to be rejected and replaced by a German brand of socialism, which would collaborate in a rebirth of the German man and the German state. Diagonally opposed to this emphasis on a strong state or on strong individuals (which concept the works of Jakob Burckhardt and Conrad Ferdinand Meyer also seemed to support) were leftist idealists like Rainer Maria Rilke and Jakob Wassermann, and mystics like Erwin Guido Kolbenheyer; yet they, too, from an entirely different angle, were *Künder einer neuen Gemeinschaft* (prophets of a new communal relationship) from which materialism and scepticism would be banished.

Paul Ernst (1866–1933). The exacting ethical teachings of Paul Ernst could but exert a great influence on his style, and because of his striving for perfect and simple art and lucid constructions he is commonly called a neoclassicist. He was a rationalist who wanted to lead the drama back to elevated and austere standards and to strict Aristotelian rules; hence the works of Hebbel rather than those of the naturalists were his models. In his straight-lined dramas and tales he liked to extol a heroic conception of life; his disillusionment about modern corruption and weakness is expressed in an astoundingly timed essay *Der Zusammenbruch des Marxismus* (The Collapse of Marxism, 1918).

His short stories often depict an Italian or a Spanish background—*Der Tod des Cosimo* (The Death of Cosimo), *Ein Familienbild von Goya* (A Family Portrait by Goya); but Ernst is at his best in his *Geschichten von deutscher Art* (Stories of German Ways and Manners, 1928), for he is fond of German medieval tales and of humorous anecdotes of the type of Till Eulenspiegel. In *Grün aus Trümmern* (Hope amidst Ruins, 1923), *Der Schatz im Morgenbrotstal* (The Treasure in the Morgenbrot Valley, 1926), and *Das Glück von Lauental* (The Luck of Lauental, 1931) he portrays the misery of Germany after 1918 and 1648 respectively, yet keeps on insisting that real folk unity can bring about recovery and strength. That recovery cannot come without heroic hardships, though; for in *Saat auf Hoffnung* (Seed and Hope, 1914) a millionaire does not help those who are poor and bitter by distributing his wealth among them.

Ernst's neoclassical dramas, which disregard milieu and elaborate on heroic ethics alone, include *Demetrios* (1905), a Russian theme which Schiller and Hebbel had already tried to treat and which Ernst now transformed into a Greek tale by describing the dilemma and the social and personal problems of a Spartan usurper about 150 B.C., *Canossa* (1908), *Manfred und Beatrice* (1912), *Preussengeist* (Prussian Spirit, 1914), *Kassandra* (1915), and *York* (1917, dealing with the dilemma of a Prussian general in Napoleon's service in 1812)—all of them dramas which teach us that man can be cured only if he is strong enough to overcome his sufferings. *Brunhild* (1909) and *Chriemhild* (1910) demonstrate anew Ernst's efforts to achieve somber classical simplicity and to underscore the role which character and fate play in dramatic conflicts. Ernst has been hailed as an early forerunner of National Socialism.

230

Wilhelm von Scholz (1874–   ). Scholz, another neo-classicist, who formulated his new theories in *Gedanken zum Drama* (Thoughts on the Drama, 1905), is considerably more mystical than was the strictly rational Paul Ernst.

Among his early works we can point to *Der Gast* (The Guest, 1900), which resembles greatly Gerhart Hauptmann's *Die versunkene Glocke* in that this drama about a plague-ridden medieval city deals with an inspiring female who lures a master architect away from his wife; *Der Jude von Konstanz* (The Jew of Constance, 1905), which depicts the futility of the efforts of a Jew to desert his race and religion and deals with the problems of anti-Semitism—rampant in the Middle Ages no less than in our days. *Meroë* (1906) anticipates Ernst's *Canossa* in portraying the conflict between state and Church and the eternal antagonism between father and son, because the latter, for a while, supports the priests against his own father.

Adaptations from Calderón de la Barca—*Das Leben ein Traum* (Life Is a Dream)—and Tirso de Molina—*Vertauschte Seelen* (Exchanged Souls, 1910)—indicate Scholz's increasing love for mystic and mysterious themes. Thus, in *Das Herzwunder* (The Heart-Wonder, 1918), a harlot who has taught the meaning of love to a monk turns out to be the Virgin Mary; in *Der Wettlauf mit dem Schatten* (The Race with the Shadow, 1921) occult forces bind together an author and the hero of a novel not yet finished by him, whose lives hitherto had been exactly alike.

Scholz's love of mysticism and of medieval themes is seen in his edition of *Deutsche Mystiker* (German Mystics, 1908); in his lyric poems contained in *Hohenklingen* (1898), *Die Balladen und Königsmärchen* (Ballads and Kings' Tales), and *Minnesang* (1917); and in his short stories—*Die Beichte* (The Confession, 1919)—and his novels of the type of *Das Zwischenreich* (The Realm Between, 1919) and *Perpetua* (1926).

Minor Neoclassical Authors.

a. SAMUEL LUBLINSKI was the author of yet another Nibelungen drama, *Gunther und Brunhild* (1908), and important also for his antinaturalistic essays *Die Bilanz der Moderne* (The Balance of Naturalism, 1904), *Ausgang der Moderne* (The Decline of Naturalism, 1909), and *Holz und Schlaf,* "a painful chapter of literary history."

b. HANS FRANCK in his medieval drama *Godiva* (1919) takes sides with the husband rather than with the legendary English lady; in *Kleist* (1933) he glorifies Prussianism and the poet's duty to serve his fatherland.

c. WILHELM SCHMIDTBONN's *Mutter Landstrasse* (The Highway, 1904) deals with an unreconciled prodigal son whom too deep an abyss separates from the older generation; *Der Graf von Gleichen* (1908) analyzes the man between two women by presenting the story of the Count of Gleichen, a crusader, who returns to his wife with a second wife he has acquired among the Saracens; *Der Zorn des Achilles* (The Wrath of Achilles, 1909) portrays the anger of a superman.

d. WILHELM SCHÄFER, a Rhinelander, in his remarkable *Die dreizehn Bücher der deutschen Seele* (The Thirteen Books of the German Soul, 1922) a glorifier of the heroic qualities of the German race, is also noteworthy for his biographies of great Swiss and German thinkers and artists: *Der Lebenstag eines Menschenfreundes* (The Life of a Humanitarian, 1915), in which he hails Pestalozzi for being the first to educate a nation to service and to real unity, *Winckelmanns Ende* (Winckelmann's Death, 1925), *Hölderlins Einkehr* (Hölderlin's Homecoming, 1925), and *Huldreich Zwingli* (1926).

e. RUDOLF BINDING, author of brooding war poems—*Stolz und Trauer* (Pride and Mourning, 1922), is at his best in his *Legenden der Zeit* (Legends of the Ages, 1909) in which he opposes the life-killing austerity of the Christian Church. His *Antwort eines Deutschen an die Welt* (Answer of a German to the World, 1933) in defense of the Nazi revolution indicates the confusion of thought prevailing at that time even among German intellectuals of proved integrity.

Carl Spitteler (1845–1924). Spitteler, the great but often unfathomable Swiss poet and Nobel Prize winner from Basel, like Nietzsche was a scorner of middle-class morality and greedy materialism. A student of Jakob Burckhardt, who had imbued him with pessimism and a titanic defiance of the mediocrity of our world, he forms the bridge between the Nietzscheans and the later circle around Stefan George.

In his *Conrad der Leutnant* (1898) and *Imago* (1905) there is already noticeable his proud rebellion against the powers that be. In the first novel the son rises against a dictatorial father; in the second novel the hero, disappointed to see his ideal girl gradually become a Mrs. Babbitt, refuses to let himself be drawn in by the philistines, and escapes from her and all she stands for in order to save his soul. Rather than be a "Tasso amidst democrats," as Spitteler stated it, he preferred to remain aloof and idealistic.

But his two greatest works are *Prometheus und Epimetheus* (1881) and *Olympischer Frühling* (Olympian Spring, 1905)—the former published even ahead of Nietzsche's great works, whose aphoristic and proud style it may have influenced. Disgusted by the utilitarianism of modern mentality, and rebellious even against God and the many imperfections of his world, Spitteler strives to be a new priest, a herald of a new cosmic myth, a prophet of man's intellectual regeneration. He tells us the story of the first Gods who lived amidst impressive and invigorating mountains resembling the Swiss Alps: in the first epic he hails the defiant and strong Prometheus, the idealist, the rebellious battler who, though defeated, is far superior to the clever and unscrupulous Epimetheus (no matter how much Goethe, in *Pandora,* may have praised the latter) ; in the second epic he likewise extols Apollo over the crafty Zeus. Depth of thought and boldness of fantasy permeate the two works; though Spitteler speaks in oracles and is hence not appreciated by the reading public at large, he endeavors to convince us that not matter but the spirit shall prevail, and that the idealist, the regenerated heroic man, will ultimately win out in our daily battle against the soul-killing mediocrity of our civilization.

Stefan George (1868–1933). George, a worshiper of beauty in whom the cult of Nietzschean titanism and of somewhat decadent and superrefined symbolism are strangely blended, like Hölderlin dreamed of a German rebirth, and like Platen and Meyer strove after pure, cold, and perfect form. Surrounded by a chosen circle of disciples, he kept aloof from the follies and weaknesses of the world ; the poet, according to him, is a seer, a prophet, who speaks for the chosen few only and who refuses to attract the mob. Hence the intended refinement and occasionally obscure symbolism of his language, the archaic forms, the unique spelling and punctuation. He believed in a terse, symmetrical, architectural, and finely chiselled form, an art for art's sake, in which the thought may well remain hidden to the casual reader—a trait which distinguishes him from the neoclassical epigones of the Munich School. The close study of Dante, Petrarch, and Torquato Tasso, of Shakespeare, the French symbolists, Edgar Allan Poe, and other supreme artists alienated him more and more from the crude vitality of Naturalism; as a poet-priest he, like Spitteler, felt that he had a higher mission to fulfill. In 1890 there began to appear his collections of poems (*Hymnen, Pilgerfahrt, Algabal*), and in the same year he published the first issue of the *Blätter für die Kunst* (Periodical for Art), the mouthpiece of the distinguished George circle of aesthetes to which also the great literary critics Friedrich Gundolf and Ernst Bertram belonged. The cult, indeed the holiness, of the word forms one of the main tenets of the school; such austerely classical later works as *Die Bücher der Hirten- und Preisgedichte* (The Books of Eclogues and Eulogies, 1895), *Das Jahr der Seele* (The Year of the Soul, 1897), *Der Teppich des Lebens* (The Carpet of Life, 1899), and also his careful and stately translations from Verlaine, Swinburne, d'Annunzio, and, later, from Dante's *Divina Commedia* and Shakespeare's *Sonnets* give ample proof of that. Like Nietzsche, George was opposed to middle-class mentality; in spite of his rather decadent aestheticism he belonged to those who preach of superhuman strength and will power, of the deification of man, of Apollonian restraint and a stern will to quality. His worship of male beauty as the greatest source of inspiration is seen especially in *Der siebente Ring* (The Seventh Ring, 1911); in it George rejects woman in favor of an ideal youth, Maximin, who to him represented God incarnated—for proud and strong and godlike men alone seemed worthy of song. To the internally split and disorganized Germany of World War I this Spartan poet addressed harsh words in *Der Krieg* (War, 1917): not comfort and effeminacy, but loyalty and obedience to a called leader alone can win wars. George's last collections of poems are *Der Stern des Bundes* (The Star of the Order, 1914), *Der Dichter in Zeiten der Wirren* (The Poet in Times of Chaos, 1921), and *Das neue Reich* (The New Reich, 1929) ; they restate his ever increasing emphasis on the necessity of a spiritual rebirth of man—a tenet which, together with his espousal of the *Führerprinzip* and the cult of the state, induced the Nazis to assume that Stefan George was one of their prophets, though his insistence on being buried in Switzerland rather than in Germany indicates clearly his deep aversion to their rowdyism.

Molo. Walter von Molo loves to bring out the heroic qualities of the German people; thus in his historical works: *Ein Schiller Roman,* in four volumes (1912) ; *Friedericus* (1918), *Luise* (the undaunted queen of Prussia during the Napoleonic invasion, 1919), *Das Volk wacht auf* (The People Awakens, 1924)—all three novels collected under the title of *Der Roman meines Volkes* (The Tale of My People) ; *Mensch Luther* (Brother Luther, 1928) ; and *Ein Deutscher ohne Deutschland* (A German without Germany, 1931), a novel dealing with the great economist Friedrich List. Among Molo's essays and speeches mention might be made of *Wie ich Deutschland möchte* (How I Should Like Germany To Be, 1932).

Erwin Guido Kolbenheyer (1878–   ). With Kolbenheyer, a generally accepted author of the Third Reich, mysticism and the theme of man's inner regeneration or *Wandlung* enter into the field of the historical novel.

Paracelsus, a trilogy (1917–1925) treating the famed Swiss scholar of the sixteenth century who was the first modern physician, evolves before our eyes a truly Faustian and heroic character who struggles against obsolete traditions and hostile reactionaries in order to formulate his own philosophy of life and religion.

Giordano Bruno, too, the great Italian pantheist and rebel of the late Renaissance, in the drama *Heroische Leidenschaften* (Heroic Passions, 1929) grapples with problems and dogmas. Not even the death sentence by the Inquisition that he be burned at the stake can alter his proud and individualistic religious convictions.

Among Kolbenheyer's other works, all of them analyses of historical characters, are *Amor Dei* (1908), an excellent interpretation of the pantheistic and unorthodox thinker Spinoza, the greatest modern philosopher of the Jewish race; *Meister Joachim Pausewang* (1910), depicting a hero who, like Jakob Böhme, the great Silesian mystic of the seventeenth century, was a shoemaker in Breslau; *Karlsbader Novelle* (1934), an analysis of the crisis in Goethe's life shortly before his flight to Italy; and *Gregor und Heinrich* (1934), another modern interpretation of the age-old feud between Church and state.

Brod. Max Brod, noteworthy for his book on *Heinrich Heine* (1934) and for the posthumous publication, against their author's expressed wishes, of Franz Kafka's *Gesammelte Schriften* (Collected Writings, 1935–1937), is especially to be remembered for his *Tycho Brahes Weg zu Gott* (Tycho Brahe's Road to God, 1916), the tale of a Godseeker. The contrast between the great astronomers Tycho Brahe and Johann Kepler is very well worked out; the former is ardent and mystic, the latter cool and rational.

Rainer Maria Rilke (1875–1926). Rilke, born in Bohemia and one of the greatest poets in German literature, distinguished himself in the role of poet as prophet, as philosopher, as seer. He was religious, but unorthodox; philosophic, but unsystematic; mystic, but aesthetic rather than ascetic. Like Stefan George, he was a symbolist, a perfect artist, and opposed to Naturalism. He endeavored to express the inexpressible, to extend the boundaries of language by his search for external symbols of his internal insights and visions.

Rilke made two trips to Russia which had a tremendous impact upon him; he became a mystic, a humanitarian, a poet who dreams of man's regeneration not in terms of Nietzschean supermen and blond demigods, but in terms of humility, compassion, and brotherhood. The *Wandlung* of the individual, the complete obliteration of foolish bourgeois pride and egotism, means everything to him. Not the plastic gods of Greece, not the amoral characters of the Italian Renaissance, but the half-Oriental mysticism, the endless plains, the communistic dreams of Russia inspire him most deeply. Every human being is created in the image of God; like

Buddha and Christ we must go out among the sick and the poor if we want to find again the nobility of our souls. Not radical theories, not arrogant titanism, not smug bourgeois self-complacency (so contrary to the real spirit of religion, though we continue to call ourselves Christians) can help us; the spirit of fraternal love, the theme of *Bruder Mensch* (Brother Man), alone can. For quite different reasons from those of the proud aesthetes of the type of Hofmannsthal and George, Rilke had to stay alone and be lonely in order to fathom the very depth of his ardent soul: sickly and delicate, like a restless prophet, he wandered all over Europe, stayed in France, Spain, Italy, Denmark, Sweden, and died finally in Switzerland. Also, marriage did not agree with this oversensitive poet and he left his wife after little more than one year (1901). Though Rilke is an accomplished artist, he cannot be called merely a decadent aesthete and symbolist; his message is too earnest, his convictions are too strong and too pure. Spiritually he is antipodal to all proud Nietzscheans; many of his heroes are indeed physical weaklings. His reformatory zeal justifies us in calling him a forerunner of the ardent expressionists.

Among Rilke's first lyrical collections are *Traumgekrönt* (Dream-crowned, 1897), *Mir zur Feier* (In My Honor, 1899), and then especially his immortal *Das Stundenbuch* (The Book of Hours, 1905): they contain poems about his native Bohemia expressing a simple, subservient relationship to nature, but mainly sincere, mystic, and pantheistic stanzas full of irrational fervor, of simple and childlike faith, and of genuine love and infinite commiseration for the poor and the oppressed, especially those in the slums of the big, soul-killing cities.

Of his prose tales are to be mentioned *Am Leben hin* (On the Rim of Life, 1898), a series of short stories demonstrating mainly that those who do not possess ideal love merely live on the rim of life; *Der Totengräber* (The Grave-digger), which teaches that unselfishness alone must be the basis of love; *Kleine Novellen* (Little Tales), which preach that dream and death are more real and more important than life; and the famous and childlike *Geschichten vom lieben Gott* (Tales about the Dear Lord, 1904), in which we see that God seeks man as desperately as man ought to seek Him—the concept of an imperfect, future God, ultimately the creation of his creatures.

Especially important for our understanding of Rilke is his autobiographical *Die Aufzeichnungen des Malte Laurids Brigge* (Notebook of Malte Laurids Brigge, 1909), a *Künstlerroman* of a very unusual type, the story of a Danish youth, a morbid and poor artist, who has a frightful aversion to the godless big cities (Paris). Life and death, to Malte, are parts of a greater whole; death alone is the supreme consummation and perfection of our existence, the moment when our yearned-for *unio mystica* with God at last becomes real.

Among his later works are *Das Buch der Bilder* (The Book of Pictures, 1902), *Die Weise von Liebe und Tod des Cornets Christoph Rilke* (Tale of the Love and Death of Cornet Christopher Rilke, 1906—a romantic, rhapsodic account of an early ancestor), and, a great turning point in his conception of art, his *Neue Gedichte* (New Poems, 1907 and 1908). The *Neue Gedichte* show the supreme influence of the great French sculptor Auguste Rodin, whose secretary Rilke had been (cf. his *Auguste Rodin,* 1903); for poetry, besides containing an earnest message, shall also be a flawless piece of art, impeccable in alliteration, vowel harmony, rime, and rhythm. Here, too, Rilke revealed a new attitude toward objective reality in his attempt to apprehend the very essence of things, both animate and inanimate, and to recreate such objects in poems. The *Neue Gedichte* contain many of the "thing-poems" (*Dinggedichte*) for which Rilke is so celebrated: *Der Panther, Die Gazelle, Persische Heliotrop, Archäischer Torso Apollos, Die Fensterrose,* etc.

After the tragedy of the Great War, which seemed to have crushed him and paralyzed his genius, there appeared, in 1923, *Die Sonette an Orpheus* and especially *Die Duineser Elegien,* named after Duino on the Dalmatian coast where he had stayed in 1912 and had written the earliest of these supremely important elegies. These Rilke considered his best work, and most critics begin to agree that they, rather than the *Stundenbuch* or the *Geschichten vom lieben Gott,* deserve our fullest appreciation. They indicate in verses whose intense concentration and profundity of thought are unparalleled in modern lyrics a greater affirmation of life than his previous works, for even life and the sufferings of life are God-willed and should hence be borne proudly. In this final phase of Rilke's attitude toward outward things, subordination and penetration are superseded by transformation; he endeavors to perceive unity in disparity in the same way in which he has seen life and death as component parts of a greater whole. In these poems he coupled what has been called "lamentation over the limitations and deficiencies of human nature" with celebration of existence itself despite deficiency and limitations.

Of Rilke's translations (besides Baudelaire, Verlaine, Mallarmé, and, later, Paul Valéry and André Gide) should be mentioned his version of Elizabeth Barrett Browning's *Sonnets from the Portuguese;* also *Die vierzig Sonnette der Louise Labé Lyoneserin* (a French poetess of the sixteenth century), and his translation of various poems of Michelangelo Buonarroti. Furthermore, in his *Portugiesische Briefe* (Portuguese Letters, 1913), he rendered into German the celebrated love letters of the seventeenth century Portuguese nun Marianne Alcoforada. Although Rilke's independence and strongly developed individuality prevented him from producing superior translations through his inability to subject himself sufficiently to secondary inspiration, the same qualities combined with his sensitiveness, his receptiveness, and his responsiveness contributed to make Rilke a superlative letter writer, supreme in his own time and seldom ever equaled.

Morgenstern. In the last analysis also the poetry of Christian Morgenstern (1871–1914) should perhaps be grouped here. To be sure, he is a satirist and writes lyrical verses that are whimsical and intellectual and far above the ordinary run of humorous verses (e.g. his *Galgenlieder*); but, like most satirists, Morgenstern is more often than not a melancholy man who in his philosophical speculations and in his efforts to find a spiritual meaning in earthly life dwells on the relativity of man's knowledge, and who finally ends up as a mystic. Especially noteworthy are his humorous plays on words and his fine gift for weaving mood into rhythm.

Hermann Stehr (1864–   ). This advocate of man's spiritual rebirth rejects the shallow materialism of modern civilization; sturdy peasants and craftsmen, rather than modern Babbitts, will through their strength and faith bring about a regeneration of man's communal life. Among his early novels, written in the naturalistic manner, can be named *Der begrabene Gott* (The Buried God, 1905).

Der Heiligenhof (Heiligenhof Farm, 1917) betrays a mysticism and a visionary fervor which among Stehr's fellow Silesians had been revealed already by the great Baroque authors of the seventeenth century and by some of Gerhart Hauptmann's works. The theme, developed in a laborious and cumbersome style, is man's belated but not futile quest of God. As in *Und Pippa tanzt,* only the blind see the supreme truth; but the blind and saintly daughter of the farmer commits suicide because her love for Peter Brindeisener, the son of her father's inveterate enemy, seems so utterly hopeless. In atonement and faith alone does the old man then find peace and salvation. In 1924 Stehr continued this tale in *Peter Brindeisener.*

Stehr's mysticism and close attachment to Silesian peasantry, plus his demand that an individual should completely subordinate himself to the welfare of his community (as expressed, e.g., in his *Nathanael Mächler,* 1929), contributed to make him one of the most widely accepted authors of the Third Reich.

Jakob Wassermann (1873–1934). Wassermann is one of the best German-Jewish authors of modern times, a man who tries to analyze and cure sick souls, and to spread among them the gospel of good fellowship and compassion. As early as 1921, in his *Mein Weg als Deutscher und Jude* (My Life as German and Jew), Wassermann proudly declares that even as a Jew he is part and heir of the great German culture. His earliest work, *Die Juden von Zirndorf* (The Jews of Zirndorf, 1897) deals with the history and myths of the Jews in his native Franconia.

Caspar Hauser oder die Trägheit des Herzens (Caspar Hauser or the Sluggishness of the Heart, 1908) reminds us of Rousseau's teachings that man is naturally good and has fallen upon evil solely through corruption by modern society.

Like Sigismund in Hofmannsthal's *Turm,* the hero, who has grown up as a secluded captive and against whom wicked crimes have been committed, would indeed, isolated as he was from the world, have become perfect and saintly if the contact with outsiders, men and women of mean and sluggish hearts, were not trying to corrupt and destroy him.

Das Gänsemännchen (The Goose Man, 1915), a daring study of bigamy, is modelled after the somewhat notorious life of the Storm and Stress poet Bürger, though the hero of this novel supposedly is a musician from Nürnberg who ignores the spiritual meaning of life and good fellowship by living for his art and his selfish ego alone.

Christian Wahnschaffe (The World's Illusion, 1919), one of the great novels of postwar Germany, shows best Wassermann's faith in humanity and his ardent teachings of true brotherhood among men—teachings which he, like Rilke, bases upon the idealistic communism of the early Christians and the saintly, unselfish life of Buddha. After a lost war Germany was desperately groping for new ideals and values to hold on to ; Christian Wahnschaffe, who scorns the millions of his father in order to help and associate with murderers and prostitutes, thinks he has found the answer to the old charge that the modern bourgeoisie, though Christian, is in effect anti-Christian in its greed, niggardliness, and heartlessness. Christian, like Christ, goes out among the lepers who really need him; his story, like the one of Stehr's *Heiligenhof* farmer, is the story of a *Wandlung.* Quite rightly, this novel has frequently been compared to Dostoevski's *Brothers Karamazov.*

The same quest for spiritual redemption, for new values in our valueless world, forms the nucleus of the cycle of tales *Der Wendekreis* (The Tropic), the most significant of which is *Oberlins drei Stufen* (Oberlin's Three Stages).

Der Fall Maurizius (The Maurizius Case, 1928), later followed by *Etzel Andergast* (1931), is an ambitious though somewhat incoherent detective novel in which the unraveling of a murder takes the reader among hypnotics and homosexuals and other physical and moral wrecks of the modern world. It is also a bitter castigation of so-called justice and judicial fallacies.

241

As in the *Maurizius* cycle, Wassermann's faith in the idealistic nobleness of young people is expressed in a charming
earlier short story, *Der Aufruhr um den Junker Ernst* (The
Rebellion for Young Squire Ernst), in which the youngsters
of a medieval village flock together to rescue their beloved
young master.

EXPRESSIONISM

Characteristics of Expressionism

Like the naturalists, the expressionists stand in the midst
of the battle of life; theirs is a militant and aggressive type
of literature. Morbid, sexual, and perverse themes, the unfortunate characteristics of modern "literature," are particularly frequent among them. In stating their problems the
expressionists, in contrast to the naturalists, detach themselves completely from the visual, external picture and dwell
only on the souls, the sensations, and the inner reactions of
their heroes. Thus elevated, their art threatens to become
abstract, allegorical, mysterious; and many commentaries are
indeed often necessary to explain the visions, the ecstatic
concepts, and the hallucinations in the hero's soul. Impressionism, being still essentially realistic, had been proceeding
from the exterior to the interior; Expressionism, however,
being essentially romantic and a postulate of the soul, tries
to proceed from the interior to the exterior, and to give
expression to man's mental phenomena. Though many traits
of the expressionists may still be naturalistic, the poets now
animate the drab pictures of Naturalism with their own fire
and passion. Expressionism is thus unique among the literary
schools, because its representatives do not claim that their
art should imitate nature. Instead, they want to emphasize
the forcefulness of their outcries; their thoughts are written
down in white heat and resist being molded into clear pictures or into a calm and symmetrical style. The wild social
and political protests of this type we have met already among
the poets of the Storm and Stress, of Young Germany, and
of Naturalism, except that the naturalistic sobriety of these
latter schools now is superseded by the haze of subjective
and lyrical emotionalism to which the term *Rauschkunst*

(Dionysian outbursts, as Nietzsche would call them) can well be applied. Especially the tragedy of World War I and the dawn of the Russian Revolution lend a tremendous impetus to this new movement. Every poet feels like a prophet and a leader; with his dire prophecies about the impending downfall of Western civilization and its soul-killing big-city life, he mingles glowing descriptions of the coming brotherhood of all men and fervent utopias of a communistic paradise.

Forerunners of Expressionism

Foremost among the stylistic forerunners of Expressionism must be named the great Swedish novelist and dramatist August Strindberg, in whose works men are driven to crimes or saintliness by some omnipotent force that dominates us all (*The Father, Confessions of a Fool, Inferno, Damascus*). Like the three great German woman-haters Schopenhauer, Nietzsche, and Wedekind, Strindberg is fanatically opposed to women and to the frightful sexual power they hold over the ever present instincts of men; hence his bitter scorn of the efforts of such naturalists as Ibsen or Sudermann to grant them equal rights. As to the spiritual forerunners of Expressionism: they are to be found almost exclusively in Russia, in Dostoevski and Tolstoi no less than in the newest Messiah, Lenin. Leading German impressionists who veered towards Expressionism and who were deeply influenced by Russia are Rilke and Wassermann.

Expressionist Authors

Among the outstanding expressionistic works can be mentioned the poems of Franz Werfel, the novels of Klabund, Franz Kafka, and Alfred Döblin, and the dramas of Frank Wedekind, Georg Kaiser, Ernst Toller, and Fritz von Unruh. The great theater director whose bold genius contributed most to stage the lofty and difficult visions of the expressionists was Max Reinhardt. Quite noteworthy also are modern communistic adaptations of older plays (e.g. of Schiller's *Räuber* in the garb of proletarians and gangsters, 1926)— most of them done by Erwin Piscator, a pioneer in modern staging. The majority of the expressionists are today in exile, if not dead.

243

Frank Wedekind (1864–1918). Wedekind's naturalistic dramas are filled with grotesque thoughts and tempestuous messages; even more than by Ibsen and Shaw, he was influenced by Strindberg. He began as a naturalist, but veered ever more towards symbolism and may well be considered the earliest great representative of Expressionism, which he introduced as early as 1891, shortly after Naturalism had come to the fore and some time before Impressionism put in an appearance. In his bitter struggle against the bourgeois world Wedekind was obsessed by the mania of the omnipotence of sex. In battling for sexual enlightenment, for free love, and for equal rights for unmarried mothers, he repeated sexual themes *ad absurdum*. His plays often tend to become bizarre and grotesque; through hyperbolic exaggerations and under the mask of a clown he tries to revolutionize society and to push through his very limited reforms. He loves to depict a world of harlots, clowns, and charlatans which he opposes to the well-groomed society of his day. He does not show any evidence of the social pity of the naturalists and the later expressionists; in contrast to the documentary objectivity of the former he does, however, like the latter, tend to become ever more subjective, violent, rhetorical in his style. His ways of expression are often confusing; the distinction between reality and hallucination is less clearly marked than, e.g., in Gerhart Hauptmann. In his frenzied efforts to establish the legitimacy of sex and to justify the power of man's instincts (to which power modern decadents and hypocrites should return) Wedekind preaches a gospel of amorality which resembles a one-sided interpretation of Nietzsche.

Frühlings Erwachen (The Awakening of Spring, 1891) is a pathetic tragedy about the struggles and catastrophes in the lives of adolescent children. What they need is sexual enlightenment rather than hypocrisy and reform schools.

In *Der Erdgeist* (Earth-Spirit, 1895) and *Die Büchse der Pandora* (Pandora's Box, 1903) Wedekind creates his most famous heroine, the vampire-like Lulu, the very incarnation of womanhood and sex—not a sinner, as the bourgeois so stupidly believe, not a product merely of her milieu, as the naturalists maintain, but the embodiment of life and desire, the driving power behind all creations of nature which yearn for life and procreation.

Hidalla (1904) is Nietzschean in its vision of a new race of supermen. The play deals with Karl Hetman, secretary to the "International Union for the Breeding of Beautiful Thoroughbreds," and the promiscuous, amorous adventures of the eugenically certified members of that sect.

Der Marquis von Keith (1900) is a drama about an impostor, which demonstrates well the utter irony, the bawdiness, and the clownishness of Wedekind's way of looking at life.

Minor Novelists. The expressionistic novel is represented by the following minor authors:

a. KASIMIR EDSCHMID, author of *Die sechs Mündungen* (The Six Channels, 1915) and *Das rasende Leben* (Frenzied Life, 1916), two collections of short stories, and yet another *Lord Byron, Roman einer Leidenschaft* (A Passionate Rebel, the Life of Lord Byron, 1929), whose ecstatic style is typical of the new school. Noteworthy also is Edschmid's programmatic essay *Über den dichterischen Expressionismus* (On Expressionism in Literature, 1919).

b. KLABUND (Alfred Henschke), a lover of exotic names and exotic poems, excelled in his Oriental translations and adaptations—*Dumpfe Trommel und berauschtes Gong* (Dull Drum and Frenzied Gong, 1915), *Li-Tai-Pe* (1916), *Das Sinngedicht des persischen Zeltmachers* (The Wisdom of the Persian Tent Maker, 1917). Also Oriental and fairy-like are his drama *Der Kreidekreis* (The Circle of Chalk, 1925) and his short tale *Der letzte Kaiser* (The Last Emperor). In his rather autobiographical *Bracke, ein Eulenspiegel-Roman* (1918) Klabund then turned to German themes. His communistic ideas were revealed in his *Störtebecker,* a short story which glorifies the well-known north German pirate. His stories in *Krankheit* (Illness, 1916) tell of life in a Swiss sanatorium where he died of consumption in 1926, at the age of only 35.

c. RENÉ SCHICKELE, an Alsatian and half French, editor of the expressionistic periodical *Die weissen Blätter* (The White Pages) and during the First World War a pacifist refugee in Switzerland, bitterly denounced the stupidity of war in his *Benkal der Frauentröster* (Benkal the Comforter of Women, 1914). It is a novel which resembles Clara Viebig's *Weiberdorf* and *Die Töchter der Hekuba* in emphasizing the sexual needs of women. Schickele is especially fine and significant in his treatments of the sadly perplexing Alsatian problem—e.g. in his cycle of stories *Das Erbe am Rhein* (The Heirloom on the Rhine) and in his drama *Hans im Schnackenloch*.

d. In connection with Schickele may be mentioned another author who tried to act as a mediator between France and Germany: ANNETTE KOLB, who in her *Exemplar* (The Model) gives a tender character sketch, while her biography *Briand* does homage to the great French diplomat who fought for Franco-German friendship.

e. Beginning with such expressionistic novels as *Tiere in Ketten* (Animals in Chains) and *Nahar,* emphasizing the animalistic wildness of man, the Austrian ERNST WEISS wrote in later years penetrating studies of social and human ills in his doctor novel *Georg Letham, Arzt und Mörder* (George Letham, Physician and Murderer, 1933) and in *Der arme Verschwender* (The Poor Spendthrift, 1936).

f. Other novelists veering from the extreme right to the extreme left include HERMANN BURTE, who in *Wiltfeber der ewige Deutsche* (Wiltfeber the Eternal German, 1912) preached a turning away from Christianity and Marxism and a return to Germanic principles and racial purity; ARNOLD ULITZ, author of *Ararat* (1921), a description of the communistic utopia which will arise after the new deluge that will engulf the world; JOSEF WINCKLER, who in his *Trilogie der Zeit* (Trilogy of Our Time, 1924) bitterly assailed our modern machine age which makes man an industrial robot.

g. Novels of a different type are concerned with Satanism. They combine fantastic ideas with repulsive naturalistic details; in their glorification and worship of that which is evil they are utterly un-Christian. Among the sundry descendants of Ernst Theodor Amadeus Hoffmann and Edgar Allan Poe, who mix gruesomeness with lewdness, vulgarity, and supernatural elements, we can point to

Hanns Heinz Ewers, author of *Die Alraune* (Mandrake, 1913) and *Der Vampir* (The Vampire, 1920), and to Gustav Meyrink, whose *Der Golem* (1916) deals with the horrible tale of a robot. The sexual aberrations of Satanism are represented in the notorious novels of Leopold von Sacher-Masoch, e.g. in his *Das Vermächtnis Kains* (The Legacy of Cain).

Franz Kafka (1883–1924). Kafka, perhaps the most unusual figure in contemporary German literature, has come into his own only after his premature death. During his lifetime he published but a handful of short stories; his three great novel fragments *Amerika, Der Prozess* (The Trial), and *Das Schloss* (The Castle) were edited posthumously by his friend Max Brod. It is almost impossible to place Kafka within the literary schools of our time. His language is minutely realistic, showing sometimes even a cumbersome meticulousness. But this extreme prosaicness only tends to heighten the effect of strangeness which the dreamlike superreality, the allegoric fantasy, of Kafka's stories and characters exerts. It is a pedantically realistic world, but a world which seems strangely suspended in empty space. And this quality of "suspense" is, indeed, the main characteristic of Kafka's work. Every single story of Kafka is an allegorical treatment of man in his crises. Every single one of them depicts a passionate attempt of man to integrate himself in the world, in a world, however, which is still one with God. Man is "out of focus"—and this obliqueness gives Kafka's work a painfully tragic and at times gruesomely grotesque note. The hero of *Die Verwandlung* (The Metamorphosis) wakes up and finds himself transformed into a huge insect, cut off from the community of his family, trying in vain to make himself understood. There is no redemption for aloneness and from guilt, because God is inaccessible, a judge who can never be reached and who never pronounces the final judgment. The crisis is insoluble. In *Amerika* it seems as if there might be a way out, but in *Der Prozess* man, awakened to the consciousness of his original sin, tries in vain to stand trial, although he knows that he is indicted. In *Das Schloss* the newcomer to the village tries in vain to get access to the castle where the supreme master dwells. God is hopelessly beyond, and since the world is cut off from God's grace, all the happenings in Kafka's stories and all the movements of his characters strike us as undecipherable ciphers and as grotesque reflexes of marionettes. But these weird allegories betray one of the profoundest religious thinkers and seekers of our time. Although some of his stories read like parables from the Talmud (Kafka was born the son of a middle-class Jewish family in Prague), he belongs in the company of the great Christian theologians, of the Frenchman Pascal and the Dane Kierkegaard.

Frank. Leonhard Frank contributed to the vigorous anti-war propaganda of the expressionists in his withering and very effective pamphlet *Der Mensch ist gut* (Man is Good, 1917). In *Der Bürger* (The Citizen, 1924) he repeated the doctrine that man is deformed and debased by modern bourgeois society; to accept the conventional mold of the world means to destroy that which is best in our character. A similar motif is found in Frank's novel *Die Räuberbande* (The Band of Robbers, 1914), which portrays the rebellion of youth against its elders and teachers. Best known is Frank's *Karl und Anna* (1928): of two German prisoners in Russia, Richard longs for his wife Anna in terms of physical comfort only, whereas Karl, who listens to his friend's nostalgic descriptions, conceives of Anna as a lover, a dreamer, an idealist; and when both men return to Germany it is as if she had been waiting for Karl all her life, and Richard loses her.

Alfred Döblin (1878–   ). Döblin, formerly a physician in Berlin, teaches Asiatic passivity in the face of sufferings in his Chinese novel *Die drei Sprünge des Wang-lun* (The Three Leaps of Wang-lun, 1915); and the problem of to do or not to do is found also in his long historical novel *Wallenstein* (1920).

Man's desperate struggle against the machine, a Frankenstein monster which threatens to destroy him, is presented in *Wadzeks Kampf mit der Dampfturbine* (Wadzek's Struggle with the Steam Turbine, 1918) and in the futuristic *Berge, Meere und Giganten* (Mountains, Oceans, and Giants, 1924). Only man's return to nature may help him avert a catastrophe —that belief is typical of the expressionistic dogma.

248

Best known of Döblin's novels is his *Berlin Alexanderplatz* (Alexander Square, Berlin, 1929) ; it is the depressing story of an ex-convict who struggles in vain to regain a place in society. The picture of life among the scum of Berlin makes the book very readable; its style is unusual, very detailed, and influenced by James Joyce.

After Döblin joined the great exodus of authors from Germany he wrote *Babylonische Wanderungen* (1934), *Das Land ohne Tod* (The Land without Death—i.e. South America, 1938) and a very level-headed essay on *Die deutsche Literatur im Auslande seit 1933* (German Literature Abroad since 1933, 1938). Most promising is his *Bürger und Soldaten* (Citizens and Soldiers), the opening volume of a broad epic canvas about the German Revolution of 1918 and the first years of the Weimar Republic.

Franz Werfel (1890–1945). Werfel, like Kafka a Jewish author from Prague, is famous not only for his novels and dramas, but also because he was perhaps the greatest lyric poet of Expressionism, a man who in his all-embracing and enthusiastic love of mankind is suggestive of Walt Whitman.

Even the titles of his lyric collections are symbolic of the ardent feeling of altruism and religion that animated the expressionists: *Der Weltfreund* (The Friend of the World, 1911), *Wir sind* (We Are, 1913), *Einander* (Each Other, 1915), *Der Gerichtstag* (The Day of Judgment, 1919).

Die Troerinnen (1914), an adaptation of Euripides' *Trojan Women,* forms Werfel's contribution to the antiwar literature of his age, for it draws a dismal picture of the sufferings of defeat.

Der Spiegelmensch (The Mirror-Man, 1920), a trilogy, is a drama about the eternal dualism between man's real nature and his outer mask—a conflict between *Sein* and *Schein* (reality and appearance) which is memorably presented in the Janus-faced Faust-Mephistopheles of Goethe, and which is found also well expressed (if we may refer to a great American contemporary of Werfel's) in many dramas by Eugene O'Neill.

The novel *Nicht der Mörder, der Ermordete ist schuldig* (Not the Murderer But the Murdered Man Is Guilty, 1920) does more than present the favorite topic of the *Generation-*

enkonflikt: by its very title it also indicates the expressionists' revaluation of all moral values.

In *Verdi* (1924) Werfel wrote a fine piece of musical criticism in which he distilled the quintessence of the opera. In particular the novel effectively contrasts the genius of Verdi with that of Wagner, to the detriment of the latter.

Among Werfel's minor works are the tragedy *Juarez und Maximilian* (1924), in which the problem of republic versus monarchy is weighed; and the two religious works, the play *Paulus unter den Juden* (Paul among the Jews, 1926) and the novel *Höret die Stimme* (Hearken unto the Voice, 1937), the latter Jeremiah's warning of the doom of all that is.

Die vierzig Tage des Musa Dagh (The Forty Days of Musa Dagh, 1933), a gripping novel about the Turkish persecutions of the Armenians, is a fine example of the pleading of modern refugees (like that which Stefan Zweig made in his *Erasmus*) against the spirit of intolerance and bigotry. The same warmhearted espousing of the cause of the poor and the oppressed appears also in Werfel's *Der Weg der Verheissung* (The Eternal Road, 1936), a drama about Jewish sufferings in medieval ghettos.

In his intense religious feeling Werfel came ever closer to the Catholic faith (although he did not actually become a convert) and so his works ever more consistently extolled simple and childlike piety which acts as a bulwark against the aberrations of our times. In his great novel *Barbara oder die Frömmigkeit* (The Pure in Heart, 1929) he erects a monument to a simple old nurse to whom the hero can always return after having exposed himself to the sophistication and confusion of the world; in *Der veruntreute Himmel* (Embezzled Heaven, 1939) he tells the touching story of an old, simple-hearted woman who sacrifices everything to give her foster son the chance to become a priest; and in *Das Lied von Bernadette* (The Song of Bernadette, 1942) he piously glorifies the saintly maid of Lourdes to whom the Holy Virgin appeared in a lonely grotto.

After *Jacobowsky und der Oberst* (Jacobowsky and the Colonel, 1944), a "comedy of a tragedy" dealing with the odyssey of a shrewd little Jew and a Polish nobleman through France after the German invasion, Werfel ended his literary career with the novel *Stern der Ungeborenen* (Star of the Unborn, 1946), a visionary trip into the far remote future in which mankind has finally realized the lofty tenets of Christianity.

Minor Dramatists. In the field of the expressionistic drama the following minor representatives are noteworthy:

a. ANTON WILDGANS combines crass Naturalism with an expressionistic message in *Armut* (Poverty, 1915). His *Dies irae* (1919) ends the eternal father-son conflict with the suicide of the latter. *Liebe* (Love, 1919) draws a depressing picture of matrimonial boredom and increasing frigidity.

b. CARL STERNHEIM in his dramas *Die Hose* (The Trousers), *Bürger Schippel* (Citizen Schippel, 1913), and *Der Snob* most acidly castigates what is ridiculous, perverse, or lowly in the lives of the small bourgeoisie—that selfsame social stratum which Raabe, Stifter, and Keller had hailed as the backbone of any nation.

c. In WALTER HASENCLEVER's *Der Sohn* (The Son, 1914) the father, at the height of his conflict with his son, is saved by a stroke of apoplexy. Hasenclever's inspiring adaptation of Sophocles' *Antigone* (1916) reiterates the rebellious and daring viewpoint that the laws of God and of our hearts are more important than the hateful laws of monarchs. Hasenclever spent the last years of his life in France; he died miserably on his flight after the fall of France in 1940.

d. REINHARD GOERING describes the naval aspects of the war and its aftermath in the dramas *Seeschlacht* (Sea Battle, 1917) and *Scapa Flow* (1919)—the former interesting because it shows that even among revolutionists military discipline is so deep-seated that it cannot be disregarded. The latter deals with the scuttling of the German Navy after the armistice.

e. FRIEDRICH WOLF, after condemning the folly of war in *Die Matrosen von Cattaro* (The Sailors of Cattaro, 1930) turned to social problems and proletarian misery in *Kolonne Hund*, the presentation of the life of a team of coal miners. His strongest drama, *Cyankali* (Potassium Cyanide) lashes out against the cruel and bigoted para-

HISTORY OF GERMAN LITERATURE

graphs of the laws which forbid abortion and which thus force desperate proletarian girls to be at the mercy of ignorant quacks who will cause their death. Wolf's pronouncedly leftist tendencies show themselves also in his *Floridsdorf* (1935), dealing with the revolt of the Vienna workers, and in his famous anti-Nazi play *Doktor Mamlocks Ausweg* (Professor Mamlock, 1935).

Georg Kaiser (1867–1945). Kaiser, together with Werfel and Toller a leader in the field of the expressionistic drama, repeats in *Rektor Kleist* (1905) the frequent condemnation of the school system in which tyrannical teachers can drive pupils to suicide. Turning to the ever present problem of sex, Kaiser, in *Die jüdische Witwe* (The Jewish Widow, 1911) presents the famed Judith, the slayer of Holofernes, as a sex-starved and desperately passionate female, and in *König Hahnrei* (King Cuckold, 1913) he gives a new interpretation of the story of Tristan and Isolde and of the impotent yet erotic king Mark.

Die Bürger von Calais (The Citizens of Calais, 1914), one of the striking plays of the new school, best embodies Kaiser's expressionistic gospel that man should be ever willing for self-sacrifice if thereby he can enable his fellow men to live on. The drama takes place against the bloody background of the Hundred Years' War between France and England.

Von Morgens bis Mitternachts (From Morn till Midnight, 1916) joins other expressionistic works in asserting that our machine age will reduce man to a mere automaton whose work will be futile and worthless. The same idea pervades *Gas I* (1918) and *Gas II* (1920): men have become so mechanical and brutalized that they cannot be saved any more, for greed and cheap civilization mean more to them than simplicity and rustic happiness; and in the end they will all be exterminated through industrial catastrophes.

Die Koralle (The Coral, 1917), like *Gas,* repeats the father-son conflict against the background of capitalism versus socialism; like Wassermann's Christian Wahnschaffe, the son scorns the millions and the false ideas of his father.

Ernst Toller (1893–1939). At the beginning of his literary career, Toller was the leading communist among the expressionistic dramatists. In his dramas—so typical of all expressionists—heroes and heroines are to such an extent submerged among the nameless masses that often they appear as nameless characters, distinguished only by their professions. Many of his scenes are on the borderline between reality and unreality, like scenes watched distantly in a dream.

Die Wandlung (The Inner Change, 1919) depicts a soldier who after the war becomes a revolutionary leader. *Masse Mensch* (Masses and Man, 1920) brings up the fundamentally important problem of conflicts that will arise between revolutionary leaders and the masses of their followers and that will force the individual to pit himself against the mob. This play marks Toller's doubts of the desirability of a dictatorship of the masses.

Die Maschinenstürmer (The Machine Wreckers, 1922) about an insurrection of English weavers in 1812, repeats the expressionists' thesis that machines destroy men's souls; again the leader tries to restrain the destructive masses and is therefor slain.

Der deutsche Hinkemann (Hobbleman, 1923) discusses another bitter aspect of the soldier returning to his wife after the war: wounds have made him impotent. *Feuer aus den Kesseln* (Draw the Fires, 1930) portrays the ominous rebellion in the German Navy in 1917; it is also a bitter attack on the German courts of justice.

Of a completely different type is *Das Schwalbenbuch* (The Swallow Book, 1923), a book of verse idyllically describing his animal friends which brought him comfort while he was incarcerated on account of his political ideas. These ideas he describes in his autobiography *Eine Jugend in Deutschland* (I Was a German, 1933) published several years before his suicide in New York.

Unruh. In *Offiziere* (Officers, 1912) and *Louis Ferdinand, Prinz von Preussen* (1913), Fritz von Unruh analyzes the problem of personal impulse and initiative versus military discipline and obedience—a problem which is reminiscent of Kleist's *Prinz Friedrich von Homburg*. *Ein Geschlecht* (A Family, 1917) reveals the frightful passions such as incest and rape which follow in the wake of the general demoral-

ization of war. Similarly emphatic in its opposition to the
degradation and cruelty of war is a prose epic about the
slaughterings before Verdun, *Der Opfergang* ('The Way of
Sacrifice, 1918). The drama *Der Platz* (The Square, 1920)
—a continuation of *Ein Geschlecht*—evolves the only cure
possible in a mad world of greed and shallow civilization:
a return to nature, to the *Bruder Mensch* theme which Wassermann and also Rilke already had advocated. Noteworthy
also is Unruh's *Vor der Entscheidung* (Before the Decision),
a dramatic poem giving expression to his pacifistic ideas.

Brecht. Among the most gifted and original German expressionists must be counted Bertolt Brecht, whose political
vigor (he is an extreme leftist) is matched by the raciness
and poetic vitality of his style. In his *Hauspostille* (Domestic Handbook, 1927) he revives and modernizes the ballad,
approximating the mischievous sauciness of the late medieval
French vagabond poet Villon and the down-to-earth political
verve of Rudyard Kipling. After stormy expressionistic experiments like *Trommeln in der Nacht* (Drums in the Night,
1923), the story of a returning soldier, and *Im Dickicht der
Städte* (In the Jungle of the Cities), he reached the apex of
his dramatic career with *Die Dreigroschenoper* (1928), a
musical satire (music by Kurt Weill) based on John Gay's
Beggar's Opera (1728), ingeniously burlesquing modern society under the disguise of an empire ruled by gangsters. No
less devastating is his attack on capitalism in the allegorical
musical comedy *Aufstieg und Fall der Stadt Mahagonni*
(Rise and Fall of the City of Mahagonni, 1932) and in his
Die heilige Johanna der Schlachthöfe (St. Joan of the Stock-
yards). Among his most recent works is his powerfully sinister sequence of scenes in *Furcht und Elend des Dritten
Reiches* (The Private Life of the Master Race, 1944).

PRESENT TRENDS IN GERMAN LITERATURE

The greater calmness and objectivity, the new matter-of-
factness (*die neue Sachlichkeit*), of the most recent German
authors are signs of a natural reaction against the often-
times stammering outbursts of the expressionists. Quite a
few among the newer writers were still pacifists, socialists,
or Jewish, as so many expressionists had been, and hence

lived abroad; others, however, accepted the irrational creed of National Socialism. The ardent nationalism of Ulrich von Hutten, the back-to-nature movement of the great folklorist Johann Gottfried Herder, the glorification of the Middle Ages of the *Deutschromantiker,* the philosophical works of Fichte and Hegel, the tenor of so many *Heimat* novelists of the nineteenth century, the cult of the superman in Friedrich Nietzsche and Stefan George, the naturalists' and expressionists' attacks against materialism and egotism—they all were used and traduced to formulate the creed of the Nazis. The term "Neoromanticism"—inappropriately applied to Austrian aesthetes of the type of Hugo von Hofmannsthal, inasmuch as Hofmannsthal's colorful beauty and escapism represent only one certain aspect of Romanticism—might better be used for the Nazis, because in their hero worship, their mysticism, and their glorification of race and soil they borrowed largely from the romantic past. All critical, analytical, or cosmopolitan works and authors were banished; instead, the "positive" qualities of history, the soil, and the achievements of the men and women of Germany were to be emphasized. Literature henceforth was ordered to be *ein Dienst am Volke,* written in the service of the people; rather than analyze the diseases of society and of individual heroes, the poet should extol the community and the race.

Minor Writers. In the treatment of World War I the difference between the eruptive nature of the expressionists and the greater composure of the poets of *die neue Sachlichkeit* becomes particularly striking. Many among them are still ardent pacifists, but the stylistic presentation of their theme becomes calmer and clearer.

a. WALTER FLEX, who fell on the eastern front in 1917, deserves our attention because of his sincere and fine collections of poems, *Vom grossen Abendmahl* (On the Lord's Supper, 1915) and *Im Felde zwischen Tag und Nacht* (At the Front between Day and Night, 1918); because of his novel *Der Wanderer zwischen beiden Welten* (The Wanderer between Two Worlds, 1916) and his partly autobiographical *Wolf Eschenlohr* (1919); and also because of his *Weihnachtsmärchen des fünfzigsten Regimentes* (Christmas Tales of the Fiftieth Regiment).

b. Ludwig Renn is a militant pacifist in *Krieg* (War, 1928) and *Nachkrieg* (After War, 1930); his *Vor grossen Wandlungen* (Before Great Changes, 1936) attacks fascism and preaches communism.

c. Edwin Erich Dwinger's trilogy deals with prison life in Siberia, the merciless mutual slaughter of Red and White Russians, and the German soldiers' final return to their fatherland and their old militaristic ideas: *Armee hinter Stacheldraht* (The Army behind Barbed Wire, 1929), *Zwischen Weiss und Rot* (Between White and Red, 1930), and *Wir rufen Deutschland* (We Call Germany, 1932).

d. Particularly touching is the great documentary collection *Kriegsbriefe gefallener Studenten* (War Letters by Students Killed in Action), published by Philipp Witkop in 1928.

e. Werner Beumelburg glorifies comradeship in *Gruppe Bosemüller* (1930); the hard postwar years he describes in *Deutschland in Ketten* (Germany in Chains, 1931).

f. The problem of the home front, the loneliness of women, and especially the unruliness and precociousness of half-grown boys who lack their fathers' steadying guidance are described in Ernst Gläser's *Jahrgang 1902* (Class of 1902, 1928). His fine novel *Der letzte Zivilist* (The Last Civilian, 1935) is the story of an elderly German-American who, full of hopes and expectations, returns to the country of his ancestors, but who flees again after witnessing the outrages of the Third Reich.

Jünger. Undoubtedly one of the strongest literary talents in contemporary German literature is Ernst Jünger (born in 1895), whose war book *In Stahlgewittern* (Storm of Steel, 1920) became the gospel of the neonationalistic German youth. War is hailed here as the great liberator, the medium in which man throws off all artificial shackles and faces the absolute and ultimate challenge. Were it not for the stress on discipline and self-mastery, the book would be utterly nihilistic—but it is just this nihilism which exerts a most powerful fascination. Jünger's prose is quite unique: underneath its lucidity and its sometimes overworked discipline there is vitality, even violence. In his *Der Arbeiter* (The

Working Man, 1932) Jünger explores the emotional structure of the worker as opposed to the soldier. Although hailed by the Nazis as one of their foremost writers, Jünger gave in his weird parable *Auf den Marmorklippen* (On the Marble Cliffs, 1939) a thinly veiled denunciation of a system which mobilizes frustration, fear, and vulgar greed to the end of destroying all noble cultural values. Together with his brother, the poet Georg Friedrich Jünger, Ernst Jünger in the austere consciousness of his style and in many aspects of his philosophical creed is one of the truest and most talented disciples of Stefan George.

Remarque. Erich Maria Remarque (born in 1897) mingles misery and blood with expressionistic and pacifistic ardor in his war novel *Im Westen nichts Neues* (All Quiet on the Western Front, 1929). Even more impressive is his *Der Weg zurück* (The Road Back, 1931) : it is a typical *Heimkehrer-roman* depicting the grave social, political, and emotional readjustments awaiting the former front-soldiers—one of the best novels of this type. *Drei Kameraden* (Three Comrades, 1937) extols comradeship, love, and communism against the darkening background of postwar strife and the rise of German Nazism. *Liebe deinen Nächsten* (Flotsam, 1941) has as its theme the heartrending destinies of German refugees. The same theme, still more dramatic and agonizing by the inclusion of the German invasion of France in 1940, is reiterated in Remarque's most recent work, *Der Triumphbogen* (Arch of Triumph, 1946).

Hans Carossa (1878–   ). Carossa, a physician from Bavaria, one of the best and sanest authors of modern Germany, reveals a warm compassion for the sufferings of mankind. Perhaps because of his calmer style his books are more effective than the outcries of so many expressionists.

Die Schicksale Doktor Bürgers (The Destinies of Dr. Bürger, 1913) describes the despair and ultimate suicide of a sensitive young physician who realizes how powerless he is in trying to cure the endless miseries of mankind.

Rumänisches Tagebuch (Rumanian Diary, 1924) is one of the fine German books about World War I. It contains none of the bitter accusations, none of the filth and the frenzy of other books, but is warmhearted, sad, almost stoic in its acceptance of that which is unescapable. Even war is defended by Carossa—not for its own sake, but as a defense of the homeland, as a chance offered to all to sacrifice for an ideal.

Der Arzt Gion (The Physician Gion, 1931) tells the story of a humble servant who insists on giving birth to her child, even though she knows that that birth will kill her. Carossa here again analyzes the position of a physician in the midst of human suffering; and again he preaches courage, compassion, hope, and strength, so that men and women may be ready to sacrifice themselves and to efface their individuality for the sake of something bigger than all else: the children, the future.

With their exquisite prose, their beautiful descriptions of the Bavarian countryside, and their sincere quest for a harmonious and essential life, his two autobiographical volumes *Eine Kindheit* (A Childhood, 1922) and *Verwandlungen einer Jugend* (Metamorphoses of a Youth, 1928) are confessions of a true poet.

Arnold Zweig. Arnold Zweig (born in 1887) begins with his subtle *Novellen um Claudia* (1912), which forms a delicate study of psychological and sexual problems in the lives of two intelligent people; but his *magnum opus* is his trilogy of antiwar novels *Die Erziehung vor Verdun* (Education before Verdun), *Der Streit um den Sergeanten Grischa* (The Case of Sergeant Grischa), and *Die Einsetzung eines Königs* (The Crowning of a King)—all three of them grouped together under the title of *Trilogie des Übergangs* (Trilogy of Transition, 1927–1937). Most famous is *Der Streit um den Sergeanten Grischa;* it is a truly great war novel and describes the hopeless case of a Russian prisoner of war in the clutches of military law. The moral is depressing: even innocent men are pitilessly crushed by war, the new Frankenstein monster which men can unleash but not restrain or stop. In lieu of rhapsodic Expressionism this novel again distinguishes itself through its matter-of-fact *Sachlichkeit.* Zweig's later works, such as the *Bilanz der deutschen Judenheit* (Insulted and Exiled, the Truth about the German Jews, 1933) and *The Living Thoughts of Spinoza* (1939), represent his contribution to the fight against Hitler's Germany.

CONTEMPORARY LITERATURE

Musil and Broch. Among the great writers of the postwar period must be counted Robert Musil and Hermann Broch, whose penetrating and intellectually ambitious works have not yet been fully appreciated by the reading public. Both Musil's *Der Mann ohne Eigenschaften* (A Nondescript Man, 1930) and Broch's *Die Schlafwandler* (The Sleepwalkers, 1932) expose in the frame of huge narratives the emptiness and hollow artificiality of man in the bourgeois age. Recently Broch published a startling prose epic *Der Tod des Vergil* (The Death of Virgil, 1945), rendering the profound and involved vision of the decaying Roman Empire and of the dawn of the Christian era.

Roth. The Austrian novelist Joseph Roth is memorable for his excellent *Radetzkymarsch* (Radetzky, March, 1932), the story of a young officer and at the same time a delicate and melancholy analysis of the gradual dissolution of the Austro-Hungarian Empire.

Fallada. Hans Fallada (Rudolf Ditzen) is objective, though deeply touching, in *Kleiner Mann, was nun?* (Little Man, What Now?, 1932)—the story of a brave and lovable young couple and their baby who, after 1929, seem to be crushed by the machine of economic catastrophe and political revolution, just as Zweig's Sergeant Grischa had been crushed by the merciless machine of war. Other works of Fallada's include *Wer einmal aus dem Blechnapf frisst* (The World Outside, 1934), the story of the pathetic efforts of an ex-convict to rehabilitate himself in society; *Wir hatten mal ein Kind* (Once We Had a Child, 1934), the tragedy of children begotten without love; *Altes Herz geht auf die Reise* (An Old Heart Goes A-Journeying, 1936), written in a lively and youthful vein and depicting the battle of youth against the tyrannous older generation: and *Wolf unter Wölfen* (Wolf among Wolves, 1937), a somber description of meanness and misery during the German inflation.

Kästner. Erich Kästner is not only the humorous author of *Emil und die Detektive* (1929), *Das fliegende Klassenzimmer* (The Flying Classroom, 1933), and *Drei Männer im Schnee* (Three Men in the Snow, 1934), for which he is famous in America. He reveals his truer self in the collection *Lyrische Hausapotheke* (Lyrical Medicine Chest, 1938),

259

which contains poems resembling those of Morgenstern in form and those of Bert Brecht in their scathing irony and sauciness. Kästner's novel *Fabian, die Geschichte eines Moralisten* (Fabian, the Story of a Moralist, 1931) presents a cynical picture of the upheavals in Germany before Hitler's triumph.

Zuckmayer. In this connection may be mentioned Carl Zuckmayer (born 1895), although his greatest achievements lie in the field of the drama. After the hilarious comedy *Der fröhliche Weinberg* (The Merry Vineyard, 1925), a realistic and frank portrayal of manners and morals among the wine growers of Hesse, he emerges with his *Schinderhannes* (1927), the story of a rustic nineteenth century Robin Hood, as one of the most genuine folklorists among the younger generation. Excellent is his celebrated *Der Hauptmann von Köpenick* (The Captain of Köpenick, 1930), a biting satire on militarism in which he pillories the Germans' blind obedience to men in uniform. Among Zuckmayer's prose works are the fine short stories *Ein Bauer aus dem Taunus* (A Peasant of the Taunus), the delicate novel *Schloss Salware oder die Magdalena von Bozen* (The Moons Ride Over, 1936), and his interesting, whimsical fable *Der Seelenbräu* (1946).

Seghers. To the outstanding younger novelists belongs Anna Seghers, whose first story, *Der Aufstand der Fischer von St. Barbara* (Revolt of the Fishermen, 1928) is distinguished by its remarkably powerful, almost abrupt prose. The novel *Der Kopflohn* (Ransom, 1934) describes the flight of a young socialist through Germany, trying to escape the Gestapo, and her stirring last novel *Das siebte Kreuz* (The Seventh Cross, 1942) deals with the escape of a political prisoner from a concentration camp. In the intensity of her style and the strength of her political convictions Anna Seghers is equaled by another refugee, the Hungarian ARTHUR KOESTLER, author of *Darkness at Noon* (1941) and *Scum of the Earth* (1941).

Reger and Hauser. The last stage of the new Matter-of-Fact School was the so-called *Reportage,* an almost scientific analysis of industrial, administrative, and professional organizations and powers. Erich Reger gave such analyses in his sober but fascinatingly interesting novels *Union der festen*

Hand (Strong-fisted Union, 1929), dealing with the monopolistic heavy industry of the Rhineland, and *Das wachsame Hähnchen* (The Vigilant Rooster, 1931), dealing with city politics and politicians. Heinrich Hauser wrote pure *Reportagen* in *Schwarzes Revier* (Black District—i.e. the Ruhr), and *Die letzten Segelschiffe* (Fair Winds and Foul, 1930).

Lyric Poets. Among the lyric poets of World War I and of the two subsequent revolutions is noticed the gradual transition from expressionistic eccentricity to greater calmness and normalcy. Many of the poets are laborers who first were socialists and later became National Socialists.

a. Of GEORG TRAKL, GEORG HEYM, PAUL ZECH, GOTTFRIED BENN, and others little need be said. They are expressionistic reformers frequently tinged with communism, poets who often love to delve into horrible, pathological, and malodorous themes (e.g. the "Ophelia" theme).

b. KARL BRÖGER, a laborer, is famous for his simple, ardent, and sincere war poems; among them his beautiful *Bekenntnis* (Credo) in particular is frequently quoted. Of his later works we can name *Deutschland* (1924) and his verse legends about postwar misery, *Die vierzehn Nothelfer* (The Fourteen Helpmates).

c. HEINRICH LERSCH, likewise a laborer, is deeply moving in his war poems *Herz! aufglühe dein Blut* (Glowing Heart) and *Deutschland;* among them his *Soldatenabschied* (Departure) and especially his *Brüder* (Brothers) are truly great. In *Mensch in Eisen* (Man in Iron, 1925) he fears lest machines destroy man's soul; but in *Im Pulsschlag der Maschinen* (Amidst the Pulse of Machines, 1935) he feels reassured: it is man, not the machine, that will win out. The poems contained in *Mit brüderlicher Stimme* (A Brother's Voice, 1933) give expression to Lersch's Nazi creed.

d. Minor poets include ALFONS PETZOLD, a Viennese, an ardent believer in the Russian Revolution—*Der feurige Weg* (The Fiery Road, 1921)—who is, in his poems, deeply influenced by Rilke, to whom he dedicates his book of verse *Franz von Assisi* (1918); MAX BARTHEL, author of notable poems about the war such as *Verse aus den Argonnen* (Verses from the Argonnes, 1916) and about

261

proletarian problems as in *Arbeiterseele* (Workingman's Soul, 1920), who in *Das unsterbliche Volk* (The Immortal People, 1933), his description of communistic Russia, is however utterly disillusioned with Marxism; and GERRIT ENGELKE, a laborer discovered by Dehmel and killed in action, author of the *Rhythmen des neuen Europa* (Rhythms of the New Europe, 1921).

e. Best among the young Nazi poets is GERHARD SCHUMANN in his *Lieder vom Reich* (1935); less deserving are HEINRICH ANACKER, RICHARD EURINGER, and BALDUR VON SCHIRACH, the Nazi Youth Leader.

Johst. The same trend, first towards *neue Sachlichkeit,* later towards National Socialism, is seen also in the field of the contemporary German drama, in the transition from Carl Zuckmayer to Hanns Johst and Hans Rehberg.

Hanns Johst (born in 1890), the leading and excessively honored dramatist of the Third Reich, began as an expressionist—e.g. *Der Einsame* (Alone, 1917), a drama dealing with the playwright Grabbe, whom alcohol had ruined. His interesting play on *Thomas Paine* (1927) glorifies a great leader whose oratory, fanaticism, and self-sacrifice help bring about the birth of a new and proud nation. *Schlageter* (1933), Johst's best known play, aims to render immortal a fervent nationalist who singlehanded had tried to sabotage the French invasion of the Ruhr in 1923; Johst indeed hails him as one of the first great National Socialists. His interpretation of Luther, the battler and popular leader, in *Die Propheten* (1923) is also worth noting.

Rehberg. Hans Rehberg, a promising dramatist of the Third Reich, is known especially for his historical plays. In *Der grosse Kurfürst* (The Great Elector, 1934) he, like Wildenbruch before him, depicts the heroic struggle of the young Hohenzollern dynasty; in *Kaiser und König* (Emperor and King, 1936) he continues his patriotic canvas and portrays Frederick the Great's fight for Silesia.

New *Heimatliteratur*. In the field of the novel the trend from Expressionism to greater objectivity, simplicity, and closeness to nature led to a renewed flourishing of *Heimatliteratur*. The strength and beauty of this type of literature we find in an unadulterated form especially among the novel-

ists of Switzerland; in Germany the provincial novels, from
the days of Stehr and Frenssen on, tend to become ever more
imbued with the mysticism and racialism of the Nazis, who
propagated these books in order to fight against the nefarious
Asphaltzivilisation of the big-city novels.

a. Swiss regionalists of some importance are JAKOB CHRIS-
TOPH HEER, author of *Der König der Bernina* (The King
of Bernina, 1900); ERNST ZAHN (*Albin Indergand,*
1901); HEINRICH FEDERER, author of *Berge und Men-
schen* (Mountains and Men, 1911); and ALFRED HUG-
GENBERGER, who wrote *Der Kampf mit dem Leben* (The
Struggle with Life, 1926). Less deserving, but more
famous, are JOHANNA SPYRI's juvenile tales about *Heidi.*
Favorite Swiss dialect authors are SIMON GFELLER from
Bern and MEINRAD LIENERT from Zurich. JAKOB SCHAFF-
NER, originally a cobbler from Basel, tries to emulate
Keller's irony and to blend regional and historical themes
in *Konrad Pilater* (1910 ff.) or *Der Bote Gottes* (The
Messenger of God, 1911)—the former, like Keller's *Der
grüne Heinrich,* largely autobiographical, and the latter,
like Enrica von Handel-Mazzetti's novels, a powerful
description of the clash between Protestantism and Ca-
tholicism in the seventeenth century. Politically, Jakob
Schaffner, like Knut Hamsun in Norway, came to espouse
the cause of German National Socialism (*Eine deutsche
Wanderschaft,* 1933).

b. RUDOLF HANS BARTSCH, an Austrian, shows his regionalism in *Zwölf aus der Steiermark* (Twelve from Styria,
1908) and also in his charming historical sketches about
Austria around 1800. *Vom sterbenden Rokoko* (The Vanishing Rococo, 1909) deals, among others, with Mozart;
other sketches deal with Schubert. Bartsch can best be
compared to RUDOLF VON TAVEL in Switzerland, whose
finely written books present the Swiss patricians of the
eighteenth century.

c. One of the really great and powerful regionalists of
recent years is the Bavarian OSKAR MARIA GRAF, a worthy
successor of Ludwig Thoma, whose autobiographical novel
Wir sind Gefangene (Prisoners All, 1927) is a stirring
protest against social injustices, while *Das bayrische*

Dekameron (The Bavarian Decameron) shows Graf's strong, down-to-earth sense of humor.

d. Minor regionalists of the past few decades include LUD-WIG GANGHOFER, a Bavarian, author of *Das Schweigen im Walde* (The Silent Forests, 1899); FRIEDRICH LIEN-HARD, an Alsatian (*Oberlin,* 1910) famous also for his *Wartburg* trilogy (1903 ff.); and TIMM KROGER, from Schleswig-Holstein, author of *Hein Wieck und andere Geschichten* (Hein Wieck, and Other Short Stories, 1900). Slightly different is RUDOLF HERZOG, who glorifies not the peasants and landscapes of Germany, but the Rhine-Ruhr district and the great men and women who made it the industrial heart of Europe—e.g., *Die Stoltenkamps und ihre Frauen* (The Stoltenkamps and Their Women, 1918), which deals with the Krupp family.

e. In connection with the new regionalism it is appropriate to emphasize the important influence of the German *Jugendbewegung,* for the *Wandervögel* of the Youth Movement were among the first to break away from big-city slums and to seek a closer contact with nature and peasantry. In its Spartan organization the Youth Movement followed the leadership principle which is so natural among the Germans; hence the relative ease with which these *Wandervögel* or "Migratory Birds" in later years were absorbed by the Hitler Youth.

Frenssen. Gustav Frenssen (1863–1946) illustrates clearly how the regionalism of certain authors of the past generation served to prepare the ground for the National Socialism of the present generation. *Jörn Uhl* (1901), one of the famous books of the modern *Heimatliteratur,* established Frenssen as the great successor to Storm in his descriptions of Schleswig-Holstein. The bitter struggle for daily existence of the sturdy peasants along the coast of the North Sea forms the bulk of the book. Racial problems between Teutonic and Slav settlers in Northern Germany are discussed to the detriment of the latter. Occasional anti-Christian utterings contribute to make this novel an early forerunner of Nazi literature. *Hilligenlei* (Holy Land, 1906) strives for a regeneration of our world by telling the story of a modern Christ who preaches practical socialism, national vigor, normalcy, and simplicity. As in *Jörn Uhl,* the sexual needs of healthy and strong Germanic beings are greatly emphasized. Among Frenssen's minor works may be named *Peter Moors Fahrt nach Südwest* (Peter Moor's Journey to Southwest Africa, 1907), treating the conquest of African colonies; and *Klaus Hinrich Baas* (1909), the story of a self-made man, a great merchant, who comes to realize that he needs more than commercial success in order to live a full life.

Löns. Though Hermann Löns was killed near Reims in 1914, he, too, is considered a forerunner of National Socialism, not only because of his strong love of the soil, especially of the Lüneburger Heath—as expressed in *Aus Wald und Heide* (From Forest and Heath, 1901) and in *Mein grünes Buch* (My Green Book, 1901) and *Mein braunes Buch* (My Brown Book, 1907)—but also because he is race-conscious and pagan rather than Christian in his philosophy. Aside from his peasant novels of the type of *Da hinten in der Heide* (Back There in the Heath, 1910) he is celebrated also for his descriptions of animal life (*Mümmelmann,* 1909). His masterpiece is *Der Wehrwolf* (Harm Wulf, 1910), a peasant chronicle at once regional, historical, and patriotic, for it praises the staunch courage and bitter perseverance of German peasants during the Thirty Years' War, who outfought, outkilled, and outlived all the foreign invaders so that they might continue living in their homesteads. Strong, race-conscious peasantry fighting like desperate wolf packs can alone outlast the vicissitudes of war. Only he who helps himself, rather than waiting for others to help him, will survive in man's struggle for existence: that is the message Löns conveys to modern readers.

Blunck. Hans Friedrich Blunck (born in 1888), a native of the region around Hamburg, displays his love for irrational, mythological, and early Germanic themes in his ballads (*Nordmark,* 1916) and in his fairy tales of the type of *Von klugen Frauen und Füchsen* (Of Wise Women and Foxes, 1926). Rich in folklore and mythology is also his trilogy *Werdendes Volk* (Our Dynamic Race, 1923 ff.) in which he depicts German history from the days of the heroic tribes on, beginning with the pagan Saxons' determined resistance to Roman culture and Christian religion. Another bulky trilogy, *Die Urvätersaga* (The Saga of Our Ancestors, 1927 ff.) reaches even farther back into the mist of the Germanic past and describes the Glacial period, the Stone Age, and the Bronze Age in fantastic volumes called *Gewalt über das Feuer* (Power over Fire), *Kampf der Gestirne* (Battle of the Constellations), and *Streit mit den Göttern* (Feud with the Gods). Minor works of Blunck's include novels describing the life of loyal German settlers in South and Central America, e.g. *Das Land der Vulkane* (The Land of Volcanos, 1929); *Volkswende* (Turning Point of a Nation, 1931), which contains autobiographical elements about his experiences during and after the First World War; and *König Geiserich* (King Genseric, 1936), a glorification of the strong leadership of the Vandal king in ancient Carthage.

Ponten. Josef Ponten (born in 1883), a Rhinelander, is, like Blunck, interested in the survival and the racial stamina of German colonists abroad. His impressive trilogy *Volk auf dem Wege* (The March of a Nation, 1933 ff.) deals with German emigrants and their descendants who, around 1700, had left the war-ridden Palatinate in order to settle in Russia. The second volume of the series, *Im Wolgaland,* about the German colonists on the Volga, is especially celebrated.

Hans Grimm. Grimm (born in 1875) is also *ein Künder des Dritten Reiches,* a prophet of the Third Reich. In his ambitious *Volk ohne Raum* (A Nation without Space, 1926) he brings to a peak the colonial novels and visions of Frenssen, Blunck, and Ponten. It is the tale of German settlers in Southwest Africa and their firm determination to hold on to their soil in spite of the decisions of the Treaty of Versailles; even more it is a plea not to throttle German expansive virility by locking her up in overpopulated Europe and by letting England occupy all the free space of other continents. Racial and pagan ideas prevail in Grimm's novel; but the main emphasis is on the colonial theme. This holds true also of such minor works of Grimm's as *Südafrikanische Novellen* (South African Short Stories, 1913), his anti-French *Der Ölsucher von Duala* (The Oil-Seeker of Duala, 1918), and *Lüderitzland* (1934).

Blubo Literature. Among contemporary Nazi authors who glorify *Blut und Boden* (Race and Soil—commonly

266

called *Blubo* literature), and in whom the expressionists' yearning for a regeneration, a *Wandlung,* of the whole of humanity is restricted to an ardent desire for a German national and racial rebirth, may be named:

a. WILL VESPER, who deals with sturdy and primitive Norsemen in *Das harte Geschlecht* (The Hard Race, 1931). Vesper is also well known for his historical novels; in *Kaiser und Herzog* (Emperor and Duke, 1936) he treats the ancient fights of Ghibellines and Guelfs; *Reich und Rom* (The Empire and the Church, 1937) deals with Luther's emancipation from the Roman yoke; and in *Der König und die Kaiserin* (King and Empress, 1938) he describes Frederick the Great's struggle for supremacy against Maria Theresa. *Die Hengstwiese* (The Steed's Meadow, 1937), an experiment in animal symbolism, might be considered a thinly veiled warning against Hitler's alliance with Italy.

b. FRIEDRICH GRIESE, from Mecklenburg, whose *Winter* (1927) tells the cruel story of the survival of the fittest, and who extols race, peasantry, and sturdy virility. *Das Dorf der Mädchen* (The Village of Maidens, 1932) deals with the age-old struggle between Teutons and Slavs in northeastern Germany.

c. Other Nazi authors, mainly *Blut und Boden* regionalists, include BENNO VON MECHOW, a Rhinelander; FRIEDRICH SCHNACK, from the Main district; HERMANN ERIS BUSSE, from the Black Forest; WILHELM PLEYER, a Sudeten German; ADOLF MESCHENDÖRFER, a Transylvanian; and others. The modern inspirer of regional and tribal literature is JOSEF NADLER, himself a Sudeten German, whose *Literaturgeschichte der deutschen Stämme und Landschaften* (Literary History of German Tribes and Landscapes) was published as far back as 1912.

"Inner Emigration." Long before National Socialism destroyed Germany physically, it had destroyed German literature, which had experienced such a promising revival during the first decades of the twentieth century and which could not exist under a dictatorship hostile to its intellectual freedom and integrity. Most of the great and internationally known German writers fled their home country; many of those who remained lived in what they called "Inner Emigration." Ricarda Huch belonged quite outspokenly to this group; of the younger generation are Hans Fallada and Erich Kästner, and writers like ERNST PENZOLDT, author of such delicate and promising novels and stories as *Der arme Chatterton* (Poor Chatterton, 1928), *Die Portugalesische Schlacht* (Portugalese Battle), and *Kleiner Erdenwurm* (Little Common Man); PAUL ALVERDES, author of the remarkable soldier story *Die Pfeiferstube* (The Whistlers' Room, 1929); MANFRED HAUSMANN with his delightfully romantic novels *Lampion küsst Mädchen* (Lampion Kisses Girls) and *Abel und die Mundharmonika* (Abel and the Mouth Organ). To this group belong also the gifted poetess MARIA LUISE KASCHNITZ, whose first novel, *Liebe beginnt* (Love Begins), was published in 1933; the Austrian KARL HEINRICH WAGGERL, in his *Brot* (Bread, 1930) influenced by Knut Hamsun, a sincere Catholic in such later tales of his as *Das Jahr des Herrn* (The Year of the Lord, 1933) and *Mütter* (Mothers, 1935); and RICHARD BILLINGER, likewise an Austrian and the author of various peasant plays and tales, such as *Die Rauhnacht* (Frost, 1931) and *Der Gigant* (The Giant, 1937). Even some of the outspoken early Nazis like Ernst Jünger and Hans Grimm in later years joined the camp of the "Inner Emigration."

Wiechert. The most outstanding figure of this group is Ernst Wiechert (born in 1887), an East Prussian, who, in a masterful and quiet prose, tries to solve the problem of man's rehabilitation. In *Die Flucht* (The Flight, 1916) he advocates a return to nature; *Die Magd des Jürgen Doskocil* (The Girl and the Ferryman, 1932) combines a mystic love of nature with the gift of woman to win man back to his place in society; in *Die Majorin* (The Baroness, 1934), he depicts the difficulties of a returned soldier in readjusting himself to the soil of his homeland. *Wälder und Menschen* (Woods and People, 1936) tells of his own youth in the silent forests and swamps of East Prussia. Admirably courageous are his three *Reden an die deutsche Jugend* (Addresses to German Youth, 1934, 1938, 1945) in which he warns his youthful followers against the godlessness and viciousness of a regime gone berserk. One of his recent publications is *Der*

Totenwald (The Forest of the Dead), published in Switzerland in 1945, the reminiscences of his internment in the Buchenwald concentration camp, one of the first books to come out of the German *Götterdämmerung* of the past few years.

TRANSLATIONS

GENERAL COLLECTIONS

Bennett, E. N. *German Short Stories.* London, 1934.

Bithell, J. *Contemporary German Poetry* (containing poems by Dauthendey, Dehmel, Hofmannsthal, Holz, Huch, Liliencron, Miegel, Morgenstern, Rilke, Spitteler, Wedekind, S. Zweig). London, 1909.

Broicher, D. *German Lyrists of Today.* London, 1912.

Busch, H. *Selected Austrian Short Stories* (including Grillparzer, Ebner-Eschenbach, Schnitzler, Bahr, etc.). New York, 1929.

Cerf, B. A. *Great German Short Stories and Novels* (containing Goethe: *The Sorrows of Werther;* Schiller: *The Sport of Destiny;* Grimm: *Hansel and Gretel, Cinderella;* Storm: *Immensee;* Keller: *The Naughty Saint Vitalis;* Sudermann: *The New Year's Eve Confession;* Schnitzler: *The Fate of the Baron;* Hauptmann: *Flagman Thiel;* Wassermann: *Lukardis;* Thomas Mann: *Death in Venice;* Stefan Zweig: *Amok;* Arnold Zweig: *The Parcel;* etc.). New York, 1933.

Crippen, H. R. *Germany: A Self-Portrait; A Collection of German Writings from 1914 to 1943.* London, 1944.

Deutsch, B., and A. Yarmolinsky. *Contemporary German Poetry: An Anthology* (containing poems by Benn, Brod, Dauthendey, Dehmel, George, Heym, Holz, Klabund, Liliencron, Morgenstern, Rilke, Schickele, Trakl, Werfel, Zech, etc.). New York, 1923.

Dickinson, T. H. *Chief Contemporary Dramatists.* Boston, 1915, 1921, 1930.

  1st series: Hauptmann: *The Weavers;* Sudermann: *The Vale of Content.*

  2nd series: Thoma: *Moral;* Schnitzler: *Living Hours;* Bahr: *The Concert.*

  3rd series: Wedekind: *Such Is Life;* Kaiser: *From Morn to Midnight;* Hofmannsthal: *Elektra.*

————, *Continental Plays* (containing Hauptmann: *The Weavers;* Schnitzler: *Light-o'-Love;* Wedekind: *Erdgeist;* Kaiser: *The Coral*). Boston, 1935.

Francke, Kuno, editor-in-chief. *The German Classics of the Nineteenth and Twentieth Centuries.* Albany, 1913 ff. 20 vols.

  Vol. XIV: Spitteler: From *Olympian Spring.*

  Vol. XVI: Schönherr: *Faith and Fireside.*

  Vol. XVII: Sudermann: *John the Baptist.*

  Frenssen: *The Life of Jesus.*

  Polenz: *Farmer Büttner.*

  Fulda: *Tête-à-Tête,* Poems.

  Hofmannsthal: *Death and the Fool, The Death of Titian,* Poems.

  Vol. XVIII: Hauptmann: *The Weavers, The Sunken Bell, Michael Kramer.*

Falke, Kurz, Dehmel, Holz, George, Strauss und Torney, Rilke, Hesse, Miegel: Poems.

Huch: *The Recollections of Ludolf Ursleu the Younger.*

Vol. XIX: Böhlau: *The Ball of Crystal.*

Viebig: *Burning Love.*

Keyserling: *Gay Hearts.*

Thomas Mann: *Tonio Kröger.*

Thoma: *Matt the Holy.*

Bartsch: *The Styrian Wine-Carter.*

Emil Strauss: *Mara.*

Hesse: *In the Old 'Sun.'*

Zahn: *Stephen the Smith.*

Schaffner: *The Iron Idol.*

Vol. XX: Wassermann: *Clarissa Mirabel.*

Kellermann: *God's Beloved.*

Halbe: *Mother Earth.*

Hofmannsthal: *The Marriage of Sobeide.*

Schnitzler: *The Green Cockatoo, Literature.*

Wedekind: *The Court Singer.*

Hardt: *Tristram the Jester.*

Katzin, W. *Eight European Plays* (including Kaiser, Heinrich Mann, Sternheim). New York, 1927.

Mann, K., and H. Kesten. *Heart of Europe; An Anthology of Creative Writing in Europe, 1920–1940.* New York, 1943.

Münsterberg, M. *A Harvest of German Verse* (containing poems by Arndt, Chamisso, Dehmel, Droste-Hülshoff, Eichendorff, Fontane, Geibel, George, Goethe, Heine, Hesse, Holz, Huch, Keller, Körner, Lenau, Liliencron, Luther, Meyer, Miegel, Mörike, Müller, Münchhausen, Novalis, Platen, Rilke, Scheffel, Schiller, Spitteler, Storm, Strauss und Torney, Uhland, etc.). New York, 1916.

Rothensteiner, J. E. *A German Garden of the Heart.* St. Louis, 1934.

Steinhauer, H., and H. Jessiman. *Modern German Short Stories* (including Binding, Ernst, L. Frank, Huch, Kafka, Schäfer, Schmidtbonn, Viebig, etc.). London, 1938.

Tomlinson, H. M. *Best Short Stories of the War* (including Alverdes, Binding, Euringer, Remarque, Unruh, etc.). New York, 1931.

Tucker, S. M. *Modern Continental Plays* (including Hauptmann, Kaiser, Schnitzler, Wedekind). New York, 1929.

Van Doren, M. *An Anthology of World Poetry.* New York, 1928.

Watson, E. B. *Contemporary Drama* (containing Hauptmann: *The Beaver Coat;* Schnitzler: *Light-o'-Love;* Sudermann: *Magda*). New York, 1932.

INDIVIDUAL AUTHORS

ALVERDES: Creighton, B., tr. *The Whistlers' Room.* New York, 1930.

BAHR: Gribble, R. T., tr. *Expressionism.* London, 1925.

BAUM: Creighton, B., tr. *Grand Hotel.* New York, 1931.
Zeitlin, I., tr. *Helene.* New York, 1934.

BEER–HOFMANN: "Lullaby for Miriam," *Poet Lore,* XLVII, 1941.
Wynn, I. B., tr. *Jacob's Dream.* New York, 1946.

CONTEMPORARY LITERATURE

BINDING: Morrow, I. F. D., tr. *Fatalist at War*. New York, 1929.

BONSELS: Chambers, W., tr. *Adventures of Mario*. New York, 1930.
Indian Journey (translator anonymous). New York, 1928.
Seltzer, A. S., tr. *Adventures of Maya the Bee*. New York, 1929.

BRECHT: Bentley, E. R., tr. *The Private Life of the Master Race*. New York, 1944.
Vesey, D. I., tr. *A Penny for the Poor*. London, 1937.

BROCH: Muir, W. and E., tr. *The Sleepwalkers*. Boston, 1932.
Untermeyer, J. S., tr. *The Death of Virgil*. New York, 1945.

BROD: Crosse, F. W., tr. *Redemption of Tycho Brahe*. New York, 1928.

BRÖGER: Williams, O., tr. *Pillbox 17*. London, 1930.

CAROSSA: Scott, A. N., tr. *Boyhood and Youth*. New York, 1932.
———, tr. *A Childhood*. New York, 1932.
———, tr. *Doctor Gion*. New York, 1933.
———, tr. *Roumanian Diary*. New York, 1930.

DEHMEL: Zeydel, E. H., tr. "Selected Verse," *Poet Lore*, XXXI, 1920.

DÖBLIN: Jolas, E., tr. *Alexanderplatz, Berlin*. New York, 1931.

DWINGER: Morrow, I. F. D., tr. *The Army behind Barbed Wire*. London, 1930.
Saunders, M., tr. *Between White and Red*. New York, 1932.

EDSCHMID: Chambers, W., tr. *A Passionate Rebel; The Life of Lord Byron*. New York, 1930.

EWERS: Endore, S. G., tr. *Alraune*. London, 1929.
Sallagar, F., tr. *Vampire*. London, 1935.

FALLADA: Owens, P., tr. *Wolf among Wolves*. New York, 1938.
Sutton, E., tr. *Little Man, What Now?* New York, 1933.
———, tr. *An Old Heart Goes A-Journeying*. New York, 1936.
———, tr. *Once We Had a Child*. New York, 1935.
———, tr. *The World Outside*. New York, 1934.

FEUCHTWANGER: Abbott, E., tr. *The Devil in France* (Unholdes Frankreich). New York, 1941.
Ashton, E. D., tr. *Three Plays*. New York, 1934.
Cleugh, J., tr. *The Oppermanns*. London, 1933.
Muir, W. and E., tr. *The Jew of Rome*. New York, 1935.
———, tr. *Josephus*. New York, 1932.
———, tr. *Power*. New York, 1926.
———, tr. *Success*. New York, 1930.
———, tr. *Two Anglo-Saxon Plays*. New York, 1928.
———, tr. *The Ugly Duchess*. New York, 1928.
Oram, C., tr. *Josephus and the Emperor*. New York, 1942.

FRANK, B.: Drake, W. A., tr. *Twelve Thousand*. New York, 1928.
Lowe-Porter, H. T., tr. *The Days of the King*. New York, 1929.
———, tr. *The Man Called Cervantes*. New York, 1936.
Paul, E. and C., tr. *Trenck, the Love-Story of a Favorite*. New York, 1928.

271

FRANK, L.: Brooks, C., tr. *Carl and Anna.* New York, 1930.
———, tr. *The Robber Band.* London, 1930.
A Middle-Class Man. London, 1930.

FRENSSEN: Delmer, F. S., tr. *Jörn Uhl.* Boston, 1905.
Hamilton, M. A., tr. *Holyland.* Boston, 1906.
Lape, E. E., and E. F. Read, tr. *Klaus Hinrich Baas.* New York, 1911.
Ward, M. M., tr. *Peter Moor's Journey to Southwest Africa.* New York, 1908.

FREUD: Brill, A. A., tr. *Interpretation of Dreams.* New York, 1933.
———, tr. *Psychopathology of Everyday Life.* New York, 1917.
Rivière, J., tr. *General Introduction to Psychoanalysis.* New York, 1935.

GEORGE: Valhope, C. N., and E. Morwitz, tr. *Poems.* New York, 1943.

GLÄSER: David, G., and E. Mosbacher, tr. *The Last Civilian.* New York, 1935.
Muir, W. and E., tr. *Class of 1902.* New York, 1929.

GRAF: Green, M., tr. *Prisoners All!* New York, 1928.

GRIESE: Hobman, L. A., tr. *Winter.* New York, 1929.

HALBE: Barrows, S. T., tr. *Youth.* Garden City, N. Y., 1916.

HANDEL–MAZZETTI: Shuster, G. N., tr. *Jesse and Maria.* New York, 1931.

HARTLEBEN: Bleichmann, R., tr. *Love's Carnival.* London, 1904.
Holmes, S. E., tr. "Hanna Jagert," *Poet Lore,* XXIV, 1913.

HAUPTMANN: Lewisohn, L., ed. *The Dramatic Works.* New York, 1912 ff. 9 vols.
Morgan, B. Q., tr. *The Heretic of Soana.* New York, 1923.
Muir, W. and E., tr. *The Island of the Great Mother.* New York, 1925.
Seltzer, A. and T., tr. *Atlantis.* New York, 1912.
Seltzer, T., tr. *The Fool in Christ.* New York, 1926.

HAUSER: Levin, B. S., tr. *Fair Winds and Foul.* New York, 1932.

HERMANN: Barwell, A., tr. *Hetty Geybert.* New York, 1924.

HERZOG: Lazell, L. T., tr. *Sons of the Rhine.* New York, 1914.

HESSE: Creighton, B., tr. *Steppenwolf.* New York, 1946.
Dunlop, G., tr. *Death and the Lover.* London, 1932.
Priday, N. H., tr. *Demian.* New York, 1923.

HOFMANNSTHAL: Kalisch, A., tr. *Ariadne on Naxos.* Berlin, 1924.
———, tr. *Elektra.* Berlin, 1910.
———, tr. *The Rose-Bearer.* Berlin, 1912.
Sterling, G., and R. Ordynski, tr. *The Play of Everyman.* San Francisco, 1917.
Stork, C. W., tr. *Lyrical Poems.* New Haven, 1918.
Walter, E., tr. "Venice Preserved," *Poet Lore,* XXVI, 1915.

HUCH: Drake, W., tr. *Eros Invincible* (Ludolf Ursleu). New York, 1931.
Phillips, C. A., tr. *Garibaldi and the New Italy.* New York, 1928–29.

CONTEMPORARY LITERATURE

JÜNGER: Creighton, B., tr. *Copse 125* (Das Wäldchen 125). London, 1930.
——, tr. *Storm of Steel*. Garden City, N. Y., 1929.
KÄSTNER: Brooks, C., tr. *Emil and the Three Twins*. London, 1935.
——, tr. *Fabian, the Story of a Moralist*. New York, 1932.
——, tr. *The Flying Classroom*. London, 1934.
——, tr. *Three Men in the Snow*. London, 1935.
Massee, M., tr. *Emil and the Detectives*. Garden City, N. Y., 1930.
KAFKA: Lloyd, A. L., tr. *The Metamorphosis*. London, 1937.
Muir, E. and W., tr. *America*. London, 1938.
——, tr. *The Castle*. London, 1930.
——, tr. *The Great Wall of China*. New York, 1947.
——, tr. *The Trial*. New York, 1937.
Slochower, H., et al. *A Franz Kafka Miscellany*. New York, 1940.
KAISER: Scheffauer, H. G., tr. *Gas*. Boston, 1924.
KLABUND: Laver, J., tr. *The Circle of Chalk*. London, 1929.
Scheffauer, H. G., tr. *Brackie, the Fool*. New York, 1927.
KOLBENHEYER: Linton, J., tr. *The God-intoxicated Man* (Spinoza). London, 1933.
Phillips, H. A., and K. W. Maurer, tr. *A Winter Chronicle* (Meister Joachim Pausewang). London, 1938.
KURZ: Dundas, L., tr. *Tales of Florence*. London, 1919.
LÖNS: Saunders, M., tr. *Harm Wulf*. London, 1931.
LUDWIG: Burke, K., tr. *Genius and Character* (containing essays on Frederick the Great, Wilson, Lenin, Leonardo, Shakespeare, Rembrandt, Voltaire, Byron, Balzac, Dehmel, etc.). New York, 1927.
Dunlop, G., tr. *Versailles*. New York, 1932.
Lindsay, M. H., tr. *The Nile*. New York, 1937.
Mayne, E. C., tr. *Goethe*. New York, 1928.
——, tr. *Kaiser Wilhelm II*. New York, 1926.
Murphy, J., tr. *Leaders of Europe* (containing essays on Nansen, Masaryk, Briand, Rathenau, Motta, Lloyd George, Venizelos, Mussolini, Stalin). London, 1934.
Mussey, B., tr. *The Mediterranean*. New York, 1942.
Norden, H. and R., tr. *The Germans*. Boston, 1941.
Paul, E. and C., tr. *Bismarck*. Boston, 1927.
——, tr. *Hindenburg*. Philadelphia, 1935.
——, tr. *Lincoln*. Boston, 1930.
——, tr. *Napoleon*. New York, 1926.
——, tr. *The Son of Man, the Story of Jesus*. New York, 1928.
Samuel, W., tr. *Roosevelt*. New York, 1938.
Tait, D. F., tr. *Schliemann*. Boston, 1931.
Three Titans (Michelangelo, Rembrandt, Beethoven). New York, 1930.
MANN, H.: *Blue Angel* (translator anonymous). New York, 1932.
Boyd, E., tr. *The Patrioteer* (Der Untertan). New York, 1921.
Clark, A. D. B., tr. *In the Land of Cockaigne*. New York, 1929.
Posselt, E., and E. Glore, tr. *Diana* (a translation of the first volume of *Die Göttinnen*). New York, 1929.

HISTORY OF GERMAN LITERATURE

Ray, W., tr. *The Little Town*. New York, 1931.
Sutton, E., tr. *Henri Quatre, King of France*. London, 1938.
———, tr. *Young Henry of Navarre*. New York, 1937.

MANN, T.: Curtis, A. C. C., tr. *Royal Highness*. New York, 1926.
Germany and the Germans. Washington, D. C., 1945.
Lowe-Porter, H. T., tr. *The Beloved Returns*. New York, 1940.
———, tr. *Buddenbrooks*. New York, 1938.
———, tr. *Essays of Three Decades*. New York, 1947.
———, tr. *Joseph and His Brothers*. New York, 1934.
———, tr. *Joseph in Egypt*. New York, 1938.
———, tr. *Joseph the Provider*. New York, 1944.
———, tr. *The Magic Mountain*. New York, 1939.
———, tr. *Past Masters and Other Papers* (containing "Cosmopolitanism"; "Culture and Socialism"; "Dürer"; "Freud's Position in the History of Modern Thought"; "Goethe, Novelist"; "Lessing"; "Nietzsche and Music"; "On the Theory of Spengler"; "The Sufferings and Greatness of Richard Wagner"; "Tolstoi"; etc.). New York, 1933.
———, tr. *Stories of Three Decades* (containing "The Blood of the Walsungs"; "Death in Venice"; "Disorder and Early Sorrow"; "Felix Krull"; "Fiorenza"; "Little Herr Friedemann"; "Mario and the Magician"; "Tonio Kröger"; "Tristan"; etc.). New York, 1936.
———, tr. *Three Essays* (containing "Goethe and Tolstoy"; "Frederick the Great and the Grand Coalition"; "An Experience in the Occult"). New York, 1931.
———, tr. *The Transposed Heads*. New York, 1941.
———, tr. *Young Joseph*. New York, 1935.
———, *et al.*, tr. *Freud, Goethe, Wagner*. New York, 1937.
———, *et al.*, tr. *Order of the Day; Political Essays* (containing "An Appeal to Reason"; "The Coming Victory of Democracy"; "Europe Beware"; "The German Republic"; "I Stand with the Spanish People"; "This Peace"; "This War"; etc.). New York, 1942.

MELL: White, M. V., tr. *Apostle Play*. London, 1934.

MEYRINK: Pemberton, M., tr. *The Golem*. New York, 1928.

MOLO: Sutton, E., tr. *Brother Luther*. New York, 1930.

NEUMANN: Balogh, B., tr. *Life of Christina of Sweden*. London, 1935.
Brooks, C., tr. *Patriot*. London, 1929.
Paterson, H., tr. *The Devil*. New York, 1928.
———, tr. *The Rebels*. New York, 1929.
Paul, E. and C., tr. *New Caesar*. London, 1934.

REMARQUE: Lindley, D., tr. *Flotsam*. Boston, 1941.
Sorrell, W., and D. Lindley, tr. *The Arch of Triumph*. New York, 1946.
Wheen, A. W., tr. *All Quiet on the Western Front*. Boston, 1929.
———, tr. *The Road Back*. Boston, 1931.
———, tr. *Three Comrades*. Boston, 1937.

RENN: Muir, E. and W., tr. *After War*. New York, 1931.
———, tr. *War*. New York, 1929.

REUTER: Tapley, R., tr. *Daughters, the Story of Two Generations*. New York, 1930.

CONTEMPORARY LITERATURE

RILKE: Barrett, R. G. L., tr. *The Life of the Virgin Mary*. Würzburg, 1922.

Deutsch, B., tr. *Poems from the Book of Hours*. Norfolk, Conn., 1941.

Greene, J. B., and M. D. Herter Norton. *Letters of Rainer Maria Rilke*. New York, 1945.

Herter Norton, M. D., tr. *Letters to a Young Poet*. New York, 1934.

——, tr. *Tale of Love and Death of Cornet Christopher Rilke*. New York, 1932.

——, and J. Linton, tr. *Journal of My Other Self* (*Malte Laurids Brigge*). New York, 1930.

——, and N. Purtscher-Wydenbruck. *Stories of God*. London, 1931.

Leishman, J. B., tr. *Poems*. London, 1934.

Lemont, J., tr. *Duino Elegies and Sonnets to Orpheus*. New York, 1945.

——, tr. *Poems*. New York, 1943.

——, and H. Transil, tr. *Auguste Rodin*. New York, 1945.

Sackville-West, E. and V., tr. *Duinese Elegies*. London, 1930.

ROTH: Dunlop, G., tr. *Radetzky March*. New York, 1933.

SACHER-MASOCH: Brownell, J., tr. *Venus in Furs*. London, 1931.

Cohen, H. L., tr. *Jewish Tales*. Chicago, 1894.

SCHAFFNER: *The Wisdom of Love*. New York, 1930.

SCHICKELE: Waller, H., tr. *The Heart of Alsace* (Part II of *Das Erbe am Rhein*). New York, 1929.

——, tr. *Maria Capponi* (Part I of *Das Erbe am Rhein*). New York, 1928.

SCHNITZLER: Björkman, E., tr. *The Lonely Way, Intermezzo, Countess Mizzie*. New York, 1915.

Drake, W. A., tr. *Flight into Darkness*. New York, 1931.

——, tr. *Theresa*. New York, 1928.

——, *et al.*, tr. *Viennese Novelettes* (containing "Daybreak"; "Fräulein Else"; "Rhapsody"; "Beatrice"; "None But the Brave"). New York, 1931.

Eisemann, F., tr. *Viennese Idylls* (containing "Blind Geronimo and His Brother"; "Flowers"; "The Farewell"; etc.). Boston, 1913.

Loving, P., tr. *Comedies of Words* (containing "The Big Scene"; "Literature"; "The Hour of Recognition"; etc.). Cincinnati, 1917.

Mannes, M., and G. I. Colbron, tr. *Reigen, Anatol, Living Hours, The Green Cockatoo*. New York, 1933.

Paul, E. and C., tr. *Casanova's Homecoming*. New York, 1930.

Pohli, E., tr. *Professor Bernhardi*. San Francisco, 1913.

Samuel, H., tr. *The Road to the Open*. New York, 1923.

SEGHERS: Galston, J. A., tr. *The Seventh Cross*. Boston, 1942.

Goldsmith, M., tr. *Revolt of the Fishermen*. London, 1929.

SEIDEL: Gribble, G. D., tr. *The Wish Child*. New York, 1935.

SPITTELER: Mayne, E. C., and J. F. Muirhead, tr. *Selected Poems*. New York, 1928.

Muirhead, J. F., tr. *Laughing Truths*. New York, 1927.

——, tr. *Prometheus and Epimetheus*. London, 1931.

SPYRI: Brooks, L., tr. *Gritli's Children*. Boston, 1887.

——, tr. *Heidi*. Boston, 1884.

HISTORY OF GERMAN LITERATURE

STERNHEIM: "A Pair of Drawers," *Transition,* nos. 6–9, 1927.

SUDERMANN: Baukhage, H. R., tr. *Honor.* New York, 1915.
"Fritzchen" (translator anonymous), *German-American Annals,* 1918.
Marshall, B., tr. *Regina.* New York, 1910.
Overbeck, B., tr. *Dame Care.* New York, 1917.

TOLLER: Crankshaw, E., tr. *I Was a German.* New York, 1934.
———, *et al.,* tr. *Seven Plays* (containing "The Machine-Wreckers";
"Transfiguration"; "Masses and Man"; "Hinkemann"; "Draw the
Fires"; etc.). New York, 1934.
Dukes, A., tr. *The Swallow Book.* London, 1924.

UNRUH: Björkman, E., tr. *Bonaparte.* New York, 1928.
Macartney, C. A., tr. *The Way of Sacrifice.* New York, 1930.
The End Is Not Yet. New York, 1947.

VIEBIG: Barwell, A., tr. *Daughters of Hecuba.* London, 1922.
Waterhouse, G., tr. *The Sleeping Army.* London, 1930.

WAGGERL: *Bread.* London, 1931.

WASSERMANN: Brainin, S. N., tr. *My Life as German and Jew.*
New York, 1934.
Brooks, C., tr. *Etzel Andergast.* New York, 1932.
———, tr. *The Jews of Zirndorf.* New York, 1933.
Lewisohn, L., tr. *The World's Illusion.* New York, 1920.
———, and A. W. Porterfield, tr. *The Goose Man.* New York, 1922.
Newton, C., tr. *Caspar Hauser.* New York, 1931.
———, tr. *The Maurizius Case.* New York, 1929.

WEDEKIND: Eliot, S. A., tr. *Tragedies of Sex* (containing "Spring's
Awakening"; "Earth-Spirit"; "Pandora's Box"; "Damnation").
New York, 1923.

WERFEL: Arlt, G. C., tr. *Star of the Unborn.* New York, 1946.
Behrman, S. N., tr. *Jacobowsky and the Colonel.* New York, 1944.
Dunlop, G., tr. *The Forty Days of Musa Dagh.* New York, 1934.
———, tr. *The Pure in Heart.* New York, 1931.
Firth, M., tr. *Embezzled Heaven.* New York, 1940.
———, tr. *Hearken unto the Voice.* New York, 1938.
Jessiman, H., tr. *Verdi.* New York, 1925.
Langner, R., tr. *Goat Song.* Garden City, N. Y., 1926.
———, tr. *Juarez and Maximilian.* New York, 1926.
Levertoff, P. P., tr. *Paul among the Jews.* London, 1928.
Lewisohn, L., tr. *The Eternal Road.* New York, 1936.
———, tr. *The Song of Bernadette.* New York, 1942.
Lowe-Porter, H. T., tr. *Twilight of a World* (containing "Not the
Murderer . . . Is Guilty"; "Class Reunion"; "The Man Who Con-
quered Death"; etc.). New York, 1937.
Snow, E. A., tr. *Poems.* Princeton, 1945.

WIECHERT: Blewitt, P. and T., tr. *The Baroness.* New York, 1936.
Stechow, U., tr. *The Forest of the Dead.* New York, 1947.
Wilkins, E., and E. Kaiser, tr. *The Girl and the Ferryman.* New York,
1947.

WITKOP: Wedd, A. F., tr. *German Students' War Letters.* New
York, 1929.

CONTEMPORARY LITERATURE

WOLF: Bromberger, A., tr. *Floridsdorf, the Vienna Workers in Revolt.* New York, 1935.

——, tr. *Professor Mamlock.* New York, 1935.

Wallis, K., tr. *The Sailors of Cattaro.* New York, 1935.

ZAHN: Trollope, M. R., tr. *Golden Threads.* London, 1908.

ZUCKMAYER: Firth, M., tr. *The Moons Ride Over.* New York, 1937.

Portman, D., tr. *The Captain of Köpenick.* London, 1932.

ZWEIG, A.: Paul, E. and C., tr. *Insulted and Exiled: The Truth about the German Jews.* London, 1937.

Sutton, E., tr. *The Case of Sergeant Grischa.* New York, 1928.

——, tr. *Claudia.* New York, 1930.

——, tr. *The Crowning of a King.* New York, 1938.

——, tr. *De Vriendt Goes Home.* New York, 1933.

——, tr. *Education before Verdun.* New York, 1936.

——, tr. *Young Woman of 1914.* New York, 1932.

ZWEIG, S.: Bithell, J., tr. *Emile Verhaeren.* Boston, 1914.

Langner, R., tr. *Volpone.* New York, 1928.

Paul, E. and C., tr. *Adepts in Self-Portraiture.* New York, 1928.

——, tr. *Amok.* New York, 1931.

——, tr. *Conflicts.* New York, 1927.

——, tr. *Erasmus of Rotterdam.* New York, 1934.

——, tr. *Jeremiah.* New York, 1929.

——, tr. *Joseph Fouché.* New York, 1930.

——, tr. *Kaleidoscope, Thirteen Stories and Novelettes* (containing "The Invisible Collection"; "The Burning Secret"; "Transfiguration"; etc.). New York, 1934.

——, tr. *Marie Antoinette.* New York, 1934.

——, tr. *Mary Queen of Scotland.* New York, 1935.

——, tr. *Mental Healers.* New York, 1932.

——, tr. *The Right to Heresy: Castellio against Calvin.* New York, 1936.

——, tr. *Romain Rolland.* New York, 1921.

——, tr. *Three Masters.* New York, 1930.

——, tr. *The Tide of Fortune* (Sternstunden). New York, 1940.

Rose, W. and D., tr. *Balzac.* New York, 1946.

St. James, A., tr. *Brazil, Land of the Future.* New York, 1941.

Theis, O. F., tr. *Paul Verlaine.* Boston, 1913.

The World of Yesterday. New York, 1943.

CHRONOLOGICAL TABLE

GERMAN HISTORY	GERMAN LITERATURE (Numerals refer to chapters)	HISTORY AND LITERATURE IN OTHER COUNTRIES
	I.	Tacitus' *Germania*.
Battle in Teutoburg Forest, 9 A.D.		
Migrations, 375–500.	Gothic Bible.	Boethius.
Fall of the Roman Empire.	German sound-shift.	Rise of Papacy.
Merovingians, 486–751.		Bonifacius.
Carolingians, 751–911.	**II.**	*Beowulf.*
Charlemagne, 768–814.		
Treaty of Verdun, 843.	*Hildebrandslied.*	
	Heliand.	
	Otfried von Weissenburg.	Inroads by the Vikings.
Saxons, 919–1024.	Ekkehard.	*Chanson de Roland.*
Otto the Great, 936–973.	Roswitha.	
Franconians, 1024–1125.		
Henry IV at Canossa, 1077.	**III.**	First Crusade.
Hohenstaufens, 1138–1254.		Chrétien de Troyes.
Guelph rebellions.	Heinrich von Veldeke.	Marie de France.
Frederick Barbarossa.	Hartmann von Aue.	
Henry VI, 1190–1197.	Wolfram von Eschenbach.	
Frederick II, 1215–1250.	*Nibelungenlied.*	
	Walther von der Vogelweide.	
	Gottfried von Strassburg.	Magna Charta.
	Albertus Magnus.	
Interregnum, 1254–1273.	**IV.**	
Rudolf I of Hapsburg.	*Meier Helmbrecht.*	Dante Alighieri.
Rebellion of Switzerland.		

GERMAN HISTORY	GERMAN LITERATURE	OTHER COUNTRIES
Charles IV of Luxemburg.	Meister Eckhart.	Babylonian Exile of the Church.
The Golden Bull, 1356.	Bohemian Humanism.	Petrarch, Boccaccio.
Hansa cities. Teutonic Knights.	University of Prague.	Chaucer.
Hussite Wars.	Heinrich von Wittenweiler.	
Hapsburgs, 1438–1740–1918.	Thomas a Kempis.	
	Redentin Easter Play.	
	Gutenberg.	
	Reineke Fuchs.	
	Meistersongs. Folk songs.	Fall of Constantinople.
		English War of the Roses.
		Burgundy destroyed.
		Castile and Aragon united.
		Discovery of America.
		French invasion of Italy.
		The Medicis in Florence.
	Reuchlin, Erasmus.	Ariosto, Machiavelli.
Charles V, 1519–1556.	Luther, Zwingli.	Sack of Rome.
Knights' Rebellion, 1522.	Hutten, Murner.	Colet, More, Wyatt, Surrey.
Peasant War, 1524–1525.	Dürer, Holbein.	Rabelais, Calvin, Ronsard.
Augsburg Credo, 1530.		Boscán, Garcilaso de la Vega.
Schmalkalden War, 1546–1555.	Hans Sachs.	Camoëns, Tasso.
German–Spanish Empire dissolved, 1556.	Fischart, Wickram.	Dutch War of Liberation, 1568–1648.
Council of Trent, 1545–1563.		Huguenot Wars. Montaigne.
		Sidney, Spenser, Shakespeare.
	V.	Cervantes, Lope, Tirso, Castro.
	Faustbuch of 1587.	Vondel, Rubens, Rembrandt, Grotius.
	Rollenhagen.	Marino, Galileo.
		Góngora, Quevedo, Calderón.
	Heinrich Julius von Braunschweig	Corneille, Boileau, Racine, Molière.
	Fruchtbringende Gesellschaft.	Louis XIV.
Thirty Years' War, 1618–1648.	Böhme, Opitz, Gryphius.	Donne, Milton, Dryden. The Mathers.
	Zesen, Grimmelshausen.	Spinoza.
The Great Elector, 1640–1688.	Lohenstein, Ziegler.	
Rise of Prussia.	Bach, Handel.	
	Leibniz, Wolff.	

GERMAN HISTORY	GERMAN LITERATURE	OTHER COUNTRIES
War of Spanish Succession. Frederick II, 1740–1786.	Gottsched, Gellert.	Montesquieu, Voltaire, Diderot.
	VI.	
Seven Years' War, 1756–1763.	The Anacreontic Poets. Wieland, Lessing. Gluck, Mozart, Haydn.	Metastasio, Goldoni, Alfieri. Marivaux. The *Encyclopédie*.
	VII.	
Divisions of Poland, 1772 ff.	Haller, Bodmer, Gessner. Klopstock, Herder. *Göttinger Hainbund.*	Defoe, Thomson, Richardson. Young, Gray, Macpherson, Burns. Rousseau. American Revolution; Franklin. French Revolution; Mirabeau.
	VIII.	
	Goethe, Schiller, Kant.	
Napoleonic Wars, 1795–1815.	IX.	Mme de Staël, Constant.
Reichsdeputationshauptschluss.	Hölderlin, Jean Paul. The Schlegels, Novalis, Tieck. Schleiermacher, Fichte. Beethoven, Weber, Schubert. Kleist, Arndt, Körner. Arnim, Brentano, the Grimms. Uhland, Chamisso. Hoffmann, Werner. Eichendorff, Lenau. Grillparzer. Schopenhauer.	Wordsworth, Coleridge, Scott. Byron, Shelley, Keats. Chateaubriand, Lamartine. Hugo, Vigny, Musset. Foscolo, Leopardi, Manzoni. Espronceda, Hartzenbusch, Zorrilla. Oehlenschläger, Tegnér. Pushkin, Lermontov. Mickiewicz, Slowacki. Irving, Poe, Hawthorne, Emerson. Margaret Fuller, Longfellow.
Defeat of Prussia; *Rheinbund.* End of First Reich, 1806. *Fürstentag* at Erfurt, 1808. Retreat from Moscow, 1812. German War of Liberation. Congress of Vienna, 1814–1815.		

GERMAN HISTORY	GERMAN LITERATURE	OTHER COUNTRIES
	X.	
Holy Alliance; Metternich.	Feuerbach, Strauss.	Carlyle, Macaulay, Thackeray.
Zollverein, 1834.	Heine, Herwegh, Gutzkow.	Pellico, Carducci.
Revolution of 1848.	Platen, Immermann.	George Sand, Balzac, Flaubert.
	Friedrich, Schwind, Richter.	Dickens, the Brontës, Meredith.
Otto von Bismarck.	Wagner, Liszt, Brahms.	War of Italian Independence.
	Hebbel, Ludwig.	Whittier, Whitman, Lanier.
	Mörike, Droste, Geibel.	American Civil War.
Prussian-Austrian War, 1866.	Freytag, Scheffel, Meyer.	Valera, Galdós, Valdés.
	Gotthelf, Stifter, Reuter.	Tennyson, Hardy, Disraeli.
Franco-German War, 1870–1871.	Storm, Keller, Anzengruber.	Zola, Maupassant, Daudet.
Establishment of Second Reich.	Raabe, Spielhagen, Fontane.	Dostoevski, Tolstoi.
African colonization, 1884 ff.	Marx, Nietzsche, Spitteler.	Ibsen, Strindberg.
William II, 1888–1918.	Liliencron, Dehmel.	Mark Twain, London, Norris.
		Butler, Moore, Shaw.
	XI.	
	Holz, Hauptmann, Sudermann.	Verlaine, Mallarmé, Rimbaud.
Entente cordiale, 1904.	Hesse, Huch, Mann, Zweig.	Maeterlinck, d'Annunzio, Wilde.
	Hofmannsthal, Schnitzler.	
World War I, 1914–1918.	Ernst, Scholz, Molo, Schaefer.	Rolland, Proust.
Weimar Republic, 1918–1933.	George, Rilke, Wassermann.	Hamsun, Undset.
	Frenssen, Stehr, Löns.	O'Neill, Lewis.
	Kafka, Döblin, Werfel.	Conrad, Wells, Galsworthy, Joyce.
	Kaiser, Toller, Unruh.	Hemingway, Steinbeck, Dos Passos.
Nazis achieve power, 1933.	Remarque, Carossa, Fallada.	
	Kolbenheyer, Blunck, Johst.	
World War II, 1939–1945.	Jünger, Wiechert.	

BIBLIOGRAPHIES

Side captions printed in **boldface** correspond to major divisions of the chapters in the text.

CHAPTER I

The German Language

Braune, W. *Althochdeutsche Grammatik.* Halle, 1925.
————. *Althochdeutsches Lesebuch.* Halle, 1928.
Brugmann, K. *Kurze vergleichende Grammatik der indogermanischen Sprachen.* Strassburg, 1904.
Childe, V. G. *The Aryans.* London & New York, 1926.
Curme, G. O. *A Grammar of the German Language.* New York, 1922.
Feist, S. *Die deutsche Sprache.* Munich, 1933.
Gordon, E. V. *An Introduction to Old Norse.* Oxford, 1927.
Grünbech, V. *The Culture of the Teutons.* 2 vols. London, 1931.
Gwatkin, H. M., *et al. The Christian Roman Empire and the Foundation of the Teutonic Kingdoms* (Vol. I of *The Cambridge Medieval History*). Cambridge, 1936.
Hoops, J. *Reallexikon der germanischen Altertumskunde.* 4 vols. Strassburg, 1911–19.
Kluge, F., and A. Götze. *Etymologisches Wörterbuch der deutschen Sprache.* Berlin, 1934.
Matthias, A. *Handbuch des deutschen Unterrichts.* Munich, 1908 ff.
Meillet, A. *Caractères généraux des langues germaniques.* Paris, 1930.
Paul, H. *Grundriss der germanischen Philologie.* Strassburg & Berlin, 1900 ff.
Priebsch, R., and W. E. Collinson. *The German Language.* London, 1934.
Prokosch, E. *A Comparative Germanic Grammar.* Philadelphia, 1939.
Schrader, O. *Reallexikon der indogermanischen Altertumsgeschichte.* 2 vols. Berlin & Leipzig, 1917–29.
Senn, A. *An Introduction to Middle High German.* New York, 1937.
Tonnelat, E. *Histoire de la langue allemande.* Paris, 1927.
Wilmanns, W. *Deutsche Grammatik, gotisch, alt-, mittel- und neuhochdeutsch.* Strassburg, 1911.
Wright, J. *A Grammar of the Gothic Language.* Oxford, 1930.

Periods of German Literature

Biese, A. *Deutsche Literaturgeschichte.* 3 vols. Munich, 1930.
Ermatinger, E. *Dichtung und Geistesleben der deutschen Schweiz.* Munich, 1933.
Francke, K. *A History of German Literature.* New York, 1907.
Goedeke, K. *Grundriss zur Geschichte der deutschen Dichtung aus den Quellen.* 11 vols. Dresden, 1884–1938.
Heinemann, K. *Die deutsche Dichtung.* Leipzig, 1927.

BIBLIOGRAPHIES

Klein, K. K. *Literaturgeschichte des Deutschtums im Ausland*. Leipzig, 1939.
Kluge, H. *Geschichte der deutschen National-Literatur*. Altenburg, 1935.
Korff, H. A., and W. Linden. *Aufriss der deutschen Literaturgeschichte*. Leipzig, 1932.
Liptzin, S. *Historical Survey of German Literature*. New York, 1936.
Merker, P., and W. Stammler. *Reallexikon der deutschen Literaturgeschichte*. 4 vols. Berlin, 1925–31.
Nadler, J. *Literaturgeschichte der deutschen Stämme und Landschaften*. 4 vols. Regensburg, 1912–28.
Nagl, J. W., and J. Zeidler. *Deutsch-österreichische Literaturgeschichte*. 4 vols. Vienna, 1899–1937.
Priest, G. M. *A Brief History of German Literature*. New York, 1910.
Robertson, J. G. *A History of German Literature*. London, 1931.
————. *The Literature of Germany* (Home University Library). London, 1913.
————. *Outlines of the History of German Literature*. London, 1911.
Röhl, H. *Wörterbuch zur deutschen Literatur*. Leipzig & Berlin, 1931.
Rose, E. *Geschichte der deutschen Dichtung*. New York, 1936.
Scherer, W., and O. Walzel. *Geschichte der deutschen Literatur*. Berlin, 1928.
Steinhausen, G. *Geschichte der deutschen Kultur*. Leipzig, 1929.
Thomas, C. *A History of German Literature*. New York, 1909.
Vogt, F., and M. Koch. *Geschichte der deutschen Literatur*. 3 vols. Leipzig, 1934–38.
Waterhouse, A. *A Short History of German Literature*. London, 1942.
Wiegand, J. *Deutsche Geistesgeschichte im Grundriss*. Frankfurt, 1932.
Wolkan, R. *Geschichte der deutschen Literatur in Böhmen und in den Sudetenländern*. Augsburg, 1925.

The Migrations

Bithell, J. *Germany. A Companion to German Studies*. London, 1932.
Classen, W. *Das Werden des deutschen Volkes*. Hamburg, 1925.
Friederich, W. P. *Kurze Geschichte des deutschen Volkes*. New York, 1939.
Gebhardt, B. *Handbuch der deutschen Geschichte*. 2 vols. Stuttgart, 1930.
Haller, J. *The Epochs of German History*. New York, 1930.
Henderson, E. F. *A Short History of Germany*. New York, 1937.
Krones, F. von. *Österreichische Geschichte*. Berlin & Leipzig, 1915–23.
Largiadèr, A. *Geschichte der Schweiz*, Berlin & Leipzig, 1927.
Ludwig, E. *The Germans: Double History of a Nation*. Boston, 1941.
Pinnow, H. *History of Germany*. New York, 1933.
Shuster, G. N., and A. Bergsträsser. *Germany: A Short History*. New York, 1944.
Steinberg, H. *A Short History of Germany*. Cambridge, 1944.

Earliest Reports about the Germanic Peoples

Chadwick, H. *The Heroic Age*. Cambridge, 1912.
Golther, W. *Handbuch der germanischen Mythologie*. Leipzig, 1895.
Grimm, J. *Deutsche Mythologie*, ed. E. H. Meyer. 3 vols. Berlin, 1930.

Heusler, A. *Altgermanische Poesie*. Berlin, 1924.

———. *Lied und Epos in germanischer Sagendichtung*. Dortmund, 1905.

Leyen, F. von der. *Deutsches Sagenbuch*. 2 vols. Munich, 1923–24.

Mogk, E. *Germanische Religionsgeschichte und Mythologie*. Berlin, 1927.

Schneider, H. *Deutsche Heldensage*. Berlin & Leipzig, 1930.

Steinhausen, G. *Germanische Kultur in der Urzeit*. Leipzig, 1917.

CHAPTER II

The Historical Background

Gwatkin, H. M., *et al. The Rise of the Saracens and the Foundation of the Western Empire; Germany and the Western Empire* (Vols. II and III of *The Cambridge Medieval History*). Cambridge, 1922.

Hodgkin, T. *Charles the Great*. London, 1903.

Russell, C. E. *Charlemagne, First of the Moderns*. Boston, 1930.

Woodruff, D. *Charlemagne*. New York, 1935.

Old High German Literature

Clark, J. M. *The Abbey of St. Gall*. Cambridge, 1926.

Golther, W. *Die deutsche Dichtung, 800–1500*. Stuttgart, 1922.

Ker, W. P. *The Dark Ages*. Edinburgh, 1911.

———. *Epic and Romance*. London, 1922.

Singer, S. *Die mittelalterliche Literatur der deutschen Schweiz*. Frauenfeld, 1930.

Stammler, W. *Die deutsche Literatur des Mittelalters*. Berlin, 1931.

Literature in Other Languages

Laistner, M. W. *Thought and Letters in Western Europe, 500–900*. New York, 1931.

Manitius, M. *Geschichte der lateinischen Literatur des Mittelalters*. 3 vols. Munich, 1911–31.

Naumann, H. *Karolingische und Ottonische Renaissance*. Frankfurt, 1926.

Raby, F. J. E. *A History of Christian-Latin Poetry from the Beginnings to the Close of the Middle Ages*. Oxford, 1927.

———. *History of Secular Latin Poetry in the Middle Ages*. Oxford, 1934.

Stammler, W. *Geschichte der niederdeutschen Literatur von den ältesten Zeiten bis auf die Gegenwart*. Leipzig & Berlin, 1920.

Traube, L. *Karolingische Dichtungen*. Berlin, 1888.

CHAPTER III

General Observations

Brinkmann, H. *Entstehungsgeschichte des Minnesangs*. Halle, 1926.

Bruce, J. D. *The Evolution of Arthurian Romance from the Beginnings down to the Year 1300*. Göttingen, 1923.

Dam, J. von. *Das Veldeke-Problem*. Groningen, 1924.

———. *Zur Vorgeschichte des höfischen Epos*. Bonn, 1923.

Eckenstein, L. *Woman under Monasticism: Chapters on Saint-Lore and Convent Life between 500 and 1500*. Cambridge, 1898.

BIBLIOGRAPHIES

Ehrismann, G. *Der Geist der deutschen Dichtung im Mittelalter*. Leipzig, 1925.

Fairley, B. *Die Eneide Heinrichs von Veldeke und der Roman d'Enéas*. Jena, 1910.

Golther, W. *Das Rolandslied des Pfaffen Konrad*. Munich, 1887.

Naumann, H., and G. Müller, *Höfische Kultur*. Halle, 1929.

Singer, S. *Die Artussage*. Bern, 1926.

Vogt, F. *Geschichte der mittelhochdeutschen Literatur*. Berlin, 1922.

The Popular Epic

Boer, R. C. *Untersuchungen über den Ursprung und die Entwicklung der Nibelungensage*. 3 vols. Halle, 1906–09.

Heusler, A. *Nibelungensage und Nibelungenlied*. Dortmund, 1929.

Holz, G. *Der Sagenkreis der Nibelunge*. Leipzig, 1920.

Panzer, F. *Hilde-Gudrun*. Halle, 1901.

Sandbach, F. E. *The Nibelungenlied and Gudrun in England and America*. London, 1903.

The Court Epic

Bacon, S. A. *The Source of Wolfram's Willehalm*. Tübingen, 1910.

Brown, A. C. L. *The Origin of the Grail Legend*. Cambridge, Mass., 1943.

Golther, W. *Die Gralsage bei Wolfram von Eschenbach*. Rostock, 1910.

———. *Parzival und der Gral in der Dichtung des Mittelalters und der Neuzeit*. Stuttgart, 1925.

———. *Tristan und Isolde in den Dichtungen des Mittelalters und der neuen Zeit*. Leipzig, 1907.

Ranke, F. *Tristan und Isolde*. Munich, 1925.

Schönbach, A. E. *Über Hartmann von Aue*. Graz, 1894.

Schoepperle, G. *Tristan and Isolt*. 2 vols. Frankfurt & London, 1913.

Singer, S. *Wolframs Willehalm*. Bern, 1918.

Weber, G. *Wolfram von Eschenbach*. Frankfurt, 1928.

Weston, J. L. *The Legend of Sir Perceval*. 2 vols. London, 1906–09.

Lyric Poetry

Becker, R. *Wahrheit und Dichtung in Ulrichs von Lichtenstein Frauendienst*. Halle, 1888.

Bielschowsky, A. *Geschichte der deutschen Dorfpoesie im 13. Jahrhundert*. Berlin, 1891.

Burdach, K. *Reinmar der Alte und Walther von der Vogelweide*. Halle, 1928.

———. *Über den Ursprung des mittelalterlichen Minnesangs, Liebesromans und Frauendienstes*. Halle, 1926.

Kraus, K. von. *Walther von der Vogelweide: Untersuchungen*. Berlin & Leipzig, 1935.

Singer, S. *Neidhart-Studien*. Tübingen, 1920.

CHAPTER IV

General Observations

Burdach, K. *Vom Mittelalter zur Reformation*. Halle, 1912.

Francke, K. *Personality in German Literature before Luther*. Cambridge, Mass., 1916.

HISTORY OF GERMAN LITERATURE

Stammler, W. *Von der Mystik zum Barock, 1400–1600*. Stuttgart, 1927.
Taylor, A. *Problems of German Literary History of the Fifteenth and Sixteenth Centuries*. New York & London, 1939.

Three Centuries of Bourgeois Realism

Bergmann, E. *Die deutsche Mystik*. Breslau, 1926.
Böckel, O. *Handbuch des deutschen Volksliedes*. Marburg, 1930.
Borcherdt, H. H. *Geschichte des Romans und der Novelle in Deutschland*, Leipzig, 1926.
Bruinier, J. W. *Das deutsche Volkslied*. Leipzig, 1927.
Creizenach, W. *Geschichte des neueren Dramas*. Halle, 1911.
Evans, M. B. *The Passion Play of Lucerne: An Historical and Critical Introduction*. New York, 1943.
French, W. *Mediaeval Civilization as Illustrated by the Fastnachtspiele of Hans Sachs*. Baltimore, 1925.
Geisler, H. W. *Gestaltungen des Faust: die bedeutendsten Werke der Faustdichtung seit 1587*. Munich, 1927.
Genee, R. *Hans Sachs und seine Zeit*. Leipzig, 1902.
Herford, C. H. *Studies in the Literary Relations of England and Germany in the Sixteenth Century*. Cambridge, 1886.
Hertling G. F. von. *Albertus Magnus. Beiträge zu seiner Würdigung*. 2nd ed. Münster, 1914.
Kettlewell, S. *Thomas a Kempis and the Brothers of the Common Life*. New York, 1882.
Landau, P. *Hans Sachs*. Berlin, 1924.
Mackensen, L. *Die deutschen Volksbücher*. Leipzig, 1927.
Mielke, H., and W. Rehm. *Geschichte des deutschen Romans*. Berlin, 1927.
Palmer, P. M., and R. P. More. *The Sources of the Faust Tradition, from Simon Magus to Lessing*. New York, 1936.
Pfeiffer, F. *Meister Eckhardt*, tr. by C. B. Evans. 2 vols. London, 1924–31.
Rajewski, Sr. M. A. *Sebastian Brant: Studies in Religious Aspects of His Life and Work*. Washington, D. C., 1944.
Reilly, G. C. *The Psychology of Saint Albert the Great Compared with That of Saint Thomas*. Washington, D. C., 1934.
Richards, A. E. *Studies in English Faust Literature*. Berlin, 1907.
Rohde, R. *Das englische Faustbuch und Marlowes Tragödie*. Halle, 1910.
Rudwin, M. J. *The Origin of the German Carnival Comedy*. New York, 1920.
Scherer, W. *Die Anfänge des deutschen Prosaromans und Jörg Wickram von Colmar*. Strassburg, 1877.
Stammler, W. *Das religiöse Drama des deutschen Mittelalters*. Leipzig, 1925.
Taylor, A. *The Literary History of the Meistergesang*. New York, 1937.
Wolf, E. *Faust und Luther,* Halle, 1912.

Humanism

Borinski, K. *Die Poetik der Renaissance und die Anfänge der litterarischen Kritik in Deutschland*. Berlin, 1886.

BIBLIOGRAPHIES

Burdach, K. *Der Dichter des Ackermann aus Böhmen und seine Zeit.* Berlin, 1926.
――――. *Reformation, Renaissance. Humanismus.* Berlin, 1926.
Ellinger, G. *Geschichte der neulateinischen Literatur Deutschlands im 16. Jahrhundert.* Berlin & Leipzig, 1929.
Froude, J. A. *Life and Letters of Erasmus.* London, 1894.
Geiger, L. *Renaissance und Humanismus in Italien und Deutschland.* Berlin, 1882.
――――. *Reuchlin.* Leipzig, 1871.
Hiller, J. H. *Albrecht von Eyb, Medieval Moralist.* Washington, D. C., 1939.
Holborn, H. *Ulrich von Hutten and the German Reformation.* New Haven, 1937.
Huizinga, J. *Erasmus.* London, 1924.
Murray, R. H. *Erasmus and Luther.* London, 1920.
Rashdall, H. *The Universities of Europe in the Middle Ages.* Oxford, 1895.
Richard, J. W. *Ph. Melanchthon.* London, 1898.
Strauss, D. F. *Ulrich von Hutten.* Leipzig, 1927.
Strauss, E. *Der Übersetzer N. von Wyle.* Berlin, 1911.
Voigt, G. *Die Wiederbelebung des klassischen Altertums.* Berlin, 1893.
Winship, G. P. *Gutenberg to Plantin: An Outline of the Early History of Printing.* Cambridge, Mass., 1926.
Zweig, S. *Erasmus of Rotterdam.* New York, 1934.

The German Reformation

Böhmer, H. *Luther im Lichte der neueren Forschung.* Leipzig, 1918.
Burdach, K. *Die Einigung der neuhochdeutschen Schriftsprache.* Halle, 1883.
Clayton, J. *Luther and His Work.* Milwaukee, 1937.
Cunz, D. *Ulrich Zwingli.* Aarau, 1937.
Fife, R. H. *Young Luther.* New York, 1928.
Hauffen, A. *Johann Fischart, ein Literaturbild aus der Gegenreformation.* Berlin, 1921.
Holstein, H. *Die Reformation im Spiegelbild der dramatischen Literatur.* Halle, 1886.
Köstlin, J. *Life of Luther.* London, 1919.
Liebenau, T. *Thomas Murner.* Freiburg, 1913.
Pascal, R. *The Social Basis of the German Reformation: Martin Luther and His Times.* London, 1933.
Schultz, H. *Luthers Stellung in der Geschichte der deutschen Sprache.* Braunschweig, 1893.
Walther, W. *Die deutsche Bibelübersetzung des Mittelalters.* Braunschweig, 1889–92.
Waring, L. H. *The Political Theories of Martin Luther.* New York, 1910.

CHAPTER V

General Observations

Reynaud, L. *Histoire générale de l'influence française en Allemagne.* Paris, 1915.
Schneider, A. *Spaniens Anteil an der deutschen Literatur des 16. und 17. Jahrhunderts.* Strassburg, 1898.

Waterhouse, G. *The Literary Relations of England and Germany in the Seventeenth Century.* Cambridge, 1914.

Baroque Literature

Bailey, M. L. *Milton and Jakob Böhme.* New York, 1914.

Blödau, C. A. von. *Grimmelshausens Simplizissimus und seine Vorgänger.* Berlin, 1908.

Brinton, H. H. *The Mystic Will, Based on a Study of the Philosophy of Jacob Boehme.* New York, 1930.

Cholevius, L. *Die bedeutendsten deutschen Romane des 17. Jahrhunderts.* Leipzig, 1866.

Cohn, A. *Shakespeare in Germany in the Sixteenth and Seventeenth Centuries.* London & Berlin, 1865.

Creizenach, W. M. A. *Die Schauspiele der englischen Komödianten.* Berlin & Stuttgart, 1889.

Cysarz, H. *Deutsche Barockdichtung.* Leipzig, 1924.

Deussen, P. J. *Böhme, sein Leben und seine Philosophie.* Leipzig, 1911.

Ermatinger, E. *Barock und Rokoko in der deutschen Dichtung.* Leipzig, 1926.

———. *Weltdeutung in Grimmelshausens Simplizissimus.* Leipzig, 1925.

Friederich, W. P. "From Ethos to Pathos: The Development from Gryphius to Lohenstein," *Germanic Review,* X (1935).

———. "German and French Dramatic Topics of the Seventeenth Century," *Studies in Philology,* XXXIV (1937).

———. "Late Renaissance, Baroque, or Counter-Reformation?", *Journal of English and Germanic Philology,* XLVI (1947).

Gebhard, J. F. *Spee, sein Leben und seine Werke.* Hildesheim, 1893.

Gundolf, F. *Andreas Gryphius.* Heidelberg, 1927.

———. *Martin Opitz.* Munich, 1923.

Hansen, T. *J. Rist und seine Zeit.* Halle, 1872.

Hartmann, F. *Life and Doctrines of Jacob Boehme.* London, 1891.

Herz, E. *Englische Schauspieler und englisches Schauspiel zur Zeit Shakespeares in Deutschland.* Hamburg, 1903.

Hewitt, T. B. *Paul Gerhardt as a Hymn Writer and His Influence in English Hymnody.* New Haven, 1918.

Ibel, R. *Hofmann von Hofmannswaldau.* Berlin, 1928.

Kretschmar, A. F. H. *Geschichte der Oper.* Leipzig, 1919.

Müller, G. *Deutsche Dichtung von der Renaissance bis zum Ausgang des Barock.* Potsdam, 1927.

———. *Geschichte des deutschen Liedes vom Zeitalter des Barock bis zur Gegenwart.* Munich, 1925.

Müller, J. *Das Jesuitendrama in den Ländern deutscher Zunge (1555–1665).* Augsburg, 1930.

Petrich, H. *Paul Gerhardt.* Gütersloh, 1914.

Rausse, H. *Geschichte des deutschen Romans bis 1800.* Kempten, 1914.

Scholte, J. H. *Philipp von Zesen.* Groningen, 1916.

Schultz, H. *Die Bestrebungen der Sprachgesellschaften des 17. Jahrhunderts.* Göttingen, 1888.

Stachel, P. *Seneca und das deutsche Renaissancedrama.* Berlin, 1907.

Strich, F. "Der lyrische Stil des 17. Jahrhunderts," *Muncker-Festschrift.* Munich, 1916.

Witkowski, G. *P. Fleming und sein Kreis.* Leipzig, 1909.

Wodeck, W. *Jakob Ayrers Dramen.* Halle, 1912.

BIBLIOGRAPHIES

Wysocki, L. G. *A. Gryphius et la tragédie allemande du XVIIe siècle.* Paris, 1893.

Zöllner, F. *Einrichtung und Verfassung der Fruchtbringenden Gesellschaft.* Berlin, 1899.

Pseudoclassicism

Bolte, J. "Die Molière-Übersetzungen," *Herrigs Archiv,* LXXXII (1889).

Kämmel, O. *Christian Weise.* Leipzig, 1897.

Mahrholz, W. *Der deutsche Pietismus.* Berlin, 1921.

Michael, G. *C. F. Gellert.* Leipzig, 1917.

Raab, R. *Pierre Corneille in deutschen Übersetzungen und auf der deutschen Bühne bis Lessing.* Heidelberg, 1910.

Uehlin, H. *Geschichte der Racine-Übersetzungen in der vorklassischen deutschen Literatur.* Heidelberg, 1903.

Waniek, G. *Gottsched und die deutsche Literatur seiner Zeit.* Leipzig, 1897.

Wolff, E. *Gottscheds Stellung im deutschen Bildungsleben.* Kiel, 1895.

CHAPTER VI

General Observations

Bruford, W. H. *Germany in the Eighteenth Century. The Social Background of the Literary Revival.* Cambridge, 1935.

Eloesser, A. *Die deutsche Literatur vom Barock bis zu Goethes Tod,* Berlin, 1930.

Köster, A. *Die deutsche Literatur der Aufklärungszeit.* Heidelberg, 1926.

Schneider, F. J. *Die deutsche Dichtung vom Ausgang des Barocks bis zum Beginn des Klassizismus, 1700–1785.* Stuttgart, 1924.

Willoughby, L. A. *The Classical Age of German Literature.* Oxford, 1926.

The Historical Background

Berger, A. E. *Friedrich der Grosse und die deutsche Literatur.* Bonn, 1890.

Langer, W. *Friedrich der Grosse und die geistige Welt Frankreichs.* Paris, 1932.

Marcus, H. *Friedrich der Grosse in der englischen Literatur.* Leipzig, 1931.

Priest, G. M. *Germany since 1740.* Boston, 1915.

The Rococo

Ausfeld, F. *Die deutsche anakreontische Dichtung des 18. Jahrhunderts.* Strassburg, 1907.

Behmer, A. *Sterne und Wieland.* Munich, 1899.

Budde, F. *Wieland und Bodmer.* Berlin, 1910.

Butler, E. *The Tyranny of Greece over Germany.* New York, 1935.

Elson, C. *Wieland and Shaftesbury.* New York, 1913.

Ermatinger, E. *Die Weltanschauung des jungen Wieland.* Frauenfeld, 1907.

Fuchs, A. *Les apports français dans l'œuvre de Wieland.* Paris, 1934.
Gerhard, M. *Der deutsche Entwicklungsroman bis zu Goethes Wilhelm Meister.* Halle, 1926.
Jahn, O. *Goethe und Leipzig.* Leipzig, 1908.
Kühn, J. *Der junge Goethe im Spiegel seiner Dichtung.* Heidelberg, 1912.
Kurrelmeyer, W. "English Translations of Wieland," *Modern Language Notes,* XXXII (1917).
Schuster, H. *Hagedorn und seine Bedeutung für die deutsche Dichtung.* Leipzig, 1882.
Stadler, E. *Wielands Shakespeare.* Strassburg, 1910.

The Enlightenment

Böhtlingk, A. *Shakespeare und unsere Klassiker.* Leipzig, 1909.
Borinski, K. *Die Antike in Poetik und Kunsttheorie.* Leipzig, 1914.
———. *Deutsche Poetik.* Berlin, 1916.
Brandl, A. "Shakespeare and Germany," *British Academy Proceedings* (1913).
Fischer, K. *Lessings Nathan.* Stuttgart, 1896.
Fittbogen, G. *Die Religion Lessings.* Leipzig, 1923.
Friederich, W. P. "Jakob von Graviseth's *Heutelia,*" *Publications of the Modern Language Association of America,* LII (1937).
Gilbert, K., and H. Kuhn. *A History of Esthetics.* New York, 1939.
Goodnight, S. H. "Lessing and Wieland in American Magazines Prior to 1846," *German-American Annals,* VI (1908).
Gundolf, F. *Shakespeare und der deutsche Geist.* Berlin, 1911.
Kenwood, S. H. "Lessing in England," *Modern Language Review,* IX (1914).
Kettner, G. *Lessings Dramen im Lichte ihrer und unserer Zeit.* Berlin, 1904.
Kinkel, H. *Lessings Dramen in Frankreich.* Darmstadt, 1908.
Korff, H. A. *Voltaire im literarischen Deutschland des 18. Jahrhunderts.* Heidelberg, 1917.
Kretschmar, E. *Über das Verhältnis Lessings in seiner "Erziehung des Menschengeschlechts" zur deutschen Aufklärung.* Leipzig, 1904.
Leisegang, H. *Lessings Weltanschauung.* Leipzig, 1931.
Nolte, F. O. *The Early Middle Class Drama (1696–1774).* Lancaster, Pa., 1935.
———. *Lessing's Laocoon.* Lancaster, Pa., 1940.
Pascal, R. *Shakespeare in Germany, 1740–1815.* Cambridge, 1937.
Robertson, J. G. *Lessing's Dramatic Theory, Being an Introduction to and Commentary on His Hamburgische Dramaturgie.* Cambridge, 1939.
Rolleston, T. W. *Life of G. E. Lessing.* London, 1889.
Schmidt, E. *Lessing, Geschichte seines Lebens und seiner Schriften.* Berlin, 1923.
Todt, W. *Lessing in England, 1767–1850.* Heidelberg, 1912.
Vail, C. C. D. *Lessing's Relation to the English Language and Literature.* New York, 1936.
Vogt, O. *Der goldene Spiegel und Wielands politische Ansichten.* Berlin, 1904.
Widmann, M. *Hallers Staatsromane und Bedeutung als politischer Schriftsteller.* Biel, 1893.

BIBLIOGRAPHIES

CHAPTER VII

General Observations

Eaton, J. W. *The German Influence in Danish Literature in the Eighteenth Century.* Cambridge, 1929.

Gjerset, F. *Der Einfluss von Thomsons Jahreszeiten auf die deutsche Literatur des 18. Jahrhunderts.* Heidelberg, 1898.

Hallemore, G. *Das Bild Laurence Sternes in Deutschland von der Aufklärung bis zur Romantik.* Berlin, 1936.

Hatzfeld, H. *Wechselbeziehungen zwischen der deutschen Literatur und den übrigen europäischen Literaturen.* Bielefeld, 1927.

Hewett-Thayer, H. W. *Laurence Sterne in Germany.* New York, 1905.

Kelly, J. A. *England and the Englishman in German Literature of the Eighteenth Century.* New York, 1921.

Kind, J. L. *Edward Young in Germany.* New York, 1902.

Price, L. M. *The Reception of English Literature in Germany.* Berkeley, 1932.

———. "The Reception of Richardson in Germany," *Journal of English and Germanic Philology,* XXV (1926).

Reynaud, L. *L'influence allemande en France au XVIIIe et au XIXe siècle.* Paris, 1922.

Stockley, V. *German Literature as Known in England, 1750–1805.* London, 1929.

Süpfle, T. *Geschichte des deutschen Kultureinflusses auf Frankreich.* Gotha, 1886 ff.

Tombo, R. *Ossian in Germany.* New York, 1901.

Wihan, J. *J. J. Bode als Vermittler englischer Geisteswerke.* Prague, 1906. (Bode was the translator of Fielding, Smollett, Goldsmith, Sterne.)

Forerunners of the Storm and Stress

Bächtold, J. *Geschichte der deutschen Literatur in der Schweiz.* Frauenfeld, 1892.

Baldensperger, F. "L'épisode de Gessner dans la littérature européenne," *Salomon Gessner, Gedenkbuch zum 200. Geburtstag.* Zurich, 1930.

Bergmann, F. *S. Gessner.* Munich, 1913.

Betz, L., et al. *Denkschrift zum 200. Geburtstag Bodmers.* Zurich, 1900. (Includes essays about Bodmer's relations to French, English, and Italian literature.)

Brandl, A. *B. H. Brockes.* Innsbruck, 1878.

Coffman, B. R. *The Influence of Salomon Gessner upon English Literature.* Philadelphia, 1905.

Friederich, W. P. "Switzerland's Contribution to the International Appreciation of Dante Alighieri," *Studies in Philology,* XLII (1945).

Heyer, A., and A. Hoffmann. *Günthers Leben.* Leipzig, 1909.

bershoff, C. H. "Bodmer and Milton Once More," *Publications of the Modern Language Association,* XLIII (1928).

enny, G. *Miltons Verlorenes Paradies in der deutschen Literatur.* St. Gall, 1890.

enny, H. E. *Die Alpendichtung der deutschen Schweiz.* Bern, 1905.

ippenberg, A. *Robinsonaden in Deutschland bis zur Insel Felsenburg.* Hannover, 1892.

Milberg, E. *Die moralischen Wochenschriften des 18. Jahrhunderts.* Meissen, 1880.

Nagel, W. *Die deutsche Idylle im 18. Jahrhundert.* Zurich, 1887.

Reynold, G. de. *Bodmer et l' école suisse.* Lausaune, 1912.

Robertson, J. G. "Milton's Fame on the Continent," *British Academy Proceedings* (1908).

———. *Studies in the Genesis of Romantic Theory in the Eighteenth Century.* Cambridge, 1928.

Schröder, K. *Schnabels Insel Felsenburg.* Marburg, 1912.

Schulze, H. G. *Miltons Verlorenes Paradies in deutschem Gewand.* Bonn, 1928.

Servaes, F. *Die Poetik Gottscheds und der Schweizer.* Strassburg, 1887.

Wagener, H. F. *Das Eindringen von Percy's Reliques in Deutschland.* Heidelberg, 1897.

Wolff, E. *J. E. Schlegel.* Berlin, 1889.

The Storm and Stress

KLOPSTOCK

Beck, T. J. *Northern Antiquities in French Learning and Literature (1755–1855): A Study in Preromantic Ideas.* New York, 1934–35.

Muncker, F. *Klopstock, Geschichte seines Lebens und seiner Schriften.* Stuttgart, 1900.

Strich, F. *Die Mythologie in der deutschen Literatur von Klopstock bis Wagner.* Munich, 1910.

Viëtor, K. *Geschichte der deutschen Ode.* Munich, 1923.

HERDER

Adler, F. H. *Herder and Klopstock.* Cleveland, 1914.

Andress, J. M. *Herder as an Educator.* New York, 1916.

Auerbach, E. "Vico und Herder," *Deutsche Vierteljahrsschrift für Literatur und Geistesgeschichte,* X (1932).

Ermatinger, E. *Die deutsche Lyrik in ihrer geschichtlichen Enwicklung von Herder bis zur Gegenwart.* Leipzig, 1925.

Francke, K. *Weltbürgertum in der deutschen Literatur von Herder bis Nietzsche.* Berlin, 1929.

Gillies, A. "Herder and the Preparation of Goethe's Idea of 'Weltliteratur,'" *Publications of the English Goethe-Society* (1933).

———. *Herder und Ossian.* Berlin, 1933.

Grohmann, W. *Herders nordische Studien.* Berlin, 1899.

Hayes, C. J. H. "Contributions of Herder to the Doctrine of Nationalism," *American Historical Review* (1927).

Horstmeyer, R. *Die deutschen Ossianübersetzungen des 18. Jahrhunderts.* Greifswald, 1926.

Kühnemann, E. *Herders Leben.* Munich, 1927.

Learned, M. D. "Herder and America," *German-American Annals,* II (1904).

Minor, J. *Hamann in seiner Bedeutung für die Sturm und Drangperiode.* Frankfurt, 1881.

Richter, H. "Blake und Hamann," *Herrigs Archiv,* CLVIII (1930).

Shelley, P. A. "Crevecoeur's Contribution to Herder's 'Neger-Idyllen,'" *Journal of English and Germanic Philology,* XXXVII (1938).

BIBLIOGRAPHIES

Siegel, K. *Herder als Philosoph*. Stuttgart, 1907.
Tieghem, P. van. *Ossian et l'Ossianisme dans la littérature européenne au XVIIIe siècle*. The Hague, 1920.
Tronchon, H. *Herder en France*. Paris, 1920.

YOUNG GOETHE

Appell, J. W. *Werther und seine Zeit*. Oldenburg, 1896.
Kleiber, L. *Studien zu Goethes Egmont*. Berlin, 1913.
Kühn, J. *Der junge Goethe im Spiegel seiner Dichtung*. Heidelberg, 1912.
Meyer-Benfey, H. "Die Entstehung des Urfaust," *Preussische Jahrbücher* (1923).
————. *Goethes Götz von Berlichingen*. Weimar, 1930.
Traumann, E. *Goethe der Strassburger Student*. Leipzig, 1923.

MINOR STORM AND STRESS WRITERS

Baldensperger, F. " 'Lenore' de Bürger dans la littérature française," *Études d'histoire littéraire*. Paris, 1907.
Blömker, F. *Das Verhältnis von Bürgers lyrischer und episch-lyrischer Dichtung zur englischen Literatur*. Münster, 1930.
Cardauns, H. *Friedrich Leopold zu Stolberg*. München-Gladbach, 1919.
Emerson, O. F. *The Earliest English Translations of Bürger's Lenore*. Cleveland, 1915.
Fleming, W. *Der Wandel des deutschen Naturgefühls vom 15. bis 18. Jahrhundert*. Halle, 1931.
Guinaudeau, O. *Jean-Gaspard Lavater*. Paris, 1924.
Hauff, G. *Schubart in seinem Leben und seinen Werken*. Stuttgart, 1885.
Herbst, W. *Johann Heinrich Voss*. Leipzig, 1872–76.
Kindermann, H. *Entwicklung der Sturm und Drang-Bewegung*. Heidelberg, 1925.
Pusey, W. W. *Louis-Sébastien Mercier in Germany*. New York, 1939.
Schmidt, E. *H. L. Wagner, Goethes Jugendgenosse*. Jena, 1879.
————. *Lenz und Klinger*. Berlin, 1878.
Wagner, A. *H. W. von Gerstenberg und der Sturm und Drang*. Heidelberg, 1920.
Walzel, O. *Vom Geistesleben des 18. und 19. Jahrhunderts*. Leipzig, 1911.

YOUNG SCHILLER

Benrubi, J. "Schiller et Rousseau," *Deutsche Rundschau*. Berlin, 1913.
Deye, E. *Shakespeare und Schiller*. Munich, 1931.
Elster, E. *Zur Entstehungsgeschichte des Don Carlos*. Halle, 1889.
Kelly, J. A. "Schiller's Attitude towards England," *Publications of the Modern Language Association*, XXXIX (1924).
Kontz, A. *Les drames de la jeunesse de Schiller*. Paris, 1889.
Lieder, F. W. C. "The Don Carlos Theme," *Harvard Studies and Notes in Philology and Literature*, XII (1930).
Thomas, A. *Don Carlos und Hamlet*. Bonn, 1933.
Willoughby, L. A. "English Translations and Adaptations of Schiller's 'Robbers,' " *Modern Language Review*, XVI (1921).

CHAPTER VIII

Goethe and Schiller Compared

Bellermann, L. *Schillers Dramen*. Berlin, 1908.
Bielschowsky, A. *Goethe*. Munich, 1929; London, 1908.
Borcherdt, H. H. *Schiller*. Leipzig, 1929.
Brandes, G. *Goethe*. New York, 1924.
Brown, P. H. *Life of Goethe*. London, 1920.
Carré, J. M. *Goethe*. Paris, 1928; New York, 1929.
Croce, B. *Goethe*. Bari, 1919; London, 1923.
Golther, W. *Schiller*. Leipzig, 1925.
Gundolf, F. *Goethe*. Berlin, 1928.
Korff, H. A. *Der Geist der Goethezeit*. Leipzig, 1930.
Kühnemann, E. *Goethe*. Leipzig, 1930.
———. *Schiller*. Munich, 1920.
Ludwig, E. *Goethe*. Stuttgart & London, 1928.
Paulsen, F. *I. Kant, sein Leben und seine Lehre*. Stuttgart, 1927.
Rabel, G. *Goethe und Kant*. Vienna, 1927.
Reich, K. *Rousseau und Kant*. Tübingen, 1936.
Robertson, J. G. *Goethe*. London, 1932.
———. *Schiller after a Century*. Edinburgh, 1906.
Thomas, C. *The Life and Works of Schiller*. New York, 1901.
Vallois, M. *La formation de l'influence kantienne en France*. Paris, 1925.
Vorländer, K. *Kant, Schiller, Goethe*. Leipzig, 1907.
Wellek, R. *Immanuel Kant in England*. Princeton, 1931.

Goethe's Evolution towards Classicism

FOREIGN INFLUENCES UPON GOETHE

Bickermann, J. *Don Quijote y Fausto. Los heroes y las obras*. Barcelona, 1932.
Barnes, B. *Goethe's Knowledge of French Literature*. New York, 1937.
Bohnenblust, G. *Goethe und Pestalozzi*. Bern, 1923.
———. *Goethe und die Schweiz*. Frauenfeld, 1932.
Boyd, J. *Goethe's Knowledge of English Literature*. New York, 1932.
Diamond, W. "Wilhelm Meister's Interpretation of Hamlet," *Modern Philology*, XXIII (1925).
Engel, H. *Goethe in seinem Verhältnis zur französischen Sprache*. Göttingen, 1937.
Heller, O. "Faust and Faustus: A Study of Goethe's Relation to Marlowe," *Washington University Studies*. St. Louis, 1931.
Hérenger, A. *Goethe en Italie*. Paris, 1931.
Justi, C. *Winckelmann und seine Zeitgenossen*. Leipzig, 1898.
Kampmann, W. "Goethes Kunsttheorie nach der italienischen Reise," *Jahrbuch der Goethe-Gesellschaft* (1929).
Klenze, C. von. *The Interpretation of Italy during the Last Two Centuries*. New York, 1907.
Kühnemann, E. "Goethe und Spinoza," *Jahrbuch der Goethe-Gesellschaft* (1929).
Loiseau, H. *Goethe et la France*. Neuchâtel, 1930.
Maass, E. *Goethe und die Antike*. Berlin, 1912.
Müllensiefen, P. "Die französische Revolution und Napoleon in Goethes Weltanschauung," *Jahrbuch der Goethe-Gesellschaft* (1930).

Pinger, W. R. R. "Laurence Sterne and Goethe," *Modern Philology,* XVIII (1920).

Prang, H. *Goethe und die Kunst der italienischen Renaissance.* Berlin, 1938.

Schmidt, E. *Richardson, Rousseau und Goethe.* Berlin, 1902.

Sulger-Gebing, E. *Goethe und Dante.* Berlin, 1907.

Trevelyan, H. *Goethe and the Greeks.* Cambridge, 1941.

Viëtor, K. "Goethe in Italien," *Germanic Review,* VII (1932).

Wadepuhl, W. *Goethe's Interest in the New World.* Jena, 1935.

————. *Goethes Stellung zur französischen Romantik.* Madison, Wis., 1924.

Wahr, F. B. "Goethe's Shakespeare," *Philological Quarterly,* XI (1932).

Schiller's Evolution towards Classicism

FOREIGN INFLUENCES UPON SCHILLER

Benrubi, J. "Schiller et Rousseau," *Deutsche Rundschau.* Berlin, 1913.

Cassirer, E. von. "Schiller and Shaftesbury," *Publications of the English Goethe-Society,* XI (1935).

Cunningham, K. *Schiller und die französische Klassik.* Bonn, 1930.

Gerhard, M. "Schiller und die griechische Tragödie," *Forschungen zur neueren Literaturgeschichte.* Weimar, 1919.

Luzzato, A. "Schiller traducteur de Racine," *Revue de Littérature Comparée,* XIX (1939).

Goethe's Classical Period

Bode, W. *Der Weimarische Musenhof.* Berlin, 1917.

Federn, E. *Christiane von Goethe.* Munich, 1920.

Hehn, V. *Über Goethes Hermann und Dorothea.* Stuttgart, 1913.

Höfer, E. *Goethe und Charlotte von Stein.* Berlin, 1923.

Reinsch, F. H. *Goethe's Political Interests prior to 1787.* Berkeley, 1923.

Ruoff, H. *Zur Entstehungsgeschichte von Goethes Tasso.* Marburg, 1910.

Steinweg, C. *Das Seelendrama in der Antike und seine Weiterentwicklung bis auf Goethe und Wagner.* Halle, 1924.

Wundt, M. *Goethes Wilhelm Meister und die Entwicklung des modernen Lebensideals.* Berlin, 1913.

Schiller's Classical Period

Belling, E. *Die Metrik Schillers.* Breslau, 1883.

Düntzer, H. *Erläuterungen zu den deutschen Klassikern.* Leipzig, 1876

Eggli, E. *Schiller et le romantisme français.* Paris, 1927.

Ewen, F. *The Prestige of Schiller in England.* New York, 1932.

Fielitz, W. *Studien zu Schillers Dramen.* Leipzig, 1876.

Fischer, K. *Schiller als Philosoph.* Heidelberg, 1891.

Harnack, O. *Die klassische Aesthetik der Deutschen. Würdigung der kunsttheoretischen Arbeiten Schillers, Goethes und ihrer Freunde.* Leipzig, 1892.

Janssen, J. *Schiller als Historiker.* Freiburg, 1879.

Ludwig, A. *Schiller und die Nachwelt.* Berlin, 1909.

Müller, E. *Regesten zu Friedrich Schillers Leben und Werken.* Leipzig, 1900.

Parry, E. C. *Friedrich Schiller in America.* Philadelphia, 1905.
Philippi, E. *Schillers lyrische Gedankendichtung in ihrem ideellen Zusammenhange beleuchtet.* Augsburg, 1888.
Rea, T. *Schiller's Dramas and Poems in England.* London, 1906.
Rochholtz, E. L. *Tell und Gessler in Sage und Geschichte.* Heilbronn, 1877.
Tomaschek, K. *Schiller in seinem Verhältnis zur Wissenschaft.* Vienna, 1862.
Viehoff, H. *Schillers Gedichte erläutert, und auf ihre Veranlassungen, Quellen und Vorbilder zurückgeführt.* Stuttgart, 1895.
Willoughby, L. A. "Schiller in England and Germany," *Publications of the English Goethe-Society,* XI (1935).

Goethe's Old Age

Bianquis, G. *Faust à travers quatre siècles.* Paris, 1935.
Bluhm, H. S. "The Reception of Goethe's Faust in England after the Middle of the Nineteenth Century." *Journal of English and Germanic Philology,* XXXIV (1935).
Burdach, K. *Goethes Westöstlicher Divan.* Halle, 1926.
Carriere, M. *Calderons Wundertätiger Magus und Goethes Faust.* Braunschweig, 1876.
Dickinson, G. L., and F. M. Stawell. *Goethe's Faust.* London, 1928.
Geissler, N. W. *Gestaltungen des Faust, die bedeutendsten Werke seit 1587.* Munich, 1927.
Hanhart, W. *The Reception of Goethe's Faust in England in the First Half of the Nineteenth Century.* New York, 1909.
Harnack, O. *Goethe in der Epoche seiner Vollendung.* Leipzig, 1901.
Haskell, J. *Bayard Taylor's Translation of Goethe's Faust.* New York, 1908.
Heinemann, W. *Goethes Faust in England und Amerika.* Berlin, 1886.
Jahn, K. *Dichtung und Wahrheit: Vorgeschichte, Entstehung, Kritik, Analyse.* Halle, 1908.
Kube, K. H. *Goethes Faust in französischer Auffassung und Bühnendarstellung.* Berlin, 1932.
Lienhard, F. *Einführung in Goethes Faust.* Leipzig, 1922.
Meek, G. J. *Faust, the Man and the Myth.* Oxford, 1930.
Petersen, J. *Die Entstehung der Eckermannschen Gespräche.* Frankfurt, 1926.
Semler, C. *Goethes Wahlverwandtschaften und des Dichters sittliche Weltanschauung.* Hamburg, 1886.
Suárez de Urbina, J. "Algunas influencias del Fausto de Goethe en España," *Revista de Cultura y Vida Universitaria.* Zaragoza, 1927.
Wendriner, K. G. *Die Faust-Dichtung vor, neben, und nach Goethe* Berlin, 1914.
Witkowski, G. *Goethes Faust; mit Kommentar und Erläuterungen* Leipzig, 1929.

Goethe's Fame Abroad

Baldensperger, F. *Goethe en France.* Paris, 1914.
———. "Goethe et la littérature mondiale," *Bulletin de l'Associatio des Amis de l'Université de Liége* (1933).
Baumgarten, O. *Carlyle und Goethe.* Tübingen, 1906.

Blankenagel, J. C. "Goethe, Mme. de Staël, and 'Weltliteratur,'" *Modern Language Notes,* XL (1925).

Bleyer, J. "Goethe in Ungarn," *Jahrbuch der Goethe-Gesellschaft,* XVIII (1932).

Böschenstein, H. *Das literarische Goethebild der Gegenwart in England.* Breslau, 1934.

Bohnenblust, G. *Das Erbe Goethes.* Lausanne, 1932.

Borelius, H. "Goethe und Skandinavien," *Germanisch-romanische Monatsschrift,* XX (1932).

Braun, F. A. "Goethe as Viewed by Emerson," *Journal of English and Germanic Philology,* XV (1916).

———. *Margaret Fuller and Goethe.* New York, 1910.

Buck, P. M. "Goethe and Shelley," *Goethe Memorial Volume.* Madison, Wis., 1932.

Carré, J. M. *Goethe en Angleterre.* Paris, 1920.

Chamberlin, W. A. "Longfellow's Attitude toward Goethe," *Modern Philology,* XVI (1918).

Ciechanowska, Z. "Goethe in Polish Literature," *Slavonic Review,* XII (1933).

Farinelli, A. *Goethe et l'Espagne.* Paris, 1936.

Fasola, G. "Goethes Werke in italienischen Übersetzungen," *Jahrbuch der Goethe-Gesellschaft,* XVI (1895).

Frenz, H. "Bayard Taylor and the Reception of Goethe in America," *Journal of English and Germanic Philology,* XLI (1942).

Frühm, T. *Gedanken über Goethes Weltliteratur.* Leipzig, 1932.

Gorlin, M. "Goethe in Russland," *Zeitschrift für slavische Philologie,* IX (1932).

Gottbrath, K. *Der Einfluss von Goethes Wilhelm Meister auf die englische Literatur.* Munich, 1937.

Grueningen, J. P. von. "Goethe in American Periodicals," *Publications of the Modern Language Association,* L (1935).

Hinz, S. M. *Goethe's Lyric Poems in English Translation after 1860.* Madison, Wis., 1928.

Holl, K. "Goethes Vollendung in ihrer Beziehung zu Byron und Carlyle," *Germanisch-romanische Monatsschrift,* IX (1921).

Howe, S. *Wilhelm Meister and His English Kinsmen, Apprentices to Life.* New York, 1930.

Klenze, C. von. "America and Goethe," *Goethe Memorial Volume.* Madison, Wis., 1932.

Krummel, C. G. "Byron and Goethe," *South Atlantic Quarterly,* XXII (1923).

Lieder, F. W. C. "Goethe in England and America," *Journal of English and Germanic Philology,* X (1911).

Long, O. W. "English and American Imitations of Goethe's Werther," *Modern Philology,* XIV (1916).

———. "Goethe and Longfellow," *Germanic Review,* VII (1932).

———. "Werther in America," *Studies in Honor of J. A. Walz.* Lancaster, Pa., 1941.

MacIntosh, W. *Scott and Goethe: German Influence on the Writings of Sir W. Scott.* Glasgow, 1924.

Mann, T. *Goethe und Tolstoi.* Berlin, 1932.

Masaryk, T. G., and A. V. Lunacharsky. "Slav Verdicts on Goethe," *Slavonic Review,* XI (1932).

Norman, F. "Henry Crabb Robinson and Goethe," *Publications of the English Goethe-Society* (1930).

Orrick, J. B. "Matthew Arnold and Goethe," *Publications of the English Goethe-Society* (1928).

Oswald, E. "Goethe in England and America," *Publications of the English Goethe-Society* (1909).

Paschall, C. "What Goethe Means to the World," *Modern Language Forum* (1933).

Pfund, H. W. "George Henry Calvert, Admirer of Goethe," *Studies in Honor of J. A. Walz.* Lancaster, Pa., 1941.

Pieper, K. "Werther und Jacopo Ortis," *Herrigs Archiv* (1925).

Plagens, H. *Carlyles Weg zu Goethe.* Berlin, 1938.

Rhyme, O. P. "Browning and Goethe," *Modern Language Notes,* XLIV (1929).

Rose, W. *From Goethe to Byron: The Development of Weltschmerz.* London, 1924.

Ross, F. *Goethe in Modern France.* Urbana, Ill., 1937.

Scholte, J. H. "Goethe und Holland," *Jahrbuch der Goethe-Gesellschaft,* XVIII (1932).

Schreiber, C. F. "Goethe in America," *Jahrbuch der Goethe-Gesellschaft,* XIV (1928).

———. "Goethe und Amerika," *Jahrbuch der Goethe-Gesellschaft,* XVIII (1932).

Simmons, L. V. T. *Goethe's Lyric Poems in English Translation prior to 1860.* Madison, Wis., 1919.

Slochower, H. "Margaret Fuller and Goethe," *Germanic Review,* VII (1932).

Sondheim, M. *Werther und der Weltschmerz in Frankreich.* Frankfurt, 1929.

Strich, F. "Goethe der West-östliche," *Dichtung und Zivilisation.* Munich, 1928.

———. "Goethes Idee einer Weltliteratur," *Dichtung und Zivilisation.* Munich, 1928.

———. *Goethe und die Weltliteratur.* Bern, 1945.

Suares, A. *Goethe, le grand Européen.* Paris, 1932.

Vaughan, C. E. "Carlyle and His German Masters," *Essays and Studies by Members of the English Association.* Oxford, 1910.

Vollrath, W. *Goethe und Grossbritannien.* Erlangen, 1932.

Wahr, F. B. *Emerson and Goethe.* Ann Arbor, Mich., 1915.

Willoughby, L. A. "Goethe's Tasso in England," *Modern Language Review,* IX (1914).

Witt, B. "Goethe und der Osten," *Ostdeutsche Monatshefte* (1932).

Wukadinovič, S. "Goethe und die slavische Welt," *Jahrbuch der Goethe-Gesellschaft,* XVIII (1932).

Wurfl, G. *Lowell's Debt to Goethe.* State College, Pa., 1936.

CHAPTER IX

The Historical Background

Gooch, G. P. *Germany and the French Revolution.* London, 1920.

Schömann, M. *Napoleon in der deutschen Literatur.* Berlin, 1931.

BIBLIOGRAPHIES

Characteristics of Romantic Literature

Breul, K. *The Romantic Movement in German Literature*. Cambridge, 1927.

Gundolf, F. *Romantiker*. Berlin, 1930.

Huch, R. *Die Romantik*. Leipzig, 1920.

Kircher, E. *Philosophie der Romantik*. Jena, 1906.

Meyer, R. M. *Die deutsche Literatur des 19. Jahrhunderts*. Berlin, 1923.

Petersen, J. *Die Wesensbestimmung der deutschen Romantik*. Leipzig, 1926.

Porterfield, A. *An Outline of German Romanticism*. Boston, 1914.

Reynaud, L. *Le romantisme des origines anglo-germaniques*. Paris, 1926.

Robertson, J. G. *The Genesis of Romantic Literary Theory*. London, 1923.

Strich, F. *Deutsche Klassik und Romantik*. Munich, 1929.

Walzel, O. *Deutsche Romantik*. Leipzig, 1926.

Wernaer, R. M. *Romanticism and the Romantic School in Germany*. New York, 1910.

Willoughby, L. A. *The Romantic Movement in Germany*. London, 1930.

German Culture at Home and Abroad

Campbell, T. M. *Longfellows Wechselbeziehungen zu der deutschen Literatur*. Leipzig, 1907.

Cartier, J. *Un intermédiaire entre la France et l'Allemagne: Gérard de Nerval*. Geneva, 1904.

Diem, H. *Das Bild Deutschlands in Chateaubriands Werk*. Bern, 1936.

Goodale, R. H. "Schopenhauer and Pessimism in Nineteenth Century English Literature," *Publications of the Modern Language Association*, XLVII (1932).

Haney, J. L. *The German Influence in Samuel Taylor Coleridge*. Philadelphia, 1902.

Harrold, C. F. *Carlyle and German Thought, 1819–1834*. New Haven, 1934.

Hatfield, J. T. "Longfellow and Germany," *American-German Review*, V (1938).

———. *New Light on Longfellow, with Special Reference to His Relations to Germany*. Boston, 1933.

Haym, R. *Hegel und seine Zeit*. Berlin, 1927.

Herzberg, M. J. "W. Wordsworth and German Literature," *Publications of the Modern Language Association*, XL (1925).

Houssonville, O. d'. *Mme. de Staël et l'Allemagne*. Paris, 1928.

Jaekh, E. G. *Mme. de Staël and the Spread of German Literature*. New York, 1915.

Koch, J. "Sir W. Scotts Beziehungen zu Deutschland," *Germanisch-romanische Monatsschrift*, XV (1927).

Kohler, P. *Mme. de Staël et la Suisse*. Lausanne, 1916.

Kronenberg, M. *Geschichte des deutschen Idealismus*. Munich, 1909.

Lotter, K. *Carlyle und die deutsche Romantik*. Nürnberg, 1932.

Lütgert, W. *Die Religion des deutschen Idealismus und ihr Ende*. Gütersloh, 1923.

Margraf, E. *Der Einfluss der deutschen Literatur auf die englische am Ende des 18. und im ersten Drittel des 19. Jahrhunderts.* Leipzig, 1901.

Mönch, W. *Charles Nodier und die deutsche und englische Literatur.* Berlin, 1931.

Morley, E. J. *Crabb Robinson in Germany, 1800–1805.* London, 1929.

Pange, Comtesse J. de. *Mme. de Staël et la découverte de l'Allemagne.* Paris, 1929.

Pochmann, H. A. "Irving's German Tour and Its Influence on His Tales," *Publications of the Modern Language Association,* XLV (1930).

Sommerkamp, F. "Walter Scotts Kenntnis und Ansicht von deutscher Literatur," *Herrigs Archiv,* CXLIX (1925).

Stokoe, F. W. *German Influence in the English Romantic Period, 1788–1818.* Cambridge, 1926.

Streuli, W. *Thomas Carlyle als Vermittler deutscher Literatur und deutschen Geistes.* Zurich, 1895.

Tengler, R. *Schopenhauer und die Romantik.* Berlin, 1923.

Ullmann, H. *Benjamin Constant und seine Beziehungen zum deutschen Geistesleben.* Marburg, 1915.

Weddigen, F. O. *Geschichte der Einwirkungen der deutschen Literatur auf die Literaturen der übrigen europäischen Kulturvölker der Neuzeit.* Leipzig, 1886.

Windelband, M. *Die Philosophie im deutschen Geistesleben des 19. Jahrhunderts.* Tübingen, 1909.

Worden, J. P. *Über Longfellows Beziehungen zur deutschen Literatur.* Halle, 1900.

Two Forerunners of Romanticism

Hölderlin

Böhm, W. *Hölderlin.* Halle, 1928–30.

Montgomery, M. *F. Hölderlin and the German Neo-Hellenic Movement.* London, 1923.

Peacock, R. *Hölderlin.* London, 1938.

Stansfield, A. *Hölderlin.* Manchester, 1944.

Stemplinger, C., and H. Lamer. *Deutschtum und Antike.* Leipzig, 1920.

Jean Paul

Brewer, E. V. "The New England Interest in Jean Paul Friedrich Richter," *University of California Publications in Modern Philology,* XXVII (1943).

Geissendoerffer, T. "Carlyle and Jean Paul Richter," *Journal of English and Germanic Philology,* XXV (1926).

Kommerell, M. *Jean Paul.* Frankfurt, 1938.

——. *Jean Pauls Verhältnis zu Rousseau.* Marburg, 1925.

Müller, J. *Jean Paul und seine Bedeutung für die Gegenwart.* Leipzig, 1923.

Sieveking, G. *Jean Pauls Stellung zur Antike.* Hamburg, 1925.

Early Romanticism

Bennett, E. K. *A History of the German Novelle from Goethe to Thomas Mann.* New York, 1934.

BIBLIOGRAPHIES

Bertrand, J. J. A. *Cervantes et le romantisme allemand*. Paris, 1914.
———. "G. Schlegel et la France," *Revue germanique,* XVIII (1922).
Blankenagel, J. C. *The Dramas of Heinrich von Kleist*. Chapel Hill, N. C., 1931.
Blume, B. "Kleist und Goethe," *Monatshefte für deutschen Unterricht,* XXXVIII (1946).
Braak, S. "Novalis et le symbolisme français," *Neophilologus,* VIII (1922).
Brandt, O. *A. W. Schlegel der Romantiker*. Stuttgart, 1919.
Corssen, M. *Kleist und Shakespeare*. Weimar, 1930.
Enders, K. *Schlegel. Die Quellen seines Wesens und Werdens*. Leipzig, 1913.
Farinelli, A. *Lope de Vega en Alemania*. Barcelona, 1936.
———. "Spanien und die spanische Literatur im Lichte der deutschen Kritik und Poesie," *Zeitschrift für vergleichende Literaturgeschichte,* VII (1893).
Friederich, W. P. "Dante's Influence upon the Poets and Philosophers of Germany, 1800–1865," *Philological Quarterly,* XXV (1946).
Genee, R. *A. W. Schlegel und Shakespeare*. Berlin, 1903.
Gillies, A. "Tieck and Shakespeare," *Journal of English and Germanic Philology,* XXXVI (1937).
Gloege, G. *Novalis' Heinrich von Ofterdingen*. Leipzig, 1911.
Gülzow, E. *Wackenroder, Neue Beiträge zur Lebensgeschichte*. Stralsund, 1929.
Gundolf, F. *Heinrich von Kleist*. Berlin, 1922.
Harrold, C. F. "Carlyle and Novalis," *Studies in Philology,* XXVII (1930).
Heilborn, E. *Novalis, der Romantiker*. Berlin, 1901.
Helmholtz, A. "The Indebtedness of S. T. Coleridge to A. W. Schlegel," *Bulletin of the University of Wisconsin* (1907).
Herzfeld, G. "A. W. Schlegel in seinen Beziehungen zu englischen Dichtern und Kritikern," *Herrigs Archiv,* CXL (1920).
Humbert, C. *Deutschlands Urteile über Molière bis zum Regierungsantritt A. W. von Schlegels*. Oppeln, 1883.
Joachimi-Dege, M. *Deutsche Shakespeare-Probleme im 18. Jahrhundert und im Zeitalter der Romantik*. Leipzig, 1907.
Kaufmann, F. W. *German Dramatists of the Nineteenth Century*. Los Angeles, 1940.
Kluckhohn, P. "Die Dramatiker der deutschen Romantik als Shakespeare-Jünger," *Shakespeare-Jahrbuch,* LXXIV (1938).
Körner, J. "F. Schlegel und Mme. de Staël," *Preussische Jahrbücher* (1934).
———. *Die Botschaft der deutschen Romantik an Europa*. Augsburg, 1929.
Lampe, K. *Studien über Iffland als Dramatiker*. Leipzig, 1899.
Lüdecke, H. *L. Tieck und das alte englische Theater*. Frankfurt, 1922.
Lussky, A. E. *Tieck's Romantic Irony*. Chapel Hill, N. C., 1932.
Mann, O. *Der junge Friedrich Schlegel*. Berlin, 1932.
Nadler, J. *Die Berliner Romantik*. Berlin, 1922.
Riesenfeld, P. *Heinrich von Ofterdingen in der deutschen Literatur*. Berlin, 1916.
Ritter, H. *Novalis' Hymnen an die Nacht*. Marburg, 1930.
Schneider, F. "Kotzebue en España," *Modern Philology,* XXV (1927).

Seuffert, B. "Wielands, Eschenburgs und Schlegels Shakespeare-Übersetzungen," *Archiv für Literaturgeschichte* (1885).

Silz, W. *Early German Romanticism. Its Founders and H. von Kleist.* Cambridge, Mass., 1929.

———. *Heinrich von Kleist's Conception of the Tragic.* Baltimore, 1923.

Stiehler, A. *Das Ifflandsche Rührstück.* Hamburg, 1898.

Stöcker, H. *Die Kunstanschauung des 18. Jahrhunderts von Winckelmann bis Wackenroder.* Berlin, 1904.

Sulger-Gebing, E. "A. W. Schlegel und Dante," *Germanistische Abhandlungen H. Paul dargebracht.* Strassburg, 1902.

Thompson, L. F. *Kotzebue. A Survey of His Progress in France and England.* Paris, 1928.

Unger, R. *Herder, Novalis und Kleist. Studien über die Entwicklung des Todesproblemes.* Frankfurt, 1922.

Walzel, O. "Der deutsche Entdecker des Camões," *Revue de littérature comparée,* XVIII (1938).

Witkowski, G. *Das deutsche Drama des 19. Jahrhunderts.* Leipzig, 1923.

Wölcken, F. *Shakespeares Zeitgenossen in der deutschen Literatur.* Berlin, 1929.

Xylander, O. *H. von Kleist und J. J. Rousseau.* Berlin, 1937.

Zeydel, E. H. "George Ticknor and Ludwig Tieck," *Publications of the Modern Language Association,* XLIV (1929).

———. *Ludwig Tieck and England.* Princeton, 1931.

———. *Ludwig Tieck, the German Romanticist.* Princeton, 1935.

Patriotic Romanticism

Benz, R. *Die deutschen Volksbücher.* Jena, 1913.

———. *Die Märchendichtung der Romantiker.* Gotha, 1908.

Berger, R. *Th. Körner.* Bielefeld, 1912.

Bergmann, E. *J. G. Fichte.* Berlin, 1928.

Bode, K. *Die Bearbeitungen und Vorlagen in Des Knaben Wunderhorn.* Leipzig, 1909.

Church, H. W. *Friedrich Rückert als Lyriker der Befreiungskriege.* New York, 1916.

Diels, J., and W. Kreiten. *Cl. Brentano.* Frankfurt, 1877.

Ehrlich, E. *Das französische Element in der Lyrik Chamissos.* Berlin, 1932.

Francke, K. *Die Brüder Grimm.* Dresden, 1899.

Fulda, K. *Chamisso und seine Zeit.* Leipzig, 1881.

Haymann, F. *Weltbürgertum und Vaterlandsliebe in der Staatslehre Rousseaus und Fichtes.* Berlin, 1924.

Liedke, H. *Literary Criticism and Romantic Theory in the Work of A. von Arnim.* New York, 1937.

Lohre, H. *Von Percy zum Wunderhorn.* Leipzig, 1902.

Pundt, A. G. *Arndt and the Nationalist Awakening in Germany.* New York, 1935.

Schellberg, W. *J. J. Görres.* Cologne, 1926.

Schmitz-Mancy, M. *Die Dichter der Freiheitskriege.* Paderborn, 1909.

Schneider, H. *L. Uhlands Leben, Dichtung, Forschung.* Berlin, 1920.

Late Romanticism

Arndt, K. "Nikolaus Lenau's American Experience (1832–33)," *Monatshefte für deutschen Unterricht,* XXIV (1932).

BIBLIOGRAPHIES

Atkins, H. G. *Heine*. London, 1929.
Baerlein, H. *Heine the Strange Guest*. London, 1928.
Baker, G. *Lenau and Young Germany in America*. Baltimore, 1897.
Berendsohn, W. A. *Der lebendige Heine im germanischen Norden*. Copenhagen, 1935.
Betz, L. P. *Heine in Frankreich*. Zurich, 1894.
Bévotte, G. de. *La légende de Don Juan. Son évolution dans la littérature des origines au romantisme*. Paris, 1906.
Bianchi, L. *Italien in Eichendorffs Dichtung*. Bologna, 1937.
Biese, A. *Das Naturgefühl im Wandel der Zeiten*. Leipzig, 1926.
Blankenagel, J. C. "Carlyle as a Critic of Grillparzer," *Publications of the Modern Language Association*, XLII (1927).
Brod, M. *Heinrich Heine*. Amsterdam, 1935.
Browne, L. *That Man Heine*. New York, 1927.
Castle, E. N. *Lenau*. Leipzig, 1902.
Cobb, P. *The Influence of E. T. A. Hoffmann in the Tales of E. A. Poe*. Chapel Hill, N. C., 1908.
Duméril, E. *Le lied allemand et ses traductions poétiques en France*. Paris, 1934.
Enzinger, M. *Das deutsche Schicksalsdrama*. Innsbruck, 1922.
——. *Die Entwicklung des Wiener Theaters*. Berlin, 1918.
Eyk, D. van. *Napoleon im Spiegel der Goetheschen und Heinischen Lyrik*. Amsterdam, 1933.
Glücksmann, H. "Grillparzer und Shakespeare," *Jahrbuch der Grillparzer-Gesellschaft* (1938).
Gorlin, M. *N. V. Gogol und E. Th. A. Hoffmann*. Leipzig, 1933.
Gudde, E. G. "E. Th. A. Hoffmann's Reception in England," *Publications of the Modern Language Association*, XLII (1927).
Hankamer, P. *Z. Werner*. Bonn, 1920.
Harich, W. *E. T. A. Hoffmann*. Berlin, 1920.
Hess, J. A. *Heine's Views on German Traits of Character*. New York, 1929.
Hock, S. *Der Traum ein Leben: eine literarische Untersuchung*. Stuttgart, 1904.
Keiter, H. *J. von Eichendorff*. Cologne, 1887.
Kieft, P. *H. Heine in westeuropäischer Beurteilung*. Zutphen, 1938.
Lambert, E. "La Juive de Tolède de Grillparzer; étude sur la composition et les sources de la pièce," *Revue de littérature comparée*, II (1922).
Marcuse, L. *Heinrich Heine*. Berlin, 1932; New York, 1933.
Minor, J. *Die Schicksalstragödie in ihren Hauptvertretern*. Frankfurt, 1883.
Möller, A. *Ferdinand Raimund*. Graz, 1923.
Mulfinger, G. A. *Lenau in Amerika*. New York, 1903.
Nolte, F. O. *Grillparzer, Lessing, and Goethe in the Perspective of European Literature*. Lancaster, Pa., 1938.
Payr, B. *Gautier und Hoffmann*. Berlin, 1932.
Pollak, G. *Grillparzer and the Austrian Drama*. New York, 1907.
Reich, E. *Grillparzers Dramen*. Dresden, 1909.
Reynaud, L. *Lenau et le lyrisme autrichien*. Paris, 1923.
Sachs, H. B. *Heine in America*. Philadelphia, 1916.
Schnapp, L. *Lord Byron im Spiegel der deutschen Dichtung*. Münster, 1923.

Schneider, F. "E. T. A. Hoffmann en España," *Estudios Eruditos.* Madrid, 1927.

Schuyler-Allen, P. *Müller and the German Volkslied.* New York, 1891.

Sittenberger, H. *Grillparzer, sein Leben und Wirken.* Berlin, 1904.

Störi, F. *Grillparzer und Kant.* Frauenfeld, 1935.

Untermeyer, L. *Heinrich Heine: Paradox and Poet.* New York, 1937.

Volkelt, J. *Grillparzer als Dichter des Tragischen.* Munich, 1909.

Wächtler, P. R. *Edgar Allan Poe und die deutsche Romantik.* Leipzig, 1911.

Walter, H. *H. Heine.* London, 1930.

Williamson, E. J. *Grillparzer's Attitude towards Romanticism.* Chicago, 1910.

Wismer, E. *Der Einfluss des deutschen Romantikers Z. Werner in Frankreich.* Neuchâtel-Affoltern, 1928.

Wolff, H. J. *Heinrich Heine.* Munich, 1922.

Wood, F. H. *Heine as a Critic of His Own Works.* New York, 1934.

Wormley, S. L. *Heine in England.* Chapel Hill, N. C., 1943.

CHAPTER X

General Observations

Brandes, G. *Main Currents in Nineteenth Century Literature.* New York, 1906.

Butler, E. M. *The Saint-Simonian Religion in Germany.* Cambridge, 1926.

Faust, A. B. *The German Element in the United States.* New York, 1927.

Kaegi, W. *Michelet und Deutschland.* Basel, 1936.

Levy, A. *La philosophie de Feuerbach et son influence sur la littérature allemande.* Paris, 1904.

Long, O. W. *Literary Pioneers: Early American Explorers of European Culture.* Cambridge, Mass., 1935.

Meyer, R. M. *Die deutsche Literatur des 19. Jahrhunderts.* Berlin, 1923.

Morel, L. *Sainte-Beuve, la littérature allemande et Goethe.* Paris, 1908.

Rosenberg, R. P. *George Sand in Germany.* Madison, Wis., 1933.

Walz, J. A. *German Influence in American Education and Culture.* Philadelphia, 1936.

Walzel, O. *Die deutsche Dichtung seit Goethes Tod.* Berlin, 1919.

Witkowski, G. *Die Entwicklung der deutschen Literatur seit 1830.* Leipzig, 1911.

Young Germany

Appelmann, M. *H. W. Longfellows Beziehungen zu Ferdinand Freiligrath.* Münster, 1916.

Arnold, R. F. *Der deutsche Philhellenismus.* Vienna, 1896.

———. *Geschichte der deutschen Polenliteratur.* Halle, 1900.

Bloesch, H. *Das Junge Deutschland in seinen Beziehungen zu Frankreich.* Bern, 1903.

Brandes, G. *Börne und Heine.* Munich, 1898.

Dresch, J. *Gutzkow et la jeune Allemagne.* Paris, 1904.

Geiger, L. *Das junge Deutschland.* Berlin, 1907.

Gudde, E. G. *Freiligraths Entwicklung als politischer Dichter.* Berlin, 1922.

BIBLIOGRAPHIES

Houben, H. *Jungdeutscher Sturm und Drang*. Leipzig, 1911.
Laserstein, K. *Der Griseldisstoff in der Weltliteratur*. Weimar, 1926.
Legge, J. G. *Rhyme and Revolution in Germany*. London, 1918.
Liddell, M. F. "F. Freiligrath's Debt to English Poets," *Modern Language Review*, XXIII (1928).
Liptzin, S. *Lyric Pioneers of Modern Germany*. New York, 1928.
————. *Shelley in Germany*. New York, 1924.
Marcuse, L. *Das Leben L. Börnes*. Leipzig, 1929.
Przygodda, P. *Laubes literarische Frühzeit*. Berlin, 1910.
Seidel, R. G. *Herwegh, ein Freiheitssänger*. Frankfurt, 1905.
Spink, G. W. *Freiligrath als Verdeutscher der englischen Poesie*. Berlin, 1925.
Whyte, J. *Young Germany in Its Relations to Britain*. Menasha, Wis., 1917.

The Epigones

Greulich, O. *Platens Literatur-Komödien*. Bern, 1901.
Maync, H. *K. L. Immermann*. Munich, 1920.
Porterfield, A. W. *Immermann: A Study in German Romanticism*. New York, 1911.
Schlösser, R. *August Graf von Platen*. Munich, 1910.

Artistic Realism

Adler, G. *Richard Wagner*. Munich, 1923.
Alberts, W. *Hebbels Stellung zu Shakespeare*. Weimar, 1908.
Andler, C. F. *Nietzsche, sa vie et sa pensée*. Paris, 1920 ff.
Bachmann, F. W. *Some German Imitators of Walter Scott*. Chicago, 1933.
Badt, B. *A. von Droste-Hülshoff, ihre dichterische Entwicklung und ihr Verhältnis zur englischen Literatur*. Breslau, 1909.
Bahr, H. *Stifter*. Vienna, 1919.
Baldensperger, F. *G. Keller, sa vie et ses œuvres*. Paris, 1899.
Barthels, A. *Klaus Groth*. Leipzig, 1899.
Becker, H. K. *Kleist und Hebbel*. Chicago, 1904.
Bekker, P. *Richard Wagner*. New York, 1931.
Bentley, E. R. *A Century of Hero-Worship: A Study of the Idea of Heroism in Carlyle and Nietzsche*. Philadelphia, 1944.
Berg, L. *Der Übermensch in der modernen Literatur*. Leipzig, 1897.
Berger, G. *Mörike und sein Verhältnis zur schwäbischen Romantik*. Kempen, 1910.
Bertram, E. *Nietzsche, Versuch einer Mythologie*. Berlin, 1929.
Bethge, H. *Deutsche Lyrik seit Liliencron*. Leipzig, 1920.
Bettelheim, A. *Auerbach, der Mann, sein Werk, sein Nachlass*. Stuttgart, 1907.
Betz, J. O. *Ludwigs Verhältnis zu den Engländern*. Frankfurt, 1929.
Bianquis, G. *Nietzsche en France*. Paris, 1929.
Brandes, G. *Friedrich Nietzsche*. New York, 1914.
Brinton, C. C. *Nietzsche*. Cambridge, Mass., 1941.
Bruns, F. *Modern Thought in the German Lyric Poets from Goethe to Dehmel*. Madison, Wis., 1921.
Burckhard, A. *Conrad Ferdinand Meyer*. Cambridge, Mass., 1932.
Campbell, T. M. *The Life and Works of F. Hebbel*. Boston, 1919.
Chamberlain, H. S. *Richard Wagner*. Munich, 1919.

Coar, J. F. *Studies in German Literature in the Nineteenth Century.* New York, 1903.

Coenen, F. E. "Problems in Theodor Storm's Novellen," *Germanic Review,* XV (1940).

Dahme, L. *Women in the Life and Art of C. F. Meyer.* New York, 1936.

Davis, A. L. "Fontane as a Political Thinker," *Germanic Review,* VIII (1933).

Djordjewitsch, M. *Sealsfields Auffassung des Amerikanertums und seine literarische Stellung.* Weimar, 1932.

Dresch, J. *Le roman social en Allemagne.* Paris, 1913.

Ermatinger, E. *Die Kunstform des Dramas.* Leipzig, 1925.

Ermisch, K. *Anzengruber und der Naturalismus.* Minneapolis, 1927.

Faust, A. B. *Ch. Sealsfield. . . . A Study of His Style, His Influence upon American Literature.* Baltimore, 1892.

———. *Ch. Sealsfield, der Dichter zweier Hemisphären.* Weimar, 1897.

Fehse, W. *Wilhelm Raabe.* Braunschweig, 1937.

Foster, G. B. *Friedrich Nietzsche.* New York, 1931.

———. "Nietzsche and Wagner," *Sewanee Review,* XXXII (1924).

Friederich, W. P. "Chief Traits of Swiss Literature from Rousseau to Spitteler," *South Atlantic Quarterly,* XLVII (1948).

Gaedertz, K. T. *Aus Reuters jungen und alten Tagen.* Wismar, 1896.

———. *E. Geibel.* Leipzig, 1897.

Griesser, G. *Nietzsche und Wagner.* Vienna, 1923.

Hauch, E. F. *Gottfried Keller as a Democratic Idealist.* New York, 1916.

Hay, M. *The Story of a Swiss Poet: A Study of Keller's Life and Works.* Bern, 1920.

Hayens, K. C. *Theodor Fontane.* London, 1920.

Henning, H. *Fr. Spielhagen.* Leipzig, 1910.

Hight, G. *Richard Wagner.* London, 1925.

Hofmann, H. *W. Hauff, Darstellung seines Werdeganges.* Frankfurt, 1902.

Hunziker, R. *J. Gotthelf.* Frauenfeld, 1927

Jacobs, R. L. *Wagner.* New York, 1935.

Jäckel, K. *Richard Wagner in der französischen Literatur.* Breslau, 1931.

Joubert, M. "Paul Heyse," *Contemporary Review,* CXXXVII (1930).

Kalischer, E. *C. F. Meyer in seinem Verhältnis zur italienischen Renaissance.* Berlin, 1907.

Klein, J. *Die Dichtung Nietzsches.* Munich, 1936.

Kleinberg, A. *L. Anzengruber.* Stuttgart, 1921.

Koch, M. *Wagner.* Berlin, 1907 ff.

Korff, H. A. *Scott und Alexis.* Heidelberg, 1907.

Krauss, R. *Schwäbische Literaturgeschichte.* Freiburg, 1897.

Landsberg, H. *Nietzsche und die deutsche Literatur.* Leipzig, 1902.

Lindau, H. *G. Freytag.* Leipzig, 1907.

Litzmann, B. *E. von Wildenbruch.* Berlin, 1913.

Macleod, N. *German Lyric Poetry.* New York, 1931.

Maync, H. *C. F. Meyer und sein Werk.* Frauenfeld, 1925.

———. *D. von Liliencron.* Berlin, 1920.

———. *E. Mörike, sein Leben und Dichten.* Stuttgart, 1927.

———. *Gottfried Keller.* Frauenfeld, 1928.

Mayne, H. *Theodor Fontane*. Berlin, 1920.

Mencken, H. L. *The Philosophy of F. Nietzsche*. Boston, 1913.

Mielke, H., and G. J. Homann. *Der deutsche Roman des 19. und 20. Jahrhunderts*. Dresden, 1921.

Mis, L. *Les œuvres dramatiques d'Otto Ludwig*. Paris, 1929.

More, P. E. *Nietzsche*. Boston, 1912.

Morgan, G. A. *What Nietzsche Means*. Cambridge, Mass., 1941.

Moser, M. *Richard Wagner in der englischen Literatur des 19. Jahrhunderts*. Bern, 1938.

Nadler, J. *Der geistige Aufbau der deutschen Schweiz*. Leipzig, 1924.

——. *Das Schrifttum der Sudetendeutschen*. Regensburg, 1924.

Newman, E. *Wagner as Man and Artist*. New York, 1929 ff.

Nieten, O. *Grabbe, sein Leben und seine Werke*. Dortmund, 1908.

O'Connor, E. *Marie von Ebner-Eschenbach*. London, 1928.

O'Donnell, "Gerstäcker in America," *Publications of the Modern Language Association*, XLII (1927).

Periam, A. *Hebbel's Nibelungen, Its Sources, Method, and Style*. New York, 1906.

Pfeiffer, F. L. "Gottfried Keller and Conrad Ferdinand Meyer," *Germanic Review*, II (1927).

Plank, E. *Die Lyriker des schwäbischen Klassizismus*. Stuttgart, 1896.

Prahl, A. *Gerstäcker und die Probleme seiner Zeit*. Wertheim a/M., 1938.

Price, L. M. *The Attitude of Gustav Freytag and Julian Schmid toward English Literature (1848–1862)*. Göttingen & Baltimore, 1915.

Proelse, J. *Scheffels Leben und Dichten*. Berlin, 1902.

Purdie, E. *Friedrich Hebbel*. New York, 1932.

Rees, G. B. *F. Hebbel as a Dramatic Artist*. London, 1930.

Rehder, H. "Nietzsche and His Place in German Literature," *Monatshefte für deutschen Unterricht*, XXXVI (1944).

Rehm, W. *Das Werden des Renaissancebildes in der deutschen Dichtung*. Munich, 1924.

Salter, W. M. *Nietzsche the Thinker*. New York, 1917.

Schlosser, A. *Peter Rosegger*. Leipzig, 1921.

Schütze, P., and E. Lange. *Storms Leben und Dichtung*. Berlin, 1924.

Shears, L. A. *The Influence of W. Scott on the Novels of Th. Fontane*. New York, 1922.

——. "Theodor Fontane as a Critic of the Novel," *Publications of the Modern Language Association*, XXXVIII (1923).

Silz, W. "Pessimism in Raabe's Stuttgart Trilogy," *Publications of the Modern Language Association*, XXXIX (1924).

Simmel, G. *Schopenhauer und Nietzsche*. Leipzig, 1907.

Spiero, H. *Geschichte der deutschen Frauendichtung*. Leipzig, 1913.

——. *Paul Heyse, der Dichter und sein Werk*. Stuttgart, 1910.

Stern, A. *O. Ludwig, ein Dichterleben*. Leipzig, 1906.

Summer, E. "Dickens and Germany," *Modern Language Review*, XXXIII (1938).

Taylor, H. L. *A Study of the Technique in C. F. Meyer's Novellen*. Chicago, 1909.

Viëtor, K. *Büchner als Politiker*. Bern, 1939.

Walzel, O. *Hebbel und seine Dramen*. Leipzig, 1927.

Weber, P. C. *America in Imaginative German Literature in the First Half of the Nineteenth Century*. New York, 1926.

Werner, R. M. *Hebbel, ein Lebensbild.* Berlin, 1913.

Wiskott, U. *Französische Wesenszüge in Fontanes Persönlichkeit und Werk.* Leipzig, 1938.

Wyzewa, J. de. *L'interprétation esthétique de Wagner en France.* Paris, 1934.

Zabeltitz, M. Z. von. *G. Büchners Leben und Schaffen.* Berlin, 1915.

CHAPTER XI

Subdivisions of Modern German Literature

Bertaux, F. *A Panorama of German Literature from 1871–1931.* New York, 1935.

Bithell, J. *Modern German Literature, 1880–1938.* London, 1939.

Eloesser, A. *Modern German Literature.* New York, 1933.

Fife, R. H. *The German Empire between Two Wars.* New York, 1916.

Hertford, C. H. *The Post-War Mind of Germany.* Oxford, 1927.

Johnson, F. *The German Mind as Reflected in Their Literature from 1870–1914.* London, 1922.

Jones, W. T. *Contemporary Thought of Germany.* London, 1930–31.

Klaiber, T. *Dichtende Frauen der Gegenwart.* Stuttgart, 1907.

Lange, V. *Modern German Literature, 1870–1940.* Ithaca, 1945.

Lewisohn, L. *The Spirit of Modern German Literature.* New York, 1916.

Naumann, H. *Deutsche Dichtung der Gegenwart.* Stuttgart, 1930.

Rose, W. *Men, Myths, and Movements in German Literature.* London, 1931.

Stammler, W. *Deutsche Literatur vom Naturalismus bis zur Gegenwart.* Breslau, 1927.

Walzel, O. *Deutsche Dichtung der Gegenwart.* Leipzig, 1925.

Naturalism

Busse, K. *H. Sudermann.* Stuttgart, 1927.

Bytkowski, Z. *Gerhart Hauptmanns Naturalismus und das Drama.* Hamburg, 1908.

Dehnau, F. *Ludwig Thoma.* Munich, 1925.

Deri, M. *Naturalismus, Idealismus, Expressionismus.* Leipzig, 1919.

Dorner, A. *Pessimismus, Nietzsche und Naturalismus.* Leipzig, 1911.

Eastlake, A. E. *The Influence of English Literature on the German Novel and Drama in the Period from 1880–1900.* London, 1937.

Eller, W. H. *Ibsen in Germany.* Boston, 1918.

Heller, O. *Studies in Modern German Literature: Sudermann, Hauptmann, Women Writers of the Nineteenth Century.* Boston, 1905.

Hoffmann, K. *Hauptmanns Symbolismus.* Charlottenburg, 1908.

Holl, K. *G. Hauptmann, His Life and Work.* Chicago, 1913.

House, R. T. "The Life and Poetry of Richard Dehmel," *Poet Lore,* XXXVIII (1927).

Hülsen, H. von. *Gerhart Hauptmann: siebzig Jahre seines Lebens.* Berlin, 1932.

Keil, G. *Max Kretzer, A Study in German Naturalism.* New York, 1928.

King, A. H. *The Influence of French Literature on German Prose and the Drama between 1880–1890.* London, 1933.

BIBLIOGRAPHIES

Klenze, C. von. *From Goethe to Hauptmann.* New York, 1926.

Koplowitz, O. *Otto Brahm als Theaterkritiker.* Zurich, 1936.

Law-Robertson, H. *Walt Whitman in Deutschland.* Giessen, 1935.

Liptzin, S. *The Weavers in German Literature.* Göttingen, 1926.

Lothar, R. *Das deutsche Drama der Gegenwart.* Munich, 1905.

Reichart, W. A. "Fifty Years of Hauptmann Study in America (1894–1944): A Bibliography," *Monatshefte für deutschen Unterricht,* XXXVII (1945).

Ress, R. *Arno Holz und seine künstlerische weltkulturelle Bedeutung.* Dresden, 1913.

Röhl, H. *Der Naturalismus.* Leipzig, 1927.

Root, W. H. *German Criticism of Zola.* New York, 1931.

Scheuffler, G. *Clara Viebig.* Erfurt, 1927.

Seidlin, O. "Gerhart Hauptmann zum Gedenken," *Monatshefte für deutschen Unterricht,* XXXVIII (1946).

Slochower, H. R. *Dehmel, der Mensch und der Denker.* Dresden, 1928.

Spiero, H. *Die Heilandsgeschichte in der neueren deutschen Dichtung.* Berlin, 1926.

Stauf von der March, O. *Carl Bleibtreu.* Berlin, 1936.

Stockius, A. *Naturalism in Recent German Literature with Special Reference to Hauptmann.* New York, 1903.

Sulger-Gebing, E. *Gerhart Hauptmann.* Leipzig, 1922.

Voigt, F., and A. Reichart. *Hauptmann und Shakespeare.* Breslau, 1938.

Zorb, E. H. *Religiöse Strömungen in der schlesischen Literatur der Gegenwart.* Leipzig, 1934.

Zucker, A. E. *Ibsen, the Master-Builder.* New York, 1928.

Impressionism

Adler, F. *Waldemar Bonsels, sein Weltbild und seine Gestalten.* Frankfurt, 1925.

Arnold, R. F. *Das deutsche Drama.* Munich, 1925.

Ball, H. *Hermann Hesse.* Berlin, 1927.

Bauer, M., and M. Morgenstern. *Christian Morgensterns Leben und Werk.* Munich, 1937.

Bettelheim, A. *Karl Schönherr.* Leipzig, 1928.

Bettex, A. W. *The German Novel of To-day.* Cambridge, 1939.

Bianchi, L. *Dante und Stefan George.* Bologna, 1935.

Bianquis, G. *La poésie autrichienne de Hofmannsthal à Rilke.* Paris, 1926.

Bing, S. *Jakob Wassermann.* Berlin, 1933.

Blankenagel, J. C. *The Writings of Jakob Wassermann.* Boston, 1942.

Boeschenstein, H. *Hermann Stehr.* Breslau, 1935.

Bowra, C. *The Heritage of Symbolism.* London, 1943.

Brennan, J. G. *Thomas Mann's World.* New York, 1942.

Breysig, H. *Eindruckskunst und Ausdruckskunst.* Berlin, 1927.

Brittin, N. A. "Stefan Zweig, Biographer and Teacher," *Sewanee Review,* XLVIII (1940).

Brodersen, A. *Stefan George, Deutscher und Europäer.* Berlin, 1935.

Buck, P. M. *Directions in Contemporary Literature.* New York, 1942.

Burkhard, A. "Stefan George," *German Quarterly,* VII (1934).

Butler, E. M. *Rainer Maria Rilke.* Cambridge, 1941.

Cämmerer, H. R. M. *Rilkes Duineser Elegien.* Stuttgart, 1937.

HISTORY OF GERMAN LITERATURE

Closs, A. *The Genius of the German Lyric.* London, 1938.

Clough, J. *Thomas Mann.* London, 1933.

Daffner, H. *Salome. Ihre Gestalt in Geschichte und Kunst.* Munich, 1912.

Dehn, F. R. M. *Rilke und sein Werk.* Leipzig, 1934.

Delp, W. E. "Christian Morgenstern," *Modern Languages,* XXIV (1942).

Droop, F. *Wilhelm von Scholz und seine besten Bühnenwerke.* Berlin, 1922.

Eloesser, H. *Thomas Mann.* Berlin, 1925.

Elster, H. M. *Walther von Molo und sein Schaffen.* Munich, 1924.

Endres, F. *Emil Strauss.* Munich, 1936.

Faesi, R. *Spittelers Weg und Werk.* Frauenfeld, 1933.

Fairley, B. "Rainer Maria Rilke, an Estimate," *University of Toronto Quarterly,* XI (1942).

Farrell, R. *Stefan Georges Beziehungen zur englischen Dichtung.* Berlin, 1937.

Gilbert, M. E. "Hugo von Hofmannsthal and England," *German Life and Letters,* I (1937).

Goertz, H. *Frankreich und das Erlebnis der Form im Werke R. M. Rilkes.* Stuttgart, 1932.

Gorr, A. C. "Paul Ernst and Classicism," *German Quarterly,* XVII (1944).

Gronicka, A. von. "Thomas Mann and Russia," *Germanic Review,* XX (1945).

Gross, F. "Heinrich Mann," *Contemporary Review,* CLX (1941).

———. "Hugo von Hofmannsthal," *Contemporary Review,* CXLIX (1936).

Gundolf, F. *George.* Berlin, 1920.

Häfele, K. *Die Godivasage und ihre Behandlung in der Literatur.* Heidelberg, 1929.

Hamann, R. *Der Impressionismus in Leben und Kunst.* Marburg, 1923.

Handl, W. *Hermann Bahr.* Berlin, 1913.

Havenstein, M. *Thomas Mann.* Berlin, 1927.

Hentschel, C. "Hermann Stehr," *German Life and Letters,* III (1939).

Hewett-Thayer, H. W. *The Modern German Novel.* Boston, 1924.

Hewitt, T. B. "The Novels of Eduard von Keyserling," *German Quarterly,* IV (1931).

Hofe, H. von. "Literature in Exile: Bruno Frank," *German Quarterly,* XVIII (1945).

Hoppe, E. *Ricarda Huch.* Hamburg, 1936.

Kawerau, S. *Stefan George und R. M. Rilke.* Berlin, 1928.

Klein, M. *Stefan George als heldischer Dichter unserer Zeit.* Berlin, 1938.

Körner, J. *Arthur Schnitzler, Gestalten und Probleme.* Vienna, 1921.

Krüger, K. J. *Hugo von Hofmannsthal und Richard Strauss.* Berlin, 1935.

Lewisohn, L. "Thomas Mann," *English Journal,* XXII (1933).

Lion, F. *Thomas Mann in seiner Zeit.* Zurich, 1938.

Liptzin, S. *Arthur Schnitzler.* New York, 1932.

———. *Germany's Stepchildren.* Philadelphia, 1944.

———. *Richard Beer-Hofmann.* New York, 1936.

BIBLIOGRAPHIES

Loose, G. "Thomas Mann and the Problem of Decadence," *University of Colorado Studies,* 1941.

Macken, M. "Hermann Bahr, His Personality and His Works," *Studies* (Dublin), XV (1926).

Mason, E. C. *Rilke's Apotheosis.* Oxford, 1938.

Muirhead, J. F. "Carl Spitteler," *London Mercury,* XVI (1927).

———. "Carl Spitteler and the New Epic," *Royal Society of Literature: Essays,* X (1931).

Naef, C. J. *Hugo von Hofmannsthals Wesen und Werk.* Zurich, 1938.

Nolte, F. *Der Todesbegriff bei R. M. Rilke, H. von Hofmannsthal und Thomas Mann.* Heidelberg, 1934.

Olivero, F. *R. M. Rilke.* Torino, 1929; Cambridge, 1931.

Potthoff, A. *Paul Ernst.* Munich, 1935.

Randall, A. W. G. "The Neo-Classic Movement in 20th-Century German Drama," *New Europe,* XIII (1919–20).

Rank, O. *Das Inzest-Motiv in Dichtung und Sage.* Vienna, 1912.

Raybould, A. N. "Stefan George and the Germany of To-day," *Contemporary Review,* CXLVII (1935).

Reichart, W. A. "Hermann Stehr and His Work," *Philological Quarterly,* X (1931).

Reik, T. *Arthur Schnitzler als Psycholog.* Minden, 1913.

Reinhardt, K. F. "Kolbenheyer a Metaphysician?", *Germanic Review,* XII (1937).

Rössner, H. *Georgekreis und Literaturwissenschaft.* Frankfurt, 1938.

Romains, J. *Stefan Zweig, Great European.* New York, 1941.

Rose, W., and G. C. Houston. *R. M. Rilke.* London, 1938.

Schinnerer, O. P. "The Early Works of Arthur Schnitzler," *Germanic Review,* IV (1929).

Schmidt, A. *Deutsche Dichtung in Österreich.* Vienna, 1935.

Schnee, H. *Enrica Freiin von Handel-Mazzetti.* Paderborn, 1935.

Schroeder, W. *Heinrich Mann.* Vienna, 1932.

Seidlin, O. "Thomas Mann and Democracy," *The South Atlantic Quarterly,* XLIII (1944).

Sievers, M. *Die biblischen Motive in der Dichtung R. M. Rilkes.* Berlin, 1938.

Slochower, H. *No Voice Is Wholly Lost.* New York, 1945.

Stenner, T. *Rudolf G. Binding, Leben und Werk.* Berlin, 1938.

Stuckert, F. *Wilhelm Schäfer.* Munich, 1935.

Thomése, I. A. *Romantik und Neuromantik mit besonderer Berücksichtigung Hugo von Hofmannsthals.* The Hague, 1923.

Wache, K. *Der österreichische Roman.* Leipzig, 1930.

Wanderscheck, H. *Deutsche Dramatik der Gegenwart.* Berlin, 1938.

Wandrey, O. *Kolbenheyer, der Dichter und der Philosoph.* Munich, 1934.

Weimar, K. S. *The Concept of Love in the Works of Hermann Stehr.* Philadelphia, 1945.

Wendt, H. G. *Max Dauthendey, Poet and Philosopher.* New York, 1936.

Expressionism

Bentley, E. R. "German Writers in Exile, 1933–1943," *Books Abroad,* XVII (1943).

Boyd, E. A. "Hasenclever," *Studies from Ten Literatures.* New York, 1925.

Brod, M. *Franz Kafka.* Prague, 1937.

Bryher, C. "Bertolt Brecht," *Life and Letters To-day,* XXXIII (1942)

Chandler, F. W. "Hasenclever," *Modern Continental Playwrights.* New York, 1931.

Danton, G. H. *Germany Ten Years After.* Boston, 1928.

Dehnow, F. *Frank Wedekind.* Leipzig, 1922.

Drake, W. A. *Contemporary European Writers.* New York, 1928.

Dukes, A. *Modern Dramatists.* London, 1911.

Duwe, W. *Deutsche Dichtung des 20. Jahrhunderts: Die Geschichte der Ausdruckskunst.* Zurich, 1936.

Eisenlohr, F. *Carl Sternheim.* Munich, 1926.

Fruchter, M. J. *Georg Kaiser's Dramatic Works.* Philadelphia, 1933.

Grothe, H. *Klabund. Leben und Werk eines Dichters.* Berlin, 1933.

Hermann, G. *Der Grosstadtroman.* Stettin, 1931.

Heuser, F. W. J. "Gerhart Hauptmann and Frank Wedekind," *Germanic Review,* XX (1945).

Hock, S. *Die Vampirsage und ihre Verwertung in der deutschen Literatur.* Berlin, 1900.

Keller, M. V. *Der deutsche Expressionismus im Drama seiner Hauptvertreter.* Weimar, 1936.

Kelly, J. "Franz Kafka's 'Trial' and the Theology of Crisis," *Southern Review,* V (1940).

Knevels, W. *Expressionismus und Religion.* Tübingen, 1927.

Knudsen, H. *Der Dichter H. Burte.* Konstanz, 1918.

Königsgarten, H. F. *Georg Kaiser.* Potsdam, 1928.

———. "The Leading Playwright of Expressionism," *German Life and Letters,* III (1939).

Kohn-Bramstedt, E. "Franz Werfel as a Novelist," *Contemporary Review,* CXLVI (1934).

Kutscher, A. *F. Wedekind.* Munich, 1924.

Meister, R. *Fritz von Unruh.* Berlin, 1925.

Paulsen, W. "The Foundations of Modern German Literature," *Durham University Journal* (1936).

———. "Klabund," *German Life and Letters,* III (1939).

Reinhardt, K. F. "The Expressionist Movement in Recent German Literature," *Germanic Review,* VI (1931).

Roger-Henrichsen, G. "German Refugee Literature," *London Mercury,* XXXIX (1939).

Rose, W. "Contemporary German Literature, the Younger Generation," *London Mercury,* XVI (1927).

Rothe, H. *Max Reinhardt, 25 Jahre Deutsches Theater.* Munich, 1930.

Samuel, R., and R. H. Thomas. *Expressionism in German Life, Literature, and the Theatre (1910–1924).* Cambridge, 1939.

Schickele, R. "Rene Schickele," *Books Abroad,* XV (1941).

Schumann, D. W. "Expressionism and Post-Expressionism in German Lyrics," *Germanic Review,* IX (1934).

Singer, P. *Ernst Toller.* Berlin, 1924.

Slochower, H. "Franz Werfel and Alfred Döblin," *Journal of English and Germanic Philology,* XXXIII (1934).

Specht, R. *Franz Werfel.* Vienna, 1926.

Sperber, H. *Motiv und Wort bei Gustav Meyrink.* Leipzig, 1918.

BIBLIOGRAPHIES

Stamm, I. A. "Religious Experience in Werfel's 'Barbara,'" *Publications of the Modern Language Association,* LIV (1939).
Tauber, H. *Franz Kafka.* Zurich, 1941.
Theis, O. F. "Frank Wedekind," *Poet Lore,* XXIV (1913).
Thomas, R. H. "Franz Kafka and the Religious Aspects of Expressionism," *German Life and Letters,* II (1938).
Thompson, L. "Bert Brecht," *Kenyon Review,* II (1940).
Warren, A. "Kosmos Kafka," *Southern Review,* VII (1942).
Weiskopf, F. C. "Bitter Bread, Exiled German Writers in the Belligerent Countries," *Books Abroad,* XIV (1940).
Whittaker, E. "Leonhard Frank," *Bookman,* LXXXI (1931).
Willibrand, W. A. *Ernst Toller, Product of Two Revolutions.* Norman, Okla., 1941.

Present Trends in German Literature

Aellen, H. *Heinrich Federer.* Heilbronn, 1928.
Atkins, H. G. *German Literature through Nazi Eyes.* London, 1941.
Baer, L. "A Study of Ernst Wiechert," *Modern Language Quarterly,* V (1944).
Baier, C. "Hans Carossa and the New Germany," *German Life and Letters,* III (1939).
Bartels, A. *Einführung in das deutsche Schrifttum für deutsche Menschen.* Leipzig, 1933.
——. *Heimatkunst.* Strassburg, 1916.
Bostock, J. K. *Some Well-known German War Novels, 1914–1930.* Oxford, 1931.
Bülow, P. *F. Lienhard.* Leipzig, 1923.
Casper, S. *Der Dramatiker Hanns Johst.* Munich, 1938.
Cunz, D. "Swiss Letters," *Books Abroad,* XIV (1940).
Cysarz, H. *Zur Geistesgeschichte des Weltkriegs.* Halle, 1931.
Danton, G. H. "Hans Grimm's 'Volk ohne Raum,'" *Monatshefte für deutschen Unterricht,* XXVII (1935).
Deimann, W. *Hermann Löns.* Dortmund, 1923.
Ebeling, H. *Ernst Wiechert.* Berlin, 1937.
Elster, H. M. *Gustav Frenssen.* Leipzig, 1913.
Evans, G. "Towards a New Drama in Germany: A Survey of the Years 1933–1937," *German Life and Letters,* II (1938).
Fishman, S. "War Novels of Arnold Zweig," *Sewanee Review,* XLIX (1941).
Flex, C. *Walter Flex, ein Lebensbild.* Stuttgart, 1937.
Forster, R. L. "The Conservative Elements in German Literature," *Contemporary Review,* CLIX (1941).
Guerster-Steinhausen, E. "The Prophet of German Nihilism—Ernst Jünger," *Review of Politics,* VII (1945).
Haneis, A. *Hans Carossa.* Weimar, 1935.
Hayens, K. C. "Gerhard Schumann, Poet of the Third Reich," *German Life and Letters,* III (1939).
Heer, G. H. *Jakob Christoph Heer.* Frauenfeld, 1927.
Hodsoll, E. R. "German Literature To-day," *Contemporary Review,* CLV (1939).
Hofrichter, R. J. "Erich Kästner as a Representative of 'Neue Sachlichkeit,'" *German Quarterly,* V (1932).

Hofrichter, R. J. *Three Poets and Reality* (Hans Carossa, Josef Weinheber, Albert Steffen). New Haven, 1942.

Hohlbaum, R. *R. H. Bartsch.* Leipzig, 1923.

Jennssen, C. *Hans Friedrich Blunck.* Berlin, 1935.

Jolas, E. "Gottfried Benn," *Transition,* V (1927).

Kindermann, H. *Deutsche Gegenwartsdichtung im Aufbau der Nation.* Berlin, 1936.

Kollmann, E. C. "Characteristics of Austrian Literature," *Monatshefte für deutschen Unterricht,* XXXIV (1942).

Korrodi, E. *Schweizer Erzähler der Gegenwart.* Leipzig, 1924.

Langenbucher, H. *Nationalsozialistische Dichtung.* Berlin, 1935.

Lehner, F. "Hermann Broch," *Life and Letters To-day,* XV (1936).

———. "Robert Musil," *Books Abroad,* XVII (1943).

Lissau, R. "Recent Austrian Literature," *German Life and Letters,* IV (1939).

"Ludwig Renn, Germany's Proletarian Novelist," *Living Age,* CCCXLIII (1933).

Mankiewicz, F. "German Literature, 1933–1938," *German Quarterly,* XII (1939).

Melcher, K. *Friedrich Griese.* Berlin, 1936.

Mulot, A. *Das Bauertum in der deutschen Dichtung unserer Zeit.* Stuttgart, 1937.

———. *Der Soldat in der deutschen Dichtung unserer Zeit.* Stuttgart, 1938.

Peacock, R. "Carossa," *German Life and Letters,* II (1938).

———. "The Great War in German Lyrical Poetry, 1914–1918," *Leeds Philosophical Society, Proceedings of the Literary and Historical Section,* III (1934).

Pfeiler, W. K. *War and the German Mind: The Testimony of Men of Fiction Who Fought at the Front.* New York, 1941.

Pongs, H. *Krieg als Volksschicksal im deutschen Schrifttum.* Stuttgart, 1934.

Roh, F. *Nachexpressionismus.* Leipzig, 1926.

Schneider, W. *Die auslanddeutsche Dichtung unserer Zeit.* Berlin, 1936.

Schuman, F. L. *Germany Since 1918.* New York, 1937.

Shears, L. A. "The Novellen of Josef Ponten," *Germanic Review,* XI (1936).

Slochower, H. "Hauptmann and Fallada: Uncoordinated Writers of Nazi Germany," *Accent,* III (1942).

Spiero, H. *Ernst Zahn.* Stuttgart, 1927.

Stirk, S. D. *The Prussian Spirit, A Survey of German Literature and Politics, 1914–1940.* London, 1941.

Utitz, T. *Die Überwindung des Expressionismus.* Stuttgart, 1927.

Vermeil, E. *Germany's Three Reichs.* London, 1944.

Wendling, K. *Der Weltkrieg in der Dichtung.* Stuttgart, 1918.

Werner, A. "Four Tragic Jews," *Jewish Outlook,* VI (1942).

Wuk, H. A. "Hans Fallada," *Living Age,* CCCXLIV (1933).

Zweig, F. "Joseph Roth and the Zweigs," *Books Abroad,* XVIII (1944).

314

INDEX

315

INDEX

BITZIUS, ALBERT (*see* GOTTHELF, JEREMIAS)

Black Forest, 169, 173, 267

Blank verse, 71, 99, 101

BLEIBTREU, KARL, 201

Blubo literature, 266–267

BLUNCK, HANS FRIEDRICH, 265–266

Boccaccio, Giovanni, 24, 33, 34, 70, 225

BODENSTEDT, FRIEDRICH, 131

BODMER, JOHANN JAKOB, 57, 64, 75, 77–78, 88, 118, 170, 177

BÖHME, JAKOB, 50, 60, 236

Boethius, 7

BÖRNE, LUDWIG, 155, 156

Bohemia, 33, 141, 142, 173, 236, 237, 248, 249, 267

BOIE, HEINRICH CHRISTIAN, 87

Boileau, Nicolas, 45, 47, 50, 55, 68

Bonifacius, 4

BONSELS, WALDEMAR, 221

Bourgeois drama, 55, 69, 166

BRAHM, OTTO, 201

Brahms, Johannes, 150

Brandenburg, 44, 169, 172, 182

BRANT, SEBASTIAN, 30, 34, 36, 39

BRAUNSCHWEIG-WOLFENBÜTTEL, ANTON ULRICH ZU, 52

BRAUNSCHWEIG-WOLFENBÜTTEL, HEINRICH JULIUS ZU, 54

BRECHT, BERTOLT, 254, 260

BREITINGER, JOHANN JAKOB, 78

Brentano, Bettina, 114

BRENTANO, CLEMENS, 104, 129, 134, 135

Brentano, Sophie, 114

Bretonne, Restif de la, 128

BROCH, HERMANN, 259

BROCKES, BARTHOLD HEINRICH, 77

BROD, MAX, 236, 247

Brodzinski, Kazimierz, 122

BRÖGER, KARL, 261

Browning, Elizabeth Barrett, 239

Bruckner, Anton, 150

Bruno, Giordano, 235

BUCHOLTZ, ANDREAS, 53

BÜCHNER, GEORG, 165

Buonarroti, Michelangelo, 239

BURCKHARDT, JAKOB, 170, 185, 216, 229, 232

BÜRGER, GOTTFRIED AUGUST, 87, 119, 241

Burgundians, 1, 2, 14, 25

BURTE, HERMANN, 246

BUSCH, WILHELM, 184

BUSSE, HERMANN ERIS, 267

Butler, Samuel, 78

Byron, George Gordon, Lord, 108, 115, 118, 121, 122, 139, 155, 161, 201, 245, 273

Byzantium, 2, 3

C

Caesar, Julius, 3, 40

Calderón de la Barca, Don Pedro, 46, 56, 130, 138, 141, 159, 223, 224, 231

Calvin, Jean, 38, 227

Camoëns, Luiz de, 131

CANITZ, FRIEDRICH RUDOLF VON, 56

Canossa, 13, 230

Capellanus, Andreas, 19

Carlyle, Thomas, 119

Carolingians, 4, 7, 8, 172

CAROSSA, HANS, 257–258

Casanova, 222, 225, 226

Cellini, Benvenuto, 130

Celtic influences (*see* Arthurian romances *and* Ossian)

CELTIS, CONRAD, 34

Cervantes Saavedra, Miguel de, 46, 64, 131, 228

CHAMISSO, ADELBERT VON, 129, 136, 150, 154, 155

Charlemagne, 4, 7, 8, 12, 19

Charles IV, 25, 33

Charles V, 25, 26, 37, 38

Charles Martel, 4

Chateaubriand, François-René Vicomte de, 120, 126

Chaussée, Nivelle de la, 57–58

Chrétien de Troyes, 11

Cid, El, 82, 83, 131

CLAUDIUS, MATTHIAS, 87

Clovis, 3, 4

Codex Argenteus, 1

Coleridge, Samuel Taylor, 117, 118

Commedia dell' arte, 54, 143

Constant, Benjamin, 118

Cooper, James Fenimore, 181

Corneille, Pierre, 47, 68

Cornelius, Peter, 151

316

INDEX

Council of Trent, 43
Crusades, 11, 12, 19, 71

D

DAHN, FELIX, 170
Dante Alighieri, 16, 23, 53, 75, 78, 89, 108, 109, 130, 171, 234
Darwin, Charles Robert, 186, 199
DAUTHENDEY, MAX, 221
DEDEKIND, FRIEDRICH, 30
Defoe, Daniel, 52, 61, 73, 77
DEHMEL, RICHARD, 183, 208–209, 229, 262
Deism, 70
Dickens, Charles, 124, 153, 174, 179, 226
Diderot, Denis, 58, 60
Dionysian literature, 128, 185, 186, 243
DITZEN, RUDOLF (see FALLADA, HANS)
DÖBLIN, ALFRED, 248–249
Don Juan, 139, 140, 162, 163, 165
Donne, John, 46, 51
Dostoevski, Fedor, 154, 198, 226, 241, 243
DROSTE-HÜLSHOFF, ANNETTE VON, 161–162
Dryden, John, 78
Dürer, Albrecht, 40, 126, 127
DWINGER, EDWIN ERICH, 256

E

East Germanic tribes, 1, 2
EBNER-ESCHENBACH, MARIE VON, 180
Ecbasis Captivi, 8
ECKERMANN, JOHANN PETER, 109, 119
ECKHART, MEISTER, 27
Edda, 1, 81
EDSCHMID, KASIMIR, 245
Egmont, 85–86, 99
Egmont, Count, 43
EICHENDORFF, JOSEPH VON, 120, 137–138, 150, 154, 175
EINHART, 8
EKKEHARD, 8, 169, 170
Eleanor of Aquitaine, 19
ELISABETH VON NASSAU-SAAR-BRÜCKEN, 29

Emerson, Ralph Waldo, 119
ENGELKE, GERRIT, 262
Engels, Friedrich, 198
England, 11, 46, 47, 61, 66, 73–74, 118, 119, 130, 152, 161, 171, 182, 184, 199, 227, 228
English Comedians, 31, 53, 54, 56
EOBANUS HESSUS, 35
ERASMUS OF ROTTERDAM, 33, 35–36, 37, 38, 227
Ernst, Duke of Swabia, 12, 13, 136
ERNST, PAUL, 229–230
Espronceda, José de, 121
EURINGER, RICHARD, 262
Euripides, 97, 222, 249
Ewald, Johannes, 121
EWERS, HANNS HEINZ, 247
EYB, ALBRECHT VON, 34

F

FALLADA, HANS, 259, 268
Faust, 31, 68, 86, 108–109, 115, 118, 119, 120, 121, 123, 124, 129, 139, 141, 160, 163, 165, 185, 205, 235, 249
FEDERER, HEINRICH, 263
FEUCHTWANGER, LION, 227–228
Feuerbach, Ludwig, 151
Fichte, Johann Gottlieb, 104, 117, 134, 255
FISCHART, JOHANN, 41
FLEMING, PAUL, 50
FLEX, WALTER, 255
Folk songs, 32, 82, 134, 136
FONTANE, THEODOR, 182–183, 184, 198, 221
Ford, John, 226
Foscolo, Ugo, 75, 98, 121
FOUQUÉ, F. (see LA MOTTE-FOUQUÉ, F. de)
France, 10, 11, 12, 14, 16, 19, 45, 47, 48, 55, 56, 57, 59, 60, 61, 62, 67, 68, 73, 97, 100, 101, 111, 120, 125, 152, 170, 183, 199, 224
FRANCK, HANS, 232
FRANÇOIS, LUISE VON, 180
Franconian dynasty, 13
FRANK, BRUNO, 228
FRANK, LEONHARD, 248
Frankfurt am Main, 27, 31, 83, 84, 148

317

INDEX

Franks, 3, 4
Frederick Barbarossa (Emperor Frederick I), 13, 119, 134, 165
Frederick II (Emperor), 13, 20
Frederick II of Prussia (King Frederick the Great), 44, 61, 62, 63, 69, 73, 119, 156, 201, 220, 235, 262, 267
Frederick William (the Great Elector), 44, 262
FREIDANK, 28
Freie Bühne, 201
FREILIGRATH, FERDINAND, 131, 155, 157, 221
FRENSSEN, GUSTAV, 264–265, 266
Freud, Sigmund, 210, 219, 220, 222, 224, 226, 228
FREYTAG, GUSTAV, 169, 180
Friedrich, Caspar David, 117
FRISCHLIN, PHILIP NIKODEMUS, 40
Fruchtbringende Gesellschaft, 50
Fuller, Margaret, 119

G

GANGHOFER, LUDWIG, 264
Gay, John, 254
GEIBEL, EMANUEL, 183–184
GELLERT, CHRISTIAN FÜRCHTE-GOTT, 57, 58, 83
GEORGE, STEFAN, 197, 211, 224, 233–235, 236, 255, 257
GERHARDT, PAUL, 50
GERSTÄCKER, FRIEDRICH, 181
GERSTENBERG, HEINRICH WIL-HELM VON, 79, 81, 89
GESSNER, SALOMON, 75, 76, 78–79, 121
GFELLER, SIMON, 263
Ghibellines (*see* Hohenstaufen)
Gide, André, 239
GLÄSER, ERNST, 256
GLEIM, JOHANN WILHELM LUD-WIG, 63
Gluck, Christoph Willibald von, 62
GOERING, REINHARD, 251
GÖRRES, JOSEPH, 134
GOETHE, JOHANN WOLFGANG VON, 20, 30, 59, 63, 75, 76, 79, 82, 83–86, 87, 88, 89, 92–109, 112, 113, 114, 116, 117, 118, 119, 120, 121, 122, 123, 124, 125, 127, 128, 129, 130, 131, 138, 140, 142, 149, 150, 158, 176, 185, 197, 204, 205, 218, 220, 226, 229, 233, 236
Göttinger Hainbund, 86–87
Goeze, Johann Melchior, 70, 71
Golden Bull, 24, 25
Goldsmith, Oliver, 74
Goths, 1, 2, 170
GOTTFRIED VON STRASSBURG, 14, 16, 19–20, 64, 135, 164
GOTTHELF, JEREMIAS, 172, 173
GOTTSCHED, JOHANN CHRISTOPH, 56–57, 65, 67, 68, 69, 77, 78, 79, 83, 96
Gozzi, Gasparo, 130
GRABBE, CHRISTIAN DIETRICH, 165, 262
GRAF, OSKAR MARIA, 263
GRAVISETH, JAKOB VON, 66
Greek influences, 33, 64, 65, 67, 68, 69, 85, 95, 97, 98, 99, 101, 115, 122, 123, 150, 155, 158, 159, 160, 162, 185, 222, 228, 233
Gregory VII, 13, 236
GRIESE, FRIEDRICH, 267
GRILLPARZER, FRANZ, 114, 141–143, 156, 158–159, 164, 206, 224
GRIMM, HANS, 266, 268
GRIMM, JAKOB, 135
GRIMM, WILHELM, 135
GRIMMELSHAUSEN, HANS JAKOB CHRISTOFFEL VON, 51, 52
GROTH, KLAUS, 174
GRÜN, ANASTASIUS, 156
GRYPHIUS, ANDREAS, 50, 51, 54, 55, 69, 79, 134
Gudrun, 14, 16
Guelfs, 13, 21, 267
GÜNTHER, JOHANN CHRISTIAN, 76
GUNDOLF, FRIEDRICH, 234
Gustavus Adolphus, 171, 228
Gutenberg, Johannes, 33
Gutzkow, Karl, 156–157, 198

H

HADLAUB, JOHANNES, 177
Häckel, Ernst, 199
Händel, Georg Friedrich, 55
HÄRING, WILHELM (*see* ALEXIS, WILLIBALD)

318

INDEX

INDEX

I

Ibsen, Henrik, 154, 198, 199, 201, 203, 204, 211, 243, 244
IFFLAND, AUGUST WILHELM, 128
IMMERMANN, KARL LEBERECHT, 160–161, 173
Indo-Europeans, 1
Inner Emigration, 267–268
Interregnum, 14
Irving, Washington, 87, 117, 118, 119
Italy, 2, 5, 13, 14, 24, 25, 33, 45, 47, 49, 61, 75, 96, 100, 121, 130, 138, 152, 159, 160, 170, 171, 181, 212, 214, 215, 216, 218, 219, 222, 225, 228, 234

J

JANSEN ENIKEL, 12
JEAN PAUL, 119, 120, 123–124, 150, 173, 176
Jena, 104, 119, 122, 131
JERSCHKE, OTTO, 203
Jesuits, 41, 53, 170
Jewish problems and writers, 35, 114, 139, 150, 156, 161, 166, 168, 173, 202, 219, 221, 222, 224, 225, 226, 227, 228, 231, 240, 248, 249, 250, 258
JOHST, HANNS, 262
Jonson, Ben, 46, 227
Joseph II, 62, 73
Joyce, James, 249
JÜNGER, ERNST, 256–257, 268
JÜNGER, GEORG FRIEDRICH, 257
Jugendbewegung, 264

K

KÄSTNER, ERICH, 259–260, 268
KAFKA, FRANZ, 236, 247–248, 249
KAISER, GEORG, 252
Kant, Immanuel, 60, 61, 93, 94, 96, 101, 102, 106, 113, 117, 119
Karl August of Saxe-Weimar, 67, 83, 94, 147
KASCHNITZ, MARIA LUISE, 268
KELLER, GOTTFRIED, 176–178, 214, 215, 251, 263
KERNER, JUSTINUS, 162
KEYSERLING, EDUARD VON, 221

Kierkegaard, Sören Aabye, 152, 248
Kipling, Rudyard, 254
KLABUND, 245
KLEIST, EWALD VON, 63, 70, 77
KLEIST, HEINRICH VON, 114, 117, 127–128, 130, 132–133, 135, 141, 148, 154, 164, 165, 205, 226, 232, 253
KLINGER, MAXIMILIAN, 88
KLOPSTOCK, FRIEDRICH GOTTLIEB, 64, 80–81, 86
König Rother, 12
KÖRNER, THEODOR, 133, 150
KOESTLER, ARTHUR, 260
KOLB, ANNETTE, 246
KOLBENHEYER, ERWIN GUIDO, 229, 235–236
KONRAD, 12
KOTZEBUE, AUGUST VON, 118, 121, 128, 207
KRAUS, KARL, 217
KRETZER, MAX, 201
KRÖGER, TIMM, 264
Krupp, Alfred and Friedrich, 216, 264
Künstlerroman, 212, 213, 221, 238
Kulturkampf, 151
KURZ, ISOLDE, 215

L

Labé, Louise, 239
LACHMANN, KARL, 135, 136
LAGARDE, PAUL DE, 229
LA MOTTE-FOUQUÉ, FRIEDRICH DE, 119, 129, 154
LAMPRECHT, 12
Lassalle, Ferdinand, 188, 198
LAUBE, HEINRICH, 156
LAVATER, JOHANN KASPAR, 87–88
Leibniz, Gottfried Wilhelm, 55, 60
Leipzig, 56, 63, 77, 83, 89, 112, 206
LEISEWITZ, JOHANN ANTON, 88
LENAU, NIKOLAUS, 114, 138–139, 150, 154
LENZ, JAKOB MICHAEL REINHOLD, 88, 165
Lermontov, Mikhail Yurievich, 122
LERSCH, HEINRICH, 261
LESSING, GOTTHOLD EPHRAIM, 49, 57, 59, 60, 67–71, 81, 82, 88, 95, 123, 157

INDEX

INDEX

INDEX

INDEX

William II, 193, 216, 229
WIMPFELING, JAKOB, 34, 35, 40
WINCKELMANN, JOHANN JOACHIM, 95, 232
WINCKLER, JOSEF, 246
WITKOP, PHILIP, 256
Wittekind (*see* Widukind)
WOLF, FRIEDRICH, 251–252
Wolf, Hugo, 138, 150, 162
Wolff, Christian, 60
WOLFRAM VON ESCHENBACH, 14, 16, 18–19, 20, 135, 136, 163, 164
Women writers, 8, 9, 29, 114, 161, 180, 208, 214, 215, 216, 243, 260, 263, 268
World War I, 208, 217, 218, 227, 232, 234, 238, 243, 246, 248, 249, 251, 253, 254, 255, 256, 257, 258, 261
Wulfila, 1
WYLE, NICHOLAS VON, 34
WYSS, JOHANN RUDOLF, 77

Y

Young, Edward, 74, 125

Z

ZAHN, ERNST, 263
ZECH, PAUL, 261
ZESEN, PHILIP VON, 50, 52
ZIEGLER, HEINRICH ANSELM VON, 52, 55
Zinzendorf, Nikolaus Ludwig von, 55
Zola, Émile, 154, 199, 201, 203, 208
ZUCKMAYER, CARL, 260, 262
Zurich, 41, 75, 77, 78, 87, 170, 176, 177, 215, 263
ZWEIG, ARNOLD, 258
ZWEIG, STEFAN, 226–227, 250
Zwingli, Huldreich, 37, 38, 232